THE PLANTAGENET ENCYCLOPEDIA

THE PLANTAGENET ENCYCLOPEDIA

AN ALPHABETICAL GUIDE TO 400 YEARS OF ENGLISH HISTORY

GENERAL EDITOR: ELIZABETH HALLAM

Weidenfeld and Nicolson
London

Created and produced by Phoebe Phillips Editions

Editorial Director: Tessa Clark

Editorial:
Editor: Cecilia Walters
Hilary Bird
Fred Gill
Jenny Overton
Timothy Probart
Liliane Reichenbach
Kevin Tongue
Picture Research:
Paul Mackintosh

Design:
Tim Scott

Production:
Hilary Curtis
Roger Multon

Text:
Paul Mackintosh

Specially commissioned photographs:
Marianne Majerus

Maps:
Jeff Edwards

General Editor:
Dr Elizabeth Hallam, *Assistant Keeper of Public
Records, Public Record Office, London*

Phototypesetting: Spectrum Typesetting Ltd.
Origination: J. Film
Printed and bound in Yugoslavia

First published in Great Britain in 1990 by
George Weidenfeld & Nicolson Ltd
91 Clapham High Street, London SW4 7TA

ISBN 0 297 83003 1

CONTENTS

Frontispiece: Henry II, first of the Plantagenet dynasty that was to rule England for almost four centuries: top left, with his sons Richard I (top right), John (bottom left), and Henry the Young King (centre), and his grandson Henry III (bottom right).

Warkworth Castle (Overleaf) Held by the influential Percy family, Warkworth helped secure Northumbria against Scots invasion.

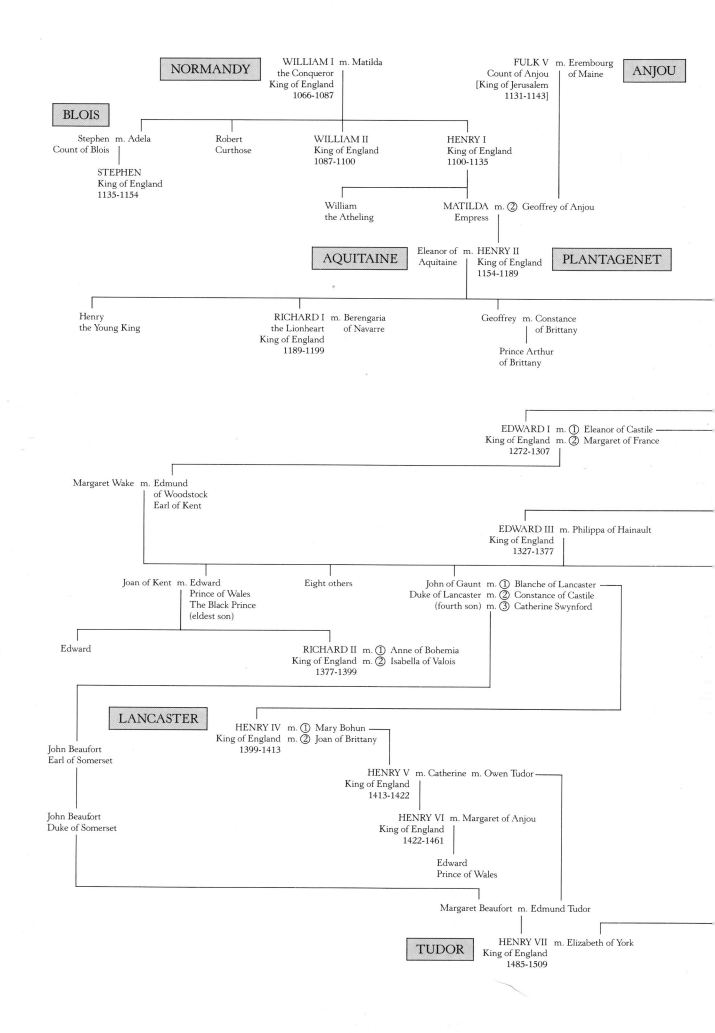

NORMANDY

WILLIAM I m. Matilda
the Conqueror
King of England
1066-1087

FULK V m. Erembourg
Count of Anjou   of Maine
[King of Jerusalem
1131-1143]

ANJOU

BLOIS

Stephen m. Adela
Count of Blois

Robert
Curthose

WILLIAM II
King of England
1087-1100

HENRY I
King of England
1100-1135

STEPHEN
King of England
1135-1154

William
the Atheling

MATILDA m. ② Geoffrey of Anjou
Empress

AQUITAINE

Eleanor of m. HENRY II
Aquitaine   King of England
1154-1189

PLANTAGENET

Henry
the Young King

RICHARD I m. Berengaria
the Lionheart   of Navarre
King of England
1189-1199

Geoffrey m. Constance
of Brittany

Prince Arthur
of Brittany

EDWARD I m. ① Eleanor of Castile
King of England m. ② Margaret of France
1272-1307

Margaret Wake m. Edmund
of Woodstock
Earl of Kent

EDWARD III m. Philippa of Hainault
King of England
1327-1377

Joan of Kent m. Edward
Prince of Wales
The Black Prince
(eldest son)

Eight others

John of Gaunt m. ① Blanche of Lancaster
Duke of Lancaster m. ② Constance of Castile
(fourth son) m. ③ Catherine Swynford

Edward

RICHARD II m. ① Anne of Bohemia
King of England m. ② Isabella of Valois
1377-1399

LANCASTER

HENRY IV m. ① Mary Bohun
King of England m. ② Joan of Brittany
1399-1413

John Beaufort
Earl of Somerset

HENRY V m. Catherine m. Owen Tudor
King of England
1413-1422

John Beaufort
Duke of Somerset

HENRY VI m. Margaret of Anjou
King of England
1422-1461

Edward
Prince of Wales

Margaret Beaufort m. Edmund Tudor

TUDOR

HENRY VII m. Elizabeth of York
King of England
1485-1509

The Plantagenet Dynasty 1154-1485

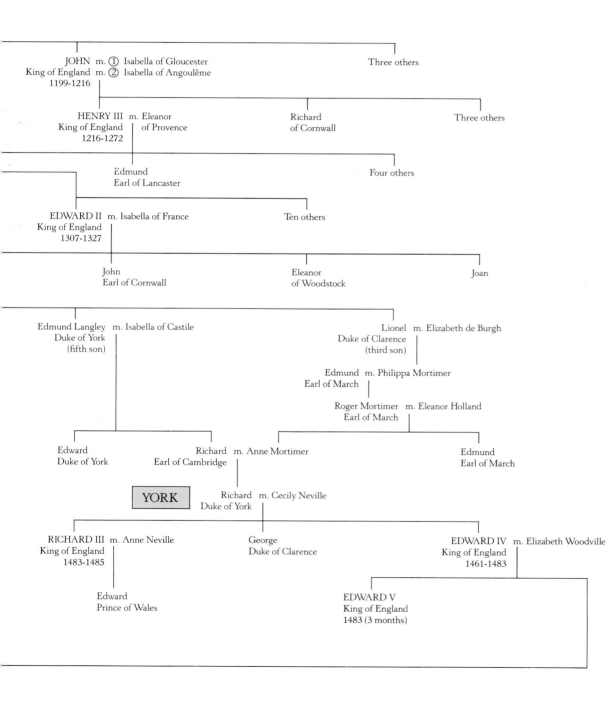

JOHN m. ① Isabella of Gloucester
King of England m. ② Isabella of Angoulême
1199-1216

Three others

HENRY III m. Eleanor
King of England of Provence
1216-1272

Richard
of Cornwall

Three others

Edmund
Earl of Lancaster

Four others

EDWARD II m. Isabella of France
King of England
1307-1327

Ten others

John
Earl of Cornwall

Eleanor
of Woodstock

Joan

Edmund Langley m. Isabella of Castile
Duke of York
(fifth son)

Lionel m. Elizabeth de Burgh
Duke of Clarence
(third son)

Edmund m. Philippa Mortimer
Earl of March

Roger Mortimer m. Eleanor Holland
Earl of March

Edward
Duke of York

Richard m. Anne Mortimer
Earl of Cambridge

Edmund
Earl of March

YORK

Richard m. Cecily Neville
Duke of York

RICHARD III m. Anne Neville
King of England
1483-1485

George
Duke of Clarence

EDWARD IV m. Elizabeth Woodville
King of England
1461-1483

Edward
Prince of Wales

EDWARD V
King of England
1483 (3 months)

EDITOR'S NOTE

Many of the scholarly works compiled in the monasteries and universities of Plantagenet England were encyclopaedic in their scope. The seven liberal arts – grammar, logic, rhetoric, arithmetic, geometry, astronomy and music – were the basis for most, but a variety of other subjects also appeared. For example, *De proprietatis rerum* (On the properties of things), an encyclopedia created *c.* 1230–40 by a Franciscan friar, Bartholomew the Englishman, begins with God and the angels, and progresses in 19 books through psychology and physiology, home economics and medicine, cosmology and chronology, to the natural history of birds, fishes, trees and animals. It then moves on to colours and scents, food and drink, and finally looks at weights and measures. Unusually for the period the book was addressed to ordinary people *(simplices et rudes)*, and was very popular for centuries: in the later Middle Ages it was hired out to students at the university of Paris, and 14 printed editions had appeared by 1500.

A great number of Bartholomew's subjects are also in **The Plantagenet Encyclopedia**, but not surprisingly for only one volume instead of 19, we have had to limit the scope of our enquiring editors and contributors. Indeed, as the title clearly indicates, we have looked at the period through the eyes of the most important family in medieval England, the Plantagenets.

The history of their rule in England and France, from its turbulent origins in 11th-century Anjou to its equally violent end on the battlefield at Bosworth, has been told by chroniclers of the time through the three-volume **Plantagenet Chronicles**, beginning with that title and going on through **The Chronicles of the Age of Chivalry, (Four Gothic Kings** in the US edition) and **The Wars of the Roses**. These books, with their cornucopia of information and options, give the reader direct access to original and contemporary sources, as well as providing modern notes to set the individual excerpts in the context of a narrative stretching from before the coronation of Henry II in 1154 to the death of Richard III in 1485.

The Plantagenet Encyclopedia is their companion, but it stands alone in providing two important focal points: immediate and alphabetical access to factual information, such as biographical and geographical notes, together with appropriate illustrations and the explanation of historical concepts and terms. It will deepen the reader's understanding of the exciting Plantagenet story in both its English and its European context, and of the feuding of its Lancastrian and Yorkist offshoots which, in the end, allowed the dynasty to be supplanted by the house of Tudor.

Edward I, Edward II and **Edward III** in York Minster (opposite): three Plantagenet kings who ruled England from 1216 to 1377.

Europe in 1100
Western Europe and the Middle East in 1100. The lands ruled by the House of Anjou are indicated. Half a century later, with the accession of Henry, count of Anjou, to the throne of England, the Angevin dominions, which also included Aquitaine and Normandy, stretched from Scotland to the Pyrenees.

KEY:

Lands ruled by the House of Anjou

Domain of the King of France

Boundaries:

Duchy

County

House of Anjou

● Paris Main town.

HUNGARY

GEORGIA

Black Sea

SELJUK SULTANATE OF RUM

Constantinople ●

EASTERN EMPIRE

Tigris

EDESSA

Edessa ○

Anitoch ●

PRINCIPALITY OF ANTIOCH

Euphrates

Athens ○

CYPRUS

SELJUK EMPIRE

CRETE

○ Damascus

Tyre ○

Acre ○

Jaffa ○   Jerusalem ●

KINGDOM OF JERUSALEM

BARKA

Alexandria ●

FATIMITE CALIPHATE

○ Cairo

EGYPT   *Nile*   *Red Sea*

Abbeville

Town in the county of Ponthieu, on the Somme in north-east France. Abbeville was an important centre of trade – it received its commercial charter as early as 1184 and was a meeting-place for diplomatic discussions between French and English kings during the Hundred Years War (1337–1453). The church of St Wulfram in Abbeville was rebuilt in the Flamboyant style in 1486.

The Wars of the Roses: 70, 147, 264

abbey

Society of monks governed by an abbot, or of nuns under an abbess; and by extension the buildings they inhabit. In the Middle Ages abbeys played an important role in society. They, and the priories and cells dependent on them, were major landholders, having control over substantial tracts of land, the peasants who farmed them and the produce from them. Abbots were highly influential in the life of the English Church, could be summoned to royal councils or parliaments and could act as justices for the Crown. Abbeys might have schools, hospitals and almshouses attached. But above all, they existed to intercede for society: and it was for this that benefactors lavished possessions and gifts upon them.

Abelard, Peter

1079–1142, French theologian and philosopher, whose brilliant teaching in the schools of Paris, from about 1108, attracted many students. He became a master at the school of Notre-Dame, but when deprived of his place after violent theological arguments with his former master, William of Champeaux, he set up his own school at Mont-Ste-Geneviève, outside the city walls (1112). He later returned to Notre-Dame; and his passionate relationship with, and secret marriage to, Héloïse, the niece of one of the canons, Fulbert, in about 1118, led to his castration at Fulbert's command. Both Abelard and Héloïse retreated into monasticism and began their celebrated correspondence. Abelard continued to work as a theologian; his application of logic to doctrine and faith led to his condemnation as a heretic by the Council of Sens in 1140. This was on the initiative of Bernard of Clairvaux, who favoured a conservative approach to theology.

Abelard died in 1142 and was buried at the Paraclete near Nogent-sur-Seine, the convent he had founded before *c.*1123 for Héloïse. On her death, in 1163–4, she was buried beside him.

The Plantagenet Chronicles: 34–5

Aberdeen

City in north-east Scotland, at the mouth of the Dee. Aberdeen became a royal burgh in 1176, and by the 14th century was an important port for trade with England and the Low Countries. The English burned the town in 1336 during a campaign against the Scots.

The Wars of the Roses: 194

Abingdon, St Edmund of

See: Edmund of Abingdon, St, archbishop of Canterbury

Acre

Port on the Bay of Haifa, in the eastern Mediterranean. The city was seized by the armies of the First Crusade, *c.*1104, and became a major port for the kingdom of Jerusalem, the principal crusader state they established. Taken by the Muslim leader Saladin in 1187, it was laid under siege by Christian forces in 1189 and recaptured by Richard I of England and Philip II of France, in 1191. Acre thereafter remained as the centre of Christian possessions in the Holy Land. The last great bastion of the crusader presence in Palestine, it was finally captured and virtually destroyed by Saracen troops in 1291.

The Plantagenet Chronicles: 198, 202, 208, 214, 216, 218-19, 222, 278

Chronicles of the Age of Chivalry/Four Gothic Kings (US edn): 18, 42, 69, 110

Acton, Sir John

d. 1414? According to the near contemporary writer Tito Livio, Sir John was a leader of the Lollard sect (followers of the teachings of Wycliffe) who conspired with Sir John Oldcastle, a prominent Lollard and a fugitive convicted of heresy, to capture Henry V at Eltham Palace in Kent on 6 January 1414. Acton was seized by the king's men and subsequently put to death, together with his co-conspirators. Only Oldcastle was able to escape.

The Wars of the Roses: 124

Adam of Murimuth

1275?–1347. Born of a family settled at Fifield in Oxfordshire. Murimuth served at Avignon as an envoy to the papal curia for Oxford University from 1312 to 1317; for the chapter of Canterbury in 1319; and for Edward II in 1323, when he opposed the Scots appeal against a papal interdict on Scotland. He gained a prebend in Hereford Cathedral in 1320, one at St Paul's in 1325, and a second, richer one there in 1328. In 1337 he became rector of Wraysbury. He completed the first version of his chronicle, *Continuatio Chronicorum,* in 1337, covering the years 1306–37; and later extended it to 1346. Though brief, it records Edward II's deposition, his death and the rumours of foul play surrounding it, Edward III's reign, the Hundred Years War (1337–1453) and England's relations with the papacy during the first part of the 14th century.

Chronicles of the Age of Chivalry/Four Gothic Kings (US edn): 180, 186, 221

Adam, Salimbene de

See: Salimbene de Adam

Adela, queen of Louis VII, king of France.

Daughter of Count Theobald of Blois and Champagne; third wife of Louis VII of France. The French king married her in 1160, two weeks after the death of his second wife. Louis hoped for a son from the match; his first two marriages had yielded only daughters. According to the chronicler Ralph of Diceto, Samson, archbishop of Reims, refused to accept or anoint her as queen because her sister's marriage to the king's brother Philip had been

Peter Abelard *The learned and passionate theologian with his beloved Héloïse.*

Agenais

County in south-west France, on the Garonne river, with Agen as its capital. Agenais was part of the duchy of Aquitaine but, as a valuable border area, was much in dispute between English and French kings during the 13th century. It had passed to Raymond VI, count of Toulouse, in 1196 as the dowry of Joan, Richard I of England's sister. In 1249 it went to Alphonse of Poitiers, Raymond's son-in-law and brother of Louis IX of France, with the rest of Raymond's lands. In 1259 it was promised to England in reversion, should Alphonse die childless, and was handed over to Edward I of England in 1279. The Agenais again became a battleground during the Hundred Years War, but passed finally to France in 1441.

The Plantagenet Chronicles: 197
Chronicles of the Age of Chivalry/Four Gothic Kings (US edn): 25, 90–1, 276

Agincourt, battle of

Battle at a village in northern France, near Calais, when Henry V of England won a great victory against the French on 25 October 1415. Henry had landed at the mouth of the Seine on 14 August, at the start of his campaign, and taken nearby Harfleur after a six-week siege; he then led a march toward Calais, also held by the English, over 150 miles to the north. Some 5–6,000 English troops met a French force of 50–60,000 near Agincourt. In the battle that followed, the French advance on the narrow English front met a hail of arrows. The English killed three French dukes, the constable of France, nine counts, 90 lords and some 5,000 lesser nobles; they lost one duke, one earl, six or seven knights and around 500 others. The highest-ranking English casualty, Edward, 2nd duke of York, suffocated in his armour. Henry's victory consolidated little territory, but enhanced his prestige, decimated and demoralized the French ruling class, and laid the basis for the Treaty of Troyes (1420) by which he became heir to the throne of France.

The Wars of the Roses: 122–3, 128–36

Aigueblanche, Peter

See: Peter of Aigueblanche, bishop of Hereford

Aigues-Mortes

Port in the Languedoc, in the Rhône delta on the Mediterranean coast of southern France. The town was built by Louis IX of France as the

---

dissolved on the grounds that the two were too closely related. Adela was mother of the future Philip II of France (b.1165), with whom she later quarrelled when he seized some of her castles. Mother and son were eventually reconciled in 1180 and Adela later acted as Philip's regent while he was on crusade (1190–91).

The Plantagenet Chronicles: 106, 112, 164–5

Adrian IV, pope

1100–59. Pope (1154–9). The only English pope; born Nicholas Breakspear, the son of a priest. He studied at Arles (then part of the Holy Roman Empire), becoming an Augustinian canon. Later he became abbot of St-Rufus near Valence, then cardinal-bishop of Albano (1149). Pope Eugenius III sent him to Scandinavia to organize the Church there. Elected pope in 1154, Adrian crowned the Holy Roman Emperor Frederick I in 1155, but later quarrelled with him over imperial claims to northern Italy. Adrian granted Ireland to Henry II of England as a papal fief (c.1155). His death in 1159 was followed by a schism, with England and France supporting Alexander III as pope and Germany Victor IV.

The Plantagenet Chronicles: 104, 106, 108

advowson

The patronage of an ecclesiastical office or benefice; the right of presentation to a benefice. The advowsons of valuable ecclesiastical livings were much prized and often in dispute, as benefices were useful gifts with which a king, magnate or bishop could reward his faithful clerical servants.

point of departure for his crusades. Aigues-Mortes was given strong walls, which still survive intact, and dominated the Camargue as a symbol of royal power.

Chronicles of the Age of Chivalry/Four Gothic Kings (US edn): 68, 69

Ailred, abbot of Rievaulx

1109–67. Abbot (1146–67) of Cistercian Rievaulx in Yorkshire; scholar and historical writer in the service of Prince Henry of Scotland. Ailred brought about a meeting of Henry II of England, Louis VII of France, and Pope Alexander III at Toucy in France in 1162. Later a missionary to the Galloway Picts, he was canonized in 1191. At his death in 1167 Rievaulx Abbey held 140 monks and 500 lay brothers and servants, typifying the success of the Cistercian order in the 12th century. The expansion of Rievaulx is a particular tribute to Ailred's qualities as an abbot, which inspired his community and were vividly portrayed by his biographer Walter Daniel, a monk of Rievaulx.

The Plantagenet Chronicles: 106, 266

alchemy The alchemists' attempts to produce gold proved fruitless, but their researches prefigured scientific chemistry.

Albertus Magnus, St

1193/1206?–1280. Eminent Dominican scholastic philosopher and doctor of the Church. Known as the 'Universal Doctor', Albertus introduced much of Aristotle's scientific thought to Europe, and attempted to reconcile Aristotelian and Christian ideas. His breadth of knowledge and his outstanding contribution to scientific thought gave him a pre-eminent role in 13th-century intellectual history.

Chronicles of the Age of Chivalry/Four Gothic Kings (US edn): 115

Albigensians

Another name for the Cathars, a heretical sect which arose in southern France in the 12th century. The name derived from the city of Albi in the Languedoc region, a centre of the heresy. The Albigensian Crusade, launched in 1208, had by 1245 crushed all but a few groups of the heretics, but some continued to exist into the late Middle Ages.

Chronicles of the Age of Chivalry/Four Gothic Kings (US edn): 65, 69

d'Albini, William, 3rd earl of Arundel

1173–1221. 3rd earl of Arundel and Sussex (1193–1221). Originally one of King John of England's favourites, he joined the baronial party opposing the king in 1216 after the sealing of Magna Carta. According to the Barnwell annalist, when the barons met in London (1216) to plan the division of England between them, they assigned to d'Albini the government of Lincolnshire. In 1217 he switched his support back to the young Henry III but the next year went on crusade; he died on his travels.

The Plantagenet Chronicles: 313

alchemy

Medieval forerunner of the science of chemistry, concerned mainly with the attempt to transmute base metals into gold.

The Wars of the Roses: 67

Alcock, John, bishop of Ely

1430–1500. Cleric and civil servant under Edward IV; master of the rolls (1462); privy councillor (1470–1); bishop of Rochester (1472–6), of Worcester (1476–86), of Ely (1486–1500); chancellor of England (1475, 1485). Became tutor to Prince Edward, son of Edward IV, but was removed from this position soon after the king's death in 1483. Later served on several royal commissions under Richard III and Henry VII.

The Wars of the Roses: 282

Alexander III, king of Scotland

1241–85. King of Scotland (1249–85). Son of Alexander II of Scotland and Mary de Couci. Succeeded in 1249 at the age of eight and was enthroned on the Stone of Scone. Married Margaret, daughter of Henry III of England, in 1251, when he was knighted by the king and did homage to him. Assisted Henry against the baronial party in 1264; did homage to Edward I of England in 1278.

Chronicles of the Age of Chivalry/Four Gothic Kings (US edn): 143

Alexander III, pope

d.1181. Pope (1159–81). Born Orlando Bandinelli. After Adrian IV's death in 1159, Alexander was accepted as pope by England and France but not Germany; and in 1162 Frederick I, the Holy Roman Emperor, forced him into exile in France where he and his court settled at Sens. Alexander favoured Thomas Becket in the archbishop's quarrel with Henry II of England and following Becket's death in 1170, canonized him on 1 March 1172. Two years later, in 1174, he absolved Henry II of complicity in the saint's murder after exacting a penance from him. After Frederick's defeat by his allies, the cities of the Lombard League, at the battle of Legnano (1176), the emperor was forced to acknowledge Alexander as pope. Among other achievements, Alexander established the procedure for canonizing saints, instituted a two-thirds majority rule for papal elections, and nurtured the universities as they emerged from the schools.

The Plantagenet Chronicles: 106–8, 110–13, 131, 134, 136, 144, 168

Alexander IV, pope

d.1261. Pope (1254–61). Born Rinaldo, count of Segni, at the end of the 12th century, the gentle and ineffectual Alexander IV was elected pope in 1254. He was unable to curb the growing power of Manfred of Hohenstaufen, Frederick II's illegitimate son, who, by Alexander's death, dominated Italy and held Sicily. The pope's choice of king for Sicily (1255), Edmund, son of Henry III of England made no headway against the Hohenstaufen prince – in part because of English shortage of funds.

Chronicles of the Age of Chivalry/Four Gothic Kings (US edn): 86

Alexander V, pope

d. 1410. Pope (1409–10). Born Peter of Candia. Elected pope at the Council of Pisa in 1409 by colleges of cardinals from the Urbanist (Roman) and the Clementine (Avignon) sides of the Great Schism. This was an unsuccessful attempt to heal the rift in the papacy by deposing the two existing popes and setting up a third endowed with authority by the council. Alexander died shortly after his election.

The Wars of the Roses: 110

Alexius II, emperor of Constantinople

1167–83. The son and heir to Manuel I; emperor of Constantinople (1180–3). Alexius was married to Agnes, daughter of King Louis VII of France, in 1178. Alexius' mother, Mary of Antioch, ruled as regent for him. In 1182 his cousin Andronicus stormed Constantinople, forced Alexius to sign his mother's death warrant, and became co-emperor as Andronicus I. A month later he had Alexius strangled and married his widow.

The Plantagenet Chronicles: 152, 168, 280, 282

Alfonso V, king of Aragon

1395–1458. Son of King Ferdinand I of Aragon; king of Aragon and Sicily (1416–58) and Naples (1443–58). Queen Joanna II of Naples adopted Alfonso as her heir after he defeated her rival Louis III of Naples in 1421. They quarrelled, and after her death in 1435 Alfonso had to contest the throne with a rival claimant, René of Anjou. In 1442 he defeated René and remained for the rest of his life in Naples. A leading figure of the early Renaissance, he favoured men of letters, and his devotion to the classics was such that a reading from Quintus Curtius is said to have cured him of a severe illness.

The Wars of the Roses: 197

Alfonso VIII, king of Castile

1155–1214. Son of Sancho III of Castile; king of Castile (1166–1214). After a chaotic minority, Alfonso assumed control of his kingdom in 1166 and married Eleanor, daughter of Henry II of England, in 1169. He received the reversion of Gascony as her dowry, but in 1204 on the death of Eleanor of Aquitaine had to claim it by force, later losing it to King John of England. He endowed the royal abbey of Las Huelgas, near Burgos, in 1187, at his wife's request; the abbey was also to be their royal mausoleum. In 1195 Alfonso was defeated by the Moors at Alarcos, and Castile was invaded by the armies of neighbouring León and Navarre, but he fought back and forced their leaders to terms. In 1212 he led León and Navarre to a great victory over the Moors at Las Navas de Tolosa.

The Plantagenet Chronicles: 114–15, 260, 261

Alfonso X, king of Castile

1221–84. Son and heir of Ferdinand III of Castile; king of Castile and León (1252–84). His sister, Eleanor of Castile, married Edward I of England (then Prince Edward) in 1255. Alfonso was chosen king of the Romans (i.e. Holy Roman Emperor-elect) by a faction of German nobles in 1257, in opposition to Richard, 3rd earl of Cornwall, King John of England's second son. Papal and domestic opposition kept him in Spain and he renounced his claim in 1275. Alfonso seized several territories from the Moors, notably Cadiz in 1262; but his reign was also significant for an influx of Moorish culture into Europe, thanks to his generous patronage of Muslim scholars.

Chronicles of the Age of Chivalry/Four Gothic Kings (US edn): 80, 84, 187

Alfonso XI, king of Castile

1311–50. King of Castile and León (1312–50). Alfonso won a great victory against the Moors at Tarifa in 1340. He was the first European sovereign to found a royal order of chivalry, the Order of the Band, in 1330. Intended to enhance Alfonso's reputation as a patron of the chivalrous ideal, the idea was soon copied by Edward III of England when he founded the Order of the Garter.

Chronicles of the Age of Chivalry/Four Gothic Kings (US edn): 262

Alice, daughter of Louis VII, king of France

Daughter of Louis VII of France and his second wife, Constance of Castile. In 1161, when she was still a child, she was betrothed to Richard, duke of Aquitaine (later Richard I of England), son of Henry II of England, and was held in wardship by the English king pending the marriage. Some sources hint that she was involved in a relationship with the king, but that is unlikely to be true. She was handed back to her brother, Philip II of France, in 1189, and Richard rejected her in 1190 in favour of Berengaria of Navarre. Philip then freed Richard from his 20-year oath to marry Alice, but only in return for 10,000 marks. In 1195 Alice was eventually married to William, count of Ponthieu.

The Plantagenet Chronicles: 97, 114, 192, 195, 212–13

Alighieri, Dante

See: Dante Alighieri

almshouse

Originally houses belonging to a monastery where alms and hospitality were dispensed, almshouses later developed into hospitals for the sick and aged poor, founded by private charity.

The Wars of the Roses: 179

Alnwick castle

Castle between the Cheviot hills and the Northumbrian coast, held by the Percy family in the late Middle Ages; a centre of Percy power in the north, as well as a border stronghold against Scots incursions. Fell to Henry IV in 1405 during the rebellion of the Percys. Alnwick was held by the Lancastrian forces of Margaret of Anjou, Henry VI's queen, in 1462, and besieged by the Yorkist Edward IV. In 1463 a Scottish relief column under Pierre de Brézé made the besiegers withdraw, but the Scots, suspecting a feint, would not approach the castle; and Margaret's force abandoned it to Edward's troops.

The Wars of the Roses: 61, 106, 232

Alphonse of Poitiers

1220–71. Count of Poitiers (1241–71) and Toulouse (1249–71); brother of Louis IX of France. An able administrator, Alphonse did much to heal the wounds left in the Languedoc by the Albigensian Crusade. He took the cross with Louis in 1248 and 1270; and on his return from crusade in 1252 was regent for his brother until 1254. Under the terms of the Treaty of Paris (1259), some of Alphonse's possessions, the Agenais, Quercy and Saintonge, were to devolve to the English crown on his death, in return for Henry III of England's abandonment of claims to Normandy, Maine, Anjou, Touraine and Poitou. However, the English crown did not receive the Agenais until 1279, eight years after Alphonse's death, and

Saintonge until 1289, by which time its claim to Quercy had been abandoned.

Chronicles of the Age of Chivalry/Four Gothic Kings (US edn): 90–1

Alsace, Philip of

See: Philip of Alsace, count of Flanders

Amesbury Abbey

Nunnery founded in c. 979 by Alfrida, widow of King Edgar of England, and refounded by Henry II in 1177. He took over the existing house and replaced its occupants, reputed to be scandalously corrupt, with sisters from the austere Benedictine abbey of Fontevrault in France. Amesbury continued under royal patronage; and the Worcester annalist records that Edward I arranged for his daughter Mary, when she was still only seven years old, to take the veil there on 15 August 1285, together with 13 other girls.

The Plantagenet Chronicles: 131
Chronicles of the Age of Chivalry/Four Gothic Kings (US edn): 126, 129

Amiens, Mise of

Judgement made at Amiens on 25 January 1264 by Louis IX of France, to resolve Henry III of England's continued dispute with Simon de Montfort and his baronial followers. Louis ruled that the Provisions of Oxford were void, and that Henry should be free to choose his own councillors, thus freeing him from de Montfort's domination.

Chronicles of the Age of Chivalry/Four Gothic Kings (US edn): 96

Ancren Riwule

Middle English tract written c. 1220 by an anonymous English churchman to instruct young ladies about to become anchoresses, that is, female hermits.

Chronicles of the Age of Chivalry/Four Gothic Kings (US edn): 163

Angelico, Fra

c. 1400–55. Early Renaissance painter and Dominican friar, born in Vicchio in Tuscany. After his death he was popularly known as Il Beato Fra Angelico, although he was never officially beatified. The Medici, patrons of San

Anne of Bohemia *Anne's death deeply grieved her husband, Richard II of England.*

Marco, and other important Florentines favoured his work, which depicted only religious subjects. The style of his paintings, particularly those adorning the convent of San Marco in Florence, combined spatial clarity and solidity with spirituality. In the 1440s Fra Angelico decorated the Cappella del Sacramento in the Vatican.

Chronicles of the Age of Chivalry/Four Gothic Kings (US edn): 66–7
The Wars of the Roses: 218

Angers

Capital of the province of Anjou in western France, and centre of Angevin/Plantagenet power. Fulk Nerra, count of Anjou, founded the abbey of St Nicholas there, and built the castle of Durtal overlooking the town in c. 1040. In 1066 Fulk Rechin imprisoned his elder brother Geoffrey Martel (the Bearded) in Angers, and ruled as count of Anjou in his stead. Site of the wedding (1128) of Empress Matilda, daughter of Henry I of England, to Geoffrey the Fair (Geoffrey Plantagenet), count of Anjou, founders of the Plantagenet dynasty. Their son, Henry II of England (ruled 1154–89) endowed a leper hospital at Angers. The chronicler Ralph of Diceto contrasted the ancient glories of the town, epitomized by its fine stone walls, with the niggardliness of its modern inhabitants (c. 1200). Castle and town were lost by King John of England to Philip II of France in 1203. Louis IX of France had the castle demolished and replaced with a stronger fortification (1228–38).

The Plantagenet Chronicles: 24–5, 34, 48–52, 129, 131, 168, 252, 276

Angoulême

Port on the River Charente in western France. Site of a great Romanesque cathedral, Saint-Pierre, begun c. 1110. In 1220, after a brief period of possession by King John of England, it passed to the Lusignan counts of La Marche. In 1360 the town was ceded to England by the Treaty of Brétigny, then reconquered in 1373 by Charles V of France.

The Plantagenet Chronicles: 32, 55, 261

Angoulême, Isabella of

See: Isabella of Angoulême

Anjou

County in north-west France, seat of the Angevin dynasty from whom the Plantagenets derived. Maine was united with Anjou under Fulk V, count of Anjou, in 1109. Anjou was linked to the English crown when the son of Geoffrey the Fair (Geoffrey Plantagenet), count of Anjou (1129–51), became Henry II of England in 1154. A focus for rivalry between the Capetian kings of France and the Plantagenets, Anjou, with its capital Angers, was finally taken from Henry II's youngest son, John, by Philip II of France, in 1203–4. By the Treaty of Paris (1259), Henry III of England relinquished his rights in the county, which passed out of Plantagenet hands.

The Plantagenet Chronicles: 30, 33–4, 37, 49, 50, 94, 261, 279
Chronicles of the Age of Chivalry/Four Gothic Kings (US edn): 90

Anjou, Margaret of

See: Margaret of Anjou

Anne of Bohemia

1366–94. Eldest daughter of Holy Roman Emperor Charles IV of Luxemburg; first wife of Richard II of England.

When Anne and Richard were married at Westminster in 1382, they were both 15 years old. The match had been a major political coup for the young Richard's regency council. Anne's eldest brother, Wenceslaus IV, who succeeded

Avignon Rome *(opposite) shown as a mourning widow after the papacy moved to Avignon.*

their father in 1378 as king of Germany, looked to be a valuable counterweight against the French. Anne herself was not famed for her beauty, but was said to be gentle of character.

The new queen brought a large following of Bohemians with her, arousing English suspicions. They may have introduced the work of the English religious reformer John Wycliffe to Bohemia, where it was taken up by John Hus and many others. In England, Anne made one major blunder, when she supported the unpopular royal favourite Robert de Vere, 9th earl of Oxford, in his wish to marry one of her ladies in waiting, Agnes Launcecrona, and divorce his own wife, Philippa de Couci, who had many relatives amongst the higher English aristocracy. Nevertheless, she gradually earned trust and affection as a mediator between the king and his subjects. One of her most celebrated actions was in 1392, when she appeased the wrath of the king against the citizens of London, who had refused to grant him a loan. When Anne died of the plague at Sheen Palace in June 1394, the king was heartbroken. 'Beside cursing the place where she died,' remarked a later chronicler, 'he did also throw down the buildings.' That is, he razed the manor house to the ground. Richard also commissioned a splendid tomb for the woman who had given him constant support and understanding – if no heirs – for the 12 years of their marriage. The English people, as well as Richard, mourned her passing.

The Wars of the Roses: 23, 33, 39–40, 44, 57, 68–9, 73

Antioch

City and principality on the eastern Mediterranean coast opposite Cyprus, one of the four crusader states set up after the First Crusade (1096–99), with Bohemond I as its first prince. It had been captured by the crusaders in 1098 after an eight-month siege, despite the city's vast defensive walls with their 400 towers. Antioch was also claimed by the emperor of Constantinople, for the leaders of the First Crusade had promised to return it to the Byzantine empire to which it had formerly belonged. The promise was not honoured. The disastrous Second Crusade retreated to Antioch in 1148, after Louis VII of France and Conrad III of Germany had failed to take Damascus. Saladin's army was defeated there in 1189 by the forces of the Third Crusade, but the city was finally lost to the Muslims in 1268.

The Plantagenet Chronicles: 21, 26, 38, 61, 69, 78, 148, 168, 186

Antioch Crusaders massacre the city's Muslim citizens after its capture in 1098.

Antioch, Bohemond of

See: Bohemond of Antioch

antipope

A pope elected in opposition to one chosen according to canon law. A whole line of antipopes resided at Avignon in France during the Great Schism (1378–1417).

Aquinas, St Thomas

*c.*1225–73. Medieval Italian philosopher and theologian. A younger son of the count of Aquino, he studied at the Benedictine monastery of Monte Cassino and at the University of Naples, where he secretly joined the Dominican order. His aristocratic relations kidnapped and imprisoned him but failed to quench his vocation. Once freed, Thomas went to Cologne in 1248 to study under Albertus Magnus, where he earned the nickname 'the dumb ox' for his massive frame and amiable taciturnity. In 1252 he began teaching theology at the University of Paris, and in 1256 was admitted as a master. Aquinas's lifelong work was the reconciliation of Christianity with Aristotelian thought. In 1267 he began the *Summa Theologiae*, a summary of all theological knowledge, running to over two million words, still unfinished when he stopped writing it in 1273. He died three months later. Thomas Aquinas was canonized in 1283.

Chronicles of the Age of Chivalry/Four Gothic Kings (US edn): 112–15

Aquitaine

Duchy in south-west France stretching from the Loire to the Pyrenees, and, in the mid-12th century, including the counties of Poitou, Périgord, La Marche, Limoges, Berry, Saintonge and Gascony. It came to the Plantagenet family in 1152, when the young Henry – the future Henry II of England – married Eleanor of Aquitaine in Poitiers Cathedral.

A 12th-century chronicler commented that it 'overflows with riches of many kinds, so excelling other parts of the western world that it is considered by historians one of the most fortunate and prosperous regions of Gaul. Its fields are fertile, its vineyards productive, and its forests abound in wild life. From the life-giving waters (*aquae*) of the River Garonne, the province takes its name.'

Its richness and fertility were matched by a flourishing cultural life centred on the ducal court at Poitiers. The duchy also supported a rich religious life which manifested itself in the building of many fine churches, such as the abbey of Notre-Dame-la-Grande in Poitiers. Eleanor and Henry, who helped to fund the rebuilding of Poitiers Cathedral, Saint-Pierre, continued a tradition of ducal patronage.

Another 12th-century source, the *Pilgrim's Book of Compostella*, stressed the diversity of the duchy's inhabitants – the Poitevins were elegant and witty, the people of Saintonge uncouth, and the Gascons frivolous and debauched but generous. Their differences reflected the diversity of political life in Aquitaine, which was little more than a collection of many different lordships under the general authority of the dukes. Many of these were controlled by turbulent and often hostile castellans, such as the lords of Lusignan.

The duchy began to fall apart early in the 13th century, as Plantagenet power in France crumbled and as the county of Poitou came gradually under the control of the French kings. In 1259, by the Treaty of Paris, the English crown formally ceded Poitou to Louis IX of France and retained only Gascony – together with rights of reversion in Saintonge, Périgord, Agenais and Quercy – as the last vestiges of the great Plantagenet domains.

The Plantagenet Chronicles: 45, 55, 122
Chronicles of the Age of Chivalry/Four Gothic Kings (US edn): 228, 282, 293
The Wars of the Roses: 28–9, 210

Aquitaine, Eleanor of

See: Eleanor of Aquitaine

Aragon

Kingdom in north-east Spain, bordering on France and including the southern Pyrenees. Ruled initially by the kings of Navarre, Aragon was first set up as a kingdom in 1035, for Ramiro I of León, the illegitimate son of Sancho III of Navarre. In its turn it annexed Navarre in

1076, and was joined with Catalonia in 1137 through the accession of Raymond Berengar IV, count of Barcelona. Aragon also expanded into the Moorish emirate of Zaragoza, and in the 12th century Zaragoza was made its capital. The name Aragon came to signify the lands held by the house of Aragon: the kingdom itself, Catalonia, Valencia, Majorca and French fiefs, notably in Roussillon, Provence and Montpellier. In 1479 Aragon was united with Castile through the marriage of Ferdinand II of Aragon and Isabella of Castile.

The Plantagenet Chronicles: 115
Chronicles of the Age of Chivalry/Four Gothic Kings (US edn): 228
The Wars of the Roses: 246–7

Arc, Joan of

See: Joan of Arc

archdeacon

The chief attendant on a bishop; his most important subordinate. Gerald of Wales, archdeacon of Brecon, always longed for promotion to the bishopric of St Davids, but Henry II of England repeatedly ignored his attempts at preferment to the higher post.

archery

In the later Middle Ages, archery was considered so important that all free men between the ages of 16 and 60 were compelled by law to own and practise with a longbow. It was the basis of England's military power during the Hundred Years War (1337–1453); Agincourt was a decisive victory for English archers.

The Wars of the Roses: 107, 190

Armagnac

County in Gascony, in south-west France, with Auch as its chief town. The counts of Armagnac originated in the 10th century, as vassals of the dukes of Gascony. Edward the Black Prince laid the county waste in 1355, when John II, count of Armagnac, led a rebellion against him on his arrival in Gascony. It passed to England with the Treaty of Brétigny in 1360; but in 1368 the counts of Armagnac and Albret refused to pay their taxes to the Black Prince and took their case to the parlement of Paris, giving Charles V of France a pretext to prolong what came to be known as the Hundred Years War. The county returned to France, and Count Bernard VII led

archery English archers at the butts; practising the skills that proved so effective at Agincourt.

the Armagnac faction in French politics from 1407 to his death in 1418.

Chronicles of the Age of Chivalry/Four Gothic Kings (US edn): 266, 294

Armagnacs

Or Orleanists, party led by Louis, duke of Orléans, at the French court during the reign of Charles VI (1388–1414). Louis, duke of Orléans, was favourite when the king was sane, and rivalry soon developed with Philip the Bold, duke of Burgundy, who took control of government during Charles' periodic bouts of insanity. Philip died in 1404, and in 1407 his son, John the Fearless, had Louis of Orléans murdered in Paris. Charles, his heir, married the count of Armagnac's daughter, and the Orleanist faction was thereafter known as the Armagnacs. In 1411 open war broke out between the factions. The Armagnacs took Paris in 1413 and led the French forces against Henry V of England in 1415. After the duke of Burgundy recognized Henry's claim to the French throne in 1419, the Armagnac/Burgundian feud was absorbed into the struggle between the house of Burgundy and the French crown.

The Wars of the Roses: 115

Arras, peace of

Treaty of 1482 between Louis XI of France and Maximilian of Austria, duke of Burgundy. Under its terms the dauphin Charles, Louis' successor, was to marry Margaret, Maximilian's daughter, who would bring with her the French counties of Artois and Burgundy. Negotiated in part to pacify Maximilian's hostile subjects in Flanders and Brabant, the treaty ended Edward IV of England's earlier alliance with Burgundy.

The Wars of the Roses: 239

Arsuf, battle of

Battle between the Muslim forces of Saladin and a crusader army under Richard I of England and Hugh, duke of Burgundy. It took place outside

the Muslim-held town of Arsuf near Jaffa in the Holy Land, on 7 September 1191. An eyewitness account by Richard, canon of Holy Trinity, Aldgate, describes the English king's great prowess and ferocity in vanquishing the Saracens, who were forced to flee, leaving the town undefended.

The Plantagenet Chronicles: 216–17

Art McMurrough

See: McMurrough, Art

Arthur, duke of Brittany

1187–1202. Posthumous son and heir of Geoffrey, fourth son of Henry II of England, and Constance, heiress of Brittany. Arthur was proclaimed duke of Brittany in 1196, and an invasion of his duchy by Richard I of England (Henry II's third son) was repulsed in 1197 with French aid. On the English king's death in 1199, Arthur's claim to the throne of England was passed over in favour of John, Henry II's youngest son. In 1202 Philip II of France declared John's French lands confiscated and conferred them on Arthur, who joined the force besieging Eleanor of Aquitaine in Mirebeau castle. John's forces attacked his camp and captured him in the battle of Mirebeau (1 August 1202). Arthur disappeared into Falaise castle and was never seen again.

The Plantagenet Chronicles: 184, 226, 260, 263, 274–8, 280

Arthur, King

Legendary 6th-century English king, first represented by the 8th-century chronicler Nennius as a Christian warrior who led the British against the pagan Saxons of Kent. The full Arthurian cycle of legends first appeared in the 12th century in the verse narrative of the clerk Wace, the *Roman de Brut*. The Arthurian legends soon became very popular: Marie de France wrote five *romans* based on them between about 1155 and 1190. The Plantagenets favoured Arthur as a useful source of prestige and propaganda. In 1191 Richard I of England gave Tancred, king of Sicily, what was said to be Arthur's sword Excalibur. Edward I was present in 1278 when the supposed tombs of Arthur and his queen Guinevere were opened at Glastonbury Abbey, and the bones ceremoniously reburied. He later took what was supposed to be Arthur's crown from the Welsh in 1283. Edward III established the Order of the Round Table – a direct reference to the legends – as a chivalric emblem of royalty.

Sir Thomas Malory's version of the story, the *Morte d'Arthur*, was published by Caxton in 1485.

The Plantagenet Chronicles: 210, 246
Chronicles of the Age of Chivalry/Four Gothic Kings (US edn): 55, 113, 125, 160, 233

Arundel, Thomas, archbishop of Canterbury

1353–1414. Bishop of Ely (1373–88); archbishop of York (1388–96); archbishop of Canterbury (1396–7, 1399–1414); chancellor of England (1386–9, 1391–6, 1399, 1407, 1412). One of the council of regency during Richard II's minority; and aligned with the lords appellant in trying to curb royal tyranny. He was nevertheless promoted to the see of Canterbury in 1396; but he lost the king's confidence in 1397, and was impeached and banished by parliament in 1397, ostensibly for involvement with the lords appellant. He was translated from Canterbury to the see of St Andrews, in Scotland, his place of exile. Arundel crowned Henry Bolingbroke as Henry IV on his return from exile in 1399 and was restored to Canterbury. Under Henry IV he served twice as chancellor, continued his earnest efforts to crush Lollardy, and prevented attempts in parliament in 1404 and 1410 to disendow the Church.

The Wars of the Roses: 56, 62, 68, 84–5, 91, 94, 106, 117

assart

To clear land; to turn woodland into arable or pastureland. Much woodland was cleared in this way throughout the Middle Ages, although the pressure for new farmland was greatest at times when the population was expanding, as in the 12th and 13th centuries. It was a grave offence to assart in the royal forest without a licence; land assarted with a licence incurred annual payments to the Exchequer.

Assisi

Town in Umbria in central Italy, situated on a commanding hill in the Apennines. Birthplace of St Francis (1182), who died there in 1226. Over his tomb were erected two churches, the lower and upper, consecrated in 1253 and decorated with frescoes by Cimabue, Giotto and others, depicting the saint's life. The mummified remains of his leading female companion, St Clare, may still be seen in the crypt of the church built nearby in her memory.

Chronicles of the Age of Chivalry/Four Gothic Kings (US edn): 41, 197

Assisi, St Francis of

See: Francis, St, of Assisi

assizes

Periodical sessions of Westminster judges in county courts; ordinances or regulations of a court (e.g. as to brewing or weaving); procedure in a court to establish possession of land.

astrolabe

Instrument used to measure the positions of heavenly bodies; much used by medieval astronomers and navigators.

The Wars of the Roses: 249–50

astrology

Ancient system of divination through the stars, known since antiquity and revived in medieval Europe in the 12th century following an influx of Arab astrological texts into Europe. In the 13th century Michael Scot completed his great encyclopedia of astrology at the court of Holy Roman Emperor Frederick II (1228), and Roger Bacon related the rise of the world's religions to astrological conjunctions. In the 14th century the French mathematician, Nicholas Oresme, used logic to disprove astrology's predictive power, but the system remained popular, receiving a fresh impetus during the Renaissance, when there was increasing interest in science and astronomy.

The Plantagenet Chronicles: 187
The Wars of the Roses: 248–9

d'Athée, Gérard

d.1213. Said to have been born a serf, Gérard d'Athée, a Frenchman from Touraine, rose in King John of England's service as a highly paid and ruthless strong-arm man. In 1204, when Philip II of France invaded John's French territories with the help of Aquitainians rebelling against the English king, d'Athée remained loyal to John and resisted the rebels at Loches until his capture in 1205. John subsequently paid his ransom of 2,000 marks and took him to England, where he became the king's lieutenant in the West Country. D'Athée died in 1213, having aroused the hatred of the English barons, but his numerous relatives were cited by name in Magna Carta (1215), when King John promised to remove them all from office.

The Plantagenet Chronicles: 280–1

Augustinians

Religious orders following the 'rule of St Augustine'. St Augustine, bishop (396–430) of Hippo, a Roman colony in North Africa, wrote letters giving detailed advice to religious communities, and in the 11th century these became the core from which a new rule was devised for communities of canons attached to cathedrals or minsters. In the 12th century the Augustinian canons emerged as a full religious order: like monks, they lived in communities and were bound by vows of poverty, chastity and obedience, but they laid greater emphasis on pastoral duties. Henry II of England was an important patron of the order: in 1177 he refounded Waltham as the richest Augustinian abbey in England. The Augustinian (or Austin) Friars emerged in the 13th century as a separate mendicant order.

The Plantagenet Chronicles: 131

Avignon

City now in south-east France on the Rhône, still surrounded by 12th- and 14th-century ramparts. Between 1309 and 1378 it housed the papal court during its exile from Rome, a period in papal history described by many contemporaries as 'the Babylonian captivity of the Church'. This was after Pope Clement V, in obedience to his sponsor Philip IV of France, had in 1309 moved his court from Rome to Avignon – conveniently situated in Provence, then just outside the boundaries of France. In 1348 his successor Clement VI bought Avignon from the countess of Provence. The fine papal palace at Avignon was built during this period. After the start of the Great Schism in 1378, Avignon became the seat of Pope Clement VII and his successors, the Avignonese popes. When the schism ended in 1408, the city remained under the nominal authority of papal legates.

Chronicles of the Age of Chivalry/Four Gothic Kings (US edn): 150–2, 197, 282, 303
The Wars of the Roses: 32–3

Babylonian captivity

The period 1309–78 during which the papacy resided at Avignon, named after the Jews' captivity in Babylon, which began when Pope Clement V, a Frenchman, fled from Rome to Avignon at the behest of Philip IV of France. During the captivity, the popes were all French, resident at Avignon, and dominated by the French kings. Pope Gregory XI finally returned the *Curia* to Rome in 1378; only for the Great Schism to begin straight afterwards.

Bacon, Roger

1214?–94, English philosopher and scientist, a Franciscan friar whose accurate observation of natural phenomena was far ahead of his time. He described the rise of the world's religions in terms of astrological planetary conjunctions.

The Wars of the Roses: 248

Bagot, William

d.?1400. One of Richard II's ministers, described by the chronicler Walsingham as avaricious, ambitious and arrogant. At the London parliament of 17 September 1397, with John Bushey and Henry Green, he led the prosecution of the lords appellant and others who opposed Richard II's despotic behaviour. One of the knights of the king's council which governed the realm during Richard's Irish expedition of 1399, Bagot escaped after Henry Bolingbroke (later Henry IV) invaded England, when Bushey and Green were beheaded as supporters of Richard. He then fled to Ireland.

The Wars of the Roses: 80, 84

Baker, Geoffrey le

14th-century lay chronicler, native of Swinbrook in Oxfordshire, and connected with Osney Abbey, also in Oxfordshire. Supported by Sir Thomas de la More of Northmoor, he obtained much of his information on Edward II of England from the chronicle of Adam of Murimuth, another Oxfordshire man. He described, in a lively but generally melodramatic and often inventive fashion, Edward II's deposition and death, Edward III's seizure of power, his struggles with Philip VI of France and the depredations of the Black Death. Royalist in his sympathies, he portrayed Edward II as an almost Christ-like saint and Queen Isabella as a 'Jezebel' allied to 'priests of Baal'. He regarded Edward III as rightful king of France and 'that tyrant' Philip VI as an usurper.

Chronicles of the Age of Chivalry/Four Gothic Kings (US edn): 16, 167, 205, 227, 236, 252, 260

Baldock, Robert

d.1327. Archdeacon of Middlesex, keeper of the Privy Seal (1320–3) and chancellor (1323–6) under Edward II. Baldock, as Edward's nominee, masterminded the reform of the Exchequer and the royal household from 1322 onwards under the direction of Hugh Despenser the son, a major beneficiary of the changes. When Isabella of France, Edward's queen, invaded England in 1326, Baldock fled to Wales with the king and Hugh Despenser the son; he

Baldwin, count of Flanders *Crusaders crown Baldwin Latin emperor of Constantinople.*

was captured and handed over to Adam of Orleton, bishop of Hereford, who in 1327 allowed a mob of angry citizens to attack Baldock. He died shortly afterwards of the injuries he had sustained.

Chronicles of the Age of Chivalry/Four Gothic Kings (US edn): 189, 210, 224

Baldwin, archbishop of Canterbury

d.1190. Cistercian abbot of Ford; bishop of Worcester (1184); archbishop of Canterbury (1184). He was a favourite of Henry II, who employed him in negotiations with Rhys ap Gruffydd, prince of South Wales. His struggle with the monks of Canterbury, who were imprisoned in their monastery in 1188–9 for their opposition to his plans to found a rival collegiate church at Hackington, became a *cause célèbre* that ended in his defeat. Baldwin officiated at Richard I's coronation in 1189. He died on crusade in the Holy Land.

The Plantagenet Chronicles: 200

Baldwin, count of Flanders

1171–1205. Count of Flanders; and emperor of Constantinople (1204–5). He made an alliance with Richard I of England in 1197 for mutual defence against Philip II of France. One of the leaders of the Fourth Crusade (1202) he was elected first Latin emperor by the crusaders after their sack of Constantinople in March 1204. According to the chronicler Ralph of Coggeshall, he promptly distributed a third of the imperial treasury (about 1,800,000 silver marks) between the Latin princes and the army; and endowed them, and others, with dignities, honours and gifts, which included two jewelled robes and a brilliant carbuncle for the king of France.

The Plantagenet Chronicles: 244, 250–2, 281–3

balinger

Small galley able to manoeuvre on rivers and used as a warship in the later Middle Ages.

The Wars of the Roses: 128

Ball, John

d.1381. Itinerant preacher and one of the leaders of the Peasants Revolt; a Kentish man repeatedly jailed by the archbishop of Canterbury for haranguing Colchester church-goers on Sundays with his subversive and heretical doctrines: he preached common ownership of goods and an end to the feudal hierarchy. With Wat Tyler, he led 30,000 men to storm John of Gaunt's Savoy palace on the Thames and invade London on 10 June 1381. He was with Tyler at Smithfield on 15 June, when the latter was killed. John Ball fled to the Midlands where he was apprehended at Coventry; brought before the king at St Albans, he was hanged, drawn and quartered.

The Wars of the Roses: 34–8

Balliol, Edward

d.1363. Son of John Balliol, king of Scotland. He shared his father's exile in Normandy until 1324, when he found shelter at the English court. Seeking to reclaim the title John had lost to Robert Bruce, he assumed the title of king of Scots in 1332, invaded Scotland, defeated the supporters of David II of Scotland, and was crowned at Scone. He was driven out within a matter of months, but returned with Edward III of England's backing in 1333 to vanquish David II's army at the decisive battle of Halidon Hill (1333). Balliol then ceded Lothian to Edward, and retired to England, leaving most of the subsequent wars in Scotland to the English. He returned to Scotland after David's defeat at Neville's Cross (1346), but surrendered his title to the kingdom of Scotland to Edward III.

Chronicles of the Age of Chivalry/Four Gothic Kings (US edn): 188–92

Bamburgh castle

Royal castle on the Northumbrian North Sea coast. It was retained by Margaret of Anjou's Lancastrian supporters after Edward IV's seizure of power in 1461. One of several bases which enabled the Lancastrians to control most of Northumberland, it was besieged by the king in December 1462, and surrendered in 1463 by its commander, Henry Beaufort, 3rd duke of Somerset, in return for a promise of 1,000 marks a year – but this was never paid.

The Wars of the Roses: 232

banking

In the 12th and 13th centuries the Jews were important as moneylenders, and the Templars were the main bankers to the English and French kings. But after the Jews were driven out of England by Edward I in 1290 and the Templars were dissolved during his son's reign, Italians – especially Florentines – built up an already major share in banking to a near monopoly. Italy dominated trade and had the added benefit of an internationally accepted currency, the Florentine florin. Interest on bank loans was disguised to circumvent the Church's ban on usury. Florence lost its dominance of European finance after 1340, when Edward III of England's huge debts ruined the English branches of his principal Florentine bankers, the Bardi and Peruzzi families. Subsequently, native bankers such as William de la Pole in England and Jacques Coeur in France catered to their sovereigns' needs. However, their resources proved inadequate in the long term and the 15th century saw the revival of Florentine financial power under the Medici.

Chronicles of the Age of Chivalry/Four Gothic Kings (US edn): 142, 234–6

banking Florentine bankers practise their profession. The gold florin served as an international currency, giving Florence's bankers a great advantage.

Bannockburn, battle of

Battle near Stirling on 23 June 1314, in which the English army under Edward II was defeated by Scottish troops led by Robert Bruce, king of Scotland. The English expedition was launched to relieve Stirling castle, held by an English garrison and besieged since 1313 by the Scots. Edward's troops, principally cavalry, first met Scots foot-soldiers in the Forth Valley plain on 22 June. Overnight, they moved to a position between the River Forth and the Bannock Burn; and at dawn the Scottish spearmen charged, trapping the English horse between the two streams. The English fled with heavy losses, many inflicted by pursuing Scots. Only Berwick was left in English hands, and Bruce was master of Scotland.

Chronicles of the Age of Chivalry/Four Gothic Kings (US edn): 281

Barbarossa

See: Frederick I Hohenstaufen, Holy Roman Emperor

Bardi

Family of Florentine bankers, whose loans did much to keep the English monarchy solvent in the first part of the 13th century. Edward III of England's bankruptcy of 1340 precipitated their collapse within a decade.

Chronicles of the Age of Chivalry/Four Gothic Kings (US edn): 281

Bardolf, Hugh

d.1203. Royal justice who assisted in the government of England during Henry II's absence in France (1188), and again (with William Marshal) between 1190 and 1194 during Richard I's absence on crusade and in captivity.

The Plantagenet Chronicles: 217, 220

Bardolf, Sir Thomas

1368–1408. Lord of Wormegay and 5th baron Bardolf. He was implicated in the ill-fated rising of Henry Percy, 'Hotspur', against Henry IV in 1403. He joined Henry Percy, 1st earl of Northumberland (Hotspur's father), in another unsuccessful revolt against Henry IV in 1405, and fled to Scotland, then in 1406 to Wales, where he assisted Owen Glendower in his uprising against the English; and then to France. Bardolf returned to Scotland in 1407 to foment rebellion against the English crown. In 1408 he joined the earl of Northumberland's invasion of northern England, and died in Yorkshire at the battle of Bramham Moor.

The Wars of the Roses: 104, 106

Barnet, battle of

Battle fought at a staging-post on the main road north from London, on 14 April 1471, in which Richard Neville, 16th earl of Warwick, 'the Kingmaker', Edward IV's most dangerous opponent, was killed. The battle ended his rebellion against Edward, whose secret marriage to the comparatively low-born Elizabeth Woodville and elevation of her relatives had angered the earl, leading him to desert the Yorkist camp. He had lent his support to the deposed Lancastrian king, Henry VI, whom he had placed on the throne in 1470. At

Barnet, Edward's victorious troops routed the Lancastrian army, inflicting a reputed 30,000 casualties.

The Wars of the Roses: 201, 224, 233, 255, 261–3

Barnwell annalist

*fl.*1210–16. Anonymous monk or canon and chronicler, whose work was kept at Barnwell Priory, but almost certainly not written there. The chronicle runs from the Incarnation to 1225 and is compiled from other authorities until 1202. The chronicler concentrates on English affairs, using documents intelligently and treating his subjects with relative objectivity. He adduces evidence rationally and provides explanations for some events, claiming, for instance, that Philip II of France aided the English barons out of greed and hatred for their king. His account of John is the fairest given by any contemporary chronicler, although he describes the king's conflict with his barons from a pro-baronial stance. His comment that John was 'deserted by his own men and, in the end, little mourned' remains the king's best-known epitaph.

The Plantagenet Chronicles: 12, 259, 265, 293
Chronicles of the Age of Chivalry/Four Gothic Kings (US edn): 23

baron

After 1066 the tenants-in-chief, the great landholders of the realm who held their lands directly from the king, were known collectively as barons. A distinction between the greater and lesser barons gradually emerged, and in the late 13th century the greater barons began to receive summonses from the Crown to attend parliament. The first use of the style of baron in an individual's title came in 1387, the second in 1433, and by the middle of the 15th century the creation of barons was frequent. Like other holders of noble titles, barons were invested by the king in person.

Bartholomew Diaz

See: Diaz, Bartholomew

Bartholomew, Lord Badlesmere

d.1322. A supporter of Thomas, 2nd earl of Lancaster, and one of the magnates who forced the Despensers, father and son, into exile in 1321. Later that year Bartholomew's wife refused hospitality to Edward II of England's queen, Isabella, at his castle of Leeds in Kent. In retaliation, the king seized Leeds and, subsequently, Bartholomew's other castles. Bartholomew was hanged at Canterbury in 1322.

Chronicles of the Age of Chivalry/Four Gothic Kings (US edn): 200, 202–3

Basle, Council of

Council of the Church (1431–49) summoned by Pope Martin V before his death in 1431. A major rift arose between Pope Eugenius IV and the council over the question of whether papal or conciliar authority was supreme in the Church. Henry VI of England supported the pope through his envoys.

The Wars of the Roses: 127, 169

Bastard of Fauconberg

See: Fauconberg, Lord (Bastard of Fauconberg)

Bath

Spa town in Somerset, colonized by the Romans in the 1st century AD. A city which shared its bishop with Wells, Bath was the centre of a flourishing wool and cloth industry in the later Middle Ages. Henry VI of England witnessed naked bathers there in 1449, and was much shocked.

The Wars of the Roses: 169

Bayeux

City in Normandy near the English Channel, inhabited since Roman times. Odo, its bishop in the late 11th century, was the half-brother of William the Conqueror, king of England. The celebrated Bayeux Tapestry was probably commissioned during his episcopate and was hung in the cathedral. Henry I of England burned Bayeux in 1105 and Henry V of England took the city during his French campaign of 1417, but it was lost with the rest of Normandy in 1449–50.

The Plantagenet Chronicles: 62
The Wars of the Roses: 24, 141

Bayonne

Port in Gascony on the River Adour in southwest France; major Gascon stronghold. Henry II of England's marriage to Eleanor of Aquitaine in 1152, and his accession to the English throne in 1154, brought Bayonne to the English crown. After almost three centuries of continuous English rule, the town capitulated to the invading French army in August 1451, but was temporarily recovered by the English under John Talbot, 4th earl of Shrewsbury, the following year. However, by 1453, Bayonne was again in French hands.

The Wars of the Roses: 209

Beauchamp, Anne

d.1493. Only daughter of Richard Beauchamp, 13th earl of Warwick, she married Richard Neville, 9th earl of Salisbury. Through her, Neville became 16th earl of Warwick and inherited the estates and power of the great Beauchamp family. Anne was the mother of Anne Neville, wife of Richard III.

The Wars of the Roses: 295

Beauchamp, Guy de, 10th earl of Warwick

d.1315. 10th earl of Warwick (1298–1315). Powerful magnate in the faction opposing Piers Gaveston, Edward II's unpopular favourite, who nicknamed him 'the Black Dog of Arden'. Guy was one of the lords who secured Gaveston's temporary banishment in 1308. In 1312, he captured Gaveston at Deddington in Oxfordshire, met with other barons at Warwick and decided on Gaveston's death. He handed his prisoner over to Thomas, 2nd earl of Lancaster, for execution on 19 June 1312.

Chronicles of the Age of Chivalry/Four Gothic Kings (US edn): 174, 177, 185
The Wars of the Roses: 196, 200, 202, 205–6, 208–10, 212, 214, 216–17

Beauchamp, Richard, 13th earl of Warwick

1382–1439. Son of Thomas, 12th earl of Warwick. Chief English lay envoy to the Council of Constance (1414), and an important military commander in France under Henry V of England. He was a member of the council of the infant Henry VI of England, in 1422, and was tutor to the young king from 1428 to 1437. Appointed Lieutenant of France in 1437, he died there two years later. His daughter, Anne Beauchamp, married Richard Neville, 'the kingmaker', 16th earl of Warwick, whose power owed much to Beauchamp wealth.

The Wars of the Roses: 148, 167, 169, 189

Beauchamp, Thomas, 12th earl of Warwick

1339–1401. 12th earl of Warwick (1369–1401). One of John of Gaunt's supporters during his regency for the young Richard II, and subsequently one of the five lords appellant. He joined their forces at Waltham Cross on 14 November 1387, and then fought at Radcot Bridge against Richard II's army. The king invited him to a banquet in 1397, then arrested and imprisoned him in the Tower, in revenge for his actions as a lord appellant. He was freed on accession of Henry IV. The Beauchamp Tower is named after him.

The Wars of the Roses: 47, 52–3, 57, 78

Beaufort, Edmund, 2nd duke of Somerset

c.1406–55. 3rd earl of Dorset (1441), 5th earl of Somerset (1444), lieutenant of France (1448), 2nd duke of Somerset (1448–55). Edmund recaptured Harfleur for the English in 1440, in the closing years of the Hundred Years War, and relieved Calais in 1442; but in 1449, he fled to Caen before a French advance which took most of Anjou, Maine and Normandy. The chronicler Capgrave alleges that, during his period as lieutenant of France, it was 'due to his misconduct, that almost the whole country was returned to the control of the king of France'. Henry VI of England protected Edmund against popular resentment, but when the king became insane in 1453 Edmund was locked up in the Tower of London. He was freed when Henry recovered his senses in December 1454, and joined the Lancastrian forces opposed to Richard, 3rd duke of York, in 1455. He was killed on 22 May in the first battle of the Wars of the Roses, at St Albans.

The Wars of the Roses: 196, 200, 202, 205–6, 208, 210, 212, 214, 216–7

Beaufort, Edmund, 'duke of Somerset'

1438?–71. Son of Edmund Beaufort. Styled himself duke of Somerset (1464–71). Exiled for siding with Henry VI after the Yorkist Edward IV's usurpation in 1461, he assumed the ducal title while abroad, on the death of his brother Henry Beaufort, 3rd duke of Somerset, in 1464. He returned to reclaim his lands and titles from Henry's queen, Margaret of Anjou, in February 1471, and became the highest-ranking noble in her Lancastrian army. He went from London to the West Country in March 1471 to raise support for Henry VI, then turned north to rally Lancashire, but was intercepted by Edward's forces in Gloucestershire. Edmund was captured at the battle of Tewkesbury on 4 May 1471, and beheaded two days later by the victorious Yorkists.

The Wars of the Roses: 252, 254, 260, 262

Beaufort, Henry, bishop of Winchester

1377?–1447. Son of John of Gaunt and his mistress Katherine Swynford; declared legitimate in 1397 after John had married Katherine. Bishop of Lincoln (1398); chancellor (1403–5, 1413–17, 1424–6); bishop of Winchester (1404); cardinal (1427–47). Henry Beaufort was a close supporter of the future Henry V during the reign of his father, Henry IV, and, as chancellor, was a leading official in his administration. Proud and ambitious, he was strongly secular in his interests as he saw them. In 1417 Beaufort attended the Council of Constance and swung English support behind the election of Pope Martin V. In 1422 he became one of the protectors of the young Henry VI and began a struggle for power with the king's uncle, Humphrey, 2nd duke of Gloucester. The first phase of this ended when he accepted a cardinal's hat in 1427 and went abroad to preach a crusade against the Hussites. Returning to the English court in 1430, he crowned Henry VI king of France in Paris in 1431. In 1432 Parliament supported Beaufort against Gloucester, who tried for a second time to remove him from his bishopric – on the grounds that a cardinal could not hold an English see. Later in the 1430s Beaufort acted as an emissary in negotiations with France but then gradually retired from public life. He died at Wolvesey Palace near Winchester in 1447 and was buried in Winchester Cathedral, whose reconstruction he had completed.

The Wars of the Roses: 117, 123, 133, 140, 157, 166–9, 172, 176–8, 188, 192, 210

Beaufort, Henry, 3rd duke of Somerset

1436–64. Lancastrian supporter. 3rd marquis of Dorset (1448–55), 3rd duke of Somerset (1455–61, 1463–4). Made captain of Calais in October 1459 in place of Richard Neville, 16th earl of Warwick, 'the Kingmaker', following Lancastrian victories that year. Having rallied Lancastrian support in the north, after the capture of Henry VI at Northampton in June 1460, he helped defeat the Yorkists at Wakefield (December 1460) and St Albans (17 February 1461), and followed Henry's queen, Margaret of Anjou, to the north after the Lancastrian defeat at Towton (29 March 1461). He held Bamburgh castle against Edward IV in 1462–3, but finally surrendered it in 1463, in return for a pension of 1,000 marks yearly (never paid). From his refuge in Scotland, Beaufort organized a raid from the north against the Yorkists that was defeated by John Neville, 1st marquis of Montagu and 12th earl of Northumberland, in May 1464. After the raid he remained in hiding until captured and executed at Hexham.

The Wars of the Roses: 220, 222–4, 232, 236

Beaufort, Joan

d.1445. Daughter of John Beaufort, 1st earl of Somerset, and queen of James I of Scotland (ruled 1406–37). James fell in love with Joan during his imprisonment in England (1406–24), wrote of her in his poem *The Kingis Quair*, and married her at Southwark before his return to Scotland in 1424.

The Wars of the Roses: 185

Beaufort, John, 1st duke of Somerset

1403–44. Son of John Beaufort, 2nd earl of Somerset. 4th earl of Somerset (1425–43); 1st duke of Somerset (1443). He had temporary command of English forces in France in 1439–40 near the end of the Hundred Years War. He was created duke of Somerset in 1443 and led an expeditionary force to attack France. Beaufort's conduct of the campaign demonstrated singular incapacity. Landing in Normandy, he crossed the frontier and attacked the Breton stronghold of La Guerche, angering the duke of Brittany (a valuable English ally). He returned to England disgraced and soon died.

The Wars of the Roses: 189

Beaufort, John, 2nd earl of Somerset

1373?–1410. 1st marquis of Dorset (1397–99); 2nd earl of Somerset (1397–1410) and 1st marquis of Somerset (1397–99). Illegitimate eldest son of John of Gaunt and Katherine Swynford, legitimized in 1397 after their marriage. He was the first to bear the name Beaufort, which John chose for his children by Katherine. Deprived of his marquisates when Richard II was deposed by Henry Bolingbroke (later Henry IV), he later became chamberlain of England and captain of Calais under Henry.

The Wars of the Roses: 117

Beaufort, Lady Margaret

1443–1509. Daughter of John, 1st duke of Somerset. She married Edmund Tudor, 14th earl of Richmond, in 1445; their son, Henry Tudor, 15th earl of Richmond, was the future Henry VII. Edmund died in 1456 and in 1472 Margaret married Henry, Lord Stanley. During Richard III's reign she began promoting a match between Henry Tudor and Elizabeth of York, daughter of Edward IV. She canvassed for her son as an alternative to Richard III and was implicated in the 1483 rebellion, which publicly established Henry as Richard's rival. After her son's accession to the throne in 1485 she lived in retirement, founded St John's and Christ's colleges at Cambridge, and was Caxton's patron.

Beaulieu Abbey *The site of the great Cistercian abbey in Hampshire.*

Beaufort, Thomas, 2nd duke of Exeter

d. 1426. 1st earl of Dorset (1412), 2nd duke of Exeter (1416–26); chancellor (1410–12). Illegitimate son of John of Gaunt and Catherine Swynford, legitimized 1397. He commanded Henry IV of England's army in 1405 against rebellious forces in the north of England and was made chancellor five years later. He resigned in 1412 and the same year was sent to assist Louis, duke of Orléans, against John the Fearless, duke of Burgundy. Thomas defended Harfleur against the French in 1416. In July of the following year he drove off the Scots who, in conjunction with Lollard rebels, were besieging Roxburgh. He was active in Henry V of England's campaigns in France (1418–20). Although one of the infant Henry VI's guardians and a protector of England after Henry V's death

in 1422, he played only a minor role in the political life of the 1420s.

Beaulieu Abbey

Cistercian abbey in the New Forest, Hampshire, founded in 1203–4 by King John of England with monks of Cîteaux (his only monastic foundation). During John's dispute with the Cistercians in 1210, following their refusal to give him money, the abbot of Beaulieu was refused licence to cross the sea to attend the Cistercian general chapter at Cîteaux. After John's death in 1216 Beaulieu's claims on his body were set aside in favour of his wish to be buried in Worcester Cathedral.

Beauvais

City in northern France, besieged by the English in 1346 and 1433. In 1227 a reconstruction of its cathedral of St-Pierre was begun on a massive scale – the vault of the choir was more than 180 feet high – but the sheer size of the building proved its undoing. Only the eastern parts of the cathedral were complete after 60 years of work and several collapses. The site destined for the nave is still occupied by a small Romanesque church of the 10th century. One transept was constructed in the 16th century.

Becket, Thomas, St, archbishop of Canterbury

1118–70. Chancellor of England (1154–62), archbishop of Canterbury (1162–70). The son of Gilbert, a middle-ranking London citizen of Norman stock, Thomas was educated in the schools of London and Paris. In about 1144 he joined the household of Theobald, archbishop of Canterbury; ten years later, in 1154, the young Henry II, on the advice of Theobald, appointed him chancellor. Thomas became the king's close companion and friend, his energy, ability, and splendid lifestyle greatly impressing his contemporaries. He also supported Henry's interests over those of the English Church, defending heavy royal taxes on the Church to pay for Henry's 1159 campaign against Toulouse, and himself fighting for Henry at Toulouse.

When, in 1162, Henry secured the election of Becket to the see of Canterbury, he fully expected Thomas to continue their partnership and to bring matters ecclesiastical more closely under royal control. However, Becket followed custom and resigned as chancellor, becoming a staunch defender of the rights of the Church. He also exchanged his life of luxury for asceticism: his biographer Herbert of Bosham revealed that he wore a monastic habit and a hair shirt under his outer garments.

In 1163 Becket resisted the king's demand at the Council of Westminster that clerks convicted of felonies in ecclesiastical courts should be handed over to the lay authorities for punishment. He also prohibited the marriage of Henry's brother, William of Anjou, to the countess of Warenne. But the next year Thomas, by assenting reluctantly to the Constitutions of Clarendon – which embodied Henry's judicial programme – partially retracted his opposition. However, Pope Alexander III refused to approve the full text of the Constitutions, and supported Becket in renewing his opposition to Henry. In November 1164 Thomas was forced into exile, after a trial at Northampton for misappropriation of funds during which he breached the Constitutions by appealing to the pope.

He stayed abroad for the next six years, spending two of them at the abbey of Pontigny, and four at Ste-Colombe at Sens. Although attempts were made to heal the breach with the king, both sides remained uncompromising: it was a clash of both principles and personalities. Henry confiscated Thomas' property and exiled his supporters. Thomas threatened the king with excommunication. The deadlock was broken when, in 1170, Henry infringed the primate's rights by allowing the archbishop of York to crown his son, the young Henry, king of England, in spite of a papal prohibition.

Thomas Becket threatened England with a papal interdict. Henry yielded to this threat, and in December 1170 Thomas was allowed to return to England. As soon as he arrived he excommunicated those bishops who had crowned Henry the Young King. News of this enraged Henry II, who reportedly exclaimed, 'Will no-one rid me of this turbulent priest?' At this, four of his knights went to Canterbury and, on 29 December, murdered Becket before the altar of St Benedict in Canterbury Cathedral.

Within three years of his death Thomas was canonized, and the king accepted a public penance for his archbishop's martyrdom. Thomas' tomb in the cathedral became the most popular place of pilgrimage in England, and was credited with many miraculous cures. Chaucer's *Canterbury Tales* is a tribute to Becket's lasting popularity as the most influential martyr in the history of the English Church.

The Plantagenet Chronicles: 82, 91, 94–6, 98, 104, 106, 108–14, 116–20, 124, 131, 134, 137, 142, 154

Bedlam

Hospital in Bishopsgate, London. The name is a corruption of St Mary of Bethlehem. Founded as a priory in 1247, it came to specialize in the treatment of lunatics; in the 15th century six out of 14 patients there were described as 'out of their senses'. John Arundel, physician to the periodically insane Henry VI, was at one time its warden during the king's reign and was succeeded in the post by William Hobbes, surgeon to Edward IV.

The Wars of the Roses: 215

Benedict XI, pope

1240–1304. Pope (1303–4). Born Niccolò Boccasini. Bishop of Ostia, and a master general of the Dominican order, he was a short-lived successor to Pope Boniface VIII. Benedict occupied the see of Rome from October 1303 to his death in July 1304 and did his best to conciliate Philip IV of France, chiefly by rescinding Boniface's excommunication of the king. However, he confirmed the excommunication of Sciarra Colonna, leader of the anti-papalists in Rome, and of Philip's envoy Nogaret, both of whom had captured Boniface and who had sacked his palace at Anagni in 1303. Benedict withdrew to Perugia to escape pressure from the Colonna faction in Rome, a prelude to his successor Clement V's flight to Avignon.

Chronicles of the Age of Chivalry/Four Gothic Kings (US edn): 151, 154

Benedict XII, pope

c.1280–1342. Pope (1334–42). Born Jacques Fournier, of humble parentage, at Saverdan near Toulouse. Cistercian abbot; bishop of Pamiers (1317), then Mirepoix (1325). Promoted cardinal-priest of St-Prisca (1327) for his skills as an inquisitor; and was made pope at Avignon in 1334. A re-organizer of the papal court and the religious orders, he tried to mediate between Philip VI of France and Edward III of England over the former's claim to the duchy of Gascony, but failed to prevent the outbreak of the Hundred Years War in 1339. Petrarch's comment that he was an unfit and drunken

Bedlam *The official seal of St Mary of Bethlehem Hospital, Bishopsgate – alias the notorious Bedlam, the asylum which became a byword for lunacy.*

helmsman of his Church was motivated by a grudge and, though unfair, reveals the extent to which his reforms aroused criticism.

Chronicles of the Age of Chivalry/Four Gothic Kings (US edn): 236, 240

Benedict XIII, antipope

1328?–1423? antipope (1394–1417). Born Pedro de Luna. Aragonese churchman and a pope of the Avignon branch of the Great Schism. Clement VII, first of the Avignon schismatic popes, made Pedro his legate in Spain, where he secured the country's adherence to Clement. The Avignonese cardinals elected Pedro pope on Clement's death in 1394, having secured his promise to abdicate if necessary to end the schism. Benedict attended the Council of Pisa in 1410 with his college of cardinals; his refusal to abdicate in favour of the council's nominee, Pope Alexander V, lost him the allegiance of all countries but Scotland, Sicily and Spain. Deposed by the Council of Constance in 1417, Benedict XIII lived on in Valencia, Spain, still claiming to be pope.

The Wars of the Roses: 110, 126, 143

Benedictines

Followers of the rule of St Benedict of Nursia, as laid down for his abbey of Monte Cassino, in Italy, early in the 6th century; known as 'black monks' from the black habits they wore. The rule emphasized obedience, communal worship and labour, and by the 8th century had superseded most other forms of monasticism in the West. Early in the 9th century, St Benedict of Aniane, with the backing of the Western Emperor Louis the Pious, promulgated a series of supplementary ordinances which were widely followed thereafter. The abbey of Cluny, founded in 910, headed a reform movement to return Benedictine monasteries to their pristine observances. During the 11th century more than 70 monastic houses accepted Cluny's guidance, establishing the first European congregation. The order remained the basis of Western monasticism: the Cistercians were reformed Benedictines who evolved into a separate order.

In the later Middle Ages the Benedictine monks, who staffed many cathedral chapters in England, were regarded – at times unfairly – as particularly idle and corrupt by critics of the religious orders.

The Plantagenet Chronicles: 29, 77, 266, 324

Benedict, St

d.547. Italian saint known as Benedict of Nursia, who founded the abbey of Monte Cassino in the first half of the 6th century, and compiled the Benedictine rule, which he described as 'a little rule for beginners'. After studying at Rome, he lived as a hermit in Subiaco, Italy. Within three years he became famous for his holiness and established a monastery there. He left this to set up the larger house at Monte Cassino, on the site of a former pagan holy place. He distilled his experience into the 73 chapters of the Rule of St Benedict, which was to become the principal rule in Western monasticism.

The Plantagenet Chronicles: 29

benefice

A position in the church with lands and an income attached. Received by the occupant in return for performing stipulated spiritualities, such as Masses.

Benet, John

d.1474? Vicar of Harlington in Bedfordshire (1443–71), rector of Broughton (1471–4), and a chronicler with Yorkist leanings. Possibly a civil lawyer, he was probably educated at Oxford – it is known that he was in Oxford during a great student riot there in 1440, of which he wrote an account. During Henry VI's reign he lived in London. Benet wrote his chronicle between 1461 and 1471, drawing on other authors for events before 1440, and writing from contemporary sources after that date. He described English campaigns and losses in France, and the civil disturbances at the end of Henry VI's reign, including Jack Cade's rebellion in 1450. He claimed that Henry VI was deposed 'because he had ruled tyrannously', and described Edward IV as being crowned 'with God's favour'.

The Wars of the Roses: 13, 188, 202, 208, 212, 216

Berengaria of Navarre

d.after 1230. Daughter of Sancho VI of Navarre; wife of Richard I of England, from 1191 to 1199. Berengaria was betrothed to Richard in 1190, and accompanied him on his way to the Holy Land for the Third Crusade in 1191. However, in April 1191 her ship was driven by a storm into Limassol harbour on Cyprus; and the island's ruler, Isaac Comnenus, threatened her. Richard overran Cyprus, and married Berengaria at Limassol on 12 May 1191. The marriage gave Richard a Spanish ally against the French in the person of Sancho VII, the Bold, of Navarre, Berengaria's brother. The couple had no children. Adam of Eynsham records her as grief-stricken at her husband's death in 1199, after which she lived at Le Mans, in France, where she was famed for alms-giving.

The Plantagenet Chronicles: 195, 206, 212–13, 224, 256

Berkeley castle

Seat of the Berkeley family since 1086; and from April 1327 the prison of the deposed Edward II. He was in the custody of Thomas Berkeley, lord of the estate, after his deposition by his queen, Isabella of France. The chronicler Geoffrey le Baker melodramatically described how Queen Isabella's agents took control of the castle from Thomas Berkeley, and, hoping to infect the king with a fatal illness, hollowed out a cellar full of corpses beneath the royal captive's cell. Edward's death was announced on 21 September 1327; how he died is not in fact known, but le Baker nevertheless wrote a detailed and horrible account describing his

murder. Edward's cell can still be seen in Berkeley castle.

Chronicles of the Age of Chivalry/Four Gothic Kings (US edn): 217–18, 220–1, 222–3

Berkeley, Lord Thomas

d.1361. Lord of the estate of Berkeley in Gloucestershire and custodian of Edward II during the latter's imprisonment in Berkeley castle in 1327, after his queen, Isabella of France, had deposed him. Geoffrey le Baker writes that he treated Edward well; but he was ordered by Isabella to have no contact with his prisoner, so withdrew to one of his other estates, leaving Edward at his persecutors' mercy. Thomas was acquitted afterwards of complicity in the king's murder. He went on to serve Edward III as a military commander in Scotland and France, and in 1361 was sent on an embassy to Pope Innocent VI.

Chronicles of the Age of Chivalry/Four Gothic Kings (US edn): 220

Berkhamsted castle

Castle built in the 11th century by Robert of Mortain, half-brother of William the Conqueror, king of England; it is now a ruin. Thomas Becket lived in the castle, and Henry II of England held court there. John II of France was briefly imprisoned at Berkhamsted after his capture by Edward of Woodstock, the Black Prince, at the battle of Poitiers (1356). The castle was one of Richard II's gifts to his favourite, Robert de Vere, 9th earl of Oxford.

The Wars of the Roses: 50

Bermondsey Abbey

Cluniac priory, founded *c.*1089, outside Southwark in London. Became an abbey in 1399. Henry V's widow, Catherine of France, retired there before her death in 1437. So too did Elizabeth Woodville, Edward IV's widow, in 1485, who died at Bermondsey in 1492.

The Wars of the Roses: 151, 182, 235

Bernard, St, abbot of Clairvaux

1090?–1153. Charismatic Cistercian abbot of Clairvaux, who was one of the leading influences in the 12th-century Church. He entered the abbey of Cîteaux (which gave the Cistercian movement its name) in 1112, and in 1115 left to found another abbey at Clairvaux,

where he remained until his death, despite many offers of promotion. A conservative opponent of Peter Abelard's theological and philosophical teachings, Bernard was ready with spiritual advice to ecclesiastics and laymen alike. He preached the Second Crusade in 1146, and later counselled Eleanor of Aquitaine in an attempt to prevent the collapse of her marriage to Louis VII of France, telling her she would conceive again only if she strove for peace. By 1133 Bernard had convinced much of Europe of the superior claim of Innocent II to the papacy, in an attempt to end a schism which had begun in 1130; and he advised several other popes, most notably the Cistercian Eugenius III.

The Plantagenet Chronicles: 34, 77, 97, 266

Bertran of Born

1140–?1204. Knight and troubadour of the Limousin, France, who benefited from Plantagenet patronage. However, he dubbed Richard I of England 'Oc-e-No' ('Yea-and-Nay') as a reflection of his duplicity.

The Plantagenet Chronicles: 229, 230

Berwick upon Tweed

Town in Northumberland at the mouth of the River Tweed. Berwick changed hands between England and Scotland many times between 1174 and 1482. In 1174 William I, king of Scots, surrendered Berwick and its castle to England after his capture by Henry II of England; King John of England retook the town in 1216, after it had passed back to the Scots, and when the English lost it once more, Edward I recaptured it in 1296. However, by 1318 Robert Bruce had re-won it for the Scots. Berwick was returned to Edward III of England by Edward Balliol, his Scots puppet-king, in 1334. Henry VI's queen, Margaret of Anjou, ceded the town to the Scots in 1461, in return for aid against the Yorkist Edward IV. In 1482 Richard, 3rd duke of Gloucester (the future Richard III) took Berwick on behalf of his brother Edward IV.

The Plantagenet Chronicles: 140, 316
Chronicles of the Age of Chivalry/Four Gothic Kings (US edn): 134, 142–5, 190, 194, 196, 230, 234, 248, 272
The Wars of the Roses: 46, 61, 106, 182, 201–2, 274, 299

Thomas Becket *The great archbishop (overleaf) challenging royal power.*

Beverley Minster

College of secular canons founded by St John of Beverley (d.721); the minster (collegiate church) was built in the 13th century. It contains the tomb of the Percy family.

The Wars of the Roses: 61

Bigod, Hugh, 1st earl of Norfolk

1095?–1177. 1st earl of Norfolk (1135–77). In 1136 he held Norwich against King Stephen of England (who had given him his earldom), then surrendered and was pardoned. In 1141 he fought under Stephen at Lincoln, against Empress Matilda's supporters but later joined the party led by Henry of Anjou (later Henry II of England) and held Ipswich against Stephen in 1153. He did homage to Henry II in 1157, but his persistent unruliness caused Henry to build Orford castle as a royal base against Hugh. In 1173 Hugh joined Henry the Young King's rebellion against Henry II and attacked Norwich with him in June 1174. Henry II besieged Hugh's castles at Framlingham and Bungay the same year and forced him to submit and to pay a large indemnity.

The Plantagenet Chronicles: 75–6, 85, 95, 129, 133

Black Death

Popular name of the first, most catastrophic outbreak of bubonic plague in Europe. In October 1347 a Genoese fleet docked at Messina in Sicily, introducing the pestilence from Constantinople, and within three years it had spread throughout Europe. Estimates of the death toll vary from two-fifths to three-quarters of the population. A Gascon sailor who landed at Melcombe Regis in Dorset in June 1348 brought the plague to England; within only 18 months it had spread throughout the country and killed over half the population of Bristol and Winchester.

Urban disorder attended the Black Death, as did religious hysteria which gave rise to extreme sects such as the Flagellants. By 1350 it had begun to abate, leaving in its wake far-reaching social and economic changes.

Chronicles of the Age of Chivalry/Four Gothic Kings (US edn): 30, 252, 254–6, 261, 264, 275
The Wars of the Roses: 37

Black Prince, the

See: Edward of Woodstock, the Black Prince

Blackheath

Common south-east of the city of London. Wat Tyler's rebels gathered there in 1381; and Jack Cade's men camped there on 11 June 1450, remaining for eight days to await Henry VI's response to their demands. After withdrawing, temporarily, the rebels returned to Blackheath on 29 June before entering central London by force. On 2 March 1452 the Lancastrian Henry VI and Richard, 3rd duke of York, were temporarily reconciled at Blackheath.

The Wars of the Roses: 36, 100, 168, 204, 207, 210

Blanche of Castile

1185–1252. Daughter of Alfonso VIII, king of Castile, queen of Louis VIII of France, mother of Louis IX of France. Blanche was married to Louis in 1200. Regent for her son from his accession at the age of 12 in 1226 to his coming of age in 1234, she retained a strong influence over him thereafter. Blanche went to London for Henry III of England's marriage to Eleanor of Provence in 1236. She and Louis IX brought what was said to be the Holy Cross to Paris from the east in 1241, and built the Sainte-Chapelle to house it. Blanche was again regent for Louis during his first crusade, which departed in 1248: when news of her son's capture reached her in 1250, she had the messengers hanged. She held discussions with the Pastoureaux mob when it reached Paris in 1251, but later had its leaders seized and put to death. She died two years before Louis' return in 1254.

The Plantagenet Chronicles: 97
Chronicles of the Age of Chivalry/Four Gothic Kings (US edn): 30, 58, 62, 68, 73, 93

Blanche of Lancaster

d.1368. Daughter of Henry, 1st duke of Lancaster, and wife of John of Gaunt, a distant cousin whom she married in 1359. Through her, John inherited the vast Lancastrian estates in northern England, the Midlands, and the Welsh marches, including more than 30 castles. Blanche died of the plague, leaving a son (Henry Bolingbroke, the future Henry IV) and two

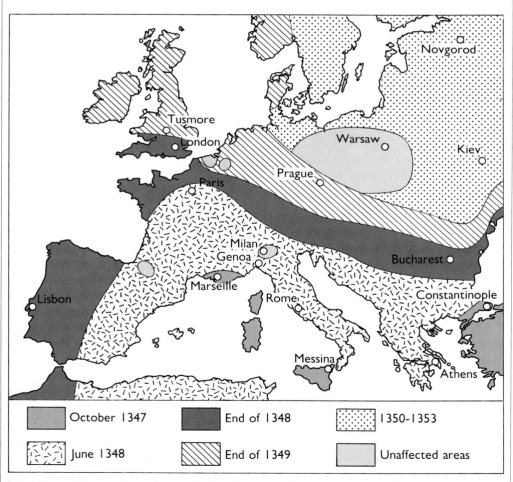

Black Death The map shows the spread of the plague from Constantinople across Europe within three years, killing around a third of the European population.

daughters. John of Gaunt was said to be deeply grieved by her death.

Chronicles of the Age of Chivalry/Four Gothic Kings (US edn): 300
The Wars of the Roses: 47

Blois

Town on the Loire and former county in central France. The counts of Blois and Champagne were among the most powerful feudal lords in France in the 11th and 12th centuries; their lands encircled the French royal domain, although they seem not to have had any ambitions to engulf it. The house of Blois gave England one king, Stephen (ruled 1135–54). The last count of Blois, childless and debt-ridden, sold his fief to Louis, duke of Orléans, who took possession in 1397.

The Plantagenet Chronicles: 28, 30

Blois, Henry of

See: Henry of Blois, bishop of Winchester

Blondel

*fl.*1190s. French minstrel and favourite of Richard I of England. Legend relates that Blondel found the king after his imprisonment by Leopold V of Austria in 1193–4, by singing verses they had composed together outside every castle in Germany until his refrain was answered.

The Plantagenet Chronicles: 228–9

Bodiam castle

Built in 1385 for Sir Edward Dallingrigge, the keeper of the Tower of London, 'in defence of the adjacent country against the king's enemies'. Sir Edward was granted a licence to crenellate in 1385, showing that he was deemed trustworthy enough to hold a fortified stronghold. The overall design, based on early 13th-century French castles, was a rectangular arrangement of rooms and halls with towers on the gatehouses and corners, built around a central courtyard and ringed by a moat. Such a layout, thin-walled with no central keep, marks a transition from such heavily fortified castles as John of Gaunt's Kenilworth in Warwickshire to less defended homes such as Sir John Pulteney's Penshurst Place in Kent.

The Wars of the Roses: 49, 124–5

Bohemia

Kingdom in western Czechoslovakia, part of the Holy Roman Empire. Bohemia reached its greatest extent under King Ottocar II (1253–78), but all his conquests were lost after his defeat by Rudolf I of Habsburg. The reign of Charles IV (1346–78), crowned Holy Roman Emperor in 1355, was Bohemia's golden age, when Prague became the hub of the empire. Richard II of England married Anne, eldest daughter of Charles IV's successor, Wenceslas IV (1378–1419), in 1382. Sigismund, king of Hungary and Bohemia (later Holy Roman Emperor) succeeded his half-brother Wenceslas, but disputes with the Hussites (followers of the Bohemian theologian John Hus) delayed his acceptance till 1434. After his death in 1437 the kingdom was riven by a dispute about the succession, not resolved until 1471 with the election of Vladislav of Poland.

The Wars of the Roses: 156, 158–9

Bohemia, Anne of

See: Anne of Bohemia

Bohemia, Wenceslas of

See: Wenceslas IV, Holy Roman Emperor

Bohemond of Antioch

c.1056–1111. Norman adventurer from southern Italy, the son of Robert Guiscard, who became the ruler of the crusader state of Antioch from 1099 to 1111. He made himself prince of Antioch in contravention of his oath of allegiance to the Byzantine emperor Alexius Comnenus in 1097 and in defiance of Raymond, count of Toulouse, leader of the crusade. He was captured by Muslims in 1100, released in 1103, and returned to Europe, where he married the daughter of Philip I of France. His campaign against the Byzantine empire was humiliatingly crushed by Alexius in 1108, and he never returned to Syria.

The Plantagenet Chronicles: 38, 61

Bohun, Humphrey de, 8th earl of Hereford

1276–1322. Son of Humphrey de Bohun, 7th earl of Hereford. 8th earl of Hereford and 10th earl of Essex (1299–1322); constable of England. Married Elizabeth, countess of Holland, widowed daughter of Edward I, in 1302. One of the 21 ordainers appointed to regulate the king's conduct of affairs in 1310, Humphrey joined the barons besieging Piers Gaveston, Edward II's favourite, at Scarborough in 1312. He fought and was captured at the battle of Bannockburn in 1314, and was exchanged by the Scots for Robert Bruce's wife, who was imprisoned in England. One of the major opponents of Edward II's later favourites, the Despensers, Humphrey joined the league of marcher lords who were demanding their exile (1321). Alarmed by Edward's massacre of rebels defending Leeds castle in 1321, Humphrey surrendered his castles to the king's troops without resistance. Retreating before Edward's northwards advance, he was killed at the battle of Boroughbridge in Yorkshire in 1322.

Chronicles of the Age of Chivalry/Four Gothic Kings (US edn): 200, 202

Bolingbroke, Henry

See: Henry IV, king of England

Boniface, archbishop of Canterbury

d.1270. Boniface of Savoy; son of Thomas I, count of Savoy; uncle of Eleanor of Provence, his sister Beatrix's daughter, who married Henry III of England in 1236. His election as archbishop of Canterbury in 1241 caused resentment among English barons because he was one of a Savoyard clique, increasingly dominating king and court. Boniface died at St Helena in Savoy while on a crusade with the future Edward I of England.

Chronicles of the Age of Chivalry/Four Gothic Kings (US edn): 58–9, 72

Boniface VIII, pope

1235–1303. Born Benedetto Caetani; pope 1294–1303. Boniface was born in Anagni, and after studying canon law became a papal notary in the late 1270s. His brilliance as a lawyer was employed on behalf of the papacy, but he earned many enemies for his arrogance, greed and thirst for power. Italy at this time was torn by factional strife, and three of the factions – the Neapolitans, the extreme Franciscans, and the Colonna family in Rome – remained bitterly hostile to Boniface after his election as pope. This was in succession to the saintly but unworldly Celestine V, most of whose acts he immediately annulled on taking office. Celestine had abdicated in December 1294, largely on the advice of Benedetto, who was elected Pope Boniface VIII in his stead. Once

pope, Boniface kept Celestine imprisoned to prevent a schism, and may have brought about his death in prison in 1296.

During his pontificate Boniface published codification of canon law, and improved the administration of the papal *Curia*. A major patron of the arts, he allowed so many statues of himself to be erected that his enemies accused him of encouraging idolatry. He declared the year 1300 a year of jubilee, and tens of thousands of pilgrims flocked into Rome to take advantage of the special indulgences offered. Boniface wore imperial insignia and boasted that he was as much emperor as pope. He saw his office as endowing him with universal authority – over lay rulers as well as the Church.

In 1296 Boniface issued a bull, *Clericis laicos*, to prevent Philip IV of France from taxing the clergy; declaring that lay authorities could not tax clergy without papal consent. Philip retaliated by cutting off all Boniface's funds from France and Edward I of England followed suit. Both kings needed to tap all possible sources to finance their conflict over Gascony, and in 1297 Boniface was compelled to agree in another bull that kings could raise a clerical subsidy in times of emergency without papal permission.

Boniface sent Bernard Saisset, bishop of Pamiers, as his legate to protest against Philip's oppressive taxation of the clergy. In 1301 Philip had Saisset arrested and prosecuted by a civil court for heresy and treason, and demanded papal confirmation of his condemnatory sentence. That was a direct contravention of the pope's exclusive rights to try and sentence prelates, and Boniface reacted angrily, demanding that Saisset should be sent to Rome for trial by an ecclesiastical court.

A major propaganda war followed, during which Philip accused Boniface of illegitimacy, sodomy, sorcery, and heresy. The pope declared in the bull *Unam Sanctam* of 1302 that 'it is altogether necessary for salvation for every human creature to be subject to the Roman pontiff', enunciating the principle that secular sovereigns were subservient to the papacy. In 1303, Philip's righthand man William de Nogaret stormed the papal palace at Anagni with a band of mercenaries led by Sciarra Colonna. Boniface confronted the invaders and was slapped by Sciarra during an attempt to browbeat him into abdicating. Although the outraged citizens rescued Boniface and escorted

him to Rome, the shock was so great that he died a month later in the Vatican, a broken man.

Chronicles of the Age of Chivalry/Four Gothic Kings (US edn): 137, 140, 148, 150–1, 154–5, 162, 281

Boniface IX, pope

*c.*1345–1404. Born Pietro Tomacelli, Boniface succeeded Urban VI as pope in the Roman line of the Great Schism in 1389. He successfully imposed his rule on the papal states, fortified Rome, and won the support of Naples in the schism.

The Wars of the Roses: 33

Bordeaux The historic capital of the English territories in Gascony, Bordeaux capitulated to French royal troops in 1453, ending English rule there.

Bordeaux

Port on the Garonne estuary in south-west France; capital of the duchy of Aquitaine (later of the duchy of Gascony). Under English rule from 1154 to 1453 – following Henry II of England's marriage to Eleanor of Aquitaine in 1152 – Bordeaux prospered from wine exports to England. Richard II of England was born there in 1367, while his father, Edward of Woodstock, the Black Prince, was prince of Aquitaine. In spring 1451 Charles VII of France's forces, campaigning to drive the English from Gascony, reached Bordeaux. The town surrendered in June on good terms, was recaptured by the English by November 1452, and fell to the French once more on 19 October 1453. Thereafter, the city remained French.

The Plantagenet Chronicles: 271
Chronicles of the Age of Chivalry/Four Gothic Kings (US edn): 73, 90, 125, 290, 293
The Wars of the Roses: 108, 188, 194, 208–10

Born, Bertran of

See: Bertran of Born

borough

Originally signifying a fortified town, the term borough came to mean a town possessing a corporation of citizens and privileges conferred by royal charter. The boroughs were of great political and economic significance during the Middle Ages – their markets and fairs were important and privileged centres of trade, and in the later Middle Ages their burgesses elected members of parliament. There were 66 boroughs in England in 1066, 350 by 1250, 480 by 1300 (the increase reflecting economic prosperity and growing patronage of their royal, noble or ecclesiastical lords) and 592 by 1500. Devon had the largest number (74), Middlesex and Rutland the smallest (1 each).

Boroughbridge, battle of

Battle in Yorkshire in 1322 between barons in revolt against Edward II, led by Thomas, 2nd earl of Lancaster, and Andrew Harclay, a north-country soldier and supporter of the king. The anonymous writer of the *Life of Edward II* described how the rebels had taken lodgings in the town and, on hearing that Harclay had arrived to seize them, met his troops at a ford nearby. Humphrey de Bohun, 8th earl of Hereford, was one of a number of nobles who died in the fighting. The rebels made a truce with Harclay until morning and returned to their lodgings. However, the sheriff of York arrived with more troops during the night and Harclay entered Boroughbridge early in the morning after the battle, and seized the rebels in their beds. Lancaster was subsequently tried and executed.

Chronicles of the Age of Chivalry/Four Gothic Kings (US edn): 196, 204

Bosworth, battle of

Battle near Market Bosworth in Leicestershire, on 22 August 1485, which resulted in the death of England's last Plantagenet ruler, Richard III. Warned by spies in France, the king had waited at Nottingham since June 1485 for Henry Tudor, 15th earl of Richmond, to invade England in an attempt to seize the throne. Richard's army was larger than his opponent's mixed French and Welsh force, but morale was low. Many nobles joined Henry and others supported neither side. Henry advanced on the royal camp at Bosworth, and when Richard led a

Burgundy Philip the Good (opposite), one of the greatest dukes of Burgundy and ally of Henry V of England.

charge aimed at his rival, the troops of the Stanley family, hitherto loyal to the king, intervened for Henry; they crushed Richard's forces and killed the king.

The Wars of the Roses: 301, 302–5

Boucicault master

Active c.1375–1400. Anonymous Franco-Flemish manuscript illuminator, famed for his work on the *Boucicault Hours* for Jean le Meingre, marshal of France (also known as Boucicault), and the *Dialogues de Pierre Salmon*.

The Wars of the Roses: 136

Bourchier, Thomas, archbishop of Canterbury

1404?–86. Bishop of Worcester (1433–43) and of Ely (1443–54); archbishop of Canterbury (1454-86) under Henry VI; chancellor in 1455–6; cardinal (1467). Although previously Lancastrian in his sympathies, Thomas, who wanted to see an end to the strife between Lancastrians and Yorkists, crowned Edward IV in 1461. He officiated at Richard III's coronation in 1483, having three weeks earlier taken Richard, 5th duke of York, the younger brother of Edward V, from sanctuary at Westminster to the Tower of London on promise of his future safety. Bourchier crowned Henry VII in 1485 and married him to Elizabeth of York in 1486.

The Wars of the Roses: 214

Bourges

City in Berry in central France, possessing one of the great French High Gothic cathedrals, built between 1195 and 1225. The master of Hungary and other leaders of the Pastoureaux crusade were captured there by French royal officials and hanged in 1251. Bourges briefly became the artistic centre of France in the 1380s, thanks to the patronage of John, duke of Berry. The Limbourg brothers probably painted the *Très Belles Heures du Duc de Berry* and the *Très Riches Heures* there. A plague in Bourges killed both the duke and the Limbourg brothers in 1416. The French royal banker, Jacques Coeur, who was born in Bourges, built his palatial town house there in the 1440s.

Chronicles of the Age of Chivalry/Four Gothic Kings (US edn): 30, 73
The Wars of the Roses: 125, 137

Bouvines

Village in northern France, near Valenciennes. Site of Philip II Augustus of France's great victory of 27 July 1214 against Otto IV, the Holy Roman Emperor. Otto had invaded France to help his ally, King John of England, recover the French dominions that Philip had seized. John remained on campaign in western France, leaving Otto to face Philip's forces. Despite his allies, the counts of Flanders and Boulogne, the emperor lost the battle, confirming the French monarchy's power and terminating John's campaigns in France.

The Plantagenet Chronicles: 205, 305–7

Bradwardine, Thomas, archbishop of Canterbury

c.1290–1349. Proctor at Oxford University (1325); chaplain and confessor to Edward III (c.1338); became archbishop of Canterbury in 1349, only 40 days before his death. Thomas was known by his learned contemporaries as the *doctor profundis* for the quality of his philosophical and theological ideas. He wrote several religious treatises, and his work in the physical sciences prefigured that of Galileo.

The Wars of the Roses: 67

Bramham Moor, battle of

A battle in Yorkshire on 19 February 1408 in which Henry Percy, the rebellious 4th earl of Northumberland, was killed fighting local Yorkshire knights loyal to King Henry IV, led by the sheriff of Yorkshire.

The Wars of the Roses: 108

Braose, William de

d.1211. Lord of Brecon, an ambitious lesser baron who rose in King John of England's service. He captured John's nephew Arthur, duke of Brittany, at Mirebeau in western France in 1202 and was rewarded with many lands and offices in South Wales, including the post of sheriff of Herefordshire (1206). His power was increasingly a threat to the crown, and in 1206 John began to curb it. The king tried to take William's sons hostage in 1208; William refused, and his family escaped to Ireland just ahead of soldiers sent to arrest them. He raised an unsuccessful rebellion in Wales (1210) and died an exile in France.

The Plantagenet Chronicles: 265

Braybrooke, Robert, bishop of London

d.1404. Bishop of London (1381–1404). In 1387 Braybrooke tried unsuccessfully to mediate in the dispute between Richard II and his barons over the king's increasingly authoritarian rule. He went to Ireland with the archbishop of York in 1395 to beg Richard to return from his successful campaign there and secure the English Church against the Lollards. He was later a privy councillor under Henry IV.

The Wars of the Roses: 68

Brembre, Sir Nicholas, mayor of London

d.1388. Mayor of London (1377, 1378, 1383). Brembre, who supported Richard II against Wat Tyler's mob on 15 June 1381, was knighted by the king at Smithfield; but on 14 November 1387 he was accused of treason by the lords appellant. Imprisoned at Gloucester, he was brought before the Merciless Parliament of February 1388 and was one of the two so-called traitors executed after its proceedings; the other was Sir Robert Tresilian.

The Wars of the Roses: 38, 52–3, 56–7

Brétigny, Treaty of

Peace treaty between Edward III of England and John II of France, concluded at Brétigny, near Chartres, in May 1360. John had been captured at the battle of Poitiers in 1356, and, when a short English campaign launched in 1359 in northern France to seize Paris, proved fruitless, Edward decided to negotiate the French king's release. Under the terms of the treaty, Edward received Poitou, Aunis, Saintonge, Angoumois, Guyenne, Gascony and Calais, and the French renounced all rights in Aquitaine. In return John's ransom was reduced from 700,000 pounds to 500,000 pounds and Edward renounced his claim to the throne of France. The treaty was operative until 1371, when certain Gascon nobles, oppressed by English taxes, sought help from Charles V of France.

Chronicles of the Age of Chivalry/Four Gothic Kings (US edn): 229, 271
The Wars of the Roses: 29, 49

Brewer, William

d.1226. Sheriff of Devon and a baron of the Exchequer (1221). One of four justices left in charge of the kingdom by Richard I during his absence (1189–94) on the Third Crusade and his imprisonment in Germany. Brewer was also an adviser to King John and Henry III.

The Plantagenet Chronicles: 217, 220

Bridlington

Port and market town on the east Yorkshire coast above Spurn Point. An Augustinian priory was established there in the early 12th century, and in the 1380s miracles began to occur regularly at the tomb of John, a former prior who was said to have walked on water and raised the dead. He was canonized in 1401 and Bridlington became an important place of pilgrimage.

The Wars of the Roses: 64, 141

Bristol

Important port in Gloucestershire, first chartered as a borough in 1188. Bristol surrendered to the army of Isabella of France, Edward II of England's queen, in 1326, and Hugh Despenser the father, one of Edward II's favourites, was put to death on the Bristol public gallows. Edward himself was held prisoner in the castle in 1327 after his forced abdication. The city lost more than half its inhabitants by the Black Death. In 1373 Edward III granted Bristol county status, giving it a sheriff of its own and immunity from other jurisdictions – it was the first provincial city to be so honoured. During his reign the manufacture of woollens, drawing in the fine wool of the Cotswolds, added to its prosperity.

Chronicles of the Ages of Chivalry/Four Gothic Kings (US edn): 125, 174, 212, 217, 249, 254–6
The Wars of the Roses: 41, 97, 109, 147, 203

Brito, Richard de

fl.1170. One of the four Norman knights who murdered Thomas Becket in Canterbury Cathedral on 29 December 1170. According to Becket's biographer William Fitzstephen, Brito struck the prone martyr in the head with such force that his sword was broken against the cathedral floor, as he said 'Take that for love of my lord William, the king's brother'. Henry II's brother was Brito's lord, and Becket had forbidden William's marriage to the countess of Warenne. In 1171 Brito was excommunicated for his sin.

The Plantagenet Chronicles: 118, 120

Brittany

North-western peninsula of France, and a duchy in the Middle Ages. Constance, the duke of Brittany's daughter, married Geoffrey Plantagenet, Henry II of England's son, in 1170. Their son Arthur was acknowledged as duke in 1196 and after his death in 1203, allegedly at the hands of King John of England, the duchy passed to Arthur's French brother-in-law, Peter, instead of to the English crown. Brittany's dukes tried to remain neutral during the Hundred Years War, but the duchy was captured by Henry V of England during his campaigns in France (1413–22). After the end of the war in 1453, the duchy remained autonomous until the rebellion of Francis II, duke of Brittany, against the French crown, led to the duchy's absorption into France in 1488. Henry Tudor, 15th earl of Richmond, the future Henry VII, spent 12 years' exile in Brittany after the Lancastrian party's collapse in 1471.

The Wars of the Roses: 209, 239, 296–7

Brittany, Joan of

See: Joan of Brittany

Bruce, Robert

d.1094? Founder of the Scottish dynasty, Bruce derived his name from his castle of Bruis near Cherbourg. He arrived in England with William the Conqueror, king of England, who granted him land in Yorkshire. His son, Robert Bruce, founded Guisborough Priory in North Yorkshire in 1119.

Chronicles of the Age of Chivalry/Four Gothic Kings (US edn): 13

Bruce, Robert, king of Scotland

See: Robert Bruce, king of Scotland

Bruges

Trading and manufacturing city in Flanders, and a major port for the Hanseatic League. At its zenith in the 13th century Bruges was the main port of exchange for Mediterranean and Baltic goods. Under Philip the Good, duke of Burgundy, who moved his court to Bruges in the 1430s, the city became a major cultural centre, home to artists such as the brothers van Eyck and van der Weyden. William Caxton, the printer who was governor of the English merchant community in Bruges (1465–9), led the English reception for Edward IV of England's sister, Margaret of York, on her marriage to Charles the Bold, duke of Burgundy, in 1468, and set up his first press there in 1472. Bruges declined when its access to the sea silted up in 1490.

The Wars of the Roses: 137, 240–2, 266

burgess

Holder of a tenement (i.e., land or a house) in a borough, with special judicial privileges and certain obligations in running the borough.

Burgh, Hubert de, 2nd earl of Kent

d.1243. Chamberlain (1201); chief justiciar (1215–32); 2nd earl of Kent (1227). According to Ralph of Coggeshall, Hubert was the jailer of the king of England's nephew Arthur, duke of Brittany, at Falaise castle (1202) and when John sentenced Arthur to blinding and castration, Hubert prevented the king's servants from carrying out the sentence. Later an adviser to Henry III, he built up a pre-eminent position in the southern marches of Wales. But he also earned the enmity of a powerful faction at court and in 1232 was briefly imprisoned in the Tower and outlawed.

The Plantagenet Chronicles: 276

Burghersh, Henry, bishop of Lincoln

1292–1340. Bishop of Lincoln (1320); chancellor (1328–30); treasurer (1327–8, 1334–7). Burghersh supported Queen Isabella of France against her husband, Edward II of England, and was one of the conspirators who welcomed her invasion of England, greeting her on her landing in Orwell on 24 September 1326. He was one of the commissioners sent by parliament to the captive king at Kenilworth in 1327, to persuade him to abdicate in favour of his son, the future Edward III. Burghersh was imprisoned in the Tower by Edward III after he had broken away from Isabella's authority (1330), but subsequently regained royal favour.

Chronicles of the Age of Chivalry/Four Gothic Kings (US edn): 214

Burgundians

Supporters of the house of Burgundy during their feud with the Armagnac (Orleanist) faction which split France between 1388 and 1435.

The Wars of the Roses: 114–16, 148

Burgundy

Region in north-east France with its capital at Dijon; was in the later Middle Ages the seat of the dukes of Burgundy. Under the Capetian kings the duchy of Burgundy had been an important and often hostile fief. (The county of Burgundy, which adjoined it, lay outside France and formed part of the Holy Roman Empire.) The duchy's golden age began in 1364 when John II of France made his son Philip the Bold duke of Burgundy, inaugurating the Valois-Burgundy dynasty. Under Dukes John the Fearless (1404–19), Philip the Good (1419–67) and Charles the Bold (1467–77), the house of Burgundy held lands both outside and within the borders of France: the Low Countries, Luxembourg and the Franche-Comté. John the Fearless's murder by his Armagnac opponents (1419) made Burgundy ally with England. The Treaty of Arras (1435) ended the alliance.

Charles the Bold died at the battle of Nancy in 1477, and Louis XI of France seized the duchy, returning it to the French crown lands.

Chronicles of the Age of Chivalry/Four Gothic Kings (US edn): 110–12, 296, 298
The Wars of the Roses: 114–16, 148, 239

Burgundy, Mary of

See: Mary of Burgundy

Burley, Sir Simon

1336–88. Companion and follower of Edward of Woodstock, the Black Prince, Burley was made a guardian to Prince Richard, the future Richard II. Accompanying him to London in 1377 on his accession. Burley carried the exhausted ten-year-old king from Westminster Abbey to Westminster Hall on his shoulders after the coronation. As adviser and tutor to the young Richard, Burley apparently encouraged the king to enhance royal prestige by exercising firm authority. When the Merciless Parliament met on 4 February 1388, Burley was impeached for treason and executed.

The Wars of the Roses: 23, 25, 57

Bury St Edmunds

An important place of pilgrimage in Suffolk during the Plantagenet era: the name derives from the remains of St Edmund, entombed in its abbey. The town became a textile centre in the reign of Edward III when Flemish immigrants introduced wool weaving. In his *Historia Anglicana* the chronicler Thomas Walsingham relates that the abbey of Bury St Edmunds suffered particularly from the visit of Richard II and his queen, Anne of Bohemia, and their household in 1383: the house was obliged to spend 800 marks (some 500 pounds) on their keep over ten days.

The Plantagenet Chronicles: 133, 208, 259
The Wars of the Roses: 44

Byzantine Empire *The Byzantine Emperor receives envoys from the western European kingdoms involved in the crusades.*

Bushey, John

d.1399. One of the speakers of the parliament of 17 September 1397. The chronicler Thomas Walsingham records that he was ambitious, arrogant and anxious to curry favour with Richard II. During Richard's absence on campaign in Ireland in 1399 he was one of the advisers summoned to organize opposition to the invasion on 4 July by Henry Bolingbroke (the future Henry IV). When Bolingbroke's forces took Bristol in July 1399 they seized Bushey and beheaded him.

The Wars of the Roses: 80, 84

Butler, James, 2nd earl of Wiltshire

1420–61. 5th earl of Ormonde (1452–61); 2nd earl of Wiltshire (1449); treasurer to Henry VI (1455, 1458–60). A zealous Lancastrian, Butler fought for Henry VI against Richard, 3rd duke of York at St Albans on 22 May 1455; escaped from the battle of Northampton on 10 July 1460; and fought at Wakefield (December 1460), Mortimer's Cross (3 February 1461). He was beheaded by the victorious Yorkists at Newcastle-on-Tyne in 1461, and his estates were forfeited.

The Wars of the Roses: 222, 224

Butler, Lady Eleanor

d.1468. Daughter of John Talbot, earl of Shrewsbury; said to have been Edward IV's mistress in her youth. A rumour allegedly put about by Richard, 3rd duke of Gloucester, later Richard III, claimed that Edward IV had contracted to marry Lady Eleanor, that his marriage to Elizabeth Woodville on 1 May 1464 was therefore invalid and that the young Edward V was consequently illegitimate and not entitled to the throne.

The Wars of the Roses: 253, 283

Byzantine Empire

The eastern half of the Roman Empire, reconstituted as a separate empire in the 4th century AD and ruled from Constantinople. The empire endured until the conquest of Constantinople by the Turks in 1453.

Chronicles of the Age of Chivalry/Four Gothic Kings (US edn): 18
The Wars of the Roses: 210

Cabot, John

1461–98, Explorer, born in Genoa. Settled in Bristol in the 1480s. Later sailed under letters patent from Henry VII of England and discovered Newfoundland in 1497, laying the basis for future English claims in America.

The Wars of the Roses: 257

Cade, Jack

d.1450. Rebel leader. Little is known about him. He may have been an Irishman in service to Sir Thomas Dacre in Sussex. Banished from England for murder in 1449. Returned from France to lead a rebellion in Kent in May 1450 in protest against Henry VI's misgovernment. He called himself John Mortimer, possibly to link himself with Richard, 3rd duke of York's Mortimer lineage. Cade met Henry's emissaries on 13 June at Blackheath, near London, and on 27 June defeated the king's troops at Sevenoaks. His demands were refused and he entered London on 2 July, after which his followers executed Lord Say (Henry's most hated adviser) and the sheriff of Kent (Say's brother-in-law). The Londoners turned against Cade because of the rebels' indiscipline and held London Bridge against his men on 5 July. The rebels dispersed after a general amnesty had been granted by the king. Cade was mortally wounded resisting capture at Heathfield on 12 July 1450.

The Wars of the Roses: 204–7

Caen

Port in Normandy, northern France. A favourite residence, and burial place, of William the Conqueror, king of England. Part of Henry II of England's French dominions; surrendered to Philip II of France in 1203, having been abandoned by King John of England. Caen was sacked by Edward III of England after his invasion force landed in Normandy in July 1346. Henry V seized it for the English in 1417. The city gained its university – one of Henry VI's foundations – in 1432 and remained under English rule until 1450, when, with the rest of Normandy, it was recaptured by the French.

The Plantagenet Chronicles: 279–80, 294
Chronicles of the Age of Chivalry/Four Gothic Kings (US edn): 246, 269
The Wars of the Roses: 141, 194, 202

Caernarfon castle

Castle built *c.*1284 in Gwynedd by Edward I of England, as part of his fortification programme to subdue Wales: one of the five principal English strongholds in Snowdonia.

Designed by Edward's architect, the Savoyard master James of St George, with polygonal towers and banded walls in imitation of Constantinople's defences, Caernarfon was also a royal residence.

Edward's queen, Eleanor of Castile, built a garden there. Edward's son, the future Edward II, was born at Caernarfon in 1284; an event celebrated with a feasting, ceremonies and tournaments inspired by the Arthurian legends. Prince Edward was later created the first prince of Wales at Caernarfon in 1301.

Chronicles of the Age of Chivalry/Four Gothic Kings (US edn): 108, 117, 121, 127, 160

Caerphilly castle

Castle in South Wales. Hugh Despenser, the son, Edward II of England's favourite, used his great wealth to make several extensions to the splendid building.

Chronicles of the Age of Chivalry/Four Gothic Kings (US edn): 212

Calais

Port in Picardy, on the French side of the Straits of Dover; an English possession from 1347 to 1558. The counts of Boulogne fortified the town in the 13th century. When Edward III of England took Calais in August 1347, after an 11–month siege, he agreed to spare the inhabitants on condition that six prominent citizens should go barefoot to him with the town's keys. Edward ordered the men to be beheaded but, according to the chronicler Froissart, relented when his wife, Philippa of Hainault, pleaded for their lives. In 1362 Edward transferred England's wool staple to Calais, making the town the main port for English wool exports to the Continent and the centre for exacting duties on wool. It finally fell to the French in 1552.

Chronicles of the Age of Chivalry/Four Gothic Kings (US edn): 229, 248–52, 278, 280, 282, 296, 298
The Wars of the Roses: 29, 46, 76, 78, 115, 130, 173, 176, 182, 202–3, 236, 244, 264, 268, 301

Cambridge

Settled since Roman times, Cambridge became an academic centre in 1209 with the emergence

Caernarfon castle One of Edward I of England's greatest Welsh castles.

of the university there, following the migration of a group of students from Oxford. Nine new colleges were founded between the mid-14th century and the 1530s; King's College was founded in 1440 by Henry V.

The Plantagenet Chronicles: 321
Chronicles of the Age of Chivalry/Four Gothic Kings (US edn): 87
The Wars of the Roses: 62–4, 194–5

canon

A clergyman living in a clerical house or within cathedral precincts and ordering his life according to rules (canons) of the church. Some canons followed the monastic life, the most noted orders being the Augustinian and Premonstratensian canons. Secular (non-monastic) canons of cathedrals held prebends, estates set aside for their support. These could produce substantial incomes.

Canterbury

City in Kent, and the centre of English Christianity since St Augustine founded an abbey there in 597. The first Norman archbishop of Canterbury, Lanfranc, began the present cathedral in 1070. Thomas Becket's murder there on 29 December 1170 made it England's principal place of pilgrimage. The cathedral choir burned down in September

Canterbury Cathedral *The Perpendicular nave of St Thomas Becket's burial place.*

1174 and was rebuilt by the Frenchman William of Sens, who retained the old aisle walls. Becket's shrine was finished in 1220; stained glass windows around the tomb depict his miraculous cures. Between 1379 and 1405 the cathedral nave was totally rebuilt in the Perpendicular style by Henry Yevele, England's leading architect.

The Plantagenet Chronicles: 98–9, 118–20, 130, 136–7, 142, 152, 172, 245, 270, 288, 317
Chronicles of the Age of Chivalry/Four Gothic Kings (US edn): 41, 56, 58, 116, 148, 206, 291
The Wars of the Roses: 64, 86–7, 117, 133

Canterbury Tales, The

Chaucer's last work, written mostly after 1387 and unfinished at his death in 1400. A prologue describing a procession of pilgrims (a cross-section of later Plantagenet society) en route to Becket's shrine at Canterbury is followed by a collection of tales narrated by each of the company. The whole gives a comprehensive portrait of the manners and views of the age.

The Wars of the Roses: 71

Canterbury, Eadwine of

See: Eadwine of Canterbury

Canterbury, Gervase of

See: Gervase of Canterbury

Cantilupe, Thomas, bishop of Hereford

1218?–82. Son of William de Cantilupe, 2nd baron; chancellor of Oxford University (1262–3); chancellor of England (1264–5) under Henry III; bishop of Hereford (1275–82). A papal chaplain in the 1240s, and an eminent lawyer, Thomas studied at the university of Paris and at Orléans, then went to Oxford to teach common law in 1255. With his uncle Walter Cantilupe, bishop of Worcester, he supported Simon de Montfort's party opposing Henry III. Elected bishop of Hereford in 1275, he was conscientious in his cure of souls. He died in Orvieto while appealing against his excommunication over bitter jurisdictional disputes with John Peckham, archbishop of Canterbury. Buried in Hereford Cathedral, he was canonized in 1320 as St Thomas of Hereford, after miracles had occurred at his tomb.

Chronicles of the Age of Chivalry/Four Gothic Kings (US edn): 86–7

Capetians

Dynasty of French monarchs which followed the Carolingians from 987 – when Hugh Capet became king – to 1328 (with the death of Charles IV). The nickname Capet, probably meaning cap or cape wearer, was attached exclusively to Hugh from the 13th century but not used for the dynasty until the 18th.

Capgrave, John

1393–1464, Augustinian friar and chronicler, resident most of his life in Norfolk at the friary in King's Lynn where he was prior. One of his works, *The Book of Illustrious Henries* (1446–7), was written for Henry VI and eulogizes the Lancastrian dynasty (Henry IV, V and VI). In *The Chronicle of England,* a compilation from the chronicle of Thomas Walsingham, written probably from 1461 to 1464 and dedicated to the Yorkist Edward IV, Capgrave switched his support to the house of York, referring to Henry IV as an usurper. Also wrote theological tracts and commentaries.

The Wars of the Roses: 12, 91, 94, 192

Carcassonne

City on the River Aude in Languedoc. The old city, originally fortified by the Romans and sited on a hilltop in southern France, was a stronghold of the Albigensians until its capture by crusaders against the heresy, under the leadership of Simon IV de Montfort l'Amaury, in 1209. In 1247 the city yielded to Louis IX of France, who built a new line of heavily fortified walls to protect the city. When this work was completed in about 1270, Carcassonne was believed to be impregnable. Edward the Black Prince failed to take Carcassonne in 1355. The walls still stand, providing a rare example of a medieval fortified city.

Chronicles of the Age of Chivalry/Four Gothic Kings (US edn): 249, 266–8

Carlisle

Town in Cumberland on the site of a Roman camp near Hadrian's Wall. Carlisle had a Franciscan friary (where perhaps the *Lanercost Chronicle* was written in the 14th century) and from 1092, when it was annexed by William II of England, was involved in sporadic border warfare between England and Scotland. Edward I of England held three parliaments there; in 1307, the last was convened while he was campaigning against Robert Bruce, king of

Scotland. The *Lanercost Chronicle* records the Scots siege of Carlisle for ten days from 22 July 1315. Both sides used stone-throwing siege engines and the Scots were beaten off, with the loss of only two Englishmen, after the wheels of their siege tower sank in soft ground. The same chronicle also records that in 1335 the Carlisle Dominicans paid ten marks for a bell stolen by Edward III of England's forces from a Franciscan friary in Dundee.

Chronicles of the Age of Chivalry/Four Gothic Kings (US edn): 13, 162, 192, 236

carrack

Large medieval vessel, commonly of about 500 tons, used both to transport cargo and for warfare.

The Wars of the Roses: 128

Carthusians

Monastic order founded by St Bruno at La Grande Chartreuse in France in 1084. It was characterized by extreme austerity and the solitude of its monks, who met only during communal worship. Henry II of England founded two Carthusian houses: at Witham in Somerset (1177) and at Le Liget near Loches in France (c.1181). When Hugh of Avallon (later St Hugh) arrived at Witham as its new prior in about 1175 he found the priory only half planned, with the monks living in a wood, but he managed to persuade the king to pay for a modest building programme. Under his leadership the priory remained a small ascetic house. The Charterhouse (English name for a Carthusian house) in London was founded in 1371, and still stands.

The Plantagenet Chronicles: 77, 131, 182–3, 324

castellan

Governor or constable of a castle.

Castile

Kingdom comprising the high plateau of central Spain and the littoral to its north. Castile's name derived from the many castles built after its reconquest from the Moors (8th–9th century). In 1367 Peter, the Cruel, king of Castile, deposed by his half-brother Henry of Trastamara two years earlier, asked Edward the Black Prince to help him regain his throne; the English defeated Henry at Najera on 3 April 1367. When John of Gaunt married Peter's daughter

Constance in 1371 he acquired a claim to the throne of Castile, but failed to secure it by diplomacy or by campaigning in Castile (1387). Isabella of Castile's marriage to Ferdinand of Aragon (later Ferdinand II of Aragon) in 1469 led to the eventual union of Castile and Aragon in 1479.

The Plantagenet Chronicles: 115
Chronicles of the Age of Chivalry/Four Gothic Kings (US edn): 66, 228, 286–93
The Wars of the Roses: 42–3, 46, 246–7

Castile, Blanche of

See: Blanche of Castile

Castile, Constance of

See: Constance of Castile

Castile, Eleanor of

See: Eleanor of Castile

Castile, Isabella of

See: Isabella of Castile

Castillon-sur-Dordogne

Port on the River Dordogne in south-west France. The town, which was, like the rest of Guyenne, consistently loyal to the English crown after 1154, was besieged by the troops of Charles VII of France in spring 1453. Jean Bureau, the French commander, routed the English relief force under John Talbot, 4th earl of Shrewsbury, on 17 July 1453, in the last great battle of the Hundred Years War. Castillon fell to the French, and remained French thereafter.

The Wars of the Roses: 209–10

Catesby, William

d.1485, Lawyer, speaker of the House of Commons (1484); squire of King Richard III of England (1484–5). In 1483 Catesby helped Richard, 3rd duke of Gloucester, capture and execute William, Lord Hastings, his former patron, thus clearing the way for Richard's usurpation as Richard III. Catesby gained from the property confiscations which followed the risings against Richard in October 1483, and managed the Commons for the king at the Westminster parliament of November 1483. A seditious ballad of 1484 lampooned him as 'the Cat', ruling England under 'the Hog' (Richard).

Catesby was taken prisoner when the future Henry VII defeated Richard's forces at Bosworth and beheaded.

The Wars of the Roses: 293, 300–1

William Catesby *The memorial brass of Richard III's protégé and devoted servant, beheaded after Bosworth.*

Cathars

Also known as the Albigensians, after the French town of Albi, a major Cathar centre. Catharism was a widespread medieval heretical movement which flourished in the 11th and 12th centuries, especially in the Languedoc region of southern France. Cathars were extreme ascetics, who held the dualist view that God ruled the spiritual world and Satan the material world. They were savagely persecuted by the Church. In 1209 Pope Innocent III preached the Albigensian Crusade (1209–29) against the Languedoc. Led by Simon IV de Montfort l'Amaury and Prince Louis, son of Philip II of France, the crusade became a rush to seize land, with northern Frenchmen massacring Cathars and Catholics alike. The crusade's failure to stamp out heresy led to the setting up of the Inquisition, whose tactics of interrogation and torture gradually wore down Catharism by the 15th century.

The Plantagenet Chronicles: 304
Chronicles of the Age of Chivalry/Four Gothic Kings (US edn): 65, 69

Cathars *The Albigensian heretics are expelled from the town of Carcassone in southern France.*

Catherine of France

1401–37. Also known as Catherine of Valois; daughter of Charles VI of France and Isabella of Bavaria. Brought up at a convent at Poissy, France, her marriage to Henry V of England (then Henry, prince of Wales) was first proposed in 1408, when she was eight and he 21. Henry met her briefly in 1419, and, according to some contemporary chroniclers, it was love at first sight. Their marriage, one of the terms of the Treaty of Troyes (1420), reinforced Henry's status as the French king's regent and heir. The ceremony took place at Troyes Cathedral in June 1420 and the future Henry VI was born at Windsor on 6 December 1421. After Henry V's death she was queen dowager until her secret marriage in about 1429 to Owen Tudor, a Welsh squire. Their eldest son, Edmund Tudor, 14th earl of Richmond, was father to the future Henry VII. In 1436 Owen was imprisoned, and Catherine entered Bermondsey Abbey where she died aged 36.

The Wars of the Roses: 124, 133, 148, 150–1, 157, 167, 182

Caxton, William

1422?–91. First English printer. Born in Kent, he was apprenticed to a London mercer. In 1441, after his master's death, Caxton went to Bruges, where he became a fully fledged mercer by 1453 and was elected governor of the English Merchants Adventurers in 1465. He went to Cologne in 1472 to learn printing and returned to Bruges some two years later with a press, type, and matrixes. He produced the first printed English book, the *Recuyell of the Historyes of Troye* (from his own translation), in about 1474. Returning to England in 1476, Caxton issued nearly 80 books from his press at Westminster (1477–91), including Ovid in translation, Malory and Chaucer's *The Canterbury Tales*. About a third were his own translations from French, Latin and Dutch.

The Wars of the Roses: 240–1

Cecily, daughter of Edward IV, king of England

1469–1507. Third daughter of Edward IV and Elizabeth Woodville. In 1474 Edward concluded a marriage alliance with James III of Scotland, betrothing the five-year-old Cecily to James's heir, the future James IV, then one year old. However, in 1475 Edward sealed the Treaty of Picquigny between England and France, isolating Scotland, and the cooling of Anglo-Scots relations which followed forestalled the marriage. Cecily was betrothed to James III's rival, Alexander Stewart, 3rd duke of Albany, in 1482, but this marriage also failed to materialize when the English withdrew their support from Albany later that year. With her mother, Elizabeth Woodville, she took sanctuary from Richard III in Westminster Abbey in 1483, after the arrest of her uncle, Anthony Woodville, Lord Rivers, but was surrendered to the king in 1484. She won Henry VII's favour after his accession in 1485. That same year she married John, Viscount Welles, and five years after his death in 1499, she married Thomas Kyme.

The Wars of the Roses: 274, 299

Celestine III, pope

?1105–98. Born Giacinto Bobo-Orsini; pope 1191–8. Celestine crowned Henry VI, son of Frederick I, as Holy Roman Emperor in 1190, but tried to keep imperial power in Italy in check. He appealed to Albert, duke of Austria, for the release of Richard I of England from captivity and, when Albert initially failed to comply, excommunicated him: Richard, as a crusader, was under the Church's protection.

The Plantagenet Chronicles: 234, 250

Celestine V, St, pope

1215–96. Born Pietro del Murrone; pope 5 July–13 December 1294. Celestine was a venerated hermit, who was elected pope as a compromise to end a 27-month election conclave, divided between Roman and Neapolitan/French interests. As pope Celestine was naïve and influenced by Charles II of Naples, who detained him in his city. Celestine granted privileges and offices to almost anyone who asked, delegated his duties to a commission of three cardinals and kept to his cell. He abdicated after five months on the advice of the ambitious Cardinal Benedetto Caetani, who succeeded him as Pope Boniface VIII, and then imprisoned him. Celestine escaped, was recaptured, and died soon after; foul play by Caetani was rumoured. Celestine V was canonized in 1313.

Chronicles of the Age of Chivalry/Four Gothic Kings (US edn): 150

Champagne

Region of north-east France, Situated at the junction of Europe's main trade routes, it was noted during Plantagenet times for its great fairs at Troyes (capital of Champagne), Provins, Lagny-sur-Marne and Bar-sur-Aube, which six times a year attracted merchants from all over Europe. The trade laws of Champagne had a profound influence on later commercial practices: troy weight (from Troyes) is still used to weigh precious metals and gems. Champagne's prosperity was at its peak when Reims Cathedral was built (1211–70). Champagne was, with Blois, a powerful fief which threatened royal interests in the early Capetian period. It was incorporated into the French royal domain in 1314, when the grandson and heir of Henry III, count of Champagne and king of Navare, ascended the throne of France as Louis X.

The Plantagenet Chronicles: 28, 237

Chancellor of England

Originally the king's chaplain and secretary, the chancellor headed Chancery, the royal secretariat, and supervised the issue of writs, the basic instruments of the royal administrative and legal system. He was usually a cleric; clergy were best schooled for writing and administration. He also held the king's great seal for authenticating solemn state documents. The chancellor was appealed to as 'keeper of the king's conscience' in legal cases not covered by common or statute law.

Charles the Bold *The last reigning duke of Burgundy, Charles (opposite) died in the battle of Nancy in 1477.*

Chancery

From the late 10th century, the secretariat responsible for writing the king's charters, writs and letters and authenticating documents with seals. It was headed by the chancellor, a cleric who was the king's secretary. Under Hubert Walter, archbishop of Canterbury and chancellor from 1199 to 1205, the office began recording its letters in long rolls. Chancery issued royal instructions of three main types: charters (making permanent grants of lands or privileges), letters patent (making temporary grants) and letters close (bearing secret orders to royal officials, usually sheriffs). Chancery also dealt with legal disputes not covered by existing common or statute law. Writs issued by Chancery governed access to the royal courts.

The Plantagenet Chronicles: 309
The Wars of the Roses: 270

Chanson de Roland

Composed *c.* 1098–1100. Most celebrated of the *chansons de geste.* These were long rhymed poems in medieval French, relating heroic deeds, composed and sung by troubadours and popular throughout Europe in the 12th and 13th centuries. Roland, the eponymous hero, was the real-life commander of the Emperor Charlemagne's forces on the Breton border; the rearguard action in which he died (778) became in the poem the legendary battle of Roncesvalles.

The Plantagenet Chronicles: 247

chantry

Endowment in a will for the maintenance of priests to sing masses, usually for the soul of the person making the endowment; also the body of priests or chapel so endowed.

The Wars of the Roses: 182

Charlemagne, emperor

742?–814. Son of Pepin the Short; king of the Franks (768–814), emperor of the west (800–14). Inheriting the leadership of the Franks from his father, Charlemagne conquered German lands, including Saxony and Bavaria and most of northern Italy, setting a framework for the future Holy Roman Empire. When Pope Leo III crowned him western emperor on Christmas Day 800, his domain comprised almost all the lands between Bohemia in the east and the Pyrenees in the west. The Carolingian

Charles of Orléans Charles' agreement to the terms of his ransom from the English.

empire was split up after the death of Charlemagne's son and heir, Louis, in 840. By the 12th century Charlemagne had become a near-mythical hero, celebrated in the *Chanson de Roland* and other legends and *chansons de geste,* and descent from him gave royal and noble houses a particular cachet.

The Plantagenet Chronicles: 21, 167

Charles II, the Bad, king of Navarre

1332–87. Grandson of Louis X of France; count of Evreux; king of Navarre (1349–87). Charles married Joan of France in 1352; for the next two years he engaged in a feud with his father-in-law John II of France over Joan's dowry and allied himself with Edward III of England. In 1356 Charles was seized and imprisoned by John, but was released after the French king's capture at Poitiers in September of the same year. In 1358 Charles helped to suppress the Jacquerie revolt, crushing the peasant forces at the battle of Mello. He earned his nickname for his rapid changes of allegiance from the French to the English kings. He played off Castile against Aragon in the 1360s, and, although chosen by the Parisians in 1358 as their champion against the French regent, the future Charles V of France, he used his position of captain general

principally to further his own interests. From 1380 to 1387 he confined his attentions to his mountain kingdom. One of his daughters, Joan, married Henry IV of England.

Chronicles of the Age of Chivalry/Four Gothic Kings (US edn): 274 276

Charles, the Bold, duke of Burgundy

1437–77. Son of Philip, the Good, duke of Burgundy; last reigning duke of Burgundy (1467–77), named the Bold or the Rash for his impetuous valour. He married Margaret of York, sister of Edward IV of England, in 1468, thereby allying himself with England against Louis XI of France. Charles sought to annexe Alsace and Lorraine (at that time outside France), which separated his lands in the Low Countries from his estates in France; but his occupation of the duchy of Lorraine in 1473 led a year later to war with a coalition, including the French and Swiss. Edward IV, bribed by Louis XI at Picquigny in 1475, deserted Charles; and a mixed Lorraine/Swiss force defeated the Burgundians at Nancy in January 1477. Charles died in the battle, and Louis seized the French portion of his possessions.

The Wars of the Roses: 238–42, 263–5, 268, 272

Charles, duke of Orléans

1391–1465. French poet, son of Louis, duke of Orléans. Charles married Isabella of France, widow of Richard II of England, in 1406. He acceded to the duchy on his father's murder in 1407 by the Burgundian faction, and led the Armagnacs (Orleanists) against the duke of Burgundy. He was captured at Agincourt in 1415, and imprisoned in England for 25 years, where he wrote many of his poems. Charles was released in 1440 for a ransom of 120,000 marks, as part of Henry VI of England's peace overtures towards the French. Snubbed by Charles VII of France on his return, he spent most of his last years in retirement at Blois, writing and befriending other literary men, including René, duke of Anjou.

The Wars of the Roses: 77, 114, 131, 134–5, 188–9, 197

Charles IV, Holy Roman Emperor

1316–78. King of Germany and Bohemia (1346-78); Holy Roman Emperor (1355–78). Married Blanche of Valois, sister of Philip VI of France. Born in Prague, Charles spent several years as a young man at the court of his uncle, Charles IV of France. After inheriting the throne of Bohemia from his father, John of Luxembourg, who was killed at Crécy in 1347, Charles brought stability and prosperity to the kingdom, increased its territories, and in 1348 founded the university of Prague. In Germany he promulgated the Golden Bull in 1356, to regulate the election of future kings. In 1373 Charles secured the choice of his son Wenceslas as king of the Romans – Holy Roman Emperor elect – and therefore his successor.

Chronicles of the Age of Chivalry/Four Gothic Kings (US edn): 237
The Wars of the Roses: 39

Charles IV, king of France

1294–1328. Count of La Marche; king of France (1322–8). Youngest son of Philip IV and last of the direct line of Capetian kings. Charles succeeded his two brothers, Louis X and Philip V, who had ruled in turn but had left no male heirs. In 1322 he repudiated his first wife, Blanche of Burgundy, and married Mary of Luxembourg, daughter of the late Holy Roman Emperor Henry VII. Two years later, in 1324, he was offered the imperial crown by Pope John XXII, but nothing came of this. In 1324 war broke out with Edward II, king of England, over rights in the bastide (fortified town) of Saint-Sardos in Gascony, and Charles declared the duchy forfeit. Isabella, Edward's queen and Charles's sister, came to Paris in 1325 to negotiate a truce on behalf of the English, and the king's young son Edward, later Edward III, was invested as duke of Gascony and count of Ponthieu. After Edward II's deposition by Isabella and her followers, Charles recovered the Agenais and Bazardais regions for the French crown. When he died, his third wife, Joan of Evreux, was pregnant. However, the child was a girl, and in accordance with recently established precedent that succession was through the male line, the throne passed to Philip VI, grandson of Philip III of France and the first French king of the house of Valois.

Chronicles of the Age of Chivalry/Four Gothic Kings (US edn): 154, 205, 227

Charles V, king of France

1337–80. Son of John II of France and Bonne of Luxembourg; regent of France from 1356, when his father was captured at the battle of Poitiers and held captive in England; king of France (1364–80). The states general – the equivalent of the English parliament – refused to grant Charles aid for the war against England without substantial reforms of the administration, and in 1358 the people of Paris, under the leadership of Etienne Marcel, openly supported Charles II, the Bad, of Navarre against him; in addition, the Jacquerie, a major revolt of the peasants, broke out. However, in 1359, when Charles repudiated the highly unfavourable Treaty of London that John II had sealed with the English, the states general rallied to him and granted him considerable aid. The peasants were savagely suppressed and Paris returned its allegiance to Charles. After John II's death in 1364, the French royal armies under the command of Bertrand du Guesclin made inroads into the Plantagenet gains in France, and by 1380 the English had retreated to a narrow strip of coastline in Gascony. The writings of Christine de Pisan endowed Charles with a reputation as a prudent and successful monarch, and with the succession of the mentally unstable Charles VI, chroniclers looked back on his reign as a golden age.

Chronicles of the Age of Chivalry/Four Gothic Kings (US edn): 270, 274, 280, 284–6, 294–8
The Wars of the Roses: 29, 49, 136

Charles VI, king of France

1368–1422. Eldest son of Charles V of France and Joan of Bourbon; king of France (1380–1422). Charles VI was only 12 years old when his father died in 1380. Detailed instructions provided for his minority were ignored and the young king's four uncles (Louis II, duke of Bourbon and the three Valois princes, Louis, duke of Anjou, John, duke of Berry and Philip, the Bold, duke of Burgundy) jostled for power. The monarchy was short of funds and revolts broke out in many parts of France. In 1388 Charles, with the help of his brother Louis, duke of Orléans, removed his uncles from power and replaced them with a group of his father's councillors – known by the uncles as the marmosets because of their humble origins. Charles had married Isabella of Bavaria in 1385, and in 1396 their daughter Isabella of Valois, aged only seven, became the second wife of Richard II of England. In 1392 Charles suffered his first attack of madness. The next year he narrowly escaped death at the Bal des Ardents, when a group of his courtiers, dressed as wild animals, were set alight by a torch and burned alive. Further bouts of insanity enabled his uncles to remove the marmosets and return to power. For the rest of his reign, Charles was little more than a pawn in a political game he scarcely understood. In 1420 he was forced by Philip, the Good, duke of Burgundy, to conclude the Treaty of Troyes with Henry V of England. One of its provisions was that Henry was to rule France as regent until Charles's death. The French king, who had been living in a state of neglect at Senlis, was brought to Paris by Henry and ended his days there.

The Wars of the Roses: 46, 48, 49, 50, 68, 72, 76, 110, 114, 115, 148, 149, 150, 183, 212, 213, 215

Charles VII, king of France

1403–61. Fifth son of Charles VI of France and Isabella of Bavaria; king of France (1429–61). Charles was bethrothed to Mary of Anjou in 1413, at the age of ten, and brought up at the Angevin court. In 1417 he became the dauphin – heir to the French crown – and in 1418, during his father's incapacity, was made regent of France, becoming leader of the Armagnac faction at court. In 1419, however, John the Fearless, duke of Burgundy and leader of the rival Burgundian faction which actually controlled the king, was murdered at Montereau – by Charles's men and in his presence. In 1420 the dauphin was, by the terms of the Treaty of Troyes, disinherited for his complicity in John's murder. That agreement was made between his father Charles VI of France, Henry V of England, and Philip, the Good, duke of Burgundy: Philip, son of John, the Fearless, and his successor as leader of the Burgundians, forced Charles VI to make Henry V regent in the dauphin's place. After his father's death in 1422, Charles was recognized as king of France only by the Languedoc, Touraine, Berry and Poitou, and was nicknamed the 'king of Bourges', after the nominal seat of his alternative government. Disputes between his followers weakened Charles's position further; he was vacillating and easily influenced by favourites such as his mistress, Agnes Sorel.

Then in 1429, after nearly a decade of intermittent fighting, when Orléans was about to fall to the English under John, 1st duke of Bedford, Joan of Arc helped the dauphin to regain the city and revitalized his cause. Charles was crowned king of France at Reims in July 1429, at Joan's insistence and with her standing at his side. In 1433 his favourites were ousted by more energetic men, who encouraged him to wage war against the English, and he gradually took land from the Lancastrian forces, helped by the new army he organized and the gradual stabilization of French royal finances. He introduced a direct land tax and measures such as loans from the great banker of Bourges, Jacques Coeur, to finance his campaigns. In 1435 he signed the Treaty of Arras, healing the rift with Philip the Good and the Burgundians. In 1436 he captured Paris and in 1450, Normandy, held by England since 1419, fell to his armies. Eventually, in 1453, the English were driven out of Gascony. During his last years Charles had to cope with the hostility of his son Louis (the future Louis XI); on his deathbed the king believed he had been poisoned by the dauphin.

The Wars of the Roses: 148–9, 156, 166, 170–5, 177, 180, 187–8, 197, 206–7, 209, 238, 239

Charles VIII, king of France

1470–98. Son and heir of Louis XI of France. Charles was king of France from 1483 to 1498 but until 1492 the country was under the regency of his sister, Anne de Beaujeu. Charles financed the invasion of England by Henry Tudor, the future Henry VII, in 1485. His expedition to Italy (1494–5) in pursuit of the throne of Naples, proved a disaster.

The Wars of the Roses: 297

Charles I, king of Naples

1227–85. Youngest brother of Louis IX of France; count of Anjou and Provence; king of Naples and Sicily (1266–85). Charles took part in Louis IX's crusades of 1248 and 1270. He was crowned king of Naples and Sicily in 1266 by Pope Clement IV in return for supporting papal rights in southern Italy against Manfred, king of Naples and Sicily; he defeated and slew Manfred in battle the same year. As leader of the Guelph, or pro-papal, faction, he gained political dominance in Italy. But his harsh tax exactions in his southern kingdom provoked the Sicilian Vespers of 1282, when Sicily rose against his rule and called in the Aragonese for help. The war between the Angevins and Aragonese was still in progress when Charles died.

Chronicles of the Age of Chivalry/Four Gothic Kings (US edn): 110, 125

Charles II, king of Naples

1248–1309. Son of Charles I of Naples; count of Anjou and Provence; king of Naples (1289–1309). Charles was an important figure in Rome, influencing the election of popes Celestine V and Boniface VIII. He subsequently struggled to gain the throne of Sicily from James II of Aragon, but in 1302 was forced to concede his rights to James's brother Frederick.

Chronicles of the Age of Chivalry/Four Gothic Kings (US edn): 150

Chartres

Town in north-west France on the River Eure. The seat of a countship, Chartres passed to the French crown in 1286, purchased by Philip III of France. St Bernard of Clairvaux preached the Second Crusade at Chartres in 1146. The great cathedral of Notre-Dame (*c*.1195–1225) is one of France's finest High Gothic cathedrals, with two great spires and stained glass windows donated by great patrons such as Blanche of Castile.

The Plantagenet Chronicles: 174, 253
Chronicles of the Age of Chivalry/Four Gothic Kings (US edn): 30–1, 78, 276

Château Gaillard

Richard I of England's 'castle of the Rock' or 'saucy castle' in eastern Normandy, on the Seine at Les Andelys. It was the lynchpin of the fortifications shielding Rouen, capital of Richard's duchy of Normandy, against the French kings. The castle cost £11,500 and was built within two years (1196–8). Richard himself oversaw its design and construction, which incorporated many innovations: concentric walls, rock-cut ditches, and an elliptical citadel with fields of fire covering all approaches. The king hoped to use his castle as a base from which to recover the Norman Vexin lost to Philip II of France. After Richard's death, Philip took the castle by storm in 1203.

The Plantagenet Chronicles: 198, 227, 239, 248, 250, 278–9

Chaucer, Geoffrey

c.1340–1400. English poet. A page in the service of Lionel, 1st duke of Clarence (1357) he went on campaign in France (1359). He was possibly educated at one of the Inns of Court in London, and by 1367 had become a yeoman of the chamber in the king's household; his duties included entertaining the court with songs and poetry. By 1374 he had married Philippa Roet, sister of Catherine Swynford, John of Gaunt's mistress and later third wife.

On a diplomatic mission to Italy in 1372–3 Chaucer discovered the works of Dante and Boccaccio, which had a major influence on his poetry. He was a controller of the customs in London until 1386, when he was dismissed during a purge of royal officials, and from 1389 to 1391 was a clerk of the royal works. After this he subsisted with difficulty on a royal pension and on his income as a royal forester until 1399, when Henry IV acceded to the throne of England and almost doubled Chaucer's previous income with a grant of 40 marks a year. But within a year Chaucer died. He was buried in Westminster Abbey.

Chaucer's works reflect the diversity of his life as a soldier, courtier, diplomat, civil servant and official poet. *The Book of the Duchess* is an early poem written in 1369 to commemorate the death of Blanche of Lancaster, wife of John of Gaunt. The *House of Fame* and the *Parliament of Fowls*, from the same period, both centre on that favourite medieval theme, the problem of love. *Troilus and Criseyde*, an adaptation of a well-known tale, completed by 1385, is a remarkable work, imbued with ideas taken from the *Consolation of Philosophy*, by Boethius, which Chaucer translated from the Latin in the early 1380s. The *Legend of Good Women* includes a charming passage on the poet's devotion to the daisy. His most celebrated work, the *Canterbury Tales*, was written between about 1387 and his death in 1400.

Chronicles of the Age of Chivalry/Four Gothic Kings (US edn): 163, 193, 284, 297
The Wars of the Roses: 12, 54–5, 71, 249

***Chivalry** A knight (opposite) offers himself to his lady.*

Chaucer, Thomas

1367?–1434. Reputedly the son of the poet Geoffrey Chaucer; speaker of the House of Commons (1407, 1410, 1411, 1414); butler to four English kings: Richard II, Henry IV, Henry V, Henry VI. Thomas fought at Agincourt (1417), and was one of Henry V's envoys to France the same year. He was a member of Henry VI's council of regency from 1424, and was reputed to be immensely rich.

The Wars of the Roses: 117

Chertsey Abbey

Benedictine abbey, founded in 666, refounded in 964. Henry VI was buried there on 23 May 1471 after his supposed murder, possibly on Edward IV's orders. His tomb became a place of pilgrimage, as a result of miracles rumoured to have occurred there from 1481. On Richard III's orders, the king's body was reburied in 1484 at St George's Chapel, Windsor.

The Wars of the Roses: 225, 264

Chester

Port on the River Dee and county town of Cheshire. The grid pattern of its streets was established by the Romans and it is unique in England in that it still has its entire medieval defensive wall. Chester was used by Edward I of England between 1275 and 1284 as a base for military operations against Llywelyn ap Gruffydd, prince of Wales. Eleanor Cobham, duchess of Gloucester, was imprisoned in Chester castle after her prosecution for witchcraft and treason in 1441. The city had a flourishing trade with Ireland, its importance as a port peaking from about 1350 to 1450. This role was curtailed after the Middle Ages by the silting up of the Dee river.

Chronicles of the Age of Chivalry/Four Gothic Kings (US edn): 116, 174, 249
The Wars of the Roses: 55, 84, 102, 192–3, 218

Chevaliers, Krak des

See: Krak des Chevaliers

chevauchée

A war tactic, a plundering raid. Several were launched by the English against France in the 1370s and 1380s, to little effect.

The Wars of the Roses: 49

Chichele, Henry, archbishop of Canterbury

1362–1443. Son of a yeoman, supported by William of Wykeham; bishop of St Davids, Wales (1408–14); archbishop of Canterbury (1414). Chichele was English envoy to the Council of Pisa (1409) and to France (1410 and 1413). He favoured war with France in 1415; arranged a special thanksgiving after Agincourt; went to France with Henry V of England in 1418; and negotiated Rouen's surrender to Henry in 1419. In 1421 he crowned Catherine of France, Henry V's queen, on her state entry into London, and did the same for her son, Henry VI, at Westminster on 6 November 1429. Chichele was suspended from office by Pope Martin V in 1427–8 for backing parliament's measures against accepting papal nominees in English benefices. He founded two colleges at Oxford, All Souls, and the later St John's College, together with a feeder school at Higham Ferrers. Chichele's tomb, the first known English example of funeral art with a cadaver carved beneath the main effigy (as a reminder of the fate of all mortals, no matter how powerful in life), was in place about 16 years before his death as a focus for his prayers.

The Wars of the Roses: 126, 151, 166, 172, 183

Children's Crusade

Mass movement of 1212, in which a visionary, 12-year-old French peasant boy, Stephen of Cloyes, led an army of French children to fight in the Holy Land. They embarked at Marseille, but never reached their destination; most were apparently sold into slavery in Egypt. German children en route to the Holy Land ended up in Italy, where most died of hunger and disease.

The Plantagenet Chronicles: 294

China

Chinese civilization was far in advance of that of Europe during the Middle Ages: the Chinese had developed printing and invented gunpowder and paper money. China was dominated by Tartar invaders for most of the 13th and 14th centuries. Attractive to Europe because of its silk, it was occasionally visited by Western merchants, such as the Polo family in the 1270s.

Chronicles of the Ages of Chivalry/Four Gothic Kings (US edn): 18, 82–3

Chinon

Town in central western France, on the River Vienne. Seized by Fulk Nerra, count of Anjou, in 987. Chinon became a Plantagenet stronghold in the 12th century, and was a bone of contention in the disputes between Henry II of England's sons in the 1170s. Henry II died at Chinon castle in 1189. Richard I of England and Philip II of France added to the fortifications; by 1203 Philip had won Chinon from King John of England during his conquests of the Angevin lands. Joan of Arc presented herself to the dauphin, later Charles VII of France, at the castle in 1429.

The Plantagenet Chronicles: 26, 28, 30, 116, 125, 173, 188, 190, 191, 192

chivalry

Medieval nobility's code of conduct, elaborated in the troubadours' *chansons de geste*, which extolled courage, loyalty, courtesy and charity as the virtues best befitting a knight.

The Plantagenet Chronicles: 154–5, 234–5
Chronicles of the Age of Chivalry/Four Gothic Kings (US edn): 160, 262–3, 273
The Wars of the Roses: 171

Chronicle of Chronicles (*Chronicon ex Chronicis*)

See: Worcester Chronicle

Chronicles of the Counts of Anjou

Chronicles mixing historical fact with myth, compiled mostly in the 12th century by several writers, including Abbot Odo of Marmoutier Abbey and Thomas of Loches (a chaplain of Count Fulk V of Anjou). They were given their final form in the 1160s by John, a monk of Marmoutier. They recount the careers of the counts of Anjou, who were to give rise to the Plantagenet dynasty, from their 10th-century beginnings to their apogee in the 12th century.

The Plantagenet Chronicles: 19

(Chronicle of Chronicles) *Chronicon ex Chronicis*

See: Worcester Chronicle

church courts

Courts introduced in England after the Norman Conquest, existing in parallel with lay courts and dealing with certain specific offences: heresy, divorce, sexual immorality, disputes over wills, and other 'cases touching the rule of souls'. They were usually held under the authority of a bishop or archdeacon, or in some cases of the archbishop or the pope. The sentences passed in them were lighter than those in their secular equivalents. Anyone who could prove 'benefit of clergy' (i.e. that he had taken even minor orders) came under their jurisdiction. It was in trying to limit the powers of the church courts that Henry II provoked strong opposition from his erstwhile chancellor Thomas Becket, who championed these institutions in his struggle with the king.

The Plantagenet Chronicles: 162
The Wars of the Roses: 270

Cinque Ports

Ports in Sussex and Kent (originally five: Hastings, Romney, Hythe, Dover and Sandwich) that were bound, because of their closeness to France, to provide ships and men to defend England. In return they received certain privileges, including their own courts and exemption from taxes. The association was first organized in the 11th century and formally chartered in the 13th. Winchelsea and Rye joined the original ports in the 12th century.

Chronicles of the Age of Chivalry/Four Gothic Kings (US edn): 58, 97, 116, 130, 136, 200–1, 240, 242

Cistercians

Religious order founded in 1098 by St Robert, abbot of Molesme, at Cîteaux in France, as a reaction against the laxity of the Cluniac order. Stephen Harding, an Englishman who became abbot of Cîteaux in 1109, and St Bernard, abbot of Clairvaux, popularized the order; its members were known as 'white monks' from the habits they wore. By the middle of the 12th century 530 Cistercian abbeys had been established across western Europe. Inspired to return to a strict interpretation of the rule of St Benedict, the Cistercians adopted a strict regimen, including much manual labour, enforced by tight discipline and regular supervisory visits by the abbots of the parent houses. Seekers of solitude, they insisted on siting their abbeys far from habitation. They became known in the 12th century as England's leading sheep farmers, as a result of efficient farming methods that employed many lay brothers.

The Plantagenet Chronicles: 77, 86, 114, 201, 250, 262–6, 267, 293, 324
Chronicles of the Age of Chivalry/Four Gothic Kings (US edn): 146–7

Cîteaux

Site of the first Cistercian abbey, founded in 1098 by Robert of Molesme in woods south of Dijon, the duchy of Burgundy.

The Plantagenet Chronicles: 77

Clairvaux

Site in the duchy of Burgundy in France, where in 1115 St Bernard founded a Cistercian abbey that became a major centre of the order.

The Plantagenet Chronicles: 77

Clarendon, Constitutions of

Set of 16 articles, issued in January 1164 during a council meeting at Clarendon Palace. By them Henry II attempted to curb the English Church's power, which had grown during the anarchy of King Stephen's rule, claiming, correctly, that the articles codified customs of Henry I's reign. The Constitutions limited clerical and papal authority in England. Two clauses ordering clerics to be punished by secular courts after trial in church courts, and forbidding appeals to Rome without royal consent, angered Thomas Becket, archbishop of Canterbury. The English clergy at first agreed to the Constitutions, but Thomas withdrew his assent when Pope Alexander III condemned them later in 1164. After Thomas's murder in 1170 Henry revoked the two contentious clauses, but otherwise the Constitutions remained law, defining the relationship of Church and state in England.

The Plantagenet Chronicles: 110, 112, 119

Clarendon Palace

An important royal residence in the Middle Ages, now a ruin. Henry II used a lodge here as a base for his hunting expeditions in the New Forest. It was here, in 1164, that he issued his Constitutions of Clarendon, which curtailed the rights of the clergy and which Thomas Becket refused to accept. In 1175–6 Henry had the palace extensively rebuilt and it was used by many of his successors.

The Plantagenet Chronicles: 110, 119
Chronicles of the Age of Chivalry/Four Gothic Kings (US edn): 253

Clement III, antipope

c.1025–1100. Born Guibert of Ravenna; imperial chancellor for Italy (1058–63); archbishop of Ravenna (1072); antipope (1080, 1084–1100). Guibert, as a servant of the Holy Roman Emperor Henry IV, supported him against the papacy. After Pope Gregory VII excommunicated Henry in 1080, at the culmination of their struggle for power over the western Church, the emperor summoned a council (1080) which declared Gregory deposed, then elected Guibert Pope Clement III, as antipope to Gregory. Clement based himself in Rome until expelled by Urban II in 1098, and promulgated Church reforms but he never managed to extend his authority much beyond Germany and northern Italy.

The Plantagenet Chronicles: 208

Clement VII, antipope

1342–94. Born Robert of Geneva; archbishop of Cambrai (1368); cardinal (1371); antipope (1378–94). As papal legate in Italy while a cardinal, Robert was responsible for several cruel massacres in the war against Florence, in particular at Cesena in 1377. Robert was elected antipope Clement VII at the fortified papal palace at Anagni, about 30 miles south-east of Rome, in opposition to Urban VI, whose attempted sweeping reform of the Church had alienated the electoral college after his election earlier that year. Clement withdrew to Avignon where he set up a separate papal court, thus beginning the Great Schism. Backed by France, Spain, Scotland and Naples, Clement's papacy was opposed in Hungary, the Holy Roman Empire and England. Portugal twice recognized and twice repudiated him, but he was unable to enlarge his body of support any further.

The Wars of the Roses: 32–3

Clement V, pope

1264–1314. Born Bertrand de Got; archbishop of Bordeaux (1299–1305); pope (1305–14). Former clerk to Edward I of England. Well disposed towards Philip IV of France, Clement was crowned pope at Lyon in 1305. In 1309, to escape the power of the Colonna family in Rome, he settled the papal court at Avignon, where it resided until 1377. Clement, under

---

Château Gaillard *Richard I's 'saucy castle' (overleaf) in Normandy.*

pressure from Philip to support him in his attacks on the order of the Knights Templar, dissolved the order in 1312, but without a direct condemnation, and transferred their estates to their rivals, the Knights Hospitaller. Clement's death was rumoured to be a result of the curse laid upon him by the Templars' Grand Master, Jacques de Molay, who, at the stake, summoned pope and king to appear with him before God's tribunal. Within the year both Clement and Philip were dead.

The Plantagenet Chronicles: 150
Chronicles of the Age of Chivalry/Four Gothic Kings (US edn): 137, 151, 165, 180–1, 186

Clement VI, pope

1291–1352. Born Pierre Roger; archbishop of Rouen (1330–42); cardinal (1338); pope (1342–52). Clement tried to heal the breach between the English and French kings after the outbreak of the Hundred Years War in 1337. He issued an order in 1349 to suppress the Flagellant sect which arose as a result of the panic attending the Black Death. In 1348 he purchased the city of Avignon from Joanna of Naples, for 80,000 florins. Already the seat of the papal court, Avignon was now embellished by the building of the magnificent Palais Neuf, which remains as a monument to papal extravagance.

Chronicles of the Age of Chivalry/Four Gothic Kings (US edn): 261

Clermont, Council of

Council of the Church called by Pope Urban II in 1095, at which he preached the First Crusade. Clermont, in the Auvergne region of central France, was an episcopal see and the site of several councils of the Church.

The Plantagenet Chronicles: 36

Clifford, Lord Robert

1273–1314. Fifth baron Clifford; 1st baron of Westmorland; warden of the marches and governor of Carlisle (1297). As warden of the border with Scotland, Clifford was involved from 1297 in constant fighting against the Scots. In 1306 he was granted part of the English estates of Robert Bruce, king of Scotland, and, in addition, Skipton castle in 1310. He became a favourite of Edward II (c.1310), but joined the baronial party against him in 1311. He made his peace with Edward in 1313, and joined him on his Scottish campaign in the following year. In

June 1314 he failed to relieve Stirling castle, besieged by the Scots, and was slain at the battle of Bannockburn.

Chronicles of the Age of Chivalry/Four Gothic Kings (US edn): 188

Clifford, Roger

d.1285? Roger succeeded to the lordship of Tenbury as a minor (c.1231). He went with Henry III to France (1259); sided with Simon de Montfort against the king in 1262–4, but fought for Henry at Lewes (1264) and Evesham (1265). He accompanied Prince Edward (later Edward I) on crusade from 1270 to 1274 and was made envoy to France by him in 1275. Appointed justice for Wales in 1279, he was captured and temporarily imprisoned by Welsh rebels at his castle at Hawarden in 1282.

Chronicles of the Age of Chivalry/Four Gothic Kings (US edn): 124

Clifford, Rosamund

d.1176? Daughter of Walter de Clifford. Mistress of Henry II of England, but not openly acknowledged until 1174 when she was in her 30s, after he had imprisoned his wife, Eleanor of Aquitaine. She lived in the royal palace at Woodstock in Oxfordshire, which was refurbished for her after her acknowledgement, until her death. She was buried in a magnificent tomb in Godstow nunnery, and both Henry and her father made the convent large gifts. St Hugh of Avallon, bishop of Lincoln, appalled to find an adulteress buried in a church, had her body reinterred outside it and her tomb removed in 1191, after Henry's death. Later, legends grew up, which related her supposed murder by Eleanor.

The Plantagenet Chronicles: 104–5

Clito, William

1100–28. Son of Robert Curthose, duke of Normandy, who had been deposed and imprisoned by his youngest brother, Henry I of England in 1106. From 1116 to 1120 William was backed by Louis VI of France in reclaiming Normandy, but Louis' efforts on his behalf were foiled by Henry I's diplomatic encounters with Pope Calixtus II; further attempts to win back the duchy in 1122–3 were frustrated by Henry's vigorous military actions. In 1127 William was married to Jeanne, a half-sister of Louis' wife, and was given the Vexin as her dowry. Later that year Louis attempted to impose William as

count on the Flemish, a group of whom had murdered their ruler, Count Charles the Good. William met considerable opposition from Thierry of Alsace, the rival claimant, and died in 1128 from a wound received at the siege of Alost.

The Plantagenet Chronicles: 36

Cluniacs

Order of Benedictine monks founded in 910 by St Berno, a Burgundian monk; centred on Cluny Abbey in eastern France. Freed by its unique constitution from the supervision of lay powers and, after 1016, from the local bishop's jurisdiction, Cluny became the centre of the first major order of western European monks: Benedictines who under the abbey's guidance adopted Cluniac customs. Between 950 and 1130 nearly 1,000 Cluniac houses were founded making the order one of the most powerful in western Europe. In addition, Cluny was a great cultural centre. From the mid-11th century the Cluniacs were both a model for a centralized Church and agents of papal reform, but by the 12th century their wealth and power had led to allegations of worldliness and, in reaction, the Cistercians and other ascetic orders were founded. The Cluniacs nevertheless remained a formidable force throughout the Middle Ages.

The Plantagenet Chronicles: 29, 77

Cluny Abbey

Abbey in eastern France, centre of an order of Benedictine monks known as Cluniacs, founded in 910 by St Berno. The abbey, completed in the early 12th century, was until the 16th century the largest church in the world. Only a part of one transept remains today, but a much smaller copy exists complete at the former Cluniac nunnery of Paray-le-Monial nearby. In the 11th and 12th centuries Cluny was one of the chief religious and cultural centres of Europe.

The Plantagenet Chronicles: 29

Cobham, Eleanor

d.1452. Daughter of Sir Reginald Cobham of Sterborough in Kent; wife of Humphrey, 2nd duke of Gloucester. An attendant on Humphrey's first wife, Jacqueline of Hainault, she married the duke in 1431, three years after his first marriage was declared invalid. Eleanor had probably already borne him two bastards. When John, 1st duke of Bedford, Henry IV's third son, died in 1435, Humphrey, his youngest brother, became Henry VI's heir. In 1441 three priests – Roger Bolingbroke (Eleanor's secretary), John Hunne (her chaplain) and Thomas Southwell – were executed for conspiring to kill the king by witchcraft. Eleanor was tried on the same charges and admitted five of the 28 counts. The authorities sentenced her to do public penance in London, divorced her from Humphrey and imprisoned her for life in Chester castle, Kenilworth castle, the Isle of Man and Beaumaris castle, where she died.

The Wars of the Roses: 192–3

Coeur, Jacques

c.1395–1456, French merchant, magnate and chief financial adviser to Charles VII of France. He had many interests in Mediterranean trade, owned workshops and mines, and amassed a fortune. In 1449–50 he financed Charles's recovery of Normandy from the English. His splendid house in Bourges still stands. Arrested in 1451 on false charges of poisoning Charles's mistress Agnes Sorel, Jacques was sentenced to imprisonment and a vast fine. He escaped to Rome in 1454–5 and died a year later leading a papal fleet against the Turks.

The Wars of the Roses: 125

cog

Ship developed in c.1300, probably by Hanseatic League traders. Broadbeamed, high-walled, with a deep draught and stern-post rudder, the cog was stable and capacious. Its high flat sides and tall bow and sterncastles made it a favourite 14th-century warship and a preferred merchantman.

Chronicles of the Age of Chivalry/Four Gothic Kings (US edn): 138

Coggeshall, Ralph of

See: Ralph, abbot of Coggeshall

coin clipping

Shaving and melting down fragments from the edges of silver pennies. Stealing silver in this way was a serious, hanging offence.

Chronicles of the Age of Chivalry/Four Gothic Kings (US edn): 122, 148

Cologne

Ancient German port on the Rhine, a Roman town since the 1st century BC. The archbishops of Cologne were princes of the Holy Roman Empire, ranked third among the college of electors (who elected the emperor); but constant feuding with the lay population drove them out of the city in the mid-13th century. The cathedral, begun in 1248, is the largest High Gothic cathedral in Europe. St Thomas Aquinas was educated at the Dominican school in Cologne between 1248 and 1252. Cologne was self-governing after 1288, becoming a free imperial city in 1475. A prosperous member of the Hanseatic League during the late Middle Ages, it traded in wine, coal, iron and textiles. Caxton learned printing at Cologne in 1471–2.

Chronicles of the Age of Chivalry/Four Gothic Kings (US edn): 54, 56, 84
The Wars of the Roses: 132, 241, 266

Colonna, Sciarra

d.1329. Member of the pre-eminent and powerful Roman family, and, by reason of their deep feuds with the Caetani, another Roman family, a bitter enemy of Pope Boniface VIII (Benedetto Caetani). In 1297 Boniface tried to break the power of the Colonna family, excommunicating and launching a crusade against them. Sciarra fled to the court of Philip IV of France. With Philip's adviser William de Nogaret, he led a mercenary force which, in September 1303, sacked Boniface's palace at Anagni in Italy, forcing the pope to flee to Rome. Boniface died shortly after this,

coin clipping Shaving silver from the edges of coins was treated as a serious crime, since control of the coin of the realm was a vital royal prerogative.

apparently from shock. Colonna power now recovered: as a senator of Rome, Sciarra crowned Louis IV of Bavaria Holy Roman Emperor in 1328 and helped him set up Nicholas V as antipope.

Chronicles of the Age of Chivalry/Four Gothic Kings (US edn): 150

Common Pleas, court of

Royal court, normally sitting at Westminster, administering both statute and common law. It gradually split away from the court of King's Bench during the 13th century: from 1224 it had its own rolls (records) and from 1272 its own chief justice.

The Wars of the Roses: 270

Commynes, Philippe de

c.1447–1511. Chronicler and diplomat, born in Flanders of a family serving the dukes of Burgundy; was chamberlain to Charles the Bold, duke of Burgundy, but switched allegiance to Louis XI, king of France (1472). Exiled to Dreux in 1489 for plotting against Louis's successor Charles VIII, he began his *Mémoires*. Philippe was well informed about English affairs: he had attended Charles the Bold's marriage to Margaret of York (1468), and kept abreast of developments through his diplomatic work for Louis XI. In his *Mémoires*, he describes Edward IV's character, the king's flight abroad from England (1470), Edward's campaign in France in 1474–5 (Philippe helped negotiate the Treaty of Picquigny), Louis XI's character, and much else.

The Wars of the Roses: 231, 238, 252, 277

Comyn, John, 7th earl of Buchan

d.1313? Constable of Scotland, loyal to Edward I of England, whom he acknowledged as king of Scotland in 1305. The rebel Robert Bruce had murdered the earl's cousin, John Comyn, lord of Badenoch, in 1306, and when Buchan's wife Isabella crowned Bruce king of Scotland at Scone on 25 March 1306 (her right as daughter of the earl of Fife), her husband proposed to kill her. Edward intervened and ordered Buchan instead to exhibit Isabella in a cage on the walls of Berwick castle for many days.

Chronicles of the Age of Chivalry/Four Gothic Kings (US edn): 158

Comyn, John, the younger

d.1306. Son of John Comyn, lord of Badenoch; elected one of the guardians of Scotland by the Scottish nobles (1299). Comyn fought for John Balliol, king of Scotland, against Edward I of England's armies at Carlisle (1296) and at Falkirk (1298). He expelled Edward's officials in 1302 but submitted to him in 1304 after being driven north by the English. The support of Comyn, as head of his family from 1300, was vital to Robert Bruce in his claim to the Scottish throne. The two met in Greyfriars church in Dumfries, in February 1306, but Bruce failed to win Comyn from his allegiance to John Balliol as rightful king of the Scots; Bruce's followers murdered Comyn.

Chronicles of the Age of Chivalry/Four Gothic Kings (US edn): 134, 157–8, 160, 190

Conrad III, king of Germany

c.1093–1152. Grandson of Holy Roman Emperor Henry IV; king of the Germans (1138-52), first of the Hohenstaufen dynasty. Conrad was declared rival candidate to Holy Roman Emperor Lothar II in 1127, and in 1128 was crowned king of Italy at Milan. But he was repudiated by the Italians and submitted to Lothar in 1135. After Lothar's death he was again elected as king of the Germans (Holy Roman Emperor elect) by a faction opposed to Lothar's heir, Henry of Bavaria. Conrad's elevation led to a civil war, from which arose the parties of the Guelphs and Ghibellines.

Since he was never crowned by a pope, Conrad was never confirmed as emperor. At Christmas 1146, St Bernard of Clairvaux induced him to join Louis VII of France on the Second Crusade. He left in 1147, took part in the unsuccessful siege of Damascus, and returned to Germany in 1149.

Conrad was succeeded by his nephew, Holy Roman Emperor Frederick I.

The Plantagenet Chronicles: 78, 167

consistory

Gathering of the college of cardinals with the pope presiding. In England a consistory court is a bishop's court, established in the 11th century by William the Conqueror, king of England.

Constance of Castile

d.1394. Daughter of Peter I, the Cruel, king of Castile; second wife of John of Gaunt (m.1372). Through Constance, John of Gaunt claimed the throne of Castile, but without success.

Chronicles of the Age of Chivalry/Four Gothic Kings (US edn): 296, 301
The Wars of the Roses: 42, 46

Constance, Council of

Council of the Church (1414–18) summoned by Pope John XXIII to end the Great Schism, at the behest of Holy Roman Emperor Sigismund III, who chose Constance in Germany as its site. The Council, attended by German, Italian, French, English and Spanish delegates, was dominated by advocates of the conciliar theory, that councils were supreme over popes, embodied in the decree *haec sancta*. The Council condemned Wycliffe's doctrines and burned John Hus for heresy. It deposed rival popes John XXIII (29 May 1415) and Benedict XIII (26 July 1417) and accepted the resignation of a third rival, Gregory XII (4 July 1415). The new pope, Martin V, was elected in 1417.

The Wars of the Roses: 33, 126–7, 132, 140–1, 143, 158

Constantinople

City on the Bosporus in present-day Turkey, founded in 330 by the Roman emperor Constantine and soon afterwards made the new capital of the eastern half of the Roman Empire. It was built on the site of a Greek town called Byzantium; and this gave its name to the eastern empire and its civilization, which continued until the 15th century.

In 1054 the Byzantine Church, under its patriarch, split away from the Catholic Church, and doctrinal differences between the two became increasingly irreconcilable. Although the First Crusade (1096–9) had been called partly in response to an appeal for help against Islam from the Byzantine emperor Alexius I Comnenus, he and his successors in Constantinople viewed the kingdom of Jerusalem and the other crusader states as a mixed blessing, since the crusaders often pursued their own interests. In 1203 the Fourth Crusade was diverted to Constantinople, where its leaders became embroiled in Byzantine politics, and the following year the crusading armies sacked the city; the reigning Greek dynasty was deposed in favour of a Latin one.

Although Emperor Michael VIII Palaeologus, rival Greek claimant to the Eastern Empire, succeeded in regaining the city from the Latins in 1261, and re-established his capital there, Constantinople had been fatally weakened. During the 14th and early 15th centuries the Ottoman Turks gradually captured more and more of its outlying lands,

and the city, ever more isolated, was forced to withstand a number of sieges. At last, however, it fell to the Turkish ruler Mehmed II in 1453, after a siege of almost two months, and was substantially rebuilt as a Turkish city – Istanbul.

The Plantagenet Chronicles: 26–7, 168–9, 171, 186, 280, 282–3
Chronicles of the Age of Chivalry/Four Gothic Kings (US edn): 70, 117, 254
The Wars of the Roses: 70, 210, 211, 275

Constitutions of Clarendon

See: Clarendon, Constitutions of

Conway castle

One of the ten major castles built by Edward I of England to control the rebellious principality of Gwynedd in North Wales. Begun in about 1283, Conway was also a royal residence, with walls almost a mile in circumference. Richard II, returning from Ireland in 1399 to meet Bolingbroke's invasion, stopped at Conway. Here he met a deputation including Henry Percy, 1st earl of Northumberland, with whom he discussed peace terms. Henry Percy treacherously swore fidelity to the king in the castle chapel, but his forces took Richard prisoner when the king had left Conway. The castle was later captured by Welsh rebels on Good Friday 1401, while the garrison was hearing mass.

Chronicles of the Age of Chivalry/Four Gothic Kings (US edn): 117, 121, 125
The Wars of the Roses: 61, 85, 89, 101

coquillards

Groups of roving bandits at large in the French countryside in the 1450s. They were rounded up in Burgundy between 1455 and 1457, and are chiefly remembered for the occasional verses which François Villon (1431–63?) the celebrated French poet, composed in their slang. Villon was probably not a coquillard himself but merely utilized their language.

The Wars of the Roses: 197

Corfe castle

Begun in the late 11th century. Here King John of England imprisoned some of the rebels who had supported his nephew, Arthur, duke of Brittany's, claim to the Angevin inheritance in 1202. Twenty-five escaped and seized the castle keep; when besieged by John's men, 22 preferred death by starvation to surrender. According to Gervase of Canterbury's chronicle, John imprisoned his wife, Isabella, in Corfe Castle in 1208. Edward II was taken there briefly after his incarceration at Kenilworth in 1327 and, legend has it, returned to Corfe for 18 months after escaping from Berkeley castle.

The Plantagenet Chronicles: 275, 290
Chronicles of the Age of Chivalry/Four Gothic Kings (US edn): 221, 230, 232

Cotswold wool

A generic term for all quality English wools (considered the best in Europe), regardless of which area they came from; the wool was so called because sheep grazed in the Cotswold region of Gloucestershire produced the greatest quantity of it. The march (borderland) of Shropshire and Leominster produced the best of 51 English quality wools listed in 1454, followed by the Cotswolds. By this time, the trade was in decline, though still very prosperous. Much Cotswold wool was exported via Calais, which held a monopoly on the English export of the best wools; but Cotswold cloth mills, such as those on the River Stroudwater, took some to weave into cloth. The fine 'wool churches' of the Cotswolds exemplify the wealth which the wool brought to the region and the whole country.

The Wars of the Roses: 202–3

Cotton, Bartholomew

d.1298? Norwich monk and chronicler. Compiled the *Historia Anglicana*, recounting both national political events and those concerning the Norwich area. Events from the period 1291–8 seem to be described from personal knowledge, but much of Bartholomew's other information was secondhand. The *Historia* tells of Simon de Montfort's death, Edward I's return from Wales (1285), his expulsion of the Jews (18 July 1290) and French raids on England (August 1295), as well as floods in nearby Yarmouth (December 1287) and other local incidents.

Chronicles of the Age of Chivalry/Four Gothic Kings (US edn): 13, 126, 136, 144

Couci, Philippa de

*fl.*1380s. Granddaughter of Edward III of England; first cousin of Richard II. Philippa married Robert de Vere, 9th earl of Oxford,

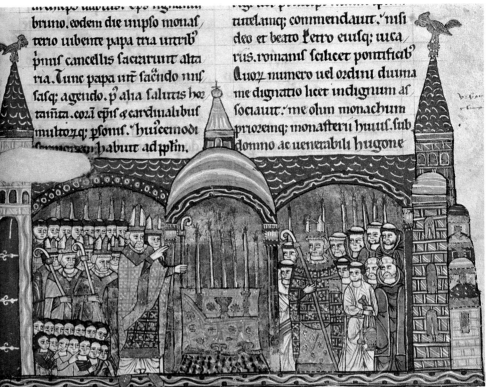

Cluny Abbey *The consecration of the great church at Cluny before the Council of Clermont in 1095. Cluniac monks followed a strict version of the Benedictine rule.*

Richard II's favourite, in 1378, but he divorced her in 1387 in order to marry Agnes Launcecrona, one of Queen Anne's Bohemian entourage. The divorce was annulled in 1389 on the grounds that it had been fraudulently obtained.

The Wars of the Roses: 39, 50

Coucy, Lady de

*fl.*1396, French governess to the young Isabella of Valois, who was married to Richard II of England in November 1396, aged seven. Lady de Coucy accompanied the young bride. She was later dismissed by Richard II on the grounds of extravagance, and Isabella's education was carried on by the widowed countess of Hereford.

The Wars of the Roses: 77

Counts of Anjou, Chronicles of the

See: *Chronicles of the Counts of Anjou*

Counts of Anjou, The Deeds of

See: *The Deeds of the Counts of Anjou*

county

In England, an administrative division of land following on from the Saxon shire and after 1066 deriving its name from the French *comté*. These had been formed in 9th-century France as administrative areas controlled by the Crown, and had soon fallen into the hands of leading families. One such was the county of Anjou.

Court of Common Pleas

See: Common Pleas, Court of

Court of Exchequer

See: Exchequer, Court of

Courtenay, John, 16th earl of Devon

*c.*1435–71. Son of Thomas Courtenay, 13th earl of Devon, and brother of Thomas, Lancastrian 14th earl of Devon; 16th earl of Devon (1470–1). John lost his inheritance when his brother Thomas was executed after the battle of Towton in 1461. Edward IV created Humphrey Stafford 15th earl of Devon in May 1469, but executed him for rebellion three months later. John was made 16th earl on 9 October 1470, immediately after Henry VI's restoration. John helped to secure London for Henry and the Lancastrians in 1471. The *Crowland Chronicle* describes his death after the battle of Tewkesbury on 4 May 1471, although it is unclear whether he died while fighting for Henry or was executed after being captured.

The Wars of the Roses: 260, 262

Courtenay, Peter, bishop of Winchester

d.1492. Dean of Windsor (1477); bishop of Exeter (1478–87); keeper of the privy seal under Henry VII (1485–7); bishop of Winchester (1487). Courtenay studied at Oxford and Padua before becoming dean of Windsor. In 1484 he was attainted – condemned to death and his estates forfeited – by Richard III for raising rebellion in the west, and fled to Brittany with other conspirators. He regained royal favour under Henry VII.

The Wars of the Roses: 296

Courtenay, Thomas de, 13th earl of Devon

1414–58. 13th earl of Devon (1423–58). John Benet's chronicle records that he calmed rioters in London threatening Edmund, 2nd duke of Somerset (blamed for losing Normandy in 1449), on 1 December 1450, in the wake of Jack Cade's revolt; and arrested their leader. Early in 1452 he marched on London with Richard, 3rd duke of York, to protest at Edmund's incompetence. He swore loyalty to Henry VI at Blackheath on 2 March 1452.

The Wars of the Roses: 206, 208

Courtenay, Thomas, 14th earl of Devon

1432–61. Son of Thomas Courtenay, 13th earl of Devon; 14th earl of Devon (1458–61). Early in 1461, after the outbreak of the Wars of the Roses the previous year, Thomas joined Henry Beaufort, 3rd duke of Somerset, in rallying support for the Lancastrian Henry VI in northern England. He was captured and executed on 3 April 1461, after the Yorkist Edward IV's triumph at the battle of Towton (29 March).

The Wars of the Roses: 222

Courtenay, William, archbishop of Canterbury

1342?–96. Fourth son of Hugh, 10th earl of Devon; bishop of Hereford (1369–75); bishop of London (1375–81); chancellor (August–December 1381); archbishop of Canterbury (1381). William was one of the council appointed in 1377 by John of Gaunt to advise the young Richard II. When in 1383 he remonstrated with Richard about his choice of unsuitable councillors, Richard angrily drew his sword and made to strike him through the heart. In 1387 he once more remonstrated with the king about his conduct; and, as a commissioner appointed by the barons to curb royal excesses, tried to mediate between Richard and his opponents. He crushed the Lollard heretics at Oxford (1382) and Leicester (1389).

The Wars of the Roses: 28

Coutances, Walter of

See: Walter of Coutances, archbishop of Rouen

Coventry

Site of the legend of Lady Godiva, who, with her husband Leofric, earl of Mercia, founded a Benedictine abbey there in 1043. It became a cathedral priory in 1102, sharing its bishop with Lichfield. A market town and textile-weaving centre, Coventry was one of the five largest towns in England by the 14th century, but in the 15th it began to decline. Henry Bolingbroke, the future Henry IV, fought a judicial duel in Coventry in 1398 against Thomas Mowbray, 1st duke of Norfolk, which resulted in Richard II exiling them both. Henry VI held a great council at Coventry after 24 June 1459, and a parliament from 20 November 1459.

The Wars of the Roses: 31, 82, 179, 218, 261

Crécy, battle of

Battle fought at a village near the Somme in northern France on 26 August 1346. Edward III of England defeated Philip VI of France in the first major English land victory of the Hundred Years War (1337–1456). The campaign began in July 1346, when Edward's invasion fleet was driven ashore in Normandy. From there the force moved east to the English king's lands at Ponthieu before turning to face the French. Edward's force of less than 10,000 was drawn up in three divisions on sloping ground behind a hedge strengthened by pits. Fifteen French assaults were mown down by English arrows as

they struggled to breach this front. Four thousand French nobles were killed; the blind John of Luxembourg, king of Bohemia, an ally of the French king, also died.

Chronicles of the Age of Chivalry/Four Gothic Kings (US edn): 244–8, 269

crockard

Forged English silver penny of reduced silver content, minted by rulers in the Low Countries and named after the 'croket', or coronet, worn in their image on the coin. Their commercial use undermined the value of English currency, and was forbidden by Edward I in 1299.

Chronicles of the Age of Chivalry/Four Gothic Kings (US edn): 148

Crouchback, Edmund

See: Edmund Crouchback, 1st earl of Lancaster

Crowland Chronicle

A history of the Benedictine abbey of Crowland in Lincolnshire. The early part purports to be the work of Abbot Ingulf (1083–1109) but is largely a later medieval forgery, giving a mythical version of the abbey's early history to substantiate its claim to various lands and rights. In the early 1470s a continuator added a more reliable account of the abbey from 1149 to 1470. The second continuation of the chronicle, written in April–May 1488, covers the years 1459–86 and contains a political history of the period; evidence in the text suggests that John Russell, bishop of Lincoln, chancellor of Oxford university, and keeper of the privy seal (1474–83) may have been its author. The *Crowland Chronicle* contains the first recorded mention of the red rose being a Lancastrian badge and the white rose a Yorkist one. It also includes details of the Treaty of Picquigny (1475), Edward IV of England's luxurious tastes, Richard III's deceitfulness and the battle of Bosworth.

The Wars of the Roses: 12, 217

crusader states

States established by Christian crusaders in and around the Holy Land to secure land conquered from the Saracens. The leading crusader state, the Latin kingdom of Jerusalem, was set up in 1099 after the First Crusade, and the principality of Antioch (1098) and counties of Edessa (1098) and Tripoli (1109) were intended as its dependent fiefs. The Saracens gradually retook the states, the last, Tripoli, falling in 1289; although Acre, a major port in the kingdom of Jerusalem, held out as the last major Christian outpost until 1291.

The Plantagenet Chronicles: 61

crusades

Series of holy wars launched by Christian western Europe from 1095 onwards. The main object of the crusades was to take the Holy Land, and in particular Jerusalem, the Holy City, from the Saracens; but over the years subsidiary aims emerged, such as wresting southern Spain from the Moors, defeating the pagan Slavs and Prussians in eastern Europe and crushing the Albigensians, a heretical sect in southern France. The term crusade derived from the crosses distributed at the Council of Clermont in 1095, when Pope Urban II preached the First Crusade. This, which lasted from 1095 to 1099, established the Latin kingdom of Jerusalem and three other crusader states. Many later crusades were undertaken to defend these states against, or recapture them from, the Saracens. The crusaders, who often undertook long and arduous journeys, were motivated by a mixture of piety, pugnacity, greed and land hunger. After the fall of Acre, the last Christian outpost in the Holy Land, in 1291, the idea of recapturing Jerusalem still remained a potent vision in the west; in addition, crusades continued to be launched against the Turks in the eastern Mediterranean, the Hussite heretics in Bohemia and the pagan Slavs in the Baltic.

The Plantagenet Chronicles: 61, 79, 148–50, 169, 184–5, 202–17, 224, 280–1, 304

Crusades

See: First Crusade, Fourth Crusade, Second Crusade, Third Crusade

Crusade of the Shepherds

See: Pastoureaux

Cuthbert, St

*c.*635–87. Celtic monk; bishop of Hexham (684–5) and Lindisfarne in Northumbria (685–6). In 676 he began a solitary retreat on Farne Island, off the coast of Northumbria, breaking it reluctantly to take up his appointment as bishop and returning to Farne to spend the last weeks of his life there. In 999 his body was taken to Durham Cathedral priory, where it became the most popular relic in northern Britain, even after 1170, when Thomas Becket's tomb at Canterbury had proved to have superior miracle-working powers.

The Plantagenet Chronicles: 134

Cyprus

Mediterranean island, ruled by Byzantine emperors until Richard I of England conquered it in 1191, while en route to the Holy Land for the Third Crusade. The conquest followed an accident at sea; when the ship carrying Richard's bride-to-be, Berengaria of Navarre, took shelter from a storm near Limassol on Cyprus, Isaac Comnenus, the island's ruler, threatened Berengaria, leading Richard to overrun the island. Cyprus became a valuable offshore supply base for operations in the Holy Land. In 1192 Richard bestowed the island on Guy of Lusignan, king of Jerusalem, and his descendants ruled it until Venice annexed it in 1489.

The Plantagenet Chronicles: 206, 213–14

Crécy *The battlefield of the first great English land victory in the Hundred Years War. Edward III oversaw the battle from the windmill on the left.*

Dafydd ap Llywelyn, prince of Gwynedd

d.1246. Son and heir of Llywelyn ap Iorwerth, Llywelyn the Great, prince of Wales; nephew of Henry III of England; prince of Gwynedd (1240–6). On Llywelyn's death, Henry allowed Dafydd to succeed only to Gynwedd, territory Dafydd held by right – and reasserted his sovereignty over the other Welsh dominions Llywelyn had claimed. In 1241 Dafydd fell out with Henry III, who supported the rival claims to Gwynedd of Dafydd's half-brother, Gruffydd. The king led an army to North Wales and crushed him, but Dafydd continued to make war against the English marcher lords. Shortly after a second campaign by Henry, in 1246, Dafydd died, without an heir.

Chronicles of the Age of Chivalry/Four Gothic Kings (US edn): 47

Dafydd, brother of Llywelyn ap Gruffydd

d.1283. Grandson of Llywelyn ap Iorwerth, Llywelyn the Great, prince of Wales; brother of Llywelyn ap Gruffydd. Dafydd conspired with the Welsh barons to kill his brother once in 1254–5 and again in about 1263; when the second plot was discovered he took refuge in England under the protection of Edward I, king of England. He was granted a lordship east of the River Conwy and had his hereditary right to part of Snowdonia recognized in Edward's treaty with his brother (1277). Angered by what he regarded as a paltry reward and having now enlisted the support of his brother, Dafydd rebelled against Edward in 1282. The rebellion failed: Dafydd was captured in Snowdonia in

1283, dragged at a horse's tail through Shrewsbury, hanged and drawn. His head was sent to London and his quarters despatched to Bristol, Northampton, York and Winchester.

Chronicles of the Age of Chivalry/Four Gothic Kings (US edn): 120–1

Dafydd, prince of North Wales

d.1203. Called 'king of Wales' by one chronicler. Dafydd claimed the lordship of Gwynedd in 1170 and won it in 1173 by his support for Henry II of England when the English barons rebelled against their king that year. In 1174 he married Emma, Henry's illegitimate sister. Dafydd was driven out of Wales in 1194 by supporters of his brother Llywelyn ap Iorwerth.

The Plantagenet Chronicles: 140

Dallingrigge, Sir Edward

*fl.*1385. Keeper of the Tower of London under Richard II. Builder of Bodiam castle in Sussex, 'in defence of the adjacent country against the king's enemies'; he acquired a licence to crenellate the castle in 1385.

The Wars of the Roses: 49, 124

Damascus

Capital of Muslim Syria, inland from the Christian states established on the eastern Mediterranean coast by the First Crusade (1096–9). The city was conquered by the Seljuk Turks in 1076. Fulk V, Angevin king of Jerusalem, made Damascus pay tribute to him in 1131. The city was besieged by Louis VII of

France and the Knights Templar in 1148, during the Second Crusade, but the siege failed. Saladin, who had been educated at the court in Damascus, seized the city in 1174. Damascus fell to the Mongols in 1206, and was sacked in about 1400 by Tamerlane.

The Plantagenet Chronicles: 38, 78–9, 148, 153

Damietta

Port and commercial centre in Egypt seized by the Christian forces of the Fifth Crusade in 1219 and held until 1221 when they were driven out by a flooding of the Nile and Egyptian resistance. The port was taken again, in 1249, by Louis IX of France; but was retaken by the Mameluke rulers of Egypt in 1250. The city's strategic importance to the crusaders lay in their conviction that security in the Holy Land rested on neutralizing Egypt; 'the keys to Jerusalem are to be found in Cairo'.

Chronicles of the Age of Chivalry/Four Gothic Kings (US edn): 62, 68–9

Dante Alighieri

1265–1321. Italian poet. Born of a noble Florentine family and an active citizen of Florence, Dante was dispossessed and banished from the city, allegedly for corruption, in 1302. When his party, the White Guelphs, was defeated by the Black Guelphs, he took refuge with a number of Italian princes – including Bartolomeo della Scale, lord of Verona – in his 19 years of exile before his death in Ravenna. His *La Vita Nuova* (*c.*1292), recounting his love for Beatrice, a noblewoman, established his literary pre-eminence; the *Divina Commedia* (Divine Comedy), relating a journey Dante

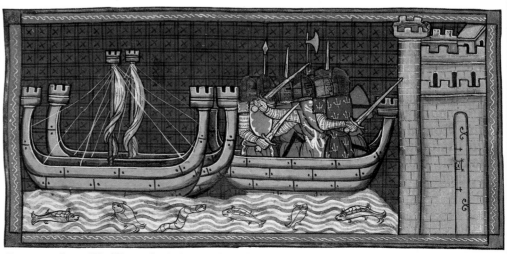

Damietta Louis IX of France leads the assault on the strategic port on the Nile delta. Damietta was a major goal for the 13th-century crusades.

supposedly took through Hell, Purgatory and Heaven in the spring of 1300, was composed during his exile. It encapsulates the medieval world-view, and yet contains references to contemporary figures and events. The *Divina Commedia* established Tuscan as the literary language of Italy.

Chronicles of the Age of Chivalry/Four Gothic Kings (US edn): 105, 154–5

David I, king of Scotland

1084–1153. Youngest son of Malcolm Canmore and St Margaret, sister of Edgar Aetheling, king of England; king of Scotland (1124–53). In 1113 his marriage to Matilda, daughter and heiress of Waltheof, 2nd earl of Northumberland brought him the earldom of Huntingdon in England. As king he was a strong supporter of Empress Matilda against King Stephen of England, but was defeated by Stephen's army at the battle of the Standard in 1138.

After narrowly escaping capture at Winchester in 1141, David confined himself to the affairs of his Scottish kingdom, where he organized the royal court on Anglo-Norman lines. He founded five bishoprics and many monasteries – and received an excellent press from the chroniclers. Ailred of Rievaulx records only one criticism of him – that he allowed his armies too much leeway in battle. David died at Carlisle and was succeeded by his grandson Malcolm IV.

The Plantagenet Chronicles: 47, 65, 68, 70–1, 74, 78, 128

David II, king of Scotland

1324–71. Son of Robert Bruce, king of Scotland, and Elizabeth de Burgh; king of Scotland (1331–71). Married to Joan, daughter of Edward II of England in 1328 at the age of four, in accordance with the terms of the Treaty of Northampton. David was crowned king at Scone when he was seven. In 1333 his army was defeated by the forces of Edward III of England and his puppet king of Scotland, Edward Balliol, at Halidon Hill, and David and Joan fled to France where they were welcomed by Philip VI of France and given Château Gaillard as a residence. Eight years later David's allies in Scotland triumphed over their opponents and he returned to his kingdom.

In 1346 he invaded England at the insistence of the French and was defeated and captured by Edward III near Durham at the battle of Neville's Cross. It was 1357 before the sum of his ransom – 100,000 marks – was agreed. He

returned to Scotland but his kingdom could not raise the amount required; David was forced to negotiate with Edward III to make a Plantagenet prince – such as Lionel, 1st duke of Clarence – his successor, in return for cancelling the debt. The Scottish parliament rejected that proposal in 1364. There was widespread hostility from the Scottish barons, who demanded administrative and judicial reforms, which David was forced to concede. The inept political activities of David's second wife, Margaret Logie, whom he married in 1362 after Joan's death, and divorced in 1369, further soured his relations with his barons in the last years. He left no heirs and was succeeded by his nephew, Robert II, the Steward.

Chronicles of the Age of Chivalry/Four Gothic Kings (US edn): 230, 234–5, 248, 272–4
The Wars of the Roses: 58

David II *The Scots king and his wife Joan, Edward II of England's daughter.*

Decorated style

An indigenous style of English Gothic architecture developed in the 14th century, characterized by complex tracery and arch forms, especially double-curved ogee arches. Initially inspired by the French *rayonnant* style, it first appeared in St Stephen's Chapel at Westminster Palace (*c.*1292) and the Eleanor Crosses (1290), both commissioned by Edward I. Exeter Cathedral (rebuilt 1280–1360) and Wells Cathedral (rebuilt in the early 14th century) typify the mature style, which reached its finest development in the central vault at Ely

Cathedral (1322–42), which is suspended over the cathedral's central crossing and built in gilded and painted wood.

Chronicles of the Age of Chivalry/Four Gothic Kings (US edn): 206–7

Deeds of the Counts of Anjou, The

A chronicle in several 11th- and 12th-century versions, by, among others, Odo, abbot of Marmoutier and Thomas of Loches, chaplain to Count Fulk V of Anjou, king of Jerusalem. It relates the history of the Angevin dynasty, much of the earlier material in the chronicle being legend. An extended version, compiled (1164–73) at Marmoutier Abbey in the Loire valley by John of Marmoutier, a monk, was dedicated to Henry II of England, patron of the abbey.

The Plantagenet Chronicles: 12

Deeds of King Henry II and King Richard I, The

A text chronicling contemporary events from 1171 to 1192; owned or commissioned by Benedict, abbot of Peterborough (1177–93), to whom it was long attributed. (More recently, Roger Howden has been suggested as the author, but the question remains open.) The chronicler records the activities of Henry II and Richard I, generally praising both kings. He is occasionally critical – for example, of Henry's dilatory way of doing business. The chronicle also contains official documents, and references to national and international events.

The Plantagenet Chronicles: 13, 208

De heretico comburendo

Title of a statute petitioned of Henry IV by the English clergy and members of the Commons and passed by parliament in 1401. Intended to combat the Lollard heresy, it forbade open or secret preaching without a licence, and the writing, teaching and dissemination of heresy. Penalties for disobedience were imprisonment or a fine, or, in the case of heretics who refused to recant, burning; however, the statute's main aim was to win heretics back to the fold. Bishops were empowered to arrest suspects and to hand them over to the local sheriff or mayor. Between 1414 and 1522 some 400 heretics renounced their heresy; only 27 were burned.

The Wars of the Roses: 112–13

demesne

Portion of manorial land kept by a lord for his own use and not granted or let out to tenants. Peasants holding lands in the rest of the manor were supposed, in return for their tenancy, to work on the lord's demesne on fixed days, but from the 13th century such obligations increasingly took the form of rent payments.

Despenser, Henry, bishop of Norwich

d.1406. Canon of Salisbury; bishop of Norwich (1370–1406). In 1381, during the Peasants Revolt, he defended Peterborough Abbey against the attack of a mob and crushed a large peasant force in Norfolk, personally supervising the hanging of its leader, Geoffrey Litster, at North Walsham. John Wycliffe, the religious reformer, denounced his martial activities as unsuitable in a bishop.

In 1382 Henry Despenser was empowered by Pope Urban VI to raise a crusade against the French followers of the antipope Clement VII. He led a force to Flanders, defeated the antipope's Flemish supporters at Dunkirk (1383) and raised the siege of Ypres, although English gains were short-lived and the crusade was seen by most contemporaries as a failure. Henry subsequently helped to repel the French invasion of Scotland in 1385 and as late as 1399 he alone tried to muster a force to defend Richard II of England against Henry Bolingbroke, the future Henry IV.

The Wars of the Roses: 40

Despenser, Hugh

d.1265. Last justiciar of England (1260–1, July–October 1263). Hugh Despenser's appointment was a result of the Provisions of Oxford, imposed on Henry III in 1258. These revived the office, which had been obsolete since 1234. He was also one of the 12 baronial commissioners who governed the realm under the Provisions. Hugh fought for the barons against Henry III at Lewes in 1264, and also against Henry at the battle of Evesham on 4 August 1265, where he was slain.

Chronicles of the Age of Chivalry/Four Gothic Kings (US edn): 98, 212

Despenser, Hugh, the father, 3rd earl of Winchester

1261–1326. Son of Hugh Despenser, the chief justiciar; 3rd earl of Winchester (1322). Hugh was established in Edward I's service in the 1290s. After Edward II's accession in 1307, he was the only baron, in 1308, to support the detested royal favourite, Piers Gaveston, against his many critics. When Gaveston died in 1312 he, and later his son Hugh, became the king's leading advisers.

Hugh gained considerable wealth and power from his position, but also earned the detestation of Thomas, 2nd earl of Lancaster, and his party, who drove him from the royal council in 1314; but he soon returned to power. In 1317 a hostile faction among the barons secured his temporary banishment abroad. After 1318, however, he returned to the council in the company of his son, also Hugh Despenser, and the two were restored as firm royal favourites.

In 1321 Thomas of Lancaster and other nobles forced Edward to dismiss Hugh and his son. Hugh was exiled and disinherited, but returned within the year and was loaded with

Hugh Despenser the son *The effigy at Tewkesbury of the younger Despenser: privateer and extortionist.*

favours by the king, including, in 1322, the earldom of Winchester. The death of Thomas of Lancaster that year left Hugh and his son unchallenged.

Hugh was less active than his son in the 'tyranny' set up under Edward II after 1322: one chronicler described him as a worthy man who was led astray by devotion to his son. However, his unpopularity grew with that of the younger Hugh. In 1326, Edward's wife Isabella of France invaded England to seize power on behalf of her son Edward, later Edward III. Hugh held Bristol for the king, but, on the approach of Isabella's forces, opened the gates and threw himself on her mercy. He was hanged and drawn on the Bristol public gallows, and his body, hung on a fork like that of a common thief, was reviled by the mob as that of a traitor.

Chronicles of the Age of Chivalry/Four Gothic Kings (US edn): 170, 172, 179, 185, 190, 196–200, 202, 206, 208-9, 212-13, 278

Despenser, Hugh, the son

c.1290–1326. Son of Hugh Despenser, 3rd earl of Winchester. Hugh was knighted with the young prince Edward (later Edward II) in 1306, and the same year Edward I betrothed him to Eleanor de Clare, daughter of Gilbert de Clare, 9th earl of Gloucester, whom he married in 1309. After Edward II's accession in 1307 Hugh at first sided with the baronial opposition to the king.

By 1313 Hugh's opposition to Edward had cooled sufficiently for him to be made king's chamberlain; his father, also Hugh Despenser, became Edward's principal adviser. In 1314 Hugh's brother-in-law Gilbert de Clare was killed at the battle of Bannockburn. Hugh inherited a third share in the great Clare barony, which brought him sudden power and status – and bitter disagreement with Hugh Audley and Roger d'Amory over the partitioning of these lands. That may have been one reason for his joining his father in the king's camp in 1318. Hugh supplanted the elder Despenser in the king's affections, and was Edward's principal favourite from 1318.

In 1320 Hugh quarrelled with the barons of the Welsh marches when he tried to gain control over the lordship of Gower having first declared it forfeit to the crown. The marcher lords considered that their privileges were thereby being breached. They appealed to the king to dismiss Hugh, and, when Edward refused, they formed a league with Thomas, 2nd earl of Lancaster, and forced Edward to exile and disinherit the Despensers, father and son. In 1321 Edward entrusted Hugh the son to

the mariners of the Cinque Ports, an open invitation to take up piracy. By the time he recalled him two months later, Hugh had seized the rich cargo of a Genoese vessel, murdering its crew, and had preyed on shipping throughout the English Channel.

Edward suppressed the marcher lords by force, and Hugh, and his father, returned to office in 1322. Thomas of Lancaster, the driving force behind the opposition to the Despensers, was executed that year, and Hugh's influence was unchecked for the next few years. In 1323 he negotiated a peace with Scotland, and directed Edward's treasurer, Walter Stapledon, bishop of Exeter, and his chancellor, Robert Baldock, in a series of highly profitable reforms to the royal household and Exchequer. Hugh also tricked one heiress out of the lordships of Gower and Usk, and terrorized Thomas of Lancaster's widow into surrendering her lands. He spent the resulting wealth on extensions to his castle at Caerphilly.

Hugh's influence, like that of his father, ended in 1326, when Isabella of France, Edward II's wife, invaded England with the intention of forcing her husband to abdicate in favour of her son, Edward (later Edward III). Hugh fled with the king to Wales and, with him, hid in Neath Abbey until they were discovered by Isabella's forces. Hugh was taken to Hereford and put to death.

Chronicles of the Age of Chivalry/Four Gothic Kings (US edn): 170, 179, 189-90, 196-202, 206, 208-10, 212-15, 224, 278

Devizes, Richard of

See: Richard of Devizes

Dialogue Concerning the Exchequer

Detailed account of the procedures of the Exchequer, written in the 1170s by Richard FitzNeal, treasurer under Henry II. FitzNeal describes the chequered cloth from which the term exchequer derives: it was used as a giant abacus to count sums of money, while the wooden tallies acted as receipts and the pipe rolls (documents) recorded the Exchequer's accounts.

The Plantagenet Chronicles: 249

Diaz, Bartholomew

d.1500. Portuguese navigator. Sailing under the patronage of John II of Portugal, Diaz became, in 1488, the first European to round the Cape

of Good Hope, which he named Capo Tormentoso. His voyage opened the way to the Indian Ocean.

The Wars of the Roses: 257

diocese

The area of jurisdiction of an individual bishop, coming under his pastoral care. In the Middle Ages some dioceses, such as Lincoln, were large, as were the incomes bishops could derive from them; others, such as St Davids, were poor and remote and less valued by career ecclesiastics.

Domesday Book

The record of the survey of England carried out in 1086, by order of William I, the Conqueror, king of England, as a summary of landholders, their holdings and the tax paid on them.

The Plantagenet Chronicles: 270, 289

Dominic, St

1170?–1221. Born Domingo de Guzman; Castilian prior of the chapter of canons at Osma Cathedral (*c*.1200); canonized 1234. Dominic and his bishop, Diego de Azevedo, went to Rome in about 1203, asking to be sent to convert the Tartars. Instead, Pope Innocent III sent them to preach to the Cathar heretics, or Albigensians, in southern France. Adopting a rule of absolute poverty and using reason to win over converts, Dominic's mission had by 1207 set up a nunnery for ex-Cathar women at Prouille. Bishop Diego died in 1207; and in 1215 Dominic established a base at Toulouse in France, planning an order of educated preaching friars (possibly after having met St Francis). In 1216 his plans were approved in Rome by Pope Honorius III, and the Dominican order was established.

Chronicles of the Age of Chivalry/Four Gothic Kings (US edn): 64–5, 66

Dominicans

An order of friars, known also as the 'domini canes' (watchdogs of God), a Latin pun on their name. Founded by St Dominic in 1217 in order

Sir Edward Dalingrigge Bodiam Castle, Sussex (overleaf), was built by Sir Edward 'against the king's enemies'.

to combat the Albigensian heresy in the Languedoc region of France. Dominicans were vowed to extreme poverty and aimed to convert heretics by reasoned argument. The order emphasized study, and produced celebrated theologians, including St Thomas Aquinas. It was also the chief agent of the Inquisition, established in 1233 with the aim of suppressing heresy. Dominicans interrogated suspects, often forcing members of a family to testify against each other, and burned unrepentant heretics. In extreme cases they even exhumed and burned the remains of persons found guilty of heresy after death.

Chronicles of the Age of Chivalry/Four Gothic Kings (US edn): 64–5, 66–7

Douglas, Archibald, 4th earl of Douglas

1369?–1424. Son of Archibald, 3rd earl of Douglas; keeper of Edinburgh castle (1400); warden of the marches; 4th earl of Douglas (1400–24), duke of Touraine (1424). In 1400 he held Edinburgh against the invasion force of Henry IV of England. Two years later he led an invasion of England and was defeated and captured at Homildon Hill by Henry Percy, 4th earl of Northumberland. Douglas joined the Percy conspiracy against Henry IV, and was captured by the king's men at the battle of Shrewsbury in 1403. Ransomed in 1408, Douglas raided the English border from 1412 to 1422. In 1423 he took a large Scots force to fight for Charles VII of France, against Henry VI of England and in 1424 was made duke of Touraine and lieutenant-general of the French army; but that same year he was killed by the English at Verneuil. His persistent bad luck earned him the nickname Tyneman (the loser).

The Wars of the Roses: 100–2, 104

Douglas, James, 2nd earl of Douglas

1358?–88. In 1385 James made war on the English with the assistance of the noted French admiral, Jean de Vienne. He commanded a Scots expedition into England in the summer of 1388, and led the diversionary force which defeated the troops of Henry Percy, 'Hotspur', at the battle of Otterburn on 5 August 1388. He fought all night by moonlight and was found dead the next morning.

The Wars of the Roses: 59, 61

Dover

Port in Kent on the Straits of Dover, in south-east England; chief of the Cinque Ports.

Its castle includes a Roman lighthouse. Throughout the Middle Ages Dover was England's main Channel port, and was often a target for French raids, as well as a haven for privateers, armed private vessels licensed by the English Crown. The chronicler Bartholomew Cotton relates that 600 French ships and 30 galleys attacked Dover in August 1295, killing 11 men and looting the city and priory.

Chronicles of the Age of Chivalry/Four Gothic Kings (US edn): 29, 41, 58, 80, 98, 104, 138–9, 148, 201, 206, 280, 284
The Wars of the Roses: 70, 172, 178, 204

Dublin

Capital of Ireland. It was a Danish possession until 1170, when Richard FitzGilbert (Strongbow), 2nd earl of Pembroke, captured it for the English. In 1172 Henry II of England came to Dublin and as a special favour granted it to the 'men of Bristol'; it became the seat of English government in Ireland and, later, the centre of the Pale, the area subject to English law throughout the Middle Ages. Henry also founded an Augustinian priory in Dublin, dedicated to Thomas Becket. After the Black Monday massacre of English residents by the Irish in 1209, King John of England built a new castle there. Edward Bruce, a claimant to the throne of Ireland, unsuccessfully assaulted Dublin in 1318, and Richard II, who made his favourite, Robert de Vere, marquis of Dublin, visited it twice, in 1394 and 1399.

The Plantagenet Chronicles: 131, 295

Duccio di Buoninsegna

c.1250–1319. Italian painter; founder of the Sienese school. Duccio's art matches the humanity of Giotto's but, unlike his contemporary, who used new naturalist techniques, Duccio transforms traditional medieval motifs by the solidity and degree of characterization of his figures. His masterpiece, the 92-panel *Maesta* altarpiece for the High Altar at Siena Cathedral (1311), consists of an enthroned Madonna and Child, surrounded by smaller scenes on the front, and scenes from Christ's Passion on the rear. The Passion panels show Duccio as a master of narrative equal to Giotto.

Chronicles of the Age of Chivalry/Four Gothic Kings (US edn): 197–9

duke

Hereditary feudal rank in the Middle Ages. Grew out of the high military commands of the

late Roman Empire, whose holders began, by the 7th century, to exercise civil functions as well. In medieval Europe a duke was a sovereign or a vassal prince ruling a dukedom, or duchy; in England the style, which was not used until the 14th century, usually gave title to a dukedom, and was next below that of a prince.

Dumfries

County town in Dumfriesshire, south-east Scotland. Robert Bruce (later Robert I of Scotland) murdered John Comyn at Greyfriars Church in the town in February 1306.

Chronicles of the Age of Chivalry/Four Gothic Kings (US edn): 134, 157, 234

Dunbar

Town on the North Sea coast in East Lothian, south-east Scotland. During Edward I of England's invasion of Scotland (1295), 6th Earl Warenne inflicted a severe defeat on the Scots at Dunbar. Edward II of England fled by boat from there to England in 1314, after his defeat by the Scots at Bannockburn. 'Black Agnes', countess of Dunbar, defended Dunbar castle against a six-week siege by Edward III of England in 1338. Alexander, 3rd duke of Albany, handed the castle over to an English garrison in 1484 when he fled to England after his intrigues against his brother, James III of Scotland, were revealed. The Scottish king negotiated with Richard III of England for the return of Dunbar, but this was refused and the Scots recaptured the castle late in 1485 after a long siege.

Chronicles of the Age of Chivalry/Four Gothic Kings (US edn): 142, 190–1, 266
The Wars of the Roses: 299

Durham Cathedral

Norman cathedral in county town of Durham in north-east England, rebuilt from 1093 by the Benedictines to house the remains of St Cuthbert. His tomb, the most popular destination for pilgrimages in northern England during the Middle Ages, was credited with many miracles. The bishops of Durham exercised palatine powers (jurisdiction such as elsewhere belonged to the Crown) in the county. Richard Poore, bishop of Durham (1228–37), commissioned the Chapel of the Nine Altars in the cathedral.

The Plantagenet Chronicles: 29, 65, 66–7, 134
Chronicles of the Age of Chivalry/Four Gothic Kings (US edn): 248, 287

Durham Cathedral *The Norman cathedral rises above the town, enshrining the bones of St Cuthbert.*

Eadwine of Canterbury

*fl.*1160. Monk, scribe and illuminator. He produced the Eadwine Psalter at Canterbury, *c.*1160, as a copy of a Carolingian manuscript, the Utrecht Psalter, then at the cathedral. His illustrations include a magnificent picture of himself at his writing desk. Bound into the volume is a plan of the waterworks installed at Canterbury in the 1160s by Prior Wybert.

The Plantagent Chronicles: 159

Earl Rivers

See: Woodville, Anthony, 2nd earl Rivers

Edinburgh

Capital of Scotland, in Lothian, since the later 15th century. Established when Malcolm III of Scotland (d.1093) built a castle there. In 1296 Edward I of England besieged the castle, which surrendered after eight days. The troops of Robert Bruce, king of Scotland, recaptured it in 1314, scaling the castle rock by night. Edinburgh was granted a charter by Robert Bruce in 1329. John of Gaunt led an army to Edinburgh in 1384 intending to hold the city to ransom. The English inflicted some fire damage, but the Scots starved them out in two weeks by burning crops that should have supplied them. Edinburgh did not become the leading city of Scotland until the reign of James II of Scotland (1437–60). James IV (1473–1513) was the first Scottish king to make it his permanent seat.

Chronicles of the Age of Chivalry/Four Gothic Kings (US edn): 142, 145
The Wars of the Roses: 58–9

Edington, William, bishop of Winchester

d.1366. Treasurer to Edward III (1344–56); bishop of Winchester (1345-66); chancellor (1356–63). He was the patron of the young William of Wykeham, a future bishop of Winchester, whom he enabled to enter Edward's service in 1349. William refused the archbishopric of Canterbury because of ill-health in 1366, the year of his death.

The Wars of the Roses: 62

Edmund of Abingdon, St, archbishop of Canterbury

1170?–1240. Archbishop of Canterbury (1234–40). Edmund studied in Paris (1185–90?), returning to Oxford (*c.*1200–20) as a divinity teacher. At Pope Gregory IX's behest he preached a crusade against the Saracens in *c.*1227. As archbishop, Edmund officiated at the coronation of Henry's wife, Eleanor of Provence, at Westminster on 20 January 1236. He mediated the peace between Henry III of England and Llywelyn ap Iorwerth, Llywelyn the Great, prince of Gwynedd, in 1234 and procured the dismissal of Henry's favourites by threatening to excommunicate the king. He alienated Henry, who persuaded Gregory IX to appoint a legate favourable to himself, isolating Edmund. Edmund died at Soissy in France, on his way to retirement as a Cistercian monk.

Miracles soon occurred at his tomb and he was canonized in 1248.

Chronicles of the Age of Chivalry/Four Gothic Kings (US edn): 53, 58

Edmund, Crouchback, 1st earl of Lancaster

1245–96. Second son of Henry III of England and Eleanor of Provence; 1st earl of Lancaster (1267–96). Pope Alexander III conferred the title of king of Sicily on him in 1255, but Henry III was unable to provide the money and men Edmund needed to pursue the claim, and in 1263 he renounced the kingship. Edward I, Edmund's brother, created him earl of Lancaster in 1267. In 1271 Edmund went on a crusade in Palestine: his nickname, Crouchback, or crossed back, refers to his crusader's cross. He fought against the Welsh (1277–82) and against the French in Gascony (1296). Edmund's great-great-grandson Henry IV, who became England's first Lancastrian king, claimed – on no strong evidence – that Edmund had been

Henry III's eldest son, disinherited because of a hunched back.

Chronicles of the Age of Chivalry/Four Gothic Kings (US edn): 35, 59, 86, 241

Edmund, 1st duke of York

See: Langley, Edmund of, 1st duke of York

Edmund of Woodstock, 3rd earl of Kent

1301–30. Youngest son of Edward I of England; half-brother of Edward II of England; 3rd earl of Kent (1321–30). In 1322 Edmund supported Edward II against the coalition of the marcher lords and Thomas, 2nd earl of Lancaster, who were seeking to force the expulsion of Edward's hated favourites, the Despensers. Edmund besieged Thomas of Lancaster's Yorkshire stronghold of Pontefract and witnessed his execution in 1322. In 1324 Edward made him lieutenant of Aquitaine, where he faced an invasion by Charles of Valois. In 1326 Edmund joined Isabella, Edward's queen, in her conspiracy against her husband, and was one of the council appointed to govern for the young Edward III in 1327 after the king's forced abdication. He resisted Isabella's ascendancy and that same year she implicated him in a plot to free Edward II. She had him beheaded in 1330.

Chronicles of the Age of Chivalry/Four Gothic Kings (US edn): 200, 209, 230, 232

Edward the Black Prince

See: Edward of Woodstock, the Black Prince

Edward, the Confessor, St, king of the English

1002/5–66. King of the English (1042–66). Edward built Westminster Abbey church (consecrated *c.*1065) to obtain papal absolution for breaking his vow to make a pilgrimage to Rome. He was buried in the abbey. His nickname was the result of his exaggerated reputation for piety. He was canonized in 1161, at the behest of Henry II. Henry III venerated Edward as his patron saint, and in 1241 ordered a pure gold shrine for his relics. In his honour Henry spent vast sums of money rebuilding Westminster Abbey: originally Norman, it was reconstructed in the French Gothic style from 1245. The saint's body was moved to its new shrine in 1269 and Henry's body was buried in his old tomb.

Edward II *A boss in Bristol Cathedral adorned with a head of Edward II. Edward was the first Plantagenet king of England to be deposed, and one of the least competent of his line.*

The Plantagenet Chronicles: 173
Chronicles of the Age of Chivalry/Four Gothic Kings (US edn): 35, 62, 80, 82, 100–1, 104

Edward, 2nd duke of York

1371–1415. Grandson of Edward II; cousin of Henry IV; 1st earl of Rutland (1390–1415); admiral of England (1392); 2nd duke of York (1402-15). Edward supported Richard II against the lords appellant in 1397 and was in return created 1st duke of Aumale and granted the office of constable. Henry IV deprived him of these rewards after his accession in 1399, but made him a privy councillor. Edward accompanied the force Henry IV sent to Normandy in August 1412, to assist the duke of Orléans against the duke of Burgundy, and in 1415 commanded the right wing at Agincourt. He was the highest-ranking English casualty; overweight, he apparently suffocated inside his armour.

The Wars of the Roses: 114, 131

Edward I, king of England

1239–1307. Eldest surviving son of Henry III of England and Eleanor of Provence; king of England (1272–1307). Characterized by one contemporary as a leopard for his deviousness and a lion for his bravery, Edward was tall, handsome and eloquent. In 1254 he married Eleanor of Castile and became duke of Gascony and 9th earl of Chester. Before her death in 1290 Eleanor gave Edward 16 children, seven of whom survived. When she died, to commemorate his love for her, he erected 12 Eleanor crosses along the route of her funeral procession from Lincoln to Westminster.

During Edward's reign royal rights and franchises were investigated and clarified and attempts were made to improve law and order. Controls were instituted over new grants of land to the Church and Edward, although pious and a generous patron of the religious orders, resisted any increase in papal authority in England. In 1277 he mounted a major campaign in Wales to bring Llywelyn ap Gruffydd, prince of Wales, to heel, but Welsh resistance continued, and the rebellion was not decisively crushed until 1282–3.

In 1290, the legitimate heir to the Scottish throne, Margaret, Maid of Norway, died, and Edward was asked to arbitrate between 13 claimants. His choice, John Balliol, was unpopular, and first William Wallace, then Robert Bruce, rebelled against him. Wallace and his followers were crushed by Edward, but Bruce seized the crown in 1306 and was to remain a problem to Edward's son and successor, Edward II.

In 1294 war erupted with Philip IV of France over Gascony and Edward, already heavily committed in Scotland, was forced to demand substantial funds from the English parliament. There was strong opposition and demands for the cessation of royal exactions. In 1297 the king re-issued Magna Carta and the Charter of the Forest, and promised to remedy the abuses meted out by his administrators. He also abolished the most detested tax of all, the 'maltote', levied on wool.

Edward reached a settlement with Philip IV in 1299 and married his sister, Margaret, who gave him three children. Edward died at Burgh by Sands in Cumbria, on his way to campaign in Scotland. He was buried in Westminster Abbey under a plain slab inscribed 'Here lies Edward I, the hammer of the Scots'.

The Plantagenet Chronicles: 202
Chronicles of the Age of Chivalry/Four Gothic Kings (US edn): 7, 13–14, 47, 69, 74, 88, 90, 96–100, 107–65

Edward II, king of England

1284–1327. Son of Edward I of England and Eleanor of Castile; king of England 1307–27. Strong and handsome, with extravagant tastes that seemed well offset by his dashing horsemanship and his martial interests, Edward II was acclaimed by his people when he came to the throne. But within eight years a member of the royal household declared openly that 'it was no wonder the king couldn't win a battle, because he spent the time when he should have been hearing mass in idling, ditching, digging and other improper occupations'.

In 1308 Edward married Isabella, daughter of Philip IV of France, a match that gave him two sons and two daughters and an uneasy alliance with the Capetian court. However, he was more interested in his male favourites – first Piers Gaveston, then the Despensers (father and son) – than in his wife. Resentful of Gaveston and concerned at the way Edward was mismanaging the affairs of state, a major coalition of barons, the Ordainers, rose in opposition to the king. In 1311 its leaders forced him to agree to a series of ordinances for the better governance of the kingdom, but its unity was destroyed when Guy de Beauchamp, 10th earl of Warwick, and Thomas, 2nd earl of Lancaster, engineered Gaveston's death in 1312. The disagreements between Edward and the barons allowed Robert Bruce to conquer large areas of Scotland. Edward led a large army north in 1314 to relieve the siege of Stirling, but was defeated by Bruce at the battle of Bannockburn.

In 1324 war broke out with France over Gascony and Edward sent Isabella and his son Edward (the future Edward III) to negotiate with Charles IV, king of France and Isabella's brother. In Paris, in liaison with one of Edward's disaffected barons, Roger Mortimer, the queen made plans to invade England. In 1326 she crossed the Channel, pursued Edward II to South Wales, and captured him. He was imprisoned, first at Kenilworth, then at Berkeley castle. Early in 1327 Edward was deposed and his son crowned in his place. One source suggests that the king escaped and wandered the continent, disguised as a hermit. However, it is more likely that he died at

Edward IV *The great seal of Edward IV, bearing his image.*

king's adviser, in preference to the Black Prince, and stirred up political opposition to the king. The conflicts of the last years of Edward's reign soured the earlier successes, but after his death, in 1377, he was remembered with pride for his great victories against the French.

Chronicles of the Age of Chivalry/Four Gothic Kings (US edn): 13–14, 186, 205–6, 208, 210, 224, 226–306.
The Wars of the Roses: 22, 29, 49, 171, 289

Edward IV, king of England

1442–83. Son of Richard, 3rd duke of York, and Cicely Neville; 7th earl of Cambridge (1460–61); 4th duke of York (1460–61); king of England (1461–83). During the 1450s, as Henry VI became increasingly ineffective as king, Edward's father Richard, a descendant of Edward III, began to prosecute the Yorkist claim to the throne. Defeated by the Lancastrians at Ludlow in 1459, Richard and Edward fled to Ireland. They returned the following year, however, and parliament acknowledged Richard as Henry's heir; but in renewed fighting between the Yorkists and Lancastrians, Richard was killed at Wakefield. Edward struck back, defeated a Lancastrian force at Mortimer's Cross in February 1461 and was acclaimed as king in London. He then won a decisive victory over the Lancastrians at Towton in March and was crowned at Westminster later in the year.

In 1470, Edward lost the throne when Richard Neville, 16th earl of Warwick, 'the Kingmaker', returned from exile in France and proclaimed Henry VI king again. Edward fled to the Low Countries but returned the following year and defeated his adversaries. For the rest of his reign he allowed some of the great nobles, such as his brother Richard, 3rd duke of Gloucester, to build up major power bases in the provinces, in return for their support. This gave them a dangerous and unprecedented independence. However, in the later years of his reign, his advisers began to restore law and order and to revitalize the royal administration.

A patron of learning and the arts and a builder of magnificent churches, Edward also had a taste for luxury and a life of pleasure. In 1464 he married Elizabeth Woodville, thus vexing his councillors, since she was a widow and not of noble blood. He also had several mistresses. After a son (the future Edward V), one of ten children, was born to Edward and Elizabeth in 1470, the Yorkist dynasty's future seemed secure. However, Edward's brother, George, 3rd duke of Clarence, intrigued against the king and Edward had him judicially

Berkeley castle in September 1327, probably murdered.

Chronicles of the Age of Chivalry/Four Gothic Kings (US edn): 13–14, 126, 137, 144, 150, 158, 160, 162, 166–225, 230

Edward III, king of England

1312–77. Eldest son of Edward II of England and Isabella of France; king of England (1327–77). Only 14 years old at the time of Edward II's deposition and his own coronation, he was at first dominated by his mother and her lover, Roger Mortimer. In 1330, however, he executed Mortimer, and exiled his mother from court.

Edward was tall, restless, energetic, a man of action, a fine warrior, but also a shrewd politician. Conventionally pious, he also had a darker side to his character, as the chronicler Jean le Bel's account of his brutal rape of the 'countess of Salisbury' suggests. In 1328 he married Philippa, daughter of William I, count of Hainault; she produced 12 children, nine of whom survived.

In 1333 Edward and Edward Balliol defeated David II of Scotland at the battle of Halidon Hill and drove him into exile. The French were in league with the Scots, and this, together with problems over Gascony and Edward's claims to the throne of France (through his mother Isabella), contributed towards the outbreak of the Hundred Years War in 1337. Edward won a major victory at Crécy in 1346 and went on to capture Calais; and in 1356 his son, Edward of Woodstock, the Black Prince, gained another success at the battle of Poitiers, which resulted in the capture of John II of France. But in 1360 Edward recognized the magnitude of the task he had set himself in conquering France and relinquished his claims to the country in return for undisputed title to Aquitaine. Financed by John's ransom, Edward now indulged his tastes for chivalry and ceremonial (in 1348 he had created the Order of the Garter). However, hostilities with France resumed in 1369 and the English gradually lost ground.

Philippa died in 1369 and in the last years of his reign Edward was firmly under the influence of his mistress, Alice Perrers. She favoured John of Gaunt, one of Edward's younger sons, as the murdered in 1478. In addition, there was intense rivalry between the future Richard III and the Woodvilles. When Edward died he left a troubled legacy behind him.

The Wars of the Roses: 128–9, 220–5, 227–77, 282, 299

Edward V, king of England

1470–83?. Eldest son of Edward IV of England and Elizabeth Woodville; proclaimed king at the age of 12, on his father's death in April 1483. Within two months, he was ousted by his paternal uncle, Richard, 3rd duke of Gloucester, who took the throne as Richard III in June 1483. Edward's maternal uncle, 2nd earl Rivers, and the earl's closest adherents, were killed by Richard, and Edward V and his brother Richard, 5th duke of York, were confined in the Tower of London. They never emerged alive, and it is probable that they had been killed by the autumn of 1483. That is what contemporaries believed, and many were convinced that it was Richard III who was responsible for their murder.

The Wars of the Roses: 235, 254, 279–87, 292, 294

Edward, prince of Wales, son of Henry VI

1453–71. Only son of Henry VI of England and Margaret of Anjou; prince of Wales (1454). Henry VI, who was mad at the time of Edward's birth, did not recognize his new-born son. In 1460, after the Lancastrian defeat at Northampton, Margaret of Anjou took her young son to Harlech castle for safety and in 1461 he was present at the second battle of St Albans. Edward IV was victorious and Prince Edward fled with his mother to Scotland (1461) and Brittany (1462). In December 1470 he was married to the 14-year-old Anne Neville, to cement the alliance between his mother and Richard Neville, 16th earl of Warwick, 'the kingmaker', who had driven Edward IV from England. He arrived in England with his mother in April 1471, a month after Edward's return from exile in France, but was slain after the battle of Tewkesbury on 4 May 1471.

The Wars of the Roses: 200–1, 212, 248, 262, 295

Edward, prince of Wales, son of Richard III

1473–84. Only child of Richard III of England and Anne Neville; prince of Wales (1483–4).

The chronicler John Rous relates that Edward died at Middleham castle in Yorkshire, in April 1484, after a brief illness. He was only ten or eleven and left his parents griefstricken and without an heir.

The Wars of the Roses: 294–5, 298

Edward, son of the Black Prince

Born *c*.1364; died in infancy. Eldest son of Edward of Woodstock, the Black Prince, and Joan, the Fair Maid of Kent. He was born in Gascony while his father was governing the region. His brother Richard eventually succeeded to the English crown as Richard II.

Chronicles of the Age of Chivalry/Four Gothic Kings (US edn): 293
The Wars of the Roses: 22

Edward of Woodstock, the Black Prince

1330–76. Eldest son of Edward III of England and Philippa of Hainault, born at Woodstock; 14th earl of Chester (1354–76); 1st duke of Cornwall (1337–76); prince of Wales (1334–76; prince of Aquitaine (1362–76). His title, the Black Prince, was not used before the 16th century and probably derived from the black armour he is said to have worn.

The prince accompanied his father on all his campaigns and soon earned a reputation as a brave and chivalrous knight. Present at the battle of Crécy (1346) and the siege of Calais (1347) and a keen participant in the tournaments organized to celebrate their success, he was made one of the first knights of the Garter when Edward III founded the order in 1348. In 1355, as the king's lieutenant in Gascony, he began a series of marauding raids from the duchy. These culminated in the battle of Poitiers (1356), a crushing defeat for the French. He played a major role in the peace negotiations that led to the Treaty of Brétigny (1360).

In 1361 the Black Prince married his cousin Joan, the Fair Maid of Kent, and the next year was made prince of Aquitaine. From here he waged a major campaign in Spain, in support of Pedro, the Cruel, deposed king of Castile; but despite a major victory at Nájera in 1367 his efforts were transitory and expensive. The opposition of Edward's Gascon subjects to the excessive taxation needed to fund the campaign gave Charles V of France the opportunity to declare war over Gascony; but Edward, whose health was in decline, retired to England in 1371.

The prince remained active in court politics, trying to counteract the influence of his brother, John of Gaunt, over the ageing Edward III. He died a year before his father and was buried in Canterbury Cathedral.

Chronicles of the Age of Chivalry/Four Gothic Kings (US edn): 4, 228, 244, 246–7, 266–72, 280, 282, 286–94, 296, 300
The Wars of the Roses: 22

Egypt

A principal target of the crusaders, who saw it as the key Muslim power that prevented them from liberating Jerusalem. The Fourth Crusade (1202–4) was initially aimed against Egypt. Crusaders twice (1219–21, 1249–50) seized Damietta, Egypt's chief Mediterranean port, but advanced no further.

The Plantagenet Chronicles: 282

Eleanor of Aquitaine

1122?–1204. Daughter of William X, duke of Aquitaine; duchess of Aquitaine (1137–1204), queen-consort to (in succession) Louis VII of France (1137–51) and Henry II of England (1154–89). Eleanor succeeded to the duchy of Aquitaine in 1137, and that year also married Louis VII of France, at her father's behest. She bore Louis two daughters, but their marriage broke down when she accompanied him to Palestine on the Second Crusade (1147–9). Pope Eugenius III tried but failed to heal the breach. Granted an annulment in 1151, the next year Eleanor married Henry Plantagenet, duke of Normandy and count of Anjou, who became king of England in 1154. Relations between Eleanor and Henry were strained by his numerous infidelities (the most notable with Rosamund Clifford), and in 1170 Eleanor established her own separate court at Poitiers, which became a centre of culture and courtly manners. She bore Henry five sons and three daughters, but also fomented strife within the family, as in 1173 when she supported her sons, Henry, the Young King, Richard (the future Richard I of England) and Geoffrey, when they rebelled against their father. From 1173 to 1185 she was kept under house arrest at Winchester and Salisbury; and was released only four years before Henry's death in 1189. In 1189 she secured Richard's uncontested accession to the English throne, and held Aquitaine for him thereafter. On his death in 1199 she backed John's claim to the throne against his nephew Arthur, duke of Brittany, whom Richard had recognized as his heir in 1190. Arthur trapped her in the Angevin stronghold of Mirebeau castle in 1202, and John won a great victory in coming to her aid. She died in 1204 and was buried in the Plantagenet funerary church at Fontevrault.

The Plantagenet Chronicles: 55, 79, 81–2, 88, 91, 97, 101–4, 108, 112, 114, 117, 121, 125, 127, 130, 144, 195–8, 208, 212–13, 226–7, 232, 235, 253, 257, 261–2, 274–6, 278
Chronicles of the Age of Chivalry/Four Gothic Kings (US edn): 90
The Wars of the Roses: 307

Eleanor of Castile

d.1290. Daughter of Ferdinand III, king of Castile. In 1254 she married the future Edward I of England at Las Huelgas, near Burgos in Castile. In return Ferdinand granted Edward his lands and rights in Ponthieu and Montreuil and relinquished his claims to Gascony. Eleanor bore Edward 16 children, only seven of whom survived to adulthood, and accompanied him on all his travels until her death. In 1270 she went on crusade with Edward in the Holy Land and is said to have lamented so loudly when he was wounded by a Muslim poisoned dagger that the doctors ordered her to leave the room. Edward's devotion to his wife was shown by the magnificent Eleanor crosses he built to her memory along the route her cortège followed from Lincoln to Westminster.

Chronicles of the Age of Chivalry/Four Gothic Kings (US edn): 80–2, 114, 119, 126–7, 132–3

Eleanor crosses

Twelve stone crosses erected in 1290 on the orders of Edward I, to mark the 12 resting places of his wife Eleanor of Castile's bier during her funeral procession from Harby in Lincolnshire, where she died, to Westminster. The crosses stood at Lincoln, Grantham, Stamford, Geddington, Northampton, Stony Stratford, Woburn, Dunstable, St Albans, Waltham, Westcheap, and Charing. Three survive: at Waltham, Northampton and Geddington. The crosses, inspired by the *Montjoies* in France commemorating Saint Louis' (Louis IX, of France) funeral procession to Paris, incorporated French features, such as the double-curved ogee arches which inspired the native English style of Decorated Gothic in the 14th century. Eleanor of Castile's portrait was originally painted on each cross.

Chronicles of the Age of Chivalry/Four Gothic Kings (US edn): 132–3, 206

Eleanor of England

1161–1216. Daughter of Henry II of England and Eleanor of Aquitaine. In 1176 she married Alfonso VIII, king of Castile. He was promised Gascony as her dowry and seized it by force in 1204 after Eleanor of Aquitaine's death. His brother-in-law, King John of England, recaptured it in 1206. The Cistercian royal nunnery of Las Huelgas in Castile was founded in 1187 at Eleanor's request. It is built in a similar style to buildings in Angers, her birthplace, suggesting that Eleanor may have employed an Angevin architect. She and Alfonso were buried there.

The Plantagenet Chronicles: 97, 114–15, 260

Eleanor of Provence

d.1291. Daughter of Raymond Berengar, count of Provence; queen of Henry III of England (m.1236). Although the marriage to Henry was prestigious – Eleanor's sister, Margaret, had become the wife of Louis IX of France in 1234 –

Exeter Cathedral The Norman fabric of the cathedral (opposite) was rebuilt between 1280 and 1360 in the Decorated style.

Eleanor of Castile The funerary effigy of Edward III's beloved queen lies in Westminster Abbey.

Eleanor brought no dowry with her. The king, however, provided generously for his young bride, who was still in her early teens, and the couple formed a strong mutual attachment, considered unusual by contemporaries. Henry showed considerable favour to two of her uncles, giving one, Peter of Savoy, the honour of Richmond in 1240, and the other, Boniface, the archbishopric of Canterbury in 1241. As a result he was drawn into a network of Savoyard intrigue, which created hostility to both king and queen. Eleanor was also extravagant: in the 1260s a payment of 20,000 marks made to her by the Londoners was swallowed up by her creditors abroad. Eleanor bore Henry two sons and three daughters. When he died, in 1272, she retired to the great nunnery at Amesbury. After her death her son, Edward I, paid off her continuing debts.

Chronicles of the Age of Chivalry/Four Gothic Kings (US edn): 56–9, 78, 96

Elizabeth of York

1465–1503. Daughter of Edward IV of England and Elizabeth Woodville; queen of Henry VII of England (1486). In 1475 her marriage to the dauphin was made a condition of peace between Edward IV and Louis XI of France, but was never performed. After her father's death in 1483, and the murder of her brothers Edward V and Richard, 5th duke of York, later that year, Elizabeth's mother promised her to Henry Tudor, 15th earl of Richmond, later Henry VII (c.1484). Henry was in exile, plotting to invade England and topple Richard III, and the proposed marriage promised to win him the loyalty of Edward IV's old servants. Richard III publicly dismissed rumours that he was planning to marry Elizabeth of York after his own wife's death in 1484. She married Henry Tudor, by then king of England, in 1486, following his successful invasion and Richard III's death. Tudor propagandists hailed the match as uniting the houses of Lancaster and York.

The Wars of the Roses: 235, 253, 295–6, 300

Elmham, Thomas

d.1426. Historian; monk and treasurer of St Augustine's, Canterbury; vicar-general of the Cluniacs for England and Scotland (1415). Elmham wrote several works, including a *Life of Henry V* in Latin verse. This criticized the Lollards and 'that satellite of hell, John Oldcastle, heresiarch and arch-Lollard', whom Elmham compared to the devil and the great beast of the Book of Revelation. He also wrote a history of the Augustinian monastery at Canterbury.

The Wars of the Roses: 145

Eltham Palace

Royal palace south-east of London. Sir John Oldcastle and his fellow Lollard conspirators made an abortive attempt to assassinate or kidnap Henry V as he celebrated Twelfth Night at the palace in 1414. Henry VI of England stayed there in 1432 after returning from his coronation as king of France. John Benet records that a thunderbolt struck the palace on 27 February 1450, between six and seven o'clock in the evening, burning down the storeroom, hall, kitchen and some chambers.

The Wars of the Roses: 73, 79, 145, 178, 202

Ely Cathedral

Cathedral built between the late 11th and the 14th centuries on the site of an abbey founded by St Aetheldreda and destroyed by the Danes in 870. It contains supreme examples of the Decorated style: the nodding ogees, curved in two planes, on the Lady Chapel. The vault of the central tower, built 1322–42, spans the 65-foot space of the cathedral's central crossing and was built in wood to an octagonal design, painted and gilded to imitate stone, which would have been too heavy to be supported over such a span.

Chronicles of the Age of Chivalry/Four Gothic Kings (US edn): 206
The Wars of the Roses: 87

Empire, Holy Roman

See: Holy Roman Empire

England, Eleanor of

See: Eleanor of England

English language

In Anglo-Saxon England Old English was the language of both court and people: of the several dialects, West Saxon predominated. The Norman Conquest saw the arrival of Latin as the language of government (it continued in use in legal records until the 18th century), and Norman French. French was the language of the court until the 14th century, when a vernacular revival exemplified by Chaucer and Wycliffe made English the tongue of all classes. Many French words, such as baron and prison, had by this time become absorbed into normal English speech. Regional dialects were so different that northerners and southerners had great difficulty in communicating, but gradually the dialect of the south-east, the day-to-day language of the administration, gained supremacy and is the ancestor of modern standard English.

Chronicles of the Age of Chivalry/Four Gothic Kings (US edn): 163, 297
The Wars of the Roses: 12

epic poetry

Long poems on a heroic theme, highly popular during the Middle Ages and typified by the *Chanson de Roland*.

escheat

Under feudal law, the reversion of a fief (an estate granted conditionally to a vassal) to the fief's overlord, usually if the vassal died without heirs or became an outlaw.

essoin

An excuse for not attending a court when summoned to perform a suit or answer an action; sickness or infirmity were considered acceptable reasons.

Eton

Town in Buckinghamshire, on the Thames, where Henry VI founded Eton College in 1440–41. The school was closely linked with his other foundation of the same year, King's College, Cambridge. The model for both was William of Wykeham's endowment of Winchester College and New College, Oxford. The chronicler John Capgrave records that Henry VI was present for the laying of Eton's foundation stone; but the college was not completed until the 1490s, at least two decades after his death. The initial plan made provision for a church as long as Lincoln Cathedral and nearly as wide as York Minster, but shortage of money forced Eton's authorities to halt the project when only the choir was completed.

The Wars of the Roses: 169, 192, 195

Eugenius III, pope

d.1153. Born Bernard of Pisa; Cistercian abbot; pope (1145–53). A friend of St Bernard of

Clairvaux, Eugenius kept his ascetic lifestyle as pontiff. From 1146 to 1149 he was exiled from Rome by Arnold of Brescia, a radical reformer favoured by the Roman people. In 1145 Eugenius promoted the Second Crusade; he also attempted to reconcile Louis VII of France with his wife Eleanor of Aquitaine when they returned from crusade, decking their bed with valuable ornaments and giving them homilies on their conjugal duties.

The Plantagenet Chronicles: 81

Eugenius IV, pope

1383–1447. Born Gabriele Condulmer, a Venetian; pope (1431–47). His papacy was disturbed by the Council of Basle, convened in 1431; when he tried to dissolve it because of mutual mistrust, it declared its powers superior to his and refused to disband. The council's supporters drove Eugenius from Rome to Florence in 1434, but the council he called at Ferrara-Florence proclaimed the reunion of Eastern and Western churches in 1439, strengthening his authority. Although the rump of the Council of Basle deposed Eugenius in 1439, electing Felix V as an antipope in his stead, he gained the support of the Aragonese in 1443, enabling him to return to Rome.

The Wars of the Roses: 169

Eustace, bishop of Ely

d.1215; chancellor (1197–99), bishop of Ely (1197–1215). In 1208 Eustace was selected by Pope Innocent III to urge King John of England to recognize Stephen Langton as archbishop of Canterbury. When John refused, he pronounced the interdict imposed by the pope, prohibiting English clergy from administering the sacraments and even burying the dead, and escaped abroad. He procured a papal sentence of deposition on John that year. He returned to England in 1213 after John had been reconciled with the pope.

The Plantagenet Chronicles: 248, 304, 306

Eustace, son of King Stephen

1130?–1153. Son of Stephen, king of England,

and Matilda of Boulogne. In 1139 he married Constance, sister of Louis VII of France. With the French king's help, he attacked the domains of Geoffrey Plantagenet, count of Anjou, in Normandy in 1151; the following year, on the accession of Geoffrey's son Henry (the future Henry II of England) as duke of Normandy, he attacked again. In the same year Stephen tried to have Eustace crowned as heir to the English throne, but Theobald, archbishop of Canterbury, fled the country rather than crown a usurper's son. Eustace's death in 1153 cleared the way for Henry II's accession.

The Plantagenet Chronicles: 65, 72, 80–2, 85–6, 88, 93

Evesham, battle of

Battle in the Vale of Evesham, in Worcestershire, on 4 August 1265, between the rebel forces of Simon de Montfort, 6th earl of Leicester, and troops loyal to Henry III. Henry was in de Montfort's custody and the king's son, Prince Edward, the future Edward I, moved to free him with the help of Gilbert de Clare, 6th earl of Gloucester and 6th earl of Hertford, formerly a loyal supporter of de Montfort. Their force, gathered in the Welsh marches, fell on the rebel troops near Evesham. De Montfort, his son Henry, and his ally Hugh Despenser were slain in the battle; de Montfort was dismembered and decapitated, and his testicles were hung on either side of his nose. The king, wounded in the battle, was rescued.

Chronicles of the Age of Chivalry/Four Gothic Kings (US edn): 23, 75, 98, 212

Exchequer, Court of

Financial office and court of the English crown; responsible for the collection of crown revenues and for hearing cases affecting them. It started after the Norman Conquest as a financial committee of the king's court, and by about 1110 had become independent. Money was held in the well-guarded lower Exchequer, while the committee of the upper Exchequer sat around a table with a giant chequered cloth – the 'exchequer' (a form of abacus) – checking the returns made by the sheriffs. Sums paid in were

recorded by notched wooden tallies, and the accounts logged on the great parchment roll of the Exchequer, or pipe roll. After Easter there was a preliminary examination of the sheriffs by the king's officials, and final accounts were rendered in late September.

The Plantagenet Chronicles: 249, 324

Exeter

County town of Devon, inhabited since Roman times and an important centre for the production and export of woollen goods from the 10th century. Exeter Cathedral, built in Norman times and rebuilt, apart from its towers, between 1280 and 1360, is a classic example of the Decorated style, with elaborate webbed window tracery and an opulent rib-laden vault.

Chronicles of the Age of Chivalry/Four Gothic Kings (US edn): 152, 206, 207
The Wars of the Roses: 296

Eyck, Jan van

c.1390–1441. Flemish painter; one of the first artists to develop the use of oils. He was active at the courts of Count John of Holland (1422–5) and Philip the Good, duke of Burgundy, for whom he made several secret diplomatic journeys. His pictures are distinguished by their extraordinary realism, attention to detail, command of perspective, and luminous tones. The Arnolfini wedding portrait (1434), of a merchant and his bride, shows both his mastery of depicting space and light and an aptitude for realistic portraiture. Other important works are: the *Rollin Madonna* (c.1433), the Ghent altarpiece (1432), and the *Madonna with Canon Van der Paele* (1436).

The Wars of the Roses: 137, 289, 291

eyre

A periodic visitation to the shires by the king's justices, usually at intervals of a few years, to hear important legal cases.

Fabyan, Robert

d.1513. Chronicler, draper, alderman and sheriff of London (1493). His principal work, *The New Chronicles of England and France* (completed 1507), starts with the Creation and ends with the accession of Henry VII in 1485. Fabyan relates material about the history of England and France, with much detail on London, and also gives the well-known story of the death of Henry IV (in a chamber called 'Jerusalem') in the abbot of Westminster's house.

The Wars of the Roses: 116

Fair Maid of Kent, Joan, the

See: Joan, the Fair Maid of Kent

fairs

Important venues for the sale of goods in medieval times. Usually held to coincide with a saint's day, or an event in the farming year such as the autumn harvest, they normally took place annually and lasted three days. Some, like the Yarmouth Herring Fair, specialized in one product, others offered a wide range of goods. Although some were held as the result of royal grants, local lords were usually lords of the fairs, and derived great profits from their levies on trade. Great fairs were held at the junctions of European trade routes, such as those held six times a year in Champagne, where Mediterranean and Northern merchants met.

The Plantagenet Chronicles: 237
The Wars of the Roses: 187

Falaise

Town in Normandy, northern France; capital of the first dukes of Normandy, who built a castle there in the 10th and 11th centuries; birthplace of William I, the·Conqueror, king of England. King John of England imprisoned Arthur, duke of Brittany, his nephew and rival for the throne, in Falaise castle in 1202 and is said to have had him murdered there. The castle was besieged and taken by Philip II of France in 1204. Henry V of England retook Falaise for England in 1417. The town was recovered by the French with the rest of Normandy in 1450.

The Plantagenet Chronicles: 67, 158, 275–6, 280, 294
The Wars of the Roses: 141

falconry

Art of hunting with birds of prey, popular with the medieval aristocracy. Royal edicts protected hawks, and each station in society had its corresponding bird: a parson, for example, was allowed a sparrow hawk.

Chronicles of the Age of Chivalry/Four Gothic Kings (US edn): 111
The Wars of the Roses: 191

Fastolf, Sir John

1378?–1459. Soldier and landowner; knight of the Garter (1426); sometimes cited as the original of Shakespeare's Falstaff. Fastolf distinguished himself at Agincourt in 1415, was knighted before 1418, became Henry V of England's lieutenant and regent in Normandy in 1423, and was governor of Anjou and Maine from 1423 to 1426. In 1429 he used herring barrels as a barricade against French attacks in the 'Battle of Herrings' near Orléans. He retired to England in 1440, and invested profits from the wars in the wool trade, setting up textile mills on his estates at Castle Combe near Bristol. A neighbour of the Pastons (a family immortalized by their private correspondence), he is often mentioned in their letters. He built a castle at Caister in Norfolk, where he spent his retirement.

The Wars of the Roses: 203, 221

Fauconberg, Lord, 'Bastard of Fauconberg'

d.1471. Born Thomas Neville; also known as Lord Falconbridge, Thomas the Bastard of Fauconberg and Thomas the Bastard. Originally a Lancastrian rebel against Edward IV, Yorkist king of England, he fought for the king with Richard Neville, 16th earl of Warwick, 'the Kingmaker', in 1460. The chronicler Jean de Waurin relates that Edward honoured Fauconberg as a friend and a father just before his coronation in 1461. Despite this, in 1471 Fauconberg allied with Neville against Edward. Ordered to raise Kent for Neville and the Lancastrian Henry VI, he burnt part of London but lost his ships at Sandwich and was captured and beheaded.

The Wars of the Roses: 220, 230

Favent, Thomas

*fl.*1388. Clerk in minor orders and chronicler. His only surviving work is *The History or Narrative of the Mode and Form of the Wonderful Parliament*, an account of the proceedings of the Merciless Parliament of 1388, written in rhetorical Latin with frequent Biblical allusions. Favent praised the parliament and the lords appellant, 'whose integrity was justly famed throughout the land', and supported their actions against the 'pseudo lords' who oppressed the land and sought to undermine the statutes of England. His narrative, despite its florid style, includes some personal observation, such as the description of the lords appellant entering parliament arm in arm, dressed in cloth of gold.

The Wars of the Roses: 52, 56

Faversham Abbey

Abbey founded in 1148 at Faversham in Kent by Stephen, king of England (reigned 1135–54) and his wife Matilda. Original plans for the building proved over-ambitious and had to be modified after Stephen's death. The abbey followed Cluniac customs but was never part of the order. Both Stephen and Matilda were buried there.

Fawkes de Bréauté

d.1226. Norman military adventurer, who became one of the counsellors of John, king of England, and was given six shires by him in 1215. Fawkes fought for Henry III of England against Prince Louis of France from 1215 to 1217 and was largely responsible for the victory at Lincoln which ended the struggle. In 1223 he joined a conspiracy of lords plotting for the overthrow of the justiciar, Hubert de Burgh, but surrendered to Henry at Northampton when Stephen Langton, archbishop of Canterbury, threatened to excommunicate him. He was

Falaise castle One of the key fortifications of Normandy, and capital of the province's first dukes.

banished, and went to France in 1225, where he died in exile.

Chronicles of the Age of Chivalry/Four Gothic Kings (US edn): 27, 34

Ferdinand I, king of Portugal

1345–83. Son of Peter I of Portugal; king of Portugal (1367–88). Ferdinand fought three wars against Castile during his reign. The first (1369–71) ended with his promise to wed the daughter of Henry II of Castile; instead, he married a Portuguese noblewoman, Leonor Teles, after having her existing marriage annulled. He fought the second war (1372) in alliance with John of Gaunt, who laid claim to the Castilian throne through his wife, Constance of Castile. A Castilian siege of Lisbon (1373) failed, ending in a humiliating peace. In 1382 Ferdinand, again in alliance with the English, began a third war against Castile, which ended in 1383 with his daughter and heiress, Beatrice, being forced to marry John I of Castile. As a result of this marriage, Portugal would have passed to Castile on Ferdinand's death, had Ferdinand's half-brother, John, not managed to seize the Portuguese throne.

The Wars of the Roses: 40–2

Ferdinand II, the Catholic, king of Aragon

1452–1516. Son of John II of Aragon; king of Sicily (1468–1516); king of Aragon

(1479–1516); king of Naples (1504–16). Ferdinand married Isabella of Castile, heir to the Castilian throne, in 1469. The pair assumed joint rule of Castile in 1474, and on Ferdinand's accession to the throne of Aragon in 1479 all Spain save Moorish Granada became united. Ferdinand and Isabella gained an additional means of imposing their will when they gave their authority to the introduction of the Inquisition into Castile in 1478 and into Aragon in 1484. Their conquest of Granada and expulsion of the Jews (both in 1492), were further stages in the process of unifying and Catholicizing Spain.

The Wars of the Roses: 246–7

fief

Under feudal law, an estate granted by its overlord to a vassal, on condition of the latter's homage and service.

Fiennes, James, Lord Say and Sele

d.1450. Constable of Dover and warden of the Cinque Ports (1447–9); chamberlain (1447–50); lord treasurer (1449–50). Lord Say served in France under Henry V of England, who rewarded him with lands there in 1418. He later became an adviser to Henry VI of England; Thomas Cheyne, a Kentish agitator executed on 9 February 1450, called Say 'a servant of the king of the faeries'. However, under pressure from Jack Cade's rebels, Henry put Say in the Tower of London in June 1450. He was indicted

for treason and extortion by the London justices when Cade's men invaded London on 4 July 1450 and handed over to Cade, who had him beheaded and his head put on a pike.

The Wars of the Roses: 202, 204–5, 207

Fiori, Joachim of

See: Joachim of Fiori

First Crusade

First holy war (1096–9) undertaken by Christian forces against the Muslims. It was initiated at the Council of Clermont in 1095, when Pope Urban II exhorted Christendom to go to war to free the Holy Sepulchre from the Saracens. The crosses distributed at the council gave the crusade its name. The crusade was preached across Europe, and the first organized groups, under Bohemond I of Taranto (later Bohemond of Antioch), Baldwin of Boulogne, Godfrey of Bouillon and other Frankish commanders, arrived in the eastern Mediterranean in early 1097. The crusader army took Nicaea in 1097, Antioch in 1098, and Jerusalem (where they massacred the city's Muslims and Jews) in July 1099, and then established the first crusader states.

The Plantagenet Chronicles: 21, 36, 38–9, 61, 69, 153

FitzAilwin, Henry

d.1212. First lord mayor of London (1191?–1193?). FitzAilwin owed his position to

Prince John's grant of the commune (the right to municipal self-government) in 1191, made while his brother Richard I was on crusade. FitzAilwin presided over a meeting of citizens in 1212, after the first great fire of London.

The Plantagenet Chronicles: 297

FitzAlan, Richard, 9th earl of Arundel and 9th earl of Surrey

1346–97. 9th earl of Arundel and 9th earl of Surrey (1376–97). In November 1387, following his attempted arrest, Arundel joined Thomas, 1st duke of Gloucester, and Thomas, 12th earl of Warwick, in opposing Richard II. The three issued a written appeal accusing Richard's supporters of treason which earned them the title 'lords appellant'. In the Merciless Parliament, which followed on 4 February 1388, Richard's queen, Anne of Bohemia, spent three hours on her knees before Arundel, pleading unsuccessfully for the life of Sir Simon Burley. During Anne's funeral service in June 1394, the earl arrived late and Richard attacked and wounded him. In 1397 Arundel was arrested for conspiring against the king yet again with Gloucester and Warwick, and was executed on Tower Hill in London.

The Wars of the Roses: 47, 52–3, 57, 68–9, 78, 80

Fitzherbert, William, St, archbishop of York

d.1154. Treasurer and canon of York (c.1130); archbishop of York (1141–7, 1153–4). William was chaplain to his uncle King Stephen of England, who secured his election as archbishop by the York chapter. A group of Cistercians, backed by Bernard of Clairvaux, who was strongly opposed to lay interference in episcopal elections, opposed Williams's preferment and he was forced to go to Rome to attempt to have his election confirmed. Pope Eugenius III suspended his appointment and he took refuge with his distant cousin Roger II of Sicily. In 1147 the Council of Reims deposed him as archbishop but in 1153 Eugenius's successor, Anastasius IV, restored him. He died suddenly the following year, possibly poisoned. He was canonized in 1227.

The Plantagenet Chronicles: 210

FitzHubert, Robert

*fl.*1140. Flemish mercenary who fought for King Stephen of England (reigned 1135–54).

Supposedly in the pay of Robert, 1st earl of Gloucester, he captured Devizes castle in Wiltshire in 1140, then attempted to set himself up as an independent leader. Gloucester had him hanged before the castle.

The Plantagenet Chronicles: 74

FitzNeal, Richard, bishop of London

d.1198. Treasurer of England (1189?–1196); bishop of London (1189–98). FitzNeal served as treasurer under Henry II and Richard I. His *Dialogue Concerning the Exchequer* is a valuable treatise explaining Exchequer practices.

The Plantagenet Chronicles: 249

FitzOsbert, William

d.1196. London agitator, nicknamed Longbeard. FitzOsbert led protests against the levies imposed by London's magnates in 1194 to pay Richard I's ransom when the English king was imprisoned in Germany. Ralph of Diceto records that in 1196 he organized a riot in St Paul's. Pursued by the authorities, he took sanctuary in St Mary le Bow, but, by order of the archbishop of Canterbury, he was dragged out and hanged in chains at Smithfield.

The Plantagenet Chronicles: 240

FitzPeter, Geoffrey, 4th earl of Essex

d.1213. Justiciar of England (1198–1213); 4th earl of Essex (1199–1213). He was one of the governors left to rule England when Richard I went on crusade in 1191. Ennobled by King John of England in 1199, he was joint vice-regent of England during John's campaign in Poitou in 1202. In 1209 he mediated between John and the clergy when Pope Innocent III threatened the king with excommunication.

The Plantagenet Chronicles: 217, 220, 292, 305

FitzStephen, William

d.1190?. Clerk in Thomas Becket's household, and his biographer. FitzStephen was present at Becket's martyrdom in Canterbury Cathedral on 29 December 1170, and wrote his *Vita Sancti Thomae* soon after. FitzStephen's account contains a eulogistic account of Becket's childhood and youth, as well as a detailed description of 12th-century London.

The Plantagenet Chronicles: 13, 94, 96, 101, 109, 118, 297

FitzWalter, Robert

d.1235. Baronial leader; lord of Baynard's castle. In 1203 he surrendered Vaudreuil castle in Normandy to Philip II of France, since no aid had come from King John of England. In 1212 FitzWalter was exiled to France for conspiracy against John, and Baynard's castle was demolished. However, he returned soon after and led the barons' army against the king in 1215, when London was seized. FitzWalter was excommunicated as one of the 25 commissioners of Magna Carta. After John's death he offered the crown to Prince Louis of France, but was defeated and captured by the forces of the young Henry III of England led by William Marshal, at Lincoln in 1217. He went on the Fifth Crusade and was present at the siege of Damietta (1219–20). On his return, he submitted to Henry III's council.

The Plantagenet Chronicles: 278, 296, 308, 313

Flagellants

Groups of Christian zealots who wandered from town to town, flagellating themselves in public places with spiked leather thongs to atone for their sins and in the hope of avoiding divine retribution. The movement arose in northern Italy around 1260 and spread into Germany and Bohemia before it was suppressed by civil and ecclesiastical authorities. The chaos following the Black Death (1348–9) caused a resurgence of the movement. Flagellants wore white robes marked with a red cross and marched in groups of 50–500. Each was under a 'master' who possessed a 'heavenly letter', warning of imminent apocalypse, which was read at the height of their ceremonies. Groups spread all over Europe, and even reached England, but when Pope Clement VI issued an order suppressing the sect in 1349, the movement died down. It was to reappear in Italy in 1389, in Germany in 1414 and in Spain, France and Italy again in the 16th century.

Chronicles of the Age of Chivalry/Four Gothic Kings (US edn): 256–61

flagellation

Beating oneself or others. It has long been practised as an act of atonement by Christian ascetics.

Flamboyant style

Style of French Gothic architecture which arose at the end of the 14th century, due to the need to replace churches destroyed during the early part of the Hundred Years War (1337–1453). The Flamboyant style borrowed double curved and richly decorated traceries from the English Decorated and Perpendicular styles, and used them in lavish patterns whose flame-like form gave the style its name. Normandy, which had lost many churches in the war, was its centre. The west front of Rouen Cathedral (begun 1370) exhibits the early style, which is also typified by the abbey of Saint-Ouen in Rouen (1380–1415). The triangular porch of the church of Saint-Maclou in Rouen (c.1436–1520), is a superb example of mature Flamboyant extravagance.

The Wars of the Roses: 147

Flanders

Historic duchy in the Low Countries. The Flemish towns of Ghent, Bruges and Ypres enjoyed many privileges and great wealth because of trade and the local cloth industry, which had by the 13th century become the foremost in Europe. England supplied wool to Flanders and was the duchy's natural ally; the two joined forces against France in 1297 and again in 1337. Flanders became a fief of the dukes of Burgundy between 1384 and 1477, when the cloth industry declined in the face of competition from English and Dutch weavers. The Burgundian court moved to Bruges in 1419 and employed many Flemish painters such as Jan van Eyck. The Yorkist Edward IV of England fled to Flanders in 1470 during the Wars of the Roses to prepare his reconquest of England.

Chronicles of the Age of Chivalry/Four Gothic Kings (US edn): 136, 144, 147, 180, 236–7, 240, 264, 276
The Wars of the Roses: 44, 137, 202, 252

fleur-de-lis

Stylized heraldic lily, symbol of both the Virgin Mary and the royal house of France. Its shape was attributed variously to an iris, a sceptre and a battleaxe's head.

Chronicles of the Age of Chivalry/Four Gothic Kings (US edn): 175

Flint castle

One of the castles of Edward I of England built c.1300, on the Dee estuary in Clwyd, north-east Wales. Richard II was taken prisoner there by Henry Bolingbroke, later Henry IV, in August 1399, despite a guarantee of safe conduct.

The Wars of the Roses: 85, 89

Florence

Capital of Tuscany in central Italy, an independent commune from the 12th century. Florence lay at the axis of trade between northern and southern Europe, and its gold florin was recognized as an international currency of fixed weight and quality. Florentine banks, whose agents spanned Europe for much of the Middle Ages, dominated European trade. Despite the Black Death, which killed 60 per cent of the population in 1348, Florence's power expanded, as it absorbed Pisa and Arezzo. Its cultural eminence, exemplified by Dante in the 14th century, was continued in the 15th by artists of the early Renaissance, including the painter Masaccio, the architect Brunelleschi and the sculptor Donatello. The Florentine Renaissance owed much to the Medici, a prominent 15th-century family who were generous patrons of many artists and scholars.

Chronicles of the Age of Chivalry/Four Gothic Kings (US edn): 30, 70, 152, 197, 249, 281
The Wars of the Roses: 110–11, 218–19

Foliot, Gilbert, bishop of London

d.1187. Bishop of Hereford (1147–63); bishop of London (1163–87). Foliot opposed Becket's election as archbishop of Canterbury in 1162, refused to yield him obedience and administered Canterbury during Becket's exile (1164–70). Foliot was excommunicated by the archbishop in 1167, 1169 and 1171 and was absolved by him in 1170 and 1172. His letters are a major source for information about the Becket dispute. Gilbert said of Becket, 'He always was a fool, and always will remain one.'

The Plantagenet Chronicles: 111, 124

Fontevrault Abbey

Abbey in Anjou founded c.1099. A double monastery, built in the Romanesque style, it contained both priests and nuns served by lay brothers. The nuns were renowned for their piety: Henry II of England replaced the sisters of Amesbury Abbey in Wiltshire with them after 1177. Eleanor of Aquitaine generously endowed Fontevrault and was buried there in 1204. Henry II, her husband, had died near the abbey in 1189 and was interred there, probably at his followers' behest. The anonymous *Deeds of Henry II* records that when Henry's son Richard I of England went to see his father's bier at Fontevrault, the corpse bled from the nose – a sign of Henry's anger with his son. Richard was also buried in the abbey after his death near there in 1199. The Plantagenet tombs are early examples of *gisants* (effigies of recumbent figures).

The Plantagenet Chronicles: 92, 117, 131, 173, 192–3, 250, 252–7

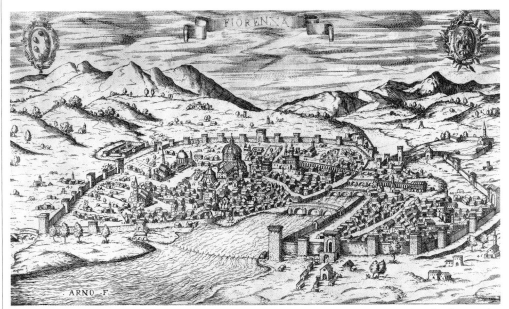

Florence Built on the banks of the River Arno in Tuscany, medieval Florence grew rich on banking and on the wool trade, buying English fleeces to be spun into yarn by Florentine workers.

forests

In medieval times, land (not necessarily woodland) reserved for the king's hunting under Forest Law and controlled by the forester instead of the sheriff.

The Plantagenet Chronicles: 325
Chronicles of the Age of Chivalry/Four Gothic Kings (US edn): 111, 165

Fountains Abbey

Cistercian abbey near Ripon in Yorkshire founded in 1132 during the first great expansion of the order. It was begun by Benedictine monks from St Mary's Abbey, York, who were moved by the laxity of life in their own house to follow the more austere rule advocated by Bernard of Clairvaux. Fountains became, and remained, the richest Cistercian monastery in medieval England, largely through the wealth earned from its great flocks of sheep.

The Plantagenet Chronicles: 77, 266

Fouquet, Jean

1415–80. French painter and illuminator; court painter to Charles VII and Louis XI of France. He was summoned to Rome in the 1440s to paint a portrait (now lost) of Pope Eugenius IV, and from this time his work showed the influence of Italian Renaissance artists such as Fra Angelico; though he was also influenced by Flemish artists such as Jan van Eyck and Rogier van der Weyden. His paintings include portraits of Charles VII, Agnes Sorel (Charles' mistress), and Etienne Chevalier (Charles' treasurer). His illuminations of works such as the *Hours of Etienne Chevalier* depict figures that are delicate yet in full perspective.

The Wars of the Roses: 136–7, 138–9

Fourth Crusade

Proclaimed by Pope Innocent III in 1198, the Fourth Crusade was preached by cardinal-legate Peter Capuano and Fulk of Neuilly, a wandering French preacher. The crusader army, which was much smaller than anticipated, was led mostly by French and Flemish nobles. It embarked from Venice in 1202 but, because its leaders owed the Venetians 34,000 marks for ships built to transport a vast army, they abandoned their original plan and instead helped the Venetians recover the port of Zara on the Dalmatian coast from the king of Hungary. Ignoring papal protests, they then advanced on Constantinople, encouraged by the Venetians and by Alexius, son of erstwhile Byzantine emperor Isaac II, who had been deposed by his own brother, Alexius III. Alexius was installed as co-emperor Alexius IV with Isaac II: but when Alexius III's son-in-law overthrew them both in March 1204, to become Alexius V, the crusaders stormed and looted Constantinople, dividing the spoils with the Venetians. The Latin empire of Constantinople was established (it endured until 1261), with Baldwin of Flanders as its first ruler; and this was the effective end of the crusade.

The Plantagenet Chronicles: 187, 282–3

Fra Angelico

See: Angelico, Fra

Frederick I The Holy Roman Emperor Frederick I with his sons.

France

France was divided for much of the Middle Ages between lands ruled directly by the kings of France, areas such as the duchy of Aquitaine that were held by the kings of England and other great fiefs such as the duchy of Burgundy. The latter stages of the Hundred Years War (1337–1453) marked France's progress to unity, and at its end left the English holding only Calais. Louis XI of France (reigned 1461–83) eroded the power of the great French magnates, and incorporated most of France into the royal domain.

Chronicles of the Age of Chivalry/Four Gothic Kings (US edn): 29–30, 50, 62, 68–70, 72–4, 78–90, 96, 112, 138–40, 144, 148, 234, 236–52, 254, 264, 266–82, 284, 294–8
The Wars of the Roses: 21–3, 28–9, 48–50, 58–9, 72, 208, 114–16, 121, 128–37, 140–1, 144–51, 165–6, 170–80, 188–9, 218, 238–9, 245–8, 268–70, 274

France, Catherine of

See: Catherine of France

France, Isabella of

See: Isabella, the she-wolf, of France

Francesco, Piero della

See: Piero della Francesco

franchise

Right, usually of quasi-regal jurisdiction, granted by the sovereign to a person, such as a lord (known as a palatine lord), or to a body of people, such as a monastery or a town.

Francis, St, of Assisi

1182?–1226. Son of Pietro Bernadone, a merchant of Assisi, Umbria, in Italy; founder of the Franciscan religious order. Baptized Giovanni, but dubbed 'Francesco' for his love of French fashions, Francis was an unexceptional, wealthy young man until his capture and imprisonment following a battle between Assisi and Perugia (c.1202). After this he fell ill, then began a life of ascetic devotion. Dressed in rags and living on alms, he set out to preach in 1209 and the following year received Pope Innocent III's support and approval for his rule. He travelled to France, Spain and the Middle East (1219–20), where he preached to the sultan at Damietta. Dissent within his order compelled his return to Assisi in 1221, and soon after he retired from active leadership of the Franciscans. He received the stigmata in 1224, following a vision during prayer, and bore them till his death.

Chronicles of the Age of Chivalry/Four Gothic Kings (US edn): 34–41, 65

Froissart The chronicler (opposite) presenting a book to Richard II of England; an incident he recorded.

Franciscans

Order of friars following the rule of St Francis, founded in 1209 and approved by Pope Honorius III in 1223; known as 'grey friars' for their homespun habits, they were vowed to preaching and extreme poverty. Two other Franciscan orders emerged during Francis' lifetime: an order of nuns, the Poor Clares (founded 1212); and the tertiaries (founded c.1221), lay people living a semi-monastic life within society. The movement expanded with great speed; by 1224 Franciscan friaries had been established in England, in Canterbury, London and Oxford – although the first Franciscans to land at Dover were arrested as vagrants. By the 1240s the grey friars had settled in most English cities.

Chronicles of the Age of Chivalry/Four Gothic Kings (US edn): 34–8, 41, 64–5, 128
The Wars of the Roses: 100

frankalmoign

Literally 'free alms'; the tenure of lands or livings granted to those devoted to the service of God. The recipient's gratitude was expressed in prayer, usually for the souls of the donor and for his kin.

Frederick I, Holy Roman Emperor

1123–90. Son of Frederick II, duke of Swabia and Judith of Bavaria; known as Barbarossa or Red Beard, king of Germany (1152–90), Holy Roman Emperor (1155–90). Frederick's mother and father belonged respectively to the two rival houses of Guelph and Ghibelline, whose rivalry had long complicated the political life of Germany and Italy.

In 1152 Frederick's uncle, Conrad III, advised on his deathbed that Frederick should succeed him, in the hope that this would end the feud. The German electors duly chose Frederick and later that year he was crowned king of Germany. To win the papacy's aid in restoring moribund imperial powers in Italy, he supported Pope Eugenius III against the Norman rulers of Sicily, and the revolutionary commune in Rome. Frederick marched into Italy, and in 1155 was crowned in Rome by Adrian IV, the new pope, as Holy Roman Emperor, amidst hostile demonstrations. Frederick's attempts to reassert imperial authority in Italy began after Adrian IV turned against him in 1156 and allied with the Sicilians. Frederick invaded Italy in 1157, seized Milan, Brescia and other towns in Lombardy, and in 1158 laid claim to all his rights as emperor and

king of the Lombards, including the right to govern all the autonomous Lombard cities. The greed of his officials led the Lombard towns to revolt in 1159, with Adrian IV's tacit support. Frederick fought back, burning Milan in 1162. Alexander III, the new pope, excommunicated the emperor (who sponsored several antipopes against him) in 1162, and Frederick drove him into exile in France. The emperor captured Rome in 1166, but was driven out of Italy in 1167 by the Lombard League, a coalition of Lombard cities.

He returned in 1174, having pacified the feuding German princes, and having made over-generous concessions to the German nobility in an attempt to buy their support. Eventually in 1177 he made a not entirely advantageous peace with the Italian cities, after a major defeat at the hands of the Lombard League at the battle of Legnano (1176). He was reconciled with Alexander III, who rescinded his excommunication in 1177. Frederick's most powerful vassal, Henry the Lion (the husband of Matilda – daughter of Henry II of England) had refused to support the campaign, and in revenge Frederick deprived him of his duchy of Saxony. In 1181 he drove him into exile at the Plantagenet court in England.

In 1184 Frederick called a diet at Mainz, a meeting of imperial princes, during which he celebrated his own powers with splendid pageantry. He crowned this triumph by marrying his son Henry, the future Holy Roman Emperor Henry VI, to Constance, heiress to the kingdom of Sicily (1186), securing peace with the Sicilian Normans. In 1189 he left for the Third Crusade at the head of a large army, but in 1190 was drowned in Cilicia in Asia Minor while on his way to Outremer. According to myth, he sleeps an enchanted sleep in a cave beneath the Kyffhäuser mountain in East Germany, ready to wake one day and restore Germany to its former greatness.

The Plantagenet Chronicles: 103, 108, 113, 153, 166–7, 176, 225

Frederick II, Holy Roman Emperor

1194–1250. Son of Holy Roman Emperor Henry VI and Constance of Sicily; king of Sicily (1198–1250), king of Germany (1212–20), Holy Roman Emperor (1220–50), king of Jerusalem (1225–28). Known by his admirers as 'the wonder of the world', and by his enemies as 'Antichrist', Frederick was brought up in Sicily under the guardianship of Pope Innocent III after his father's death in 1197 and his mother's in 1198. Despite the Hohenstaufen dynasty's history of feuding with the papacy, Innocent

promoted Frederick's coronation as German king (emperor-elect) at Mainz in 1212, as a rival to Otto IV, the incumbent emperor, who had been trying to wrest power from the pope in Italy. Frederick bought popularity in Germany with generous gifts of imperial lands. He had promised Innocent that he would divide Sicily from the Empire by conferring the Sicilian crown on Henry, his infant son. However, after his coronation as emperor in 1220 he made his son king of Germany and returned to Sicily to rule his empire from there.

Arab, Greek and Muslim worlds met in Sicily and the sophistication of Frederick's court reflected this variety of cultures. An Arab chronicler commented that 'It was clear from what he said that he was a materialist and that his Christianity was simply a game to him'. He kept a harem, and shocked Christians and Muslims alike by his scepticism. He was a gifted poet and patron of commerce, the arts and sciences; in 1225 he founded a university at Naples. His treatise on falconry, *De arte venandi cum avibus*, was the earliest systematic work of ornithology. In Sicily he cut down the powers of the nobility, transported his Muslim subjects to a colony on mainland Italy, and reformed the legal system to set up an advanced and efficient government.

Frederick married his second wife, Yolanda, heiress to the crown of Jerusalem, in 1225. He had promised Pope Honorius III that he would go on crusade, and in 1227 departed for Outremer at the insistence of the new pontiff, Gregory IX. He fell ill en route, turned back, and was excommunicated by Gregory. His second expedition, of 1228, arrived safely in the East, and the emperor made a treaty with the Saracens at Jaffa by which Jerusalem, Bethlehem and Nazareth were ceded to the Christians. The emperor, although still excommunicate, had thus succeeded by negotiation where military crusades had failed. Gregory IX denounced the treaty and despatched an army against Frederick's lands in Italy, causing the emperor's rapid return from Outremer.

Frederick's long-term strategy was to subjugate northern Italy and to unite his northern and southern territories. To that end, he revived his claim to the crown of Lombardy, and bribed the German princes to support him by allowing them a greater degree of autonomy in their own domains. This approach led to friction with his son Henry, who rebelled in 1234. Frederick defeated and imprisoned Henry (1235), and replaced him with his second son Conrad, who continued to pursue his policy in Germany. In 1236 Frederick invaded Lombardy. His campaign was successful, but in

1239 Gregory IX renewed his excommunication and aligned himself with the Lombards. Frederick overran the papal states, and was threatening Rome itself in 1241 when Gregory died. The new pope, Innocent IV (elected 1243), was offered sweeping concessions by Frederick, but fled (1244) to Lyons, declared Frederick deposed in 1245, and granted his enemies the status of crusaders.

In 1246 a German faction elected an anti-king to Conrad IV, and civil war broke out; and two years later the Italians defeated Frederick at Vittoria. Just as the war in Italy began to turn in his favour, in 1250, the emperor contracted dysentery; he died at Lucera in December 1250.

The Plantagenet Chronicles: 167, 187
Chronicles of the Age of Chivalry/Four Gothic Kings (US edn): 18, 38–44, 54, 60–2, 69–72, 86

French language

A Romance tongue derived from the Latin of Roman Gaul. By the eighth century French had become distinct even from vulgar Latin. It then developed into two main forms: the *langue d'oil*, spoken north of the Loire, and the *langue d'oc*, spoken south. Within each area there were also many local dialects. In the north, one of these, the Parisian, gradually emerged as the standard form of French, rather as, in England, the dialect of the south-east became standard English. From the 13th century, French supplanted Latin as the language of official documents.

The Plantagenet Chronicles: 149
Chronicles of the Age of Chivalry/Four Gothic Kings (US edn): 55, 163, 297

friars

Members of the mendicant (begging) religious orders: for example, Austin friars, Carmelites, Dominicans and Franciscans. Mendicant friars lived solely on alms, were forbidden to own property and differed from most cloistered monks in the centralized organization of their orders and their extensive preaching and involvement in the community. Mendicant friaries were not enclosed and were often situated in a town, attached to a school or university. Conventional orders of friars, such as the crutched friars, were closer to traditional monastic patterns.

Froissart, Jean

*c.*1337–1410? French chronicler, poet and courtier. He lived in England from 1360 to 1366, becoming a clerk to Philippa of Hainault, wife of Edward III of England, in 1362 and visiting the court of David II of Scotland in 1365. In 1366 he accompanied Edward, the Black Prince, to Gascony in south-west France and chronicled his campaign against Castile, across the border in Spain. In 1383 he was ordained as canon of Chimay in Hainault, Flanders. He revisited England in 1395, when he met Richard II and complained that his old acquaintances were gone.

Froissart's *Chroniques*, written in lively French prose, record events in western Europe from 1327 to 1400. Although he repeats gossip and is often more entertaining than accurate, he captures the spirit of his era.

Chronicles of the Age of Chivalry/Four Gothic Kings (US edn): 7, 16, 248, 253, 286
The Wars of the Roses: 13, 70, 73

Fronsac

Town and castle in the duchy of Guyenne, south-west France. In the 15th century the castle was the strongest in the duchy, according to the chronicler Jean de Waurin; it was an English royal seat and the key to the defence of Guyenne and its capital Bordeaux. On 2 June 1451 the count of Dunois laid siege to it by land and sea, using heavy artillery. The English garrison, seeing the size of the besieging force, agreed to surrender the castle if they were not relieved or beaten by 23 June and also promised that all Guyenne would surrender. The castle was given up as promised, but Bordeaux and Guyenne continued to resist. Castle and town were recovered by the English in 1452 but were taken by the French in the summer of 1453.

The Wars of the Roses: 206, 208, 210

Fulk the Good, count of Anjou

d. *c.*960. Grandson of Fulk the Red; count of Anjou (941–*c.*960). According to legend, he was learned and saintly, dressed as a cleric and said of Louis IV of France (who mocked his piety), 'an illiterate king is a crowned ass'.

The Plantagenet Chronicles: 19, 22

Fulk Nerra, count of Anjou

972–1040. Count of Anjou (987–1040). Fulk started his reign by seizing Chateaudun, to secure himself against his neighbours, Odo II, count of Blois and Champagne, and Gelduin, lord of Saumur. In 992, after winning the battle of Conquereuil against the Bretons, he pillaged and devastated the area. He took Saumur in 1026, and built many castles in Anjou: Treves, on the Loire (1020s), Durtal, also on the Loire, above Angers (*c.*1040), and a ring of forts encircling Tours for use as offensive bases. Fulk burned his first wife for infidelity but also founded two abbeys: Beaulieu-des-Loches near Tours and St Nicholas at Angers. He went on pilgrimage to Jerusalem three times (1002–3, *c.*1008, 1039).

The Plantagenet Chronicles: 19, 24–8, 30, 41, 43

Fulk Rechin, count of Anjou

d.1109. Count of Anjou (1060–1109) and chronicler. Having inherited the right to Touraine and Chateau-Landon, half of the Angevin inheritance, from his uncle, Geoffrey Martel I, Fulk went to war against his brother Geoffrey, captured and imprisoned him in 1066 and took Anjou and Saintonge, Geoffrey's half of the inheritance, into his domains. *The Chronicle of the Counts of Anjou* tells that his wife eloped with Philip I of France in 1107. Fulk himself was the initiator of this work in the 1090s, chronicling his forebears.

The Plantagenet Chronicles: 20, 30, 33–7

Fulk the Red, count of Anjou

d.941. Son of Ingelgar, a soldier of fortune; count of Anjou (*c.*941). One of the half-legendary founders of the Angevin dynasty.

The Plantagenet Chronicles: 19, 22

Fulk V, king of Jerusalem

1092–1143. Count of Anjou (1109–29); king of Jerusalem (1131–43). Fulk married the only daughter of Elias, count of Maine, in 1109, thereby ultimately uniting Anjou and Maine. In 1120 he went on pilgrimage to the Holy Land. In 1128 a delegation from Baldwin II, king of Jerusalem, arrived in France, asking Louis VII to choose one of the French nobility to marry his daughter Mélisande and become heir to the throne of Jerusalem. Fulk, by then a widower, was chosen. He married Mélisande in 1129 and succeeded as king of Jerusalem in 1131. To defend the holy city from the Muslim champion, Zengi, Fulk allied with the emir of Damascus and the emperor of Constantinople during the early 1130s. Turkish raiders took him prisoner in 1137, but then freed him.

The Plantagenet Chronicles: 19, 37–9, 46–8, 60–1

galley

Medieval ship, propelled by banks of oars but also equipped with a sail. Galleys were most suited to the calm waters of the Mediterranean.

Chronicles of the Age of Chivalry/Four Gothic Kings (US edn): 138

Gascony

Area of south-west France, whose chief towns were Bordeaux and Bayonne; the duchy of Gascony proper was the area south of Bordeaux stretching to the Pyrenees, but the name was also used interchangeably with Guyenne to encompass the Bordelais, Agenais, Bazadais and also parts of Périgord, Limousin, Quercy and Rouergue. Gascony was the principal battlefield of the English and French kings in the later Middle Ages. The only secure Plantagenet dominion in France in 1216 after King John of England's reign, it became increasingly unsettled and, in 1253, a major revolt broke out which Henry III of England settled with difficulty. Henry became Louis IX of France's vassal for the duchy under the terms of the Treaty of Paris (1259), but Gascony was coveted and fought for by Louis' successors.

Gascony then as now was a major producer of fine wines, and England was its main market. Ties between the two were strong, and it was with great reluctance that the Gascons eventually surrendered to the French in 1453.

The Plantagenet Chronicles: 32–3, 55, 261, 279. *Chronicles of the Age of Chivalry/Four Gothic Kings* (US edn): 24, 62, 74–6, 90–1, 112, 116, 136, 140–1, 154, 162, 196, 205, 228, 236, 262, 266–72, 294, 296

The Wars of the Roses: 22, 24, 29, 108, 188, 194, 206–7, 209–10

Gaveston, Piers, 5th earl of Cornwall

d.1312. Gascon knight; favourite of Edward II of England; 5th earl of Cornwall (1307); regent of England (1308). Banished by Edward I of England, in 1307, he was recalled by Edward II and created 5th earl of Cornwall on Edward's accession that year. In the same year he married the king's niece, Margaret, daughter of the late 7th earl of Gloucester. Gaveston became regent of England in 1308, during Edward's absence in France, but the English barons, resentful of the arrogant Gascon, procured his temporary exile to Ireland (1308–9). During his stay Gaveston, with Edward's connivance, pocketed the Irish crown revenues. He returned to England but was exiled to Flanders in 1311. The following year he entered England again, secretly, but was seized by the barons when he was alone at Knaresborough castle in Yorkshire. He was beheaded in the presence of Thomas, 2nd earl of Lancaster, at Blacklow Hill on 19 June 1312.

Chronicles of the Age of Chivalry/Four Gothic Kings (US edn): 167–77, 180, 185

Genghis Khan

1167?–1227. Born Temujin (Genghis Khan means 'mighty ruler'); Mongol leader and conqueror. Chieftain of one Mongol tribe, he subjugated many others and became ruler of a Mongol confederacy. Genghis established his capital at Karakorum, attacked north China in 1213, and by 1215 had conquered most of its territory, including Peking. His armies turned westwards, and by 1224 he had conquered an empire stretching from the Crimea to the Pacific. Genghis himself was tall and long-bearded, ruthless in war but faithful to his allies and convinced of his destiny to rule the world. He was tolerant of all creeds, so long as his subjects obeyed him. He was buried in a still unlocated grave on 'God's Mountain' in 1227, and his domains were divided among his heirs, the most famous of whom was Kublai Khan.

Chronicles of the Age of Chivalry/Four Gothic Kings (US edn): 41, 61

Geoffrey, archbishop of York

d.1212. Illegitimate son of Henry II (who acknowledged him at his accession); bishop-elect of Lincoln (1173–82); chancellor (1181–2); archbishop of York (1189–1212). Although elected bishop of Lincoln by the

chapter, under pressure from the king, he refused to be ordained, remained unconsecrated and in 1182 resigned under pressure from Pope Alexander III. According to one contemporary, he declared that he preferred horses and dogs to books and priests. But only as a priest was he no danger to Henry's legitimate sons, since a priest could not wear a crown.

Richard I named him archbishop of York in 1189, but Geoffrey was not finally ordained priest until 1190. In the same year, during Richard's absence on crusade, he was ordered to leave England for three years, but he returned in 1191 after being consecrated as archbishop at Tours. After his enthronement at York, Geoffrey joined the clerical opposition to King John of England in 1193. He was exiled in 1207 because of his opposition to John's taxes on the Church.

The Plantagenet Chronicles: 220, 289, 300

Geoffrey the Bearded

*fl.*1060s. Nephew of Geoffrey Martel I, who died in 1060, bequeathing him Anjou and Saintonge. His brother Fulk Rechin, who had received the other half of Geoffrey Martel's lands (Touraine and Chateau-Landon), imprisoned him in 1066 and took control of his lands. Barons including Elias, ruler of Maine, attacked Fulk with the aid of Philip I of France, in an unsuccessful attempt to obtain Geoffrey's release. Fulk's son, Geoffrey Martel II, on his accession as count of Anjou, freed Geoffrey but, according to the *Chronicle of the Counts of Anjou*, Geoffrey's wits had become addled in prison, and he did not live long after his release.

The Plantagenet Chronicles: 33–4, 36

Geoffrey, duke of Brittany

1158–86. Fourth son of Henry II of England and Eleanor of Aquitaine; duke of Brittany (1171–86). Married to Constance, heiress to Brittany, in 1167, he was recognized as heir to the duchy in 1169 and became duke on the death of Constance's father in 1170. In 1173 he joined his brothers Henry the Young King and Richard in their conspiracy against Henry II and invaded Normandy with Louis VII of France. Promised half the revenues of Brittany by his father, he repented and did homage to him in 1175. Geoffrey died suddenly in Paris on 18 August 1186, while plotting with Philip II of

Gascony Edward III (opposite) grants Gascony to his son, the Black Prince.

France, against his father. He was buried in Notre-Dame.

The Plantagenet Chronicles: 93, 116–17, 124–5, 134, 136, 140, 166, 168, 178

Geoffrey IV, the Fair, count of Anjou

1113–51. Son of Fulk V, count of Anjou and king of Jerusalem and Eremburg of La Flèche; count of Anjou (1129–51); founder of the Plantagenet dynasty. Geoffrey's nickname derived from his physical appearance – he was said to be tall, handsome, graceful and strong. He was also known as Geoffrey Plantagenet, apparently from the sprig of broom (*genêt*) he wore in his hat. In 1128, aged 15, he was married to Matilda, daughter and heiress of Henry I of England and the widow of the Holy Roman Emperor Henry V. They disliked each other, but maintained an uneasy political alliance and produced three sons, Henry (the future Henry II, king of England), Geoffrey and William.

Geoffrey spent much of his youth imposing order on his unruly vassals, including his own brother Elias, count of Maine, who rebelled against him in 1131; Geoffrey captured Elias and held him prisoner at Tours. Elias died soon after his release from a disease contracted in prison. In 1135 Henry I died, and Matilda's cousin Stephen of Blois seized the English throne, together with Normandy, traditionally coveted by the counts of Anjou. Geoffrey laid claim to the duchy in his wife's right.

Between 1135 and 1138 Geoffrey launched four expeditions into Normandy, none of which achieved great success. The expedition mounted in 1137 was stricken by dysentery, and forced to return swiftly to Anjou. In 1139 Matilda invaded England, seeking to press her claim to the English throne, and Geoffrey remained in Anjou to continue the war against Normandy. The Norman barons opposed Geoffrey, not through loyalty to Stephen, who had only visited Normandy once, but out of hatred of their traditional enemy, Anjou. However, Norman morale was weakened when Matilda captured Stephen at Lincoln in 1141, and many castles surrendered to Geoffrey, leaving him in control of most of the lands between Bayeux and the Seine. In 1142 he took the Avranchin and Mortain, and in 1143 moved east of the Seine, overrunning the Cotentin. He was invested as duke of Normandy in 1144 after the fall of Rouen, and Arques, the last castle opposing him, capitulated in 1145, leaving him unchallenged master of Normandy.

After the conquest of Normandy, Geoffrey joined Louis VII of France on the abortive Second Crusade (1147–9), returning in 1149. In 1150 he ceded Normandy to his son Henry, who also inherited the family claim to the English throne. Geoffrey died on 7 September 1151, and was buried in Le Mans Cathedral: the founder of a great dynasty of kings through his son, Henry II of England.

The Plantagenet Chronicles: 38–63, 80, 102, 140, 154

Geoffrey Greygown, count of Anjou

d.987. Son of Fulk the Good; count of Anjou (960–87). The *Chronicle of the Counts of Anjou* describes him as 'stout-hearted and strong and most successful in battle', and tells of his single-handed victory against Ethelulf the Dane, a Goliath-like figure. He was known as Greygown after a witness to the contest picked him out at the French court by the colour of his robes.

The Plantagenet Chronicles: 19, 22–4

Geoffrey Martel I, count of Anjou

d.1060. Son and heir of Fulk Nerra; count of Anjou (1040–60). Geoffrey is described by the *Chronicles of the Counts of Anjou* as 'bolder than all the rest of his family'. In 1044 he took Tours and the county of Touraine, using the ring of castles his father had built around them as jumping-off points for his attack. The same source describes his sudden illness and painful death. Geoffrey had no children and left his estates to his nephews, Fulk Rechin and Geoffrey the Bearded.

The Plantagenet Chronicles: 19, 26, 30, 33, 44

Geoffrey Martel II, count of Anjou

d.1106. Son of Fulk Rechin; count of Anjou (1103–6). The *Chronicle of the Counts of Anjou* describes him as cultivating 'everything that is good and . . . the terror of all his enemies'. Geoffrey's prowess, the source tells, earned him the love of his imprisoned uncle, Geoffrey the Bearded, who gave him title to Anjou and Saintonge, which Fulk Rechin had stolen from him. Geoffrey Martel died in an ambush near Candé castle: rumours implicated his father.

The Plantagenet Chronicles: 36–7

George, 3rd duke of Clarence

1449–78. Son of Richard, 3rd duke of York; brother of Edward IV; 3rd duke of Clarence (1461) on Edward's accession. In 1469 he married Isabel, daughter of Richard Neville, 15th earl of Warwick, 'the Kingmaker', and sided with him against Edward and in proclaiming Henry VI king of England again. In 1471, however, he rejoined Edward against Henry and fought with the Yorkists at Barnet and Tewkesbury. In 1474 he quarrelled with his brother Richard, 3rd duke of Gloucester (later Richard III) over the latter's marriage to Anne Neville.

In 1477, after his wife's death, Clarence clashed with Edward IV when the king vetoed his suit for the hand of Mary of Burgundy, heiress to the duchy of Burgundy. Edward imprisoned him in the Tower of London in June that year and he was tried for treason in January 1478. He was executed in the Tower on 19 February, perhaps by being drowned in a great butt of malmsey (a strong wine).

The Wars of the Roses: 234, 244–6, 252–4, 263–5, 272–3, 295

Gerald of Wales

1146?–1220? Son of a Norman knight and Nesta, a Welsh princess; archdeacon of Brecon (1172–1220); historian. He was bishop-elect of St Davids in 1176, but Henry II of England refused to accept the cathedral chapter's recommendation and Gerald never gained the see for which he longed. He wrote his many historical works to gain favour with contemporary notables; he dedicated his *Topography of Ireland* to Henry II, and two works to Stephen Langton, archbishop of Canterbury. His best-known work is the *Description of Wales*, written after a tour of Wales in 1188 and full of lively and informed descriptions of his countrymen. His later writings are soured by his ecclesiastical disappointment.

The Plantagenet Chronicles: 13, 22, 40, 94, 101, 122, 131, 141, 180, 284, 293
Chronicles of the Age of Chivalry/Four Gothic Kings (US edn): 36

Gervase of Canterbury

d.1210? Monk of Canterbury Cathedral priory (from 1163); sacrist (official in charge of sacred vessels) there (from 1193); chronicler in the monastic tradition. His works are imbued with loyalty to his monastery, and he began its history to provide it with ammunition in disputes with Baldwin, archbishop of Canterbury and ex officio abbot of the cathedral priory. His *Chronicle* developed from the history, as did *The Deeds of Kings*. They include accounts of the burning of Canterbury Cathedral in 1174, the building of the new cathedral and the abuses of King John against the English Church from 1208 to 1210. He also wrote a history of the archbishops of Canterbury from Augustine in the seventh century to Hubert in the 15th.

Gervase's writings, although often uncritical, contain much valuable information about England in the late 12th and early 13th centuries.

The Plantagenet Chronicles: 12, 137, 284, 293

Ghent

Capital city of Flanders. Ghent developed around an island fortress built by the first count of Flanders in the 10th century. By the 13th century it had become a major wool-producing centre, dominated by the four chief guilds: weavers, fullers, shearers and dyers. Under them Ghent enjoyed a considerable degree of independence during the 14th and 15th centuries, as when, in 1385, Philip the Bold of Burgundy, who had inherited the duchy of Flanders the previous year, was forced to make major concessions to the city to gain peace. In 1453 Ghent's liberties were curtailed and, although restored again by Mary of Burgundy in 1477, they were finally reduced by Holy Roman Emperor Maximilian I.

The Wars of the Roses: 137, 166, 274

Ghibellines

German and Italian political faction of the 12th and 13th centuries, which backed the Holy Roman Emperors against the papal (Guelph) faction. The name derives from Waiblingen, a castle belonging to the imperial Hohenstaufen dynasty, and was also used to describe Hohenstaufen supporters. It was used in Florence in the 13th century to denote supporters of Emperor Frederick II Hohen-staufen against Emperor Otto IV, during their struggle to gain the title to the Holy Roman Empire, a rivalry that also involved the papacy and split Italy. The cities of Cremona, Pisa and Arezzo were usually Ghibelline, as were the papacy's republican and other enemies in Rome. The Ghibellines were expelled from Florence late in the 13th century.

Gilbert of Clare, 6th earl of Gloucester

1243–95. Son of Richard, 8th earl of Clare; 9th lord of Clare (1262–95); 6th earl of Hertford (1262–95); 6th earl of Gloucester (1262–95). In 1263 Gilbert joined Simon de Montfort against Henry III. In 1264 he was the leading figure in the massacre of the Jews of Canterbury and soon after commanded de Montfort's centre at the battle of Lewes (14 May 1264). However, he quarrelled with de Montfort in November and joined Henry III's son Prince Edward (later Edward I). He commanded a division in the battle of Evesham (4 August 1265) in which de Montfort died. Gilbert proclaimed Edward I king in November 1272. He fought against the Welsh (1276–83) and married Edward I's daughter Joan in 1290. Rebels drove him out of Wales in 1294.

Chronicles of the Age of Chivalry/Four Gothic Kings (US edn): 75, 97, 101, 104

Gilbert of Clare, 7th earl of Gloucester

1291–1314. Son of Gilbert of Clare, 6th earl of Gloucester; 10th lord of Clare (1307–14); 7th earl of Hertford (1307–14); 7th earl of Gloucester (1307–14). A companion of Edward II, Gilbert commanded the English forces invading Scotland in 1309. He was chosen as one of the ordainers who attempted to curtail Edward's irresponsible behaviour in 1310, but nevertheless sided with Edward in his dispute with the chief ordainer, Thomas, 2nd earl of Lancaster. Gilbert tried unsuccessfully to mediate between the two in 1312–13. He accompanied Edward on his campaign against the Scots in 1314 and was slain at the battle of Bannockburn; according to the *Lanercost Chronicle,* he died fighting in the front line.

Chronicles of the Age of Chivalry/Four Gothic Kings (US edn): 172, 178, 185, 188

Gilbert Foliot, bishop of London

See: Foliot, Gilbert, bishop of London

Gilbert of Sempringham, St

1083?–1189. Founder of the Gilbertine order of nuns, lay sisters, lay brothers and canons; canonized in 1202. Gilbert began as parish priest and schoolmaster of Sempringham in Lincolnshire. In about 1131 he built a convent on his land for a group of fervently religious young women from among his pupils. The convent was a success, and others were soon established. Gilbert supported Becket against Henry II, but the king and Queen Eleanor respected him nevertheless and, in the 1160s, helped protect him when the lay brothers of Sempringham rebelled against poor conditions, alleging immorality in the order. Five bishops cleared the Gilbertines of the charge and wrote to Pope Alexander III on Gilbert's behalf. He died aged more than 100, allegedly without ever having touched a woman.

The Plantagenet Chronicles: 94, 106

Gilbertines

Exclusively English order of nuns, lay sisters, lay brothers and canons, founded by St Gilbert of Sempringham c.1131. The first Gilbertines were housed in Sempringham parish church in Lincolnshire but, by 1200, 12 Gilbertine houses had been founded. The choir nuns were ministered to by a small number of canons. Gilbertines enjoyed a high reputation for sanctity, which remained untarnished by allegations of immorality which were made in the 1160s by disaffected lay brothers, who claimed that the proximity of nuns and canons induced moral lapses. When Henry VIII dissolved the monasteries in the 16th century there were 24 Gilbertine houses.

The Plantagenet Chronicles: 106, 325

Gisors

Town on the border of the duchy of Normandy in north-east France. It changed hands several times during the 12th century, as when Geoffrey the Fair, count of Anjou, ceded it to Louis VII of France in 1144. Sixteen years later Louis returned it to Henry the Young King, son of Henry II of England, as part of his daughter Margaret's dowry. In 1198, during his campaigns in France, Richard I of England defeated Philip II of France at Gisors but in 1203 Philip seized it from King John of England and extensively refortified its castle.

The Plantagenet Chronicles: 40, 114, 124, 165, 176, 185, 192, 205, 212, 252

Glanville, Ranulf

d.1190. Chief justiciar of England (1180–9). In 1174 Glanville defeated a Scots army at Alnwick and captured William I, the Lion King of Scotland. He fought for Henry II against the Welsh, the French and Henry's own sons. Glanville went on crusade with Richard I in 1190 and died at Acre. The earliest treatise on the common law is attributed – probably erroneously – to him.

The Plantagenet Chronicles: 132

Glastonbury

Town in Somerset; ancient centre of English Christianity, identified with the Avalon of Arthurian legend and also said to be the site of England's first Christian church, founded by St Joseph of Arimathea in the 1st century AD. Glastonbury Abbey, one of England's richest Benedictine houses and a centre of learning, was a popular place of pilgrimage. It also held what were believed to be the tombs of King Arthur and Queen Guinevere, which, in 1278, were ceremoniously opened in the presence of Edward I, his queen and other dignitaries. The bones found within were reinterred with full royal pomp, as part of Edward's promotion of the Arthurian myth to enhance royal prestige.

The Plantagenet Chronicles: 132
Chronicles of the Age of Chivalry/Four Gothic Kings (US edn): 160

Glendower, Owen

*c.*1359–1415. Son of Gruffydd Vychan; the last independent prince of Wales (1400–15). Educated at the Inns of Court in London, he was also a highly proficient soldier. In 1400 he was drawn into a bitter dispute with Lord Grey of Ruthin, an English marcher lord and, backed by Welsh resentment against English occupation of the borderlands, he staged a rebellion. That year Glendower, who claimed direct descent from the princes of Powys in North Wales, was proclaimed prince of Wales.

During the next two years Henry IV of England attempted three times to crush the growing band of insurgents – but without success. Glendower allied with the treacherous Percys and negotiated with Henry's French enemies. In 1404 he captured two great English strongholds at Harlech and Aberystwyth and seemed to be in the ascendant. The following year, however, the tide turned. Prince Henry (the future Henry V) defeated the Welsh forces on the borders, and began to reconquer the principality, a process virtually completed in 1408. Glendower's wife and children were captured in 1409 and he went into hiding, where he remained until his death six years later. The obscurity of his last years fuelled legends about this remarkable man, who has become a Welsh national hero.

The Wars of the Roses: 95, 98, 100–2, 104, 108

Gloucester

City in Gloucestershire; originally a Roman town; capital of the Saxon kingdom of Mercia.

The troops of Queen Isabella of France encamped at Gloucester in 1326 after their invasion of England, and her husband, Edward II, was buried there on 21 December 1327.

The cathedral was originally a Norman abbey church begun in 1089. Rebuilding of the abbey choir and transepts began in 1330, to provide a mausoleum for Edward II. The builders stretched tracery over the Norman fabric, producing one of the first great examples of Perpendicular architecture. Fan vaults were also used – for the first time – in the cloister, built *c.*1350–1400. A lady chapel was added to the choir during the Wars of the Roses, complete with Yorkist badges.

The Plantagenet Chronicles: 104
Chronicles of the Age of Chivalry/Four Gothic Kings (US edn): 53, 207, 210, 221, 225, 254
The Wars of the Roses: 30, 56, 86–7, 109, 303

Golden Horde

Mongol state comprising most of Russia, established by Batu Khan in the 13th century and named after the Russian term for a magnificent Mongol tent camp that was set up along the Volga. The Russian principalities retained administrative autonomy as vassals of the khan. Civil war and conquest by the Mongol warlord Tamerlane caused the collapse of the Golden Horde in the 1390s.

The Wars of the Roses: 275

Good Parliament

Parliament held in 1376 at which discontent with the advisers of the ageing Edward III came to a head. The House of Commons took the lead for the first time. It elected Peter de la Mare as

Golden Horde *A Mongol khan with his court in a magnificent tent. The Golden Horde was named for the sight of its spectacular tents along the Volga river.*

the first Speaker of the Commons and refused to grant taxes to fund the king's war with France until its grievances were redressed, on the grounds that corrupt officials had diverted previous grants from the wars. The Speaker accused Lord Latimer, the chamberlain, Richard Lyons, a London banker, Alice Perrers, the king's mistress, and several others of corruption. The charges were brought collectively by the House, in the first impeachment. The Lords tried and convicted the accused: Latimer and Lyons were imprisoned and Alice Perrers was made to withdraw from court.

Chronicles of the Age of Chivalry/Four Gothic Kings (US edn): 298–9

Gothic

Dominant style of art and architecture in Europe from the 12th to the 15th century. Evolving from the Romanesque style, it included, in English architecture, the Early English, Decorated and Perpendicular styles. It was superseded by the Renaissance revival of classical styles but was revived in the 18th and 19th centuries. The term Gothic was coined pejoratively (to imply 'barbarous') in the 16th century, used with vague approbation from the 1760s and given full technical definition in 1877.

Chronicles of the Age of Chivalry/Four Gothic Kings (US edn): 48–9

Grande Chartreuse, the

Monastery high up in the Dauphiné Alps near Grenoble in south-east France. The Grande Chartreuse was the principal seat of the Carthusian order, founded by St Bruno in 1084. Hugh of Avallon (later St Hugh of Lincoln) who entered the monastery in c.1160, was a much loved figure there.

The Plantagenet Chronicles: 156, 178, 182

Grandmontines

Monastic order of extreme asceticism, founded c.1110 by Stephen of Muret at a time when many reformed religious orders were springing up throughout northern Europe. Unlike the others, the Grandmontines were forbidden to keep any animals (except for bees), lest they stimulated lust and greed for worldly goods; they lived mainly on nuts and berries, and inhabited bleak, deserted hilltops. Henry II of England, who was fond of ascetic orders,

founded several cells for the Grandmontines and in 1170 expressed his desire to be buried at the church of Grandmont, the mother house of the order, causing consternation among his barons, who declared this to be against the royal dignity. In the event, Henry was buried in Fontevrault Abbey, perhaps because of a schism in the Grandmontines in the 1180s, during which some of the choir monks at Grandmont were imprisoned by the lay brothers. Pope Clement III himself was forced to intervene in 1188, to settle the matter.

The Plantagenet Chronicles: 77, 131, 156, 173, 178, 182, 325

Great Company

Band of mercenaries which was formed in 1361, during a lull in the Hundred Years War, to provide sustenance for soldiers paid off by the two sides. Its leaders were mainly English but lesser soldiers from all over Europe formed its ranks. As the company advanced southwards through France it took towns and castles, despite preventive measures by Charles V of France. In 1366 the French king requested the aid of Edward III of England against the mercenaries, but their leaders refused to obey Edward's orders. Bertrand du Guesclin led the Great Company to Castile in 1386 and, with its help, deposed its king, Peter I, the Cruel, in favour of Peter's illegitimate brother, Henry of Trastamara. Thomas Walsingham gives the Great Company's strength as 60,000 men. Peter the Cruel later blamed their depredations for his failure to pay his ally, Edward the Black Prince.

Chronicles of the Age of Chivalry/Four Gothic Kings (US edn): 282, 284, 286, 293

Great Schism

Schism of the Western Church from 1378 to 1417, which began with the election of Pope Urban VI on 8 April 1378. His arrogant behaviour drove many cardinals to withdraw from Rome to Fondi, in southern Italy, and to depose him in 1378 in favour of a new candidate, Pope Clement VII. Clement moved north to Avignon, Urban remained at Rome, and the schism's two principal branches were established. Europe divided over the schism; England, Hungary and the Holy Roman Empire followed Urban; France and her allies supported Clement. Both sides elected successors when the popes they had chosen died. The Council of Pisa (1409), called to settle the dispute, produced a third, Pisan branch of the schism, by electing antipope Alexander V (1409–10),

succeeded by John XXIII (1410–75). The schism was resolved by the Council of Constance (1414–17), which deposed two rival claimants, Benedict XIII and John XXIII, and accepted the resignation of Gregory XII, in favour of its own choice, Martin V.

The Wars of the Roses: 11, 32–3, 40, 110, 126–7

great seal

King of England's principal seal, used to authenticate important documents, such as royal charters and letters patent. It was adopted first by Edward the Confessor. The Plantagenet kings' chancellors were known as keepers of the great seal, which they had to safeguard.

Great Yarmouth

See: Yarmouth

Gregory VII, St, pope

1020?–85. Born Hildebrand; Benedictine monk; pope (1073–85). As administrator of the Patrimony of Peter under Pope Leo IX (1049–54), Hildebrand began a reform programme which culminated under Pope Nicholas II (1058–61) with the transfer of the papal election from the citizens of Rome to the college of cardinals. His pontificate brought his reforms to fruition as he tried to purge the Western Church of what he saw as its evil practices engendered by too close a dependence on lay powers. Thus he prohibited simony (the buying or selling of ecclesiastical offices) and clerical marriage, provoking strong resistance, especially in France and Germany. He also prohibited lay investiture (the right of lay rulers to choose and install archbishops and bishops), which brought him into conflict with several rulers, particularly Holy Roman Emperor Henry IV. Gregory excommunicated Henry (1076) and even deposed him (1080). When, after years of struggle, Henry seized Rome in 1084, Gregory had to be rescued by the Normans under Robert Guiscard. Despite Gregory's intransigence, his reforming ideas were to prevail in the long run and today he is considered one of the great medieval popes.

The Plantagenet Chronicles: 27

Gregory IX, pope

1143?–1241. Born Ugolino di Segni; first cardinal protector of the Franciscans; pope (1227–41). Elected pope in about his 84th year, Gregory excommunicated Holy Roman

Emperor Frederick II in 1227 for his failure to go on his promised crusade (though in fact Frederick was ill). The emperor's supporters in Rome forced Gregory into exile in 1228 until he was reconciled with Frederick and absolved him in 1230. However, by 1239 relations between the two had again deteriorated: Gregory, fearing Frederick's growing power in Italy, which threatened papal independence, renewed his excommunication and commanded the emperor's dethronement. Gregory died when Frederick was about to attack Rome.

Chronicles of the Age of Chivalry/Four Gothic Kings (US edn): 38–44, 50–2

Gregory X, pope

d.1276. Born Teobaldo Visconti. Pope (1271–6). Gregory was archdeacon of Liège and in the Holy Land when he was elected pope after a 34-month conclave. In 1273 he helped to end civil war in Germany by supporting Rudolf of Habsburg's election as Holy Roman Emperor against several other claimants. In 1274 he convoked the Second Council of Lyon, which temporarily reunited the Catholic and Orthodox churches.

Chronicles of the Age of Chivalry/Four Gothic Kings (US edn): 112

Gregory XI, pope

1330–78. Born Pierre Roger de Beaufort; French mystic and scholar; pope (1370–8). The last Avignonese pope, Gregory was admonished in 1376 by St Bridget of Sweden and St Catherine of Siena to remove the *Curia* (papal court) from Avignon to Rome. With Florence, Milan and Perugia rebelling against papal authority in Italy, Gregory sanctioned Robert of Geneva to lead an army into the peninsula to subdue the insurgents. In January 1377 Gregory returned to Rome, ending the Babylonian Captivity (so-called by its critics) of the *Curia* by France; but he failed to secure lasting peace in Italy. Gregory's bull of 1377, sent to Oxford University, condemned the teachings of John Wycliffe – the first papal act against the Wycliffite heresy.

The Wars of the Roses: 30, 32

Gregory XII, pope

c.1327–1417. Born Angelo Correr; pope of the Roman branch of the Great Schism (1406–15); cardinal bishop of Porto (1415–17). As a condition of his election, Gregory promised to work to end the schism, and to surrender his office if necessary. He opened negotiations with Benedict XIII, the Avignon antipope, but in 1407 political pressure from his supporters forced him to break off the talks. Seven of his cardinals defected and, with a group of Avignonese cardinals, convoked the Council of Pisa in 1409 in an attempt to heal the schism – which was finally resolved by the Council of Constance in 1415, when Gregory resigned, on condition that his rivals did the same. He was cardinal bishop of Porto until his death.

The Wars of the Roses: 110, 126

Grey, Richard

d.1483. Son of John Grey, 8th baron Ferrers, and Elizabeth Woodville, later Edward IV's queen. As one of Elizabeth's two sons by her first marriage, Richard was implicated with the party surrounding the queen after Edward IV's death in 1483. In that year, according to the contemporary historian, John Rous, Richard, 3rd duke of Gloucester (later Richard III), had Richard Grey imprisoned at Pontefract in York, on charges of estranging the young Edward V (Gloucester's nephew and Richard Grey's half-brother) from his uncle. Richard Grey was found guilty and – on a new charge of plotting Gloucester's death – was beheaded.

The Wars of the Roses: 235, 279, 282

Grosseteste, Robert, bishop of Lincoln

c.1175–1253. Bishop of Lincoln (1235–53); scientific writer. A man of humble birth, Grosseteste studied in Oxford and (probably) Paris, and from 1229 headed the influential Franciscan school at Oxford. He engaged in disputes with Henry III over the king's interference in ecclesiastical appointments; in 1250 he openly attacked Pope Innocent IV for taxing the Church to finance his wars with the Holy Roman Empire; and in 1253 he refused to appoint the pope's nephew Frederick de Lavagna to a Lincoln canonry.

Grosseteste's writings on optics and motion show him to have been a talented scientific observer; his pupils included Roger Bacon. He also wrote works on theology, philosophy, and poems in French. Efforts to have him canonized after his death foundered on papal opposition.

Chronicles of the Age of Chivalry/Four Gothic Kings (US edn): 36, 76–9, 87

Gruffyd ap Llywelyn

d.1244. Son of Llywelyn ap Iorwerth, prince of Wales; Welsh prince. Gruffyd rebelled against his father and in 1223 headed an army against William Marshal, 5th earl of Pembroke. In 1239 he was seized by his brother Dafydd, who handed him over to Henry III of England in 1241. In 1244 Gruffyd attempted to escape from the Tower of London but fell and died.

Chronicles of the Age of Chivalry/Four Gothic Kings (US edn): 124

Gualo, legate

*fl.*1216. Cardinal-priest of St Martin; legate representing Pope Honorius III in England (1216–18), during Henry III's minority. One of the young king's supporters, Gualo crowned him in 1216. According to the *History of William Marshal*, he was instrumental in persuading Marshal to accept the regency for the remission of his sins. On 20 September 1217 Gualo absolved Prince Louis (later Louis VIII of France) of the sin of fighting against the child-king Henry III, a papal vassal, on condition that he abandoned his claim to the English throne; and he punished clergy who had supported Louis.

Chronicles of the Age of Chivalry/Four Gothic Kings (US edn): 26, 28–30

Guelphs

German and Italian political faction in the 12th and 13th centuries, which backed the papacy against the Holy Roman Emperors and their supporters (Ghibellines). The name derived from the Welfs or Guelphs, dukes of Saxony and Bavaria, and also described the family's supporters. In Italy it was used in 13th-century Florence to describe supporters of Holy Roman Emperor Otto IV (ruled 1209–15), in their struggle for the imperial title against Holy Roman Emperor Frederick II Hohenstaufen (ruled 1220–50); but the term later embraced Frederick's papal opponents. Milan, Genoa and Florence were usually Guelph, and by the late 13th century the Florentine Guelphs had expelled the Ghibellines. They then split into Black and White Guelph factions. Dante was exiled from Florence in 1301 when the White Guelphs (his party) were defeated by the Blacks. By the 15th century the terms had been abandoned.

Chronicles of the Age of Chivalry/Four Gothic Kings (US edn): 154

Guesclin, Bertrand du

c.1320–80). Constable of France (1370–80); greatest French soldier of his time. Du Guesclin entered the service of Charles V of France in 1364 and won a brilliant victory against Charles II of Navarre the same year, at Cocherel. In 1366 Charles V charged him to lead the free mercenary companies ravaging France, which he took to the aid of Henry of Trastamara in Castile. He fought for Henry against Edward, the Black Prince, at Najera in Castile (1367), was captured there by the English but was ransomed and won Henry the throne. He was made duke of Molina in 1369 but was summoned back to France by Charles V, who appointed him constable. Du Guesclin then recovered Poitou and Saintonge from the English and chased them into Brittany (1370–4). He died on campaign against brigands in the Languedoc, having reconquered much of France from the English.

Chronicles of the Age of Chivalry/Four Gothic Kings (US edn): 228, 286, 290, 293–4
The Wars of the Roses: 49

guild

Professional, mercantile or craft association formed in order to maintain standards and support its members. Guilds formed the basis of medieval town life. Their wealth is shown by the magnificent guildhalls that adorned medieval towns, London's being a notable example.

The Wars of the Roses: 179

Gurney, Thomas

*fl.*1327. According to the chronicler Geoffrey le Baker, one of two knights (the other was John Maltravers) sent by Queen Isabella, wife of Edward II, to remove the deposed king from Henry, 9th earl of Leicester's charge and imprison him secretly; for this purpose, the knights were given authority to take any fortress, castle or town. They removed Edward from Kenilworth to Berkeley castle in 1327 and, Geoffrey relates, Gurney placed a crown of hay on Edward's head during the journey, to mock him. Gurney fled to Marseille after Edward's murder, but was recognized by a royal servant and captured three years later. Geoffrey relates that Gurney was beheaded at sea on the way back to England, to prevent his implicating others in Edward's murder.

Chronicles of the Age of Chivalry/Four Gothic Kings (US edn): 217, 221, 224

Guy of Lusignan, king of Jerusalem

d.1194. Latin king of Jerusalem (1186–92); king of Cyprus (1192–4). Guy inherited the sovereignty of Jerusalem through his wife Sibylla, sister of Baldwin IV, king of Jerusalem; he became king after a brief regency (1183–6) for Baldwin. Only a year after being crowned he was defeated and captured by Saladin at the battle of Hattin, which led to the fall of Jerusalem. Released in 1188, he besieged Acre – in an attempt to stem Saladin's advance – from 28 August 1189 until 1191, when Richard I of England and the armies of the Third Crusade helped him to reconquer the city. Guy's wife died in 1190 and in 1192, despite Richard's support, he lost his title to Jerusalem to Conrad, marquis of Montferrat. However, Richard granted him the island of Cyprus instead.

The Plantagenet Chronicles: 202, 204, 214, 218

Guyenne

See: Gascony

Gloucester *Fan vaults in the cloister of Gloucester Cathedral dating from c.1350-1400; the first ever built in England and a fine example of the Perpendicular style.*

Hainault, Philippa of

See: Philippa of Hainault

Halidon Hill

Site of a battle, near Berwick-upon-Tweed in Northumberland, in 1333, in which the forces of Edward Balliol, claimant to the throne of Scotland, defeated the army of David II, the young Scots king. Balliol's expedition was supported by Edward III of England, who provided most of the troops for the campaign.

Chronicles of the Age of Chivalry/Four Gothic Kings (US edn): 234

Hallum, Robert, bishop of Salisbury

d. 1417. Bishop of Salisbury (1407–17), Hallum was one of the English representatives at the Council of Pisa (1409), and headed the English delegation to the Council of Constance (1414). During the latter he allied with Holy Roman Emperor Sigismund I in pressing for reforms that would limit the pope's power of taxation and protect the national clergy's interests. His death, on 4 September 1417, was a serious blow to the reform party.

The Wars of the Roses: 127

Hanseatic League

Mercantile league of German towns with both economic and political powers. In 1241 Lübeck and Hamburg formed a league for mutual trade protection, which Danzig, Brunswick, Cologne and other towns in Germany, Holland and Poland soon joined. Hanseatic merchants acquired trading privileges in Russia, Scandinavia, Germany, Flanders and England; and English representatives formed a self-governing community – the Steelyard – on the north bank of the Thames. The league won a near monopoly of trade with Scandinavia in 1370, with the Treaty of Stralsund, which lasted until 1441. England and Flanders, among other countries, exempted Hanseatic merchants from customs duties, and they enjoyed other privileges; this was to stimulate trade and supply valuable raw materials. The league enjoyed trading supremacy in northern European waters until well into the 16th century.

The Plantagenet Chronicles: 237
The Wars of the Roses: 266–7, 274–5

Harclay, Andrew, 1st earl of Carlisle

d. 1323. 1st earl of Carlisle (1322–3). As sheriff of Cumberland, Harclay defeated and captured Thomas, 2nd earl of Lancaster, in 1321, at the battle of Boroughbridge in Yorkshire, and the following year executed him at Pontefract, in the same county. Edward II made Harclay earl of Carlisle for his services, but in 1323 had him executed at Carlisle for plotting with Robert Bruce, king of Scotland.

Chronicles of the Age of Chivalry/Four Gothic Kings (US edn): 204

Hardyng, John

1378–1465? Chronicler in the service first of Henry Percy, 'Hotspur', then of Sir Robert Umfreville. A north-country soldier who turned to writing, Hardyng fought at Homildon Hill (1402), and describes the fall of 'Hotspur' at the battle of Shrewsbury (1403). He was present at Henry V of England's siege of Harfleur in France and at Agincourt (1415). Between 1418 and 1422 he went to Scotland for Henry V to collect proofs of the English claim to sovereignty, returning with a sheaf of documents, most of which he had forged. Hardyng's chronicle (begun *c*. 1440) is a history of England in verse, from the time of Brutus to 1437. He presented a first version to Henry VI in 1457 and a second one, rewritten to serve the Yorkist regime, to Edward IV in 1461.

The Wars of the Roses: 12–13, 216

Harfleur

Port at the mouth of the Seine in northern France. Harfleur was captured by Henry V of England in 1415, after a six-week siege, then defended against the French by Thomas Beaufort, 2nd duke of Exeter, in 1416. Later recovered by the French, it was recaptured for Henry VI of England by Lord Talbot in 1440, before being taken by Charles VII of France in 1449; it then remained in French hands.

The Wars of the Roses: 123, 128, 130, 132, 188, 202

Harlech castle

Castle on the east coast of Wales; one of the five principal strongholds constructed by Edward I of England after 1282 to subdue Snowdonia. Built on a cliff over 200ft above the sea, with linked pairs of towers that formed a massive gatehouse, Harlech was virtually impregnable. The castle, one of the last Lancastrian strongholds, was heroically defended against the Yorkists in 1468, but eventually fell to them.

Chronicles of the Age of Chivalry/Four Gothic Kings (US edn): 108, 117, 119, 121
The Wars of the Roses: 232

Hastings, William, Lord Hastings

1430?–83. Created a peer by Edward IV (1461); lord chamberlain (1461–83). Hastings, a devoted Yorkist, helped Edward IV escape to Holland in 1470, and was prominent among the forces fighting the Lancastrian armies at Tewkesbury and Barnet in 1471. He commanded the English force in France during Edward's brief campaign there in 1475. After Edward's death in 1483, Hastings took the king's mistress, Elizabeth (Jane) Shore, for himself. On 13 June 1483 Richard, 3rd duke of Gloucester (the future Richard III) had Hastings arrested on a false charge of treason, and beheaded without trial the same day in the Tower of London. In this way he removed one of the young Edward V's most powerful protectors, and cleared his own way to the throne of England.

The Wars of the Roses: 252–5, 263, 282, 284, 286

Haye, Nicola de la

fl. 1217. Castellan of Lincoln castle. In 1217 she was besieged by French forces at Lincoln, until relieved by a small force under William Marshal.

Chronicles of the Age of Chivalry/Four Gothic Kings (US edn): 29

Héloïse

1101–64? Beautiful and learned niece of Fulbert, canon of Notre-Dame, and mistress of Peter Abelard, Fulbert hired Abelard, famed for his learning, as Héloïse's tutor (c. 1112–18), and the two became lovers. She gave birth to a son, and she and Abelard were secretly married. Fulbert was enraged, and, when Abelard took Héloïse to the convent at Argenteuil to shield her from Fulbert's ill-treatment, her uncle assumed that Abelard intended to abandon her there. His men attacked and emasculated Abelard, and Héloïse entered the Argenteuil convent as a nun. Eventually, in 1129 she became abbess of the Paraclete, an abbey founded for her by Abelard. The letters they exchanged exemplify 12th-century learning at its most sophisticated and also give a moving insight into the lovers' predicament.

The Plantagenet Chronicles: 34–5

Henry, archdeacon of Huntingdon

1084?–1155. Historian; archdeacon of Huntingdon (1109–55). Henry's *History of the English*, compiled at the request of Alexander, bishop of Lincoln, was mostly based on Bede and other sources but is original in dealing with the period 1126–54. It includes descriptions of King Stephen of England and his turbulent reign.

The Plantagenet Chronicles: 43

Henry of Blois, bishop of Winchester

d. 1171. Son of Stephen, count of Blois, younger brother of King Stephen of England; monk of Cluny; favourite of Henry I of England; abbot of Glastonbury (1126–71); bishop of Winchester (1129–71); papal legate (1139–43). In 1135 Henry helped secure the English crown for Stephen, but by 1141 had joined the Empress Matilda against his brother, who, Henry claimed, had oppressed the Church. The two soon fell out, and in 1142 Henry besieged Matilda in Winchester, sacking the city. After the accession of her son, Henry II, in 1154 he went into voluntary exile at Cluny from 1155 until about 1158, but returned to enjoy a diminished influence in English politics. Henry was a patron of the arts, buying sculpture in Rome and commissioning books such as the Winchester Bible (c. 1160–80). On his deathbed he rebuked Henry II for Becket's death.

The Plantagenet Chronicles: 45, 72–6, 85–7, 96, 104, 108, 121, 159, 179

Henry, 3rd earl of Lancaster

1281?–1345. Second son of Edmund, 1st earl of Lancaster; 3rd earl of Lancaster and 9th earl of Leicester (1324–45). Henry inherited the titles after the execution of his elder brother Thomas by Edward II. He joined Edward II's queen, Isabella of France, and Roger Mortimer when they invaded England in September 1326 and he captured Edward at Neath Abbey in Wales. He was Edward's gaoler until 1327 when the king was presumed murdered by Thomas Gurney and John Maltravers. Henry was subsequently made guardian of the young Edward III. In 1329 he began plotting against Roger Mortimer, but was discovered. Henry went blind in 1330, but was still able to help Edward III plan the successful overthrow of Mortimer that year.

Chronicles of the Age of Chivalry/Four Gothic Kings (US edn): 208, 212, 214, 216–17, 224, 232

Henry of Grosmont, 1st duke of Lancaster

1300?–61. Son of Henry, 3rd earl of Lancaster; 7th earl of Derby (1337–61); lieutenant of Aquitaine (1345–7), 4th earl of Lancaster (1347–51); knight of the Garter (1348); 11th earl of Lincoln (1349–61); 1st duke of Lancaster (1351–61). A crusader in his youth, Henry later distinguished himself at the capture of Dalkeith in Scotland (1333), at the battle of Sluys in Flanders (1340), and against the Moors at

Hanseatic League Hamburg, whose formation of a league with Lübeck in 1241 was the basis of the Hanseatic League.

Algeciras (1343). In 1345, in the early stages of the Hundred Years War, he took 2,000 troops to Gascony, where he defeated a superior French force at Auberoche and stormed Lusignan and Poitiers (1346). Edward III's most trusted counsellor, Henry was esteemed throughout Europe as a perfect knight. He fought campaigns in Normandy and Brittany in 1356–7 and in 1360 was the chief negotiator at Brétigny, where peace was concluded between Edward III and John II of France. He died of the plague at Leicester.

Chronicles of the Age of Chivalry/Four Gothic Kings (US edn): 277

Henry IV, Holy Roman Emperor

1050–1106. King of Germany (1056–1105); Holy Roman Emperor (1084–1105). During Henry's minority the papacy embarked on an increasingly ambitious programme to reform abuses in the Church and to reduce secular rulers' power in ecclesiastical affairs; this threatened the authority of the Holy Roman Emperors, who depended heavily on the Church for support and administrators. In addition, the power of the German nobles was increasing at this time. In 1075 Henry and Pope Gregory VII quarrelled over the king's attempts to restore imperial authority in Italy by appointing his own men to key bishoprics. The following year each deposed the other and Gregory excommunicated Henry. In 1077 an alliance of German nobles forced the king to seek and receive absolution; but in 1080 Gregory joined with the nobles and renewed the king's deposition and excommunication. Henry, supported by German and Italian bishops, summoned a council, which declared Gregory deposed and elected Guibert, archbishop of Ravenna, as an antipope, Clement III.

Having quelled opposition in Germany, Henry advanced into Italy in 1081 and in 1084 took Rome, where he installed Clement, who crowned him Holy Roman Emperor. He then withdrew before Gregory's Norman allies reached the city. In 1104 Henry's son (later Holy Roman Emperor Henry V) rebelled against his father, imprisoned him and the following year forced him to abdicate.

Henry V, Holy Roman Emperor

1081–1125. Son of Holy Roman Emperor Henry IV; king of Germany (1106–25); Holy Roman Emperor (1111–25). In 1110 Henry entered Italy with his army, to be crowned Holy Roman Emperor and to settle long-running disputes with Pope Paschal II over lay investiture of bishops. But agreement proved impossible, and in 1112 Henry (still uncrowned as Holy Roman Emperor) took pope and cardinals prisoner. Paschal crowned him the same year and conceded his right to investiture, but, once Henry had left Italy, repudiated the right. In 1118 Henry elected an antipope, Gregory VIII, in opposition to Paschal's successor, Gelasius II, but in 1122, by the Concordat of Worms, the matter was finally resolved by Henry and Pope Calixtus II, who succeeded Gelasius: imperial envoys were to be present at episcopal elections, but the Holy Roman Emperor could no longer invest bishops with ring and staff.

From 1114 to 1121 rebellions in Saxony gave Henry constant trouble. In 1114 he married Matilda, daughter of Henry I of England, when she was 12; the union was childless.

The Plantagenet Chronicles: 46–7, 57, 102, 225, 232

Henry VI Hohenstaufen, Holy Roman Emperor

1165–97. Son of Holy Roman Emperor Frederick I, Barbarossa; king of Germany (1169–97); king of Italy (1186–97); Holy Roman Emperor (1191–7); king of Sicily (1194–7). In about 1186 Henry ravaged central Italy, forcing it to submit to imperial rule. In 1192 he took custody of Richard I of England, captured on his way home from the Third Crusade, releasing him, in 1194, only in return for a 100,000 mark ransom and an oath of fealty. In 1194 Henry assaulted and conquered Sicily, which Tancred, illegitimate son of Roger II of Sicily, had held since 1191, but to which Henry's wife Constance was the rightful heir. He died in 1197, having failed to secure his son, the future Holy Roman Emperor Frederick II, as his undisputed successor.

The Plantagenet Chronicles: 167, 224–5, 232, 236
Chronicles of the Age of Chivalry/Four Gothic Kings (US edn): 42

Henry I, king of England

1068–1135. Youngest son of William the Conqueror; king of England (1100–35), William bequeathed Henry no lands, but left him a substantial sum of money. During the reign of his brother William II, Rufus (1087–1100), Henry supported Rufus against Robert Curthose, duke of Normandy, their eldest brother. William Rufus died in 1100, while Robert was on crusade, and Henry took

advantage of the latter's absence to seize the treasury at Winchester and have himself elected and crowned king. At his coronation he issued a charter promising just rule. In 1100 his marriage to Matilda of Scotland, descended from the old English kings, won him English support.

In 1101 Robert invaded England, but renounced his claim to the throne in return for a pension and Henry's Norman lands. However, in 1105, Henry invaded Normandy and the following year defeated Robert Curthose and consequently secured the duchy. Robert was imprisoned, and died in captivity in 1134. Henry married his daughter Matilda to Henry V, Holy Roman Emperor, and after his death in 1128, to Geoffrey of Anjou; their eldest son was the future Henry II of England.

Henry I is remembered for his development of the English judicial system and for laying the foundations of the royal administration.

The Plantagenet Chronicles: 36–8, 40, 46–8, 60, 63–5, 69–70, 74–5, 154, 173

Henry II, king of England

1133–89. Son of Geoffrey Plantagenet, count of Anjou, and the Empress Matilda; count of Anjou (1151–89), duke of Normandy (1150–89) and Aquitaine (1152–89), king of England (1154–89). In 1153 he was recognized by Stephen, king of England, as his heir and the next year succeeded him as king. Henry had already inherited Normandy, Anjou and Maine from his parents, and in 1152 on his marriage to Eleanor, duchess of Aquitaine, added her duchy to his domain. Eleanor bore Henry five sons (William, Henry, Richard, Geoffrey and John) and three daughters (Matilda, Eleanor and Joan), all born between 1153 and 1167. However, she also fomented plots against him with her sons, aiding Henry, Richard and Geoffrey's revolt of 1173. From 1174 to 1185 Henry kept her under house arrest in Winchester and Salisbury.

The sheer size of his dominions (comprising most of France west of Rouen, plus much of the central eastern regions) gave Henry power and prestige in France – where he overshadowed his overlord, Louis VII of France – and in Europe, where he aided Pope Alexander III against the Holy Roman Emperor Frederick I (d.1190). But to defend and rule his lands he had to be constantly on the move, and one contemporary described him as a human chariot which drew all behind him.

Henry's abilities as a warrior and an administrator earned him widespread respect. In England, he created a sophisticated administrative and financial organization,

revitalizing the English Exchequer by 1158 and enforcing the superiority of the royal court (*curia regis*) over the private courts of feudal lords. He gradually changed and clarified the common law, and in 1170 dismissed incompetent sheriffs, the king's representatives at county level.

However, in 1164, Henry had attempted to subordinate Church courts to his royal courts by the Constitutions of Clarendon, and, as a result, fell into conflict with Thomas Becket, archbishop of Canterbury, formerly Henry's chancellor and close companion, who fled to France that same year after rousing the king's anger. Becket returned in 1170, having made peace with Henry, but excommunicated Henry's loyal supporter, Roger, archbishop of York, for his part in crowning Henry the Young King earlier that year. Henry, who was in Normandy, was enraged by the news and four of his knights went to Canterbury and slew Becket, although not acting on the king's direct orders. Henry was absolved of the murder by Pope Alexander III's legates in 1172, and in 1174 submitted to a penitential flogging at Becket's tomb.

In 1173 Henry's three eldest surviving sons, Henry the Young King, Richard and Geoffrey, rebelled against him. The foremost rebel, encouraged by his mother Queen Eleanor, was Henry the Young King. The principal reason for rebellion was Henry's will of 1169, which had divided his lands between his sons. The Young King was to have Normandy, England and Anjou; Geoffrey was to hold the duchy of Brittany as his vassal; and Richard was to have the duchy of Aquitaine. John, the youngest, received nothing in the will, but his father's later decision to give him the castles of Chinon, Loudon and Mirebeau in Anjou provoked the Young King's opposition in 1173. Many nobles in England and France joined the revolt, and the three brothers fled to join forces with Louis VII of France. The rebellion failed, and Louis, anxious to end the costly campaign, arranged a settlement (11 October 1174). Henry the Young King remained hostile to his father until his death from fever in 1183. Geoffrey also died suddenly in 1186, while conspiring against his father with Philip II of France, who had succeeded Louis in 1180.

The conflict was continued by Richard, who in 1188 allied with Philip II of France. Together they attacked Henry in 1189, forcing him to abandon his camp at Le Mans, and imposed a humiliating peace on him after seizing his city of Tours. The final blow came when Henry learned that John, his youngest son, had joined them. He retired to Chinon where he died on 6 July 1189 – it was said of grief. He was buried in the Plantagenet mausoleum at the abbey of Fontevrault.

The Plantagenet Chronicles: 52, 60, 74, 78, 80–8, 90–193, 253, 257, 294
Chronicles of the Age of Chivalry/Four Gothic Kings (US edn): 81, 90

Henry III, king of England

1207–72. Son of King John of England and Isabella of Angoulême; king of England (1216–72). Henry III was nine years old when he was crowned at Gloucester in 1216. A French army was rampaging over England, led by Prince Louis (later Louis VIII), who, in alliance with a powerful faction of English barons alienated by King John, seemed poised to seize power. However, the barons' hostility towards John was not transferred to his heir, and in 1217 William Marshal, the English regent, with the help of Gualo the papal legate, negotiated peace with Louis. Henry was crowned again at Westminster in 1220.

Henry was declared of age in 1227 but remained under the influence of advisers who succeeded William on the latter's death in 1219, until 1234, when his personal rule began. In 1236 he married Eleanor of Provence, who gave him two sons and four daughters. The Savoyard followers she brought with her won a reputation for greed and extravagance and strengthened English prejudices against foreigners.

Henry was noted for his piety; he gave alms generously, in the 1240s feeding 500 paupers every day. From 1245 he spent enormous sums rebuilding Westminster Abbey, in honour of Edward the Confessor, his patron saint, after whom his heir, the future Edward I, was named. He mounted an unsuccessful campaign to regain Poitou in 1242, which he claimed as his hereditary possession, but Louis IX of France's army forced him to retreat to Gascony. In 1248 he sent his brother-in-law Simon de Montfort, 6th earl of Leicester, to restore England's authority over Gascony's warring barons, but recalled him later to answer charges of maladministration. Prince Edward replaced Simon, but the region continued to be restive, and in 1259, by the Treaty of Paris, Henry accepted that he held Gascony as a fief of the French crown. He also agreed to abandon his claims to Normandy, Maine, Touraine, Anjou and Poitou.

In England, Henry's political ineptitude provoked widespread hostility, and in 1258 a group of barons under the leadership of Simon de Montfort forced him to accept the Provisions of Oxford, an ambitious and wide-ranging programme of reform. For a while, a council of 15 imposed their will on the king, who was denied control of the royal treasury and chancery; but their ranks gradually became disunited, since many feared the Provisions gave too much scope for Simon de Montfort's ambition.

In 1261 Henry regained power, the greatest political triumph of his reign, and obtained a papal bull absolving him from adhering to the Provisions. The barons refused to accept this decision, and those who had assented to the Provisions erupted in revolt (1263). Simon de Montfort marched to London and resumed control of the government, and Henry asked Louis IX to arbitrate. The French king's decision, the Mise of Amiens (1264), declared the Provisions void, and Simon's party renewed the war. This struggle led to Henry's capture at the battle of Lewes (1264), after which Simon compelled the king to call a parliament (1265) to approve the barons' reforms, summoning commoners to Parliament for the first time to broaden his base of support.

Simon's arrogance had alienated many barons, especially Gilbert of Clare, 6th earl of Gloucester, who joined Prince Edward in the Welsh marches and gathered an army to free the king. They fell on Simon's party at Evesham on 4 August 1265. Henry escaped from Simon during the battle, and was wounded fighting on his son's side; Simon himself died in the battle. Henry revoked the recent reforms, and by 1267 had overcome residual baronial opposition.

Henry was accounted 'simple' by his people, that is, weak and foolish, yet his reign defined the position of the English monarchy until the end of the 15th century – kingship limited by law. His fine work at Westminster Abbey was well advanced by 1269, when Edward the Confessor's body was moved to a new and magnificent shrine. When Henry died in 1272 he was buried in the saint's vacant tomb.

The Plantagenet Chronicles: 288, 292, 323
Chronicles of the Age of Chivalry/Four Gothic Kings (US edn): 7, 13–14, 22–105, 110, 214
The Wars of the Roses: 72

Henry IV, king of England

1367–1413. Son of John of Gaunt (fourth son of Edward III) and Blanche of Lancaster; knight of the Garter (1377), 9th earl of Derby (1377–99), 12th earl of Hereford (1384–97), 1st duke of Hereford (1397–9), king of England (1399–1413). Henry was born at Bolingbroke in Lincolnshire. Styled earl of Derby by 1377, in 1380 he married Mary Bohun, a co-heiress of the great earldom of Hereford. He was one of the five lords appellant who, in the Merciless Parliament of 1388, forced Richard II to dismiss the favourites associated with his tyrannical rule. Adventurous and enterprising, he joined the Teutonic Knights fighting in Lithuania in 1390, and also went to Prussia, Cyprus and on pilgrimage to Jerusalem (1392–3) – before returning to the political turmoil of Richard II's court. To his renown as a fighting man, he added a reputation for generosity, elegance and well-developed literary and musical tastes.

Henry III The king's effigy in Westminster Abbey, where he was buried in 1272 in the vacant tomb of St Edward the Confessor, his much venerated patron.

Henry regained Richard's favour after his return, and was created duke of Hereford in 1397. In 1398 he quarrelled with one of the other former lords appellant, Thomas Mowbray, 1st duke of Norfolk, and attempted to fight a duel with him. Richard, increasingly suspicious of Henry, banished him for ten years.

In 1399, when John of Gaunt died and Richard II confiscated his vast Lancastrian estates, the exiled Henry, as Gaunt's heir, found himself at the head of Richard's growing band of enemies, who had suffered similar wrongs. In June 1399, while the king was campaigning in Ireland, Henry invaded England. Richard abdicated on his return in August and was imprisoned at Pontefract castle in Yorkshire, where he died in 1400, presumed murdered, leaving no heirs as rivals to the new royal house of Lancaster.

Henry found it easier to gain than to retain his throne. For nearly a decade he fought to keep it – against Richard II's supporters in 1400; against the Welsh under Owen Glendower, from 1400 to 1408; against the powerful Percy family, from 1403 to 1408; and even against Richard Scrope, archbishop of York, who proclaimed his opposition in 1405.

The execution of the archbishop (1405) was a major political blunder by Henry. The king fell prey after 1408 to a mysterious disease, perhaps leprosy. Many of his subjects believed this was God's vengeance upon the king for such a misdeed.

Henry married Joan, regent of Brittany, in 1402 (Mary had died in 1394), but she bore him no children and the succession fell to Henry, prince of Wales, the eldest of his four sons by Mary. Henry relied increasingly on him to crush his rivals, and by 1410 Prince Henry effectively ruled in his ailing father's place. In 1411 the king, perhaps fearing an impending coup, briefly resumed power, but in 1413 he took to his sickbed once more, and died at Westminster. A later chronicler recounts that the king expected to die in Jerusalem in fulfilment of a prophecy, but instead ended his days in the Jerusalem chamber in Westminster Abbey. He was buried at Canterbury Cathedral, and despite the problems of his reign, left his son an undisputed succession.

The Wars of the Roses: 10, 47, 54, 57, 61, 82–9, 91–117, 119

Henry V, king of England

1387–1422. Eldest son of Henry IV of England and Mary Bohun; prince of Wales (1400–13), warden of the Cinque Ports and constable of Dover (1409), king of England (1413–22). From the time of his father's accession in 1399, Henry was drawn into English politics. Wales was governed in his name from 1400, when he was only 13 years old, and three years later he fought Owen Glendower and the Percys in the principality. He was wounded at Shrewsbury in 1403 while helping to crush the Percy family's revolt against his father.

Henry's successes on the battlefield were matched by those in the king's council; as Henry IV was progressively weakened by illness after 1408, the young prince took an even greater share in government, and ruled England on his father's behalf from 1410 to 1411, sending an expedition to France to support the house of Burgundy in its feud with the house of Orléans. Henry IV reversed that alignment after 1411, during his temporary recovery from illness, switching English support from the Burgundians to the Orleanists. Although Henry withdrew from the king's council in 1412, his disagreements with his father seem to have been political rather than personal and on the king's death in 1413 Henry won wide acceptance from the English nobility.

Henry V was an imposing and charismatic king. Described by one contemporary as tall, clean shaven, sinewy and agile, he was also said to be more clerical than military in appearance. Well educated (he was patron of the poets Lydgate and Hoccleve) and pious, he revivified the royal administration, scrupulously managing his household finances, and took considerable interest in ecclesiastical affairs, supporting a statute against the Lollard heretics in 1414 and reforming the Benedictine monasteries in 1420. Above all, he strove to fulfil what he saw as his God-given destiny, the conquest of France and the uniting of Europe in a great crusade to the Holy Land.

Having crushed a major Lollard rising in 1413–14 and a plot by nobles loyal to the memory of Richard II to assassinate him, Henry embarked on his first great expedition to France in August 1415. He had proposed to marry Catherine of Valois, daughter of Charles VI of France, and demanded the old Plantagenet lands of Anjou and Normandy as her dowry, together with lands yielded to France at the Treaty of Brétigny (1360). Charles refused these proposals, and Henry declared war. He took Harfleur in September, offering the dauphin Charles (later Charles VII) single combat, then led his depleted force on a march to Calais, pursued by the French. On 24 October he won a great victory at Agincourt, fighting in the thick of the battle. His English subjects celebrated with great rejoicing. He returned to England in November, and made a triumphal entry into London.

In 1416 Henry allied with the emperor-elect Sigismund, king of Germany, and the house of Burgundy, preparatory to another French campaign. War was renewed in 1417, and Henry, profiting from divisions between the Burgundian and Armagnac (Orleanist) camps, had by 1419 reached Paris. He had captured Normandy, and much of Picardy and the Ile-de-France, starving out the city of Rouen by a long siege (1418–19).

In May 1420, by the Treaty of Troyes, Henry was adopted as heir to Charles VI of France, and betrothed to his daughter Catherine. Their marriage took place at Troyes Cathedral in June 1420, and on 6 December 1421 their first and only son, the future Henry VI, was born at Windsor. In 1421 Henry returned to France to reassert his authority, but in 1422, while besieging the dauphin's forces at Meaux, the key to Champagne, he contracted dysentery, and died in the Bois de Vincennes. The French asked for his body to be buried at St-Denis, but instead it was taken to Westminster Abbey, where his shield, helmet and saddle were hung above it in memory of his martial achievements. His chantry tomb was erected as close as possible to the shrine of St Edward the Confessor, the abbey's patron.

The Wars of the Roses: 10, 69, 91, 101, 112, 114, 116–17, 119–61, 163, 167, 169

Henry VI, king of England

1421–71. Only son of Henry V of England and Catherine of Valois; king of England (1422–61, 1470–1). Henry VI came into a glittering inheritance when still an infant. Born in 1421, he became king of both England and France in 1422, aged nine months. Authority in his two realms was vested in his uncles, John, 2nd duke of Bedford, who was protector in France, and Humphrey of Lancaster, 2nd duke of Gloucester, who ruled with a council in England. The young king was from 1428 put in the hands of the cultivated Richard Beauchamp, 13th earl of Warwick, who oversaw his education.

Crowned at Westminster in 1429 and in Paris in 1432, Henry VI was an attractive, intelligent child who could recite the religious services at the age of six. His strong piety, which made him avoid women before his marriage to Margaret of Anjou, daughter of René, duke of Anjou, in 1445, was a conventional kingly

---

Henry II *The abbey of Fontevrault (opposite), last resting place of Henry II after his death in 1189.*

quality, as was his role as a patron of learning and the arts: he founded King's College, Cambridge, and Eton College in 1440. Otherwise, however, Henry cut a poor figure as a king. As he grew to manhood, signs of cowardice, weakness and naïvety became apparent. He detested the battlefield, and was the first English sovereign never to take the field against a foreign foe. From the late 1430s, when he began to take a role in government, officially assuming royal powers in 1437, he showed himself weak, vacillating and easily influenced. In 1448 he surrendered the English fief of Maine to Charles VII of France, an unpopular decision prompted by his wife. In 1453 he fell victim to his first attack of madness – an unhappy legacy inherited from his grandfather Charles VI of France.

Henry VI *Henry's effigy in King's College, Cambridge, which he founded in 1440.*

In the 1420s the English had continued to make gains in France, but the turning-point came in 1429 when the dauphin Charles, with the help of Joan of Arc, raised the siege of Orléans, and was crowned Charles VII at Reims. Henry favoured peace with France, and was encouraged in this by his wife and Henry Beaufort, bishop of Winchester (d.1447), his influential counsellor. The English gradually lost ground in France, as the French captured Brittany in 1449, Normandy in 1450, and the

historic English possession of Gascony in 1453. By that time all England's former French territories save Calais had been lost. The queen's lack of political judgement produced dissension at court and further weakened royal authority; her faction at court controlled Henry and was linked with the débâcle in France. Jack Cade's revolt of 1450 demonstrated public anger at the regime's failure.

In 1453 Richard, 3rd duke of York, England's most powerful noble, was temporarily made protector of the realm while the king was insane, but on Henry's recovery on Christmas Day 1454 was excluded from power by the queen and her ally Edmund Beaufort, 2nd duke of Somerset. Richard and his supporters, the Yorkists, took to arms, and won the first battle of St Albans on 22 May 1455, the first engagement in the Wars of the Roses. Somerset was killed and Henry, slightly wounded during the battle, renewed Richard's protectorship. He later founded a chantry chapel for those slain at St Albans.

After 1455 Margaret gradually rebuilt her faction, persuading Henry to dismiss Richard from office in 1456, and moved the seat of government to the West Midlands, where loyalty to Henry's Lancastrian line was strongest. In 1459 war broke out again. Henry was captured at the battle of Northampton in July 1460, and forced to acknowledge Richard as his heir, displacing his own son Prince Edward (b.1453). However, Richard was slain at the battle of Wakefield in December 1460, and in February 1461 Henry escaped from the field of the second battle of St Albans to rejoin his wife and the Lancastrian forces. The war ended in the defeat of the Lancastrian forces at Towton in March 1461. Edward, 4th duke of York, Richard's son, became king as Edward IV and Henry and Margaret of Anjou were driven into exile in Scotland.

In 1465 Henry was captured in northern England and imprisoned in the Tower of London, from whence he was brought out and restored to power in 1470–1. Edward IV, as king, had alienated many of his supporters by favouring the family of his queen, Elizabeth Woodville, and in September 1470 Richard Neville, 16th earl of Warwick, once Edward's ally but now aiding Margaret, landed at Plymouth and proclaimed Henry king. Henry was released in October 1470, by Richard Neville, but after Edward IV's final victory at the battle of Tewkesbury on 20 May 1471, the last Lancastrian king was returned to the Tower where he was put to death on 21 May. His only son, Edward, prince of Wales, had died at Tewkesbury.

Henry was buried in Chertsey Abbey, where his tomb was venerated as that of a martyred saint, working its first miracle in 1481. Richard III, anxious to legitimize his own regime, had Henry reburied at St George's Chapel, Windsor, in 1484. Henry VII later attempted, unsuccessfully, to have him canonized.

The Wars of the Roses: 151, 157, 163–225, 230, 232, 236, 238, 248, 252–60, 263–4

Henry VII, Henry Tudor, king of England

1457–1509. Son of Edmund Tudor, 13th earl of Richmond, and Margaret Beaufort; 14th earl of Richmond (1456–62); king of England (1485–1509). In 1471, when Henry VI's death made him a leader of the Lancastrian party, Henry Tudor fled to Brittany. After Edward IV's death in 1483 and the disappearance of his young heirs in the Tower of London, Henry emerged as principal rival to the usurper Richard III, on the basis of his mother's Beaufort descent from John of Gaunt. After a Lancastrian uprising in 1483 had failed, he went to France, buying Yorkist support by vowing to wed Elizabeth of York. The following year Charles VIII of France promised help, and on 7 August 1485 Henry landed at Milford Haven in Wales with an Anglo-French force. On his march towards Richard III at Nottingham, he was joined by other Lancastrian and Yorkist rebels. On 22 August the two forces met at Bosworth, where Richard was slain. Henry went on to be crowned in London on 30 October 1485, England's first Tudor monarch.

Chronicles of the Age of Chivalry/Four Gothic Kings (US edn): 301
The Wars of the Roses: 225, 286–7, 293, 296–7, 302–5

Henry, 'the Lion', duke of Saxony and Bavaria

1129–95. Son of Henry the Proud; duke of Saxony (1142–80); duke of Bavaria (1156–80). In 1147 Henry went on crusade against the pagan Wends in the Elbe region of Germany. The duchy of Bavaria was granted to him on the accession of Holy Roman Emperor Frederick I Barbarossa. In 1168 he married Matilda, daughter of Henry II of England. His power in Germany was considerable, as was his reputation throughout Western Europe and Frederick began to see him as a dangerous rival. In 1176 Henry refused to join Frederick's campaign to secure his power in Italy, and in 1178–9 the emperor used Henry's tardiness in returning lands he had seized from the bishop of Halberstadt as a pretext to move against him.

Henry's lands were confiscated by force in 1180, and he was banished to Henry II's court in England (1182–5). In 1189 he attempted to reoccupy Saxony, while Frederick was on the Third Crusade, but failed. He made peace with Holy Roman Emperor Henry VI Hohenstaufen in 1190, but rebelled again in 1193, again unsuccessfully. His last years were spent at Brunswick, in Germany, in intellectual and artistic pursuits.

The Plantagenet Chronicles: 113, 167–8, 172, 176, 225

Henry, the Navigator, prince of Portugal

1394–1460. Son of John I of Portugal. Henry was created duke of Viseu by his father in 1415 because he showed great valour in the conquest of Ceuta in North Africa. In 1416 he established a base for exploration at Sagres in south-west Portugal, and sponsored several voyages, including that which discovered Madeira (1418–20); in this way he gradually mapped the West African coast. Between 1444 and 1446 30–40 vessels left for Africa under Henry's authority, mainly on voyages of exploration but also in search of slaves and gold. In 1455 Henry forbade the kidnapping of Negroes. By 1460 his explorers had reached Sierra Leone. He led a disastrous military expedition to Tangier in 1437, but recovered his prestige with a successful Moroccan campaign in 1458.

The Wars of the Roses: 257

Henry de Reynes

*fl.*1245. First architect of the 13th-century rebuilding of Westminster Abbey. He was employed by Henry III in 1245 to reconstruct the abbey as a shrine to St Edward the Confessor. It is not known whether he was English or French, but he undoubtedly worked at Reims Cathedral and he built Westminster with high vaults and flying buttresses in the French style.

Chronicles of the Age of Chivalry/Four Gothic Kings (US edn): 101

Henry of Trastamara, king of Castile

1333?–79. Illegitimate son of Alfonso XI of Castile; king of Castile and León (1369–79). In 1366 Henry ousted his brother Peter I, the Cruel, as king of Castile, with the aid of Bertrand du Guesclin's army of mercenaries, the Great Company, and Peter IV of Aragon. Peter

the Cruel won England's help, and Edward, the Black Prince, went to his aid; at Najera, on 3 April 1367, he defeated Henry, who in his turn lost the throne to Peter. However, in 1369, after the Black Prince's departure, he defeated and killed his brother at Montiel and became king again. John of Gaunt (Peter's son-in-law) and Ferdinand I of Portugal tried unsuccessfully to contest Henry's title as king. He bought the loyalty of the Castilian nobility, with large grants of land, and was hence known as the Generous.

Chronicles of the Age of Chivalry/Four Gothic Kings (US edn): 228, 286, 290–3

Henry, the Young King

1155–83. Second and eldest surviving son of Henry II of England and Eleanor of Aquitaine. In 1160 he married Margaret, daughter of Louis VII of France, and was educated by Thomas Becket. Henry II had arranged in 1169 that the Young King was to be his heir to England, Normandy and Anjou, and in 1170 he had him crowned king of England. In 1173 the Young King, encouraged by Eleanor, rebelled against his father and fled to Louis VII of France with his brothers Richard and Geoffrey. They gave as their reason Henry II's reluctance to let his sons enjoy their lands, and his plan to give his son John the important castles of Chinon, Loudon and Mirebeau. The rebellion failed; the following year the Young King and his father were reconciled. In 1182 he made war on his brother Richard of Aquitaine, and later on his father again. He died suddenly of fever at Martel in France. He had asked to be buried at Rouen, but as his cortege passed through Le Mans, the citizens seized his body and buried it in their cathedral. The people of Rouen threatened to raze Le Mans to the ground, and Henry II was forced to intervene in favour of the city his son had chosen.

The Plantagenet Chronicles: 93, 97, 101–2, 108, 112, 116, 118–19, 122, 124–5, 127–8, 133–4, 136, 140, 142, 152, 154, 164–6, 168–73

heraldry

Systematic use of hereditary devices, introduced into England by the Normans. Among the earliest known hereditary blazons are the lions (*c.*1127) of Geoffrey the Fair, count of Anjou in France, founder of the Plantagenet dynasty. By the late 13th century heraldry had its own Norman French terminology and specialist expositors, the heralds. Coats of arms were indispensable for identification in battle or in a

tournament and also symbolized the bearer's prestige. When a mob rioted against John of Gaunt in London in 1377, they hung his arms upside down in the streets to insult him. Henry V forbade the private assumption of arms, and in 1483 Richard III established the Royal College of Heralds to regulate and govern English heraldry.

Chronicles of the Age of Chivalry/Four Gothic Kings (US edn): 278–9

herbal remedies

The use of herbs and plants in medieval medicine derived from folk tradition and from the *De Materia Medica* of the 1st-century Greek, Dioscorides. His work, adapted by the 12th-century German nun Hildegard of Bingen and others, provided a wealth of recipes. Some herbs, such as feverfew, a cure for headaches, had demonstrable powers; others, such as the mandrake, with its man-shaped root, had a mystical significance. The herbal (a book listing the properties of plants) was a popular type of medieval book.

The Plantagenet Chronicles: 285–6
The Wars of the Roses: 66–7

Herbert, Sir William, 18th earl of Pembroke

1423?–69. Privy councillor to Edward IV; created Baron Herbert (1461); chief justice of South Wales (1461) and North Wales (1467); knight of the Garter (1462); 18th earl of Pembroke (1468–9). William was captured by the French at Formigny in 1450, in one of the last battles of the Hundred Years War. In the Wars of the Roses he took the Yorkist side, and in reward Edward IV gave him his judicial post in North Wales and made him earl of Pembroke. From 1461 to 1469 he had custody of Henry Tudor (later Henry VII), who had been captured in 1461, aged four. In 1469 William took a Welsh force to oppose the Lancastrian invading force led by Richard Neville, 16th earl of Warwick, 'the Kingmaker', and George, 3rd duke of Clarence, but was defeated in Yorkshire at the battle of Edgecote, and executed by Neville, as an act of revenge, on 26 July 1469.

The Wars of the Roses: 232, 244, 255, 297

heresy

A theological doctrine or opinion held in opposition to the orthodox doctrine of the Christian Church. Notable medieval examples were the Albigensian heresy, as followed by the Cathars in southern France, and the teachings of John Wycliffe, embraced by the Lollards. In France, in the mid-13th century, the Inquisition was established to combat heresy, and it later extended to Germany, Italy and Spain. In England, heresy was rare until the late 14th century, but after the emergence of Lollardy the secular authorities took action. The statute *De heretico comburendo*, passed in 1401, made heresy punishable by burning.

The Wars of the Roses: 11, 31, 112–13, 156, 247

Heretico Comburendo, De

See: De Heretico Comburendo

hermit

Christian ascetic living in solitude, usually in the countryside. The Carthusians were an order of hermits living as a community. A renowned hermit, Pietro del Morrone, was elected Pope Celestine V, in 1294.

High Gothic style

In architecture, fully developed form of the Gothic style, arising out of the design of Chartres Cathedral (begun *c*.1194) and typified by other great French cathedrals, such as Bourges, Beauvais and Reims.

Chronicles of the Age of Chivalry/Four Gothic Kings (US edn): 286–9

Hoccleve, Thomas

1370?–1437. Poet and clerk in the privy seal office. An imitator of Chaucer, Hoccleve wrote lyrics to the Virgin, ballads to patrons and moral tales. Henry IV granted him an annuity. His principal works were *De Regimine Principum* (*c*.1411–12), an English treatise for the future Henry V on the rule of princes; *Mother of God*; and the autobiographical *La Male Regle*.

The Wars of the Roses: 71, 123

Hohenstaufen, Manfred of

See: Manfred of Hohenstaufen

Holand, John, 1st duke of Exeter

1352?–1400. Son of Thomas Holand and Joan, the Fair Maid of Kent; half-brother of Richard II; knight of the Garter (1381); 12th earl of Huntingdon (1388–1400); chamberlain of

England (1389); 1st duke of Exeter (1397–99). John Holand married Elizabeth, daughter of John of Gaunt, and was part of the royal entourage until 1384, when he fell out of favour for his violent murder of Ralph Stafford. He distinguished himself as a soldier under John of Gaunt in Spain in 1386. Richard II made him duke of Exeter in return for his support against the lords appellant, Thomas of Woodstock, 1st duke of Gloucester, and Richard Fitzalan, 9th earl of Arundel. In 1399 he accompanied Richard to Ireland.

In the first parliament of Henry IV's reign (1399), John lost his dukedom and was demoted to earl of Huntingdon. He joined a conspiracy to restore Richard II, but was captured at Pleshey and beheaded there on 15 January 1400, at the spot where three years earlier Richard had arrested Gloucester.

The Wars of the Roses: 94–6

Holand, John, 3rd duke of Exeter

1395–1447. Second son of John Holand, 1st duke of Exeter; 13th earl of Huntingdon (1416–47); knight of the Garter (1416); admiral of England (1435); governor of Aquitaine (1439); (restored) duke of Exeter (1443–7). An important figure in the later stages of the Hundred Years War, John Holand fought for Henry V with distinction in France: at Agincourt in 1415 and in command of a fleet against the Genoese off Harfleur in 1417. He took part in the sieges of Caen and Rouen, distinguished himself again at Pontoise (1419) and won a victory at Fresney (1420). He was captured by the dauphinists in 1421, and ransomed in 1425. He represented England at the conference at Arras in 1435, which reconciled Charles VII of France and Philip the Good, duke of Burgundy, and commanded an expedition to relieve Guisnes in 1438.

The Wars of the Roses: 188

Holand, Sir Thomas

d.1360. 6th earl of Kent (1360); one of the first knights of the Garter (1344). Thomas became earl of Kent through his wife, Joan, the Fair Maid of Kent, 5th holder of the title, daughter of Edmund of Woodstock, 3rd earl of Kent. He fought against the French at Sluys (1340).

The Wars of the Roses: 22

Holderness, Robin of

See: Robin of Holderness

Holy Land

Western Palestine, especially Judaea; the historic land of the Bible, centred on Jerusalem. From 640 Palestine was ruled by Islamic Arabs, and its liberation from Muslim control was the goal of the First Crusade (1096–9). The success of this brought into being the Latin kingdom of Jerusalem and other crusader states. The Muslims gradually regained Palestine and in 1291 Acre, the last Christian stronghold, fell, ending the crusader presence. Even so, the liberation of Jerusalem remained a Christian aim as late as the 17th century.

Chronicles of the Age of Chivalry/Four Gothic Kings (US edn): 69

Holy Roman Empire

Political entity that originated in 962 when Pope John XII invited Otto I, king of Germany, to renew the empire founded in 800 by Charlemagne, king of the Franks, who had revived the notion of empire in the West. This Carolingian state was itself a restoration of the western Roman Empire which had collapsed in the 5th century. Henceforth the king of Germany was also deemed to be the king of the Romans, holding land in both Germany and Italy. He was elected by the German princes, and could not assume the title of Holy Roman Emperor until crowned by the pope, whose advocate or secular representative he was. His dominions theoretically included Germany, northern Italy, Austria, Bohemia, Belgium and Burgundy, but in practice imperial authority over the Italian city-states was limited, and the German princes jealously guarded their autonomy.

In the late 11th century the papacy tried to free itself from secular tutelage and began a series of damaging disputes with its emperors. Holy Roman Emperor Henry IV (d.1106) precipitated the feud in 1075 by investing a new archbishop of Milan without Pope Gregory VII's assent. The emperors were dazzled by the prospect of ruling Italy as well as Germany, and in the 12th and 13th centuries the Hohenstaufen dynasty – in particular Frederick I and Frederick II – pursued the chimera of power south of the Alps to the detriment of their own authority and the ruination of the finances of their German kingdom. The attempts of Holy Roman Emperor Frederick I to subjugate the Italian cities, which, with papal backing, formed the Lombard League and defeated him at Legnano in 1176, typified the pattern.

Germany increasingly fell under the power of its princes, who by 1250 were firmly established as a college of electors for their king. Conradin, duke of Swabia, the last legitimate Hohenstaufen, was killed by Charles of Anjou in 1268, and in 1273 Rudolf I, the first Habsburg, was established on the German throne. Although they had no strong interests in Italy, and no particular connections with the papacy, the Habsburgs and their successors as kings of Germany continued to use the title of Holy Roman Emperor – in practical terms largely an empty gesture.

Some later medieval emperors were conscious of the significance of their title, and even tried to revive its powers: Sigismund III (Holy Roman Emperor 1433–7) called the Council of Constance to heal the Great Schism in 1414 and travelled round Europe attempting to make peace between its rulers. However, his efforts foundered in the face of hostility from Europe's kings and princes. The Holy Roman Empire was finally destroyed by Napoleon in 1806.

The Plantagenet Chronicles: 167
Chronicles of the Age of Chivalry/Four Gothic Kings (US edn): 237
The Wars of the Roses: 142–3, 164

Homildon Hill, battle of

Battle fought in Northumberland in 1402, in which a Scots invasion force led by Archibald, 4th earl of Douglas, was defeated by troops led by Henry Percy, 9th earl of Northumberland, and his son Henry, 'Hotspur'. The chronicler Walsingham described how the Percys cut off the Scots' retreat, forcing them to battle, and showered them with arrows; the victory was won by archery alone.

The Wars of the Roses: 60, 100–1

Honnecourt, Villard de

*fl.*1220s. French connoisseur whose sketchbook records buildings, sculpture, paintings and mosaics seen during his extensive wanderings across Europe. His slightly amateurish drawings and catholic interests suggest the leisured dilettante, but his sections and elevations of the choir of Reims Cathedral are the earliest known European architectural drawings.

Chronicles of the Age of Chivalry/Four Gothic Kings (US edn): 84, 286, 289

Honorius III, pope

d.1227. Born Cencio Savelli; pope (1216–27). Famed for his learning, he was tutor to the future Holy Roman Emperor Frederick II.

Through his legate Gualo, Honorius supported the young Henry III of England (a papal ward) against the attempts of Prince Louis of France to seize the English throne in 1216–18. He supported the later stages of the crusade successfully launched in 1208 against the Albigensians, a French heretical sect, and sanctioned the Dominicans' preaching against them. Honorius also organized the Fifth Crusade against Egypt (1217–21), but this was a failure. In 1220 Honorius crowned Frederick II Holy Roman Emperor on condition he went on crusade, which Frederick finally agreed to do in 1227.

Chronicles of the Age of Chivalry/Four Gothic Kings (US edn): 26, 30, 42

Hospitallers

Knights of the Order of the Hospital of St John of Jerusalem, an order formed after the capture

Hospitallers *The Grand Master and senior members of the Order of the Hospital of St John in Jerusalem, after their removal to Rhodes in 1307.*

of Jerusalem in 1099, during the First Crusade, and recognized by Pope Paschal II in 1113. The order existed to protect pilgrims in the Holy Land but also took part in most major crusading campaigns. After Jerusalem fell to Saladin in 1187 they re-established themselves first in Acre, and, when that was conquered by the Muslims in 1291, in Cyprus. They became a naval power and took Rhodes (1308–10) from the Saracens, where they established their headquarters and eventually formed an independent state. Rhodes was used as a base to continue convoying pilgrims and fighting the Muslims. They seized and briefly held Smyrna in 1344 and Alexandria in 1365. The order's great wealth was enlarged when after 1307 they were allowed to take over, from Philip IV of France, confiscated estates of the Knights Templar.

Chronicles of the Age of Chivalry/Four Gothic Kings (US edn): 181, 185

'Hotspur'

See: Percy, Henry ('Hotspur')

House of Commons

Lower house of the English parliament, which emerged in the 13th century. County representatives were first called to parliaments in 1258, 1264 and 1265; in the latter year burgesses from the towns were also summoned. Edward I's Model Parliament of 1295 established a pattern for the Commons, with two knights from each county and two burgesses from each town. The later Middle Ages saw a gradual increase in the power of the Commons.

Chronicles of the Age of Chivalry/Four Gothic Kings (US edn): 99

House of Lancaster

See: Lancaster, House of

House of York

See: York, House of

Howard, John, 6th duke of Norfolk

1430?–85. 6th duke of Norfolk (1483–5); earl marshal (1483); admiral of England, Ireland and Aquitaine (1483). John Howard entered the service of his relative John Mowbray, 3rd duke of Norfolk, and on 17 February 1461 fought under him at St Albans for the Lancastrians

against the House of York. However, by 26 February, he had abandoned Henry VI and joined Edward IV, whom he accompanied to London. Under Edward he served against the Lancastrians and acted as envoy to France and Flanders. In 1470 he was created Baron Howard by the restored Henry VI, but commanded a fleet against the Lancastrians in 1471. Richard III made him a privy councillor, and he died commanding Richard's vanguard at the battle of Bosworth in 1485.

The Wars of the Roses: 224, 302

Howden, Roger of

See: Roger of Howden

Hubert Walter, archbishop of Canterbury

See: Walter, Hubert, archbishop of Canterbury

Huelgas, Las

Royal Cistercian abbey in Castile, Spain, founded in 1187 at the request of Eleanor of England, wife of Alfonso VIII of Castile, and built in the Angevin style. The abbey's nuns were nobly born; its second abbess (1205–18) was Constance, daughter of Eleanor and Alfonso. The order was almost completely cut off from the world, and the royal couple could tour the whole abbey only once a year; on other occasions they were restricted to the choir and transepts. Eleanor and Alfonso were buried in the abbey.

The Plantagenet Chronicles: 115

Hugh of Avallon, St, bishop of Lincoln

1140–1200. Born of noble Burgundian parents at Avallon in France; bishop of Lincoln (1186–1200). Hugh, pious from childhood, joined the Carthusians at La Grande Chartreuse monastery in about 1160, rising to be procurator general. In 1176 he came to England at Henry II's request to be prior of the king's new Carthusian monastery at Witham, Somerset. In 1186 Henry appointed him bishop of Lincoln, one of England's richest sees; but each year he returned to Witham for a month as a monk. Although Hugh opposed Henry on many issues, such as his forest laws, and excommunicated his chief forester, he retained the king's respect, as he later did that of Richard I. In 1192 he began rebuilding Lincoln Cathedral. Twenty years after his death he was canonized as St Hugh of Lincoln.

The Plantagenet Chronicles: 13, 94, 104, 156–60, 178–84, 198, 244–50, 252–6, 266–8, 277

Hugh of Lusignan

See: Hugh X, the Brown

Hugh X, the Brown, of Lusignan, count of La Marche

d.1249. Lord of Lusignan; count of La Marche. In 1201 King John of England seized the county of La Marche on behalf of his new queen, Isabella. Her father had contested the county with Hugh, who had been her fiancé. With his younger brother Ralph, Hugh appealed for justice to Philip II of France, who declared John's French lands confiscated.

Hugh joined Philip and Arthur, duke of Brittany, against John and was captured by him at Mirebeau in August 1202. He was released after surrendering castles and hostages and swearing obedience to John, but, in 1204, helped Philip to take John's French lands. His son Hugh married Isabella, then John's widow, in 1220.

The Plantagenet Chronicles: 263, 270, 272, 274, 280

Humphrey of Lancaster, 2nd duke of Gloucester

1390–1447. Youngest son of Henry IV; 2nd duke of Gloucester (1414–47); lieutenant of England (1430–2). Humphrey, who was wounded at Agincourt (1415), became regent of England on the death of Henry V in 1422 but subsequently exercised power only as deputy of John, 1st duke of Bedford, with the title of protector. In 1422 Humphrey married Jacqueline, countess of Hainault in Flanders, which was claimed by Philip, the Good, duke of Burgundy. Two years later Humphrey invaded the county, in an unsuccessful attempt to establish it as his wife's possession. In 1428 the marriage was declared invalid and Humphrey married Eleanor Cobham; he was divorced from her in 1441, after her conviction for witchcraft.

In the 1420s and 1430s Humphrey was involved in a power struggle with his uncle, Henry Beaufort, bishop of Winchester. Henry VI suspected Humphrey of treason and in 1435 had him arrested; he died in custody. He was an active patron of culture and learning and is remembered as the founder of the Bodleian Library in Oxford.

The Wars of the Roses: 140, 163, 166–8, 177, 187–8, 192–3, 200

hundred

Subdivision of an English shire. First created in the 10th century, hundreds each had their own court.

The Plantagenet Chronicles: 161, 325

Hundred Years War

Conflict between England and France from 1337 to 1453. In 1337 Edward III assumed the title of king of France. His invasion of the country, two years later, started a war which, despite periods of truce, ended only with the fall of Bordeaux, England's last French outpost bar Calais, in 1453.

Chronicles of the Age of Chivalry/Four Gothic Kings (US edn): 236–48, 266–73, 276–82, 294–8
The Wars of the Roses: 29, 49, 68–70

Hungary, Master of

See: Master of Hungary

Hunne, John

d.1441. Chaplain to Eleanor Cobham, second wife of Humphrey, 2nd duke of Gloucester. In 1441 Hunne was found guilty, together with his mistress and Roger Bolingbroke and Thomas Southwell, of conspiring to kill Henry VI by witchcraft. He was executed, along with his fellow conspirators.

The Wars of the Roses: 193

Hus, John

1369?–1415. Bohemian religious reformer; rector of the Bethlehem Chapel in Prague (1402–10). Hus translated into Czech the heretical doctrines of John Wycliffe, the English

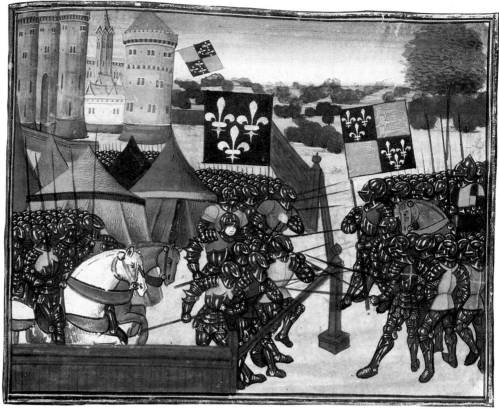

Hundred Years War Castillon, an English possession, besieged by the French in 1453.

religious reformer, and, in more than 3,000 sermons, also attacked clerical laxity; in 1410, the archbishop of Prague excommunicated him, ordered his books to be burnt and forbade preaching at the Bethlehem Chapel. By 1414 Hus had become a hero in Bohemia and was summoned to the Council of Constance. Although he was protected by a safe conduct guaranteed by Holy Roman Emperor Sigismund, the council imprisoned him and tried him for heresy. Hus refused to recant his views and on 6 July 1415 was burned at the stake.

The Wars of the Roses: 39, 126, 158–9

Hussites

Followers of John Hus, the Bohemian religious reformer. Five years after his death, in the Four Articles of Prague (1420), the Hussites demanded freedom to preach, communion of both bread and wine for lay people, limits on church property and civil punishment for offences such as simony (buying or selling ecclesiastical offices). Despite persecution and internal divisions, the Hussites survived to the time of the Reformation, the only medieval reform movement to do so.

The Wars of the Roses: 156, 158–9

Ightham Mote

Manor house in Kent begun during the 14th century with the construction of a hall. Additional wings were built over the next two centuries to create an enclosed courtyard. The house, apart from its moat, was unfortified, typifying the transformation of castle into domestic dwelling.

The Wars of the Roses: 125

Ilchester, Richard of

See: Richard of Ilchester, bishop of Winchester

Île de France

Province of northern central France, in which Paris is situated; the name dates from the 14th century, when it was first used to describe the land bounded by the rivers Seine, Oise and Marne. In 987 Hugh Capet, duke of France and count of Paris, became king of France, and his domains in the Île de France became the nucleus of French crown lands. In Philip I's reign (1060-1108), the area was the limit of effective royal authority. Philip II, who made Paris his capital city (c.1190), gave the Île de France its central importance. By the death of Louis XI in 1483, French crown lands had been expanded to include nearly all of France, and the Île de France was constituted into a province that was subject, like other French provinces, to the Paris parlement.

The Plantagenet Chronicles: 34, 115, 241
Chronicles of the Age of Chivalry/Four Gothic Kings (US edn): 274

Ingelgar

*fl.*880. Semi-legendary founder of the Angevin dynasty in France; father of Fulk the Red, count of Anjou, and possibly himself the first count of Anjou. The estate he seized in the Loire valley late in the 9th century was the foundation of the house of Anjou's later holdings.

The Plantagenet Chronicles: 19, 22

Innocent III, pope

1160?–1216. Born Lothario di Segni, son of Trastimondo, count of Segni; cardinal (1190–8), pope (1198–1216). Lothario was the first of three members of the Segni family to be elected pope: the others were his nephew Gregory IX (1207–41) and Alexander IV (1254–61), Gregory's nephew. Lothario trained as a theologian and jurist under Pope Celestine III, his uncle, who made him a cardinal in 1190. He was a man of remarkable talents, combining intelligence, determination and flexibility; and he seems to have formed an elevated view of the role of the Vicar of Christ before his election as pope in 1198.

He was elected pope at the remarkably young age of 37, and named himself Pope Innocent III. He soon began to pursue the ideal of extending the spiritual authority of the papacy over secular rulers. Therefore he intervened frequently with the rulers of western Europe on the moral plane – as when he tried to heal the divisions between King John of England and Philip II of France which opened when Philip invaded John's territory in 1199. But his direct political interventions were, on the whole, made only where the lay rulers were his vassals.

In 1198 Innocent made Constance, wife of Holy Roman Emperor Henry VI and successful claimant to the Sicilian throne, yield Sicily to him as a papal fief, in return for acknowledging her infant son Frederick of Hohenstaufen (Holy Roman Emperor Frederick II from 1212) as king of Sicily.

In 1201, the pope chose Otto of Brunswick rather than Philip of Swabia as king of Germany and Holy Roman Emperor-elect. Although within six years Innocent had come to favour Philip, by 1209, Philip had become a threat to papal power in Italy and the pope switched his support to Otto. Philip was murdered in 1209, and Innocent crowned Otto IV as Holy Roman Emperor, only to excommunicate him in 1210 and dictate the election of Frederick of Hohenstaufen, his ward since 1198, as German king in 1212.

In 1204 Innocent recognized Joannitza as king of Bulgaria and sent him a crown, and

during his pontificate the kingdoms of Aragon, Portugal and Poland all became vassal states of the papacy. England also became a vassal state, in 1213 after many years of wrangling over elections to bishoprics between Innocent and King John. In 1206 the cathedral chapter at Canterbury had chosen one candidate as archbishop, John a second, and the king had refused to accept Innocent's nominee, Stephen Langton, as a compromise candidate. Innocent had declared an interdict over England, which ran from 1208 to 1213, excommunicated the king (1209) and threatened to depose him before John finally came to terms. Innocent later stood by the king when the English barons made John seal Magna Carta in 1215; he immediately declared the charter void on the grounds that it was a forced treaty and a promise given by a vassal (John) without his overlord's knowledge. Innocent was also preoccupied with the crusading movement, with the extirpation of heresy and with attempts to reform abuses within the Church.

He preached the Fourth Crusade, which ended disastrously when the crusaders sacked Constantinople in 1204, and protested vainly against the crusaders' excesses. In 1208, after the murder of Peter of Castelnau, his legate in the south of France, with the alleged complicity of the count of Toulouse, Innocent invoked the Albigensian Crusade against the Cathar heretics who inhabited the area around Albi. This protracted, bloody and violent strife did little in the short term to extirpate the Albigensian heresy from the south of France.

On a more peaceful plane, Innocent gave his approval to St Francis's foundation of the Franciscan order (*c.*1210), which popularized the idea of apostolic poverty. The climax of his pontificate came with the Fourth Lateran Council, in 1215, which enacted a wide range of reforming decrees: marriage, the nature of the eucharist, confession, and the religious orders were among the matters covered. Within a year, however, Innocent was struck down by a bout of fever and died at Perugia in 1216.

The Plantagenet Chronicles: 250, 252, 282, 288, 290–2, 304, 323
Chronicles of the Age of Chivalry/Four Gothic Kings (US edn): 36, 38

Innocent IV, pope

d.1254. Born Sinibaldo Fieschi; cardinal (1227–43); pope (1243–54). A supporter of Holy Roman Emperor Frederick II before becoming pope, Innocent turned against him after his election and fled from Rome to Lyons, where in 1245 he convened a council that declared Frederick deposed. Innocent sponsored various measures against the emperor, even a plot to murder him, and tried to persuade an English or French prince to take the kingdom of Sicily, Frederick's power base, as a fief. Innocent was preparing a crusade against the emperor in 1250, when Frederick died. The pope continued the struggle against the emperor's sons, Conrad and Manfred.

Innocent taxed the clergy and laity heavily to pay for his struggle with the emperor and earned the opposition of many, including Robert Grosseteste, bishop of Lincoln. In 1252 he established the Inquisition in Italy, promulgating a bull which allowed torture to further its objectives. In 1254 news of a papal army's defeat by Manfred at Foggia hastened Innocent's end.

Chronicles of the Age of Chivalry/Four Gothic Kings (US edn): 43, 76–7, 79

Innocent VI, pope

d.1362. Born Etienne Aubert; cardinal (1342–52); pope (1352–62). A well-known jurist, Innocent (who resided at Avignon) was one of the few reforming popes of his time, striving to eliminate venality from church administration. He introduced important reforms, but his attempts to subjugate the papal states, so that he could return to Rome, met with failure, as did his efforts to stop the Hundred Years War between France and England in its early stages.

Chronicles of the Age of Chivalry/Four Gothic Kings (US edn): 273

Inns of Court

Four legal societies in London with exclusive right of admission to the English Bar. Originating in the 13th century, they arose as schools of law where apprentice lawyers gathered to learn from masters, as in a guild, and took their names (Lincoln's Inn, Gray's Inn, Inner Temple and Middle Temple) from the buildings where they met.

The Wars of the Roses: 195

Inquisition

Ecclesiastical tribunal that dealt with the detection and punishment of heretics. Continuing the activities performed earlier by papal legates, it was established in France in 1233 by Pope Gregory IX, as an institution run largely by Dominican friars, to combat the Albigensians, a

Ireland Richard II crosses to Ireland in 1394. He subdued the Irish chieftains, but his efforts to secure the province were curtailed by his fall in 1399.

French heretical sect. The friars interrogated suspects and passed a sentence of penance, imprisonment, confiscation of goods, or even burning, on unrepentant heretics. The sentence was enforced by the local secular ruler, who received any goods seized. In 1252 Pope Innocent IV established the Inquisition in Italy and allowed the introduction of torture to extract confessions.

During the 14th and 15th centuries its scope was widened to include investigations into sorcery and magic and its geographical sphere was extended into Bohemia and the Balkans. In Spain the Inquisition was not established until 1478, by Ferdinand and Isabella, with Pope Sixtus IV's grudging approval.

Controlled by the Spanish crown, it originally aimed to uncover Jews and Muslims who had returned to their own religions after being converted to Catholicism, but soon it began investigating society at large. It gained a terrible reputation for torture throughout Europe, now thought to be somewhat exaggerated.

Chronicles of the Age of Chivalry/Four Gothic Kings (US edn): 65
The Wars of the Roses: 247

interdict

Ecclesiastical censure, often used in the Middle Ages, as, for example, by Pope Innocent III against England in 1208, during King John's reign. In a parish or state under interdict, no public church service may be held, no corpse buried with Christian rites and only certain sacraments (notably baptism) administered. The papacy often used the interdict to sway a populace against erring rulers.

Ireland

The early 12th century saw Ireland as a collection of warring chieftainships, with a Norse presence in Dublin, and in the hope of bringing the country to order Pope Adrian IV made Henry II overlord of Ireland (*c*.1154–9). Henry invaded Ireland in 1171 and granted lordships to his followers in the area around Dublin; however, many of the chieftains remained rebellious. In 1185 Henry sent his son John to subdue them, dubbing him Lord of Ireland; but John was quickly forced to retire by the Irish, who united against him. In 1210 he returned, imposed royal authority on Norman lords there and built castles at Carrickfergus and Dublin. Ireland was split into shires ruled by the Crown from Dublin, domains held by Norman lords and independent native kingdoms. In the same century the English set up an Irish parliament at Dublin.

After an invasion of Ireland by Edward Bruce, king of Scotland (1315–18), a claimant to the Irish throne, English royal authority was reduced to the Pale, a small district around Dublin. In 1394 Richard II invaded the country to re-establish royal power. The Irish chieftains surrendered, but lack of funds forced the king to return to England in 1395. His next visit, in 1399, was curtailed by news of the invasion of England by Henry Bolingbroke (soon to be Henry IV) and he returned to England, his deposition and death, leaving Ireland to its great Anglo-Norman earls.

The Plantagenet Chronicles: 121, 293–5
Chronicles of the Age of Chivalry/Four Gothic Kings (US edn): 174, 176, 264
The Wars of the Roses: 68, 82–4, 92

Isabella of Angoulême

*c.*1188–1246. Daughter of Audemar, count of Angoulême; second wife of King John of England. The king was said to have become besotted with her during a visit to France in 1200, after his divorce from Isabella of Gloucester, and married her the same year, when she was only about 12. She had been betrothed to Hugh X, the Brown, of Lusignan, count of La Marche, and the marriage, followed by John's seizure of La Marche in 1201, led Hugh take up arms against John. The marriage helped John to secure Isabella's father's fickle allegiance and, with it, the strategically important county of Angoulême. After John's death in 1216 Isabella married Hugh, son of Hugh the Brown; Henry III, her son from her previous marriage, introduced many of his half-brothers, from Isabella's second marriage, into English offices in the 1240s. Isabella was buried in Fontevrault Abbey in France, the Plantagenet family mausoleum.

The Plantagenet Chronicles: 253, 257, 263–4, 272
Chronicles of the Age of Chivalry/Four Gothic Kings (US edn): 59

Isabella, empress, consort of Frederick II

1214–41. Daughter of King John of England and Isabella of Angoulême; sister of Henry III of England. Isabella was betrothed to Holy Roman Emperor Frederick II in 1235, after an approach from his two Templar envoys. The chronicler Roger of Wendover records that she was sent to Worms in Germany in the care of the archbishop of Cologne and William, bishop of Exeter, and that the wedding took place at Worms on Sunday 30 July 1235. After her marriage, Isabella was kept in seclusion. She died at Foggia in Italy.

Chronicles of the Age of Chivalry/Four Gothic Kings (US edn): 43, 54, 56

Isabella of Gloucester

d.1217. Daughter of William, 2nd earl of Gloucester; second cousin and first wife of the king of England. John was betrothed to Isabella in childhood and married her in 1189, receiving the counties of Somerset, Gloucester, Devon and Cornwall as her dowry. Their close blood kinship necessitated papal permission for the marriage. She bore no children and was not crowned with John at his accession in 1199; the king divorced her that year. Isabella later married Geoffrey Fitzpeter, and, after his death, Hubert de Burgh.

The Plantagenet Chronicles: 259, 263

Isabella, queen of Castile

1451–1504. Daughter of John II of Castile; queen of Castile and León (1474–1504). After her accession following the death of her brother, Henry IV of Castile, her reputedly illegitimate half-sister Joanna contested the succession with her. Isabella's victory in 1479 coincided with her husband Ferdinand II of Aragon's accession to the throne of Aragon. Isabella subdued the lawless Castilian nobility by confiscating their estates and making Ferdinand grand master of the powerful military religious orders. With her husband she instituted the Spanish Inquisition in 1478 – under royal rather than ecclesiastical control – and engineered the expulsion of the Jews from Spain in 1492.

The Wars of the Roses: 246–7

Isabella 'the She-wolf', of France

1292?–1358. Daughter of Philip IV, the Fair, of France, and Joan of Champagne; wife of Edward II of England (1308–27). Betrothed to Edward, son of Edward I of England, in 1303, Isabella was married to him in 1308, shortly after his accession to the English throne.

Contemporaries praised Isabella's beauty, but immediately after their marriage Edward showed his preference for his male favourite, Piers Gaveston, who received all the best jewels, rings and other treasures Isabella had brought with her from France as wedding presents. Isabella wrote to her father, complaining bitterly of Gaveston's avarice. After Gaveston's death in 1312, Edward and Isabella became closer, and their first child, the future Edward III, was born later that year (he was followed by another son and two daughters). In that year also, they visited Philip IV's court in France together to attend the ceremonial knighting of Isabella's brothers.

In 1313 Isabella intervened in the continuing dispute between Edward and the baronial faction known as the lords ordainers, who in 1311 had imposed ordinances on Edward, restricting royal power. The upshot was a formal reconciliation between Edward and the chief ordainers at London on 22 September. Isabella went to France as an envoy for her husband in 1314 and was probably at the centre of a plot to condemn her two sisters-in-law for adultery, hoping perhaps to discredit their issue and increase the chances of her son Edward succeeding to the French throne.

For much of her married life Isabella was occupied in managing her estates at Castle Rising and elsewhere and her household of some 180 people. She accompanied her husband when he tried unsuccessfully to subdue Scotland in 1322, but when Scots counter-attacks forced him to flee south he abandoned her at Tynemouth priory; to escape, she was forced to endure a rough sea voyage. In 1324, when war broke out with France, the king, on the advice of the Despensers, took possession of her estates, reduced her retinue and put her on a small daily allowance. When in 1325 Isabella visited France as an envoy to her brother Charles IV, she joined forces with Roger Mortimer, who became her lover, and prepared an invasion force. She lured Prince Edward to France in September 1325, claiming he should do homage to the French crown for the English fief of Gascony, then refused to return to England until the Despensers were dismissed.

Isabella and Mortimer landed at Orwell in September 1326, and within four months Edward II had been deposed and imprisoned (his death followed the next year, probably instigated by Isabella and Mortimer). Although Prince Edward was crowned in his stead as Edward III of England, in January 1327, Isabella and Mortimer ruled on his behalf for the next three years. They were hated for their rapaciousness and for the execution (1330) of Edmund, 3rd earl of Kent, who had been plotting to free Edward III from their tutelage. That same year, the young king staged a coup, executed Mortimer, and retired Isabella from public life. She lived in comfort at her manor of Castle Rising until her death in 1358. Her body was buried in London, but her heart was taken to Gloucester Abbey, burial place of Edward II.

Chronicles of the Age of Chivalry/Four Gothic Kings (US edn): 137, 162, 170–3, 177, 186, 208–14, 216–21, 224, 230–2

Isabella of Valois

1389–1409. Eldest daughter of Charles VI of France; second wife of Richard II of England (1396–1400). Isabella was married to Richard II in 1396 when she was seven years old, in order to secure peace between England and France.

She brought with her 50,000 pounds, the first part of a large dowry. Richard reportedly grew attached to Isabella, but she was left to the care of a French governess, Lady de Coucy. After Richard's deposition and death in 1399, Henry IV moved her to Wallingford in Berkshire, while attempting to marry her to his son, the future Henry V. Isabella, now aged ten, remained loyal to her dead husband and refused the match. She returned to France in 1401, with 4,000 pounds of her dowry.

In 1406 she married her cousin Charles, later duke of Orléans. She died bearing his child in 1409, aged nineteen.

The Wars of the Roses: 72–7, 95–6, 100, 115

Islip, Simon, archbishop of Canterbury

d.1366. Keeper of the privy seal to Edward III (1347–50); ambassador to France (1342), archbishop of Canterbury (1349–66). An ecclesiastical lawyer and administrator, Simon founded Canterbury College at Oxford to try to remedy the dearth of clergy after the Black Death. In 1356 he defeated Edward's demands for taxes on the clergy and in 1362 supported the opposition to the royal right of purveyance (by which the Crown could buy household items at a price fixed by itself). Simon celebrated Mass for the first meeting of the Order of the Garter in 1350.

Chronicles of the Age of Chivalry/Four Gothic Kings (US edn): 262

Istanbul

Name given to Constantinople after its conquest in 1453 by the Ottoman Turks and its conversion into the Turkish capital.

Italy

Nominally a domain of the Holy Roman Emperors in the Middle Ages, Italy was in fact divided between many different rulers and was almost impossible to dominate. The south of Italy, centred on Naples, and the island of Sicily were from the 11th century kingdoms ruled successively by the Normans, imperial Hohenstaufens, Angevins and Aragonese. Central Italy was overshadowed by the turbulent papal states, and further north, great cities like Venice, Genoa, Pisa, Florence and Milan built up a patchwork of powerful states, each striving to increase its considerable political and economic powers at the others' expense. Italy was the birthplace, in the late

Isabella of France Isabella, 'the she-wolf' of France (right) with her husband Edward II of England; she deposed and imprisoned him with the help of her lover Roger Mortimer.

14th century, of the Renaissance.

Chronicles of the Age of Chivalry/Four Gothic Kings (US edn): 197–9
The Wars of the Roses: 218–19

Ivan III, first tsar of Russia

1440–1505. Grand duke of Moscow (1462–1505). Founder of the Russian state. Ivan subjugated Novgorod, Moscow's northern rival and a rich centre of the Hanseatic fur trade, in 1478, and two years later he renounced Moscow's allegiance to the Mongol khanate of the Golden Horde. To prevent rebellion in his new lands, Ivan forcibly resettled their ruling classes to remote regions and replaced them with loyal Muscovites. After the death of his first wife, Maria of Tver, in 1467, he married Sophia, niece of Constantine XI, the last Byzantine emperor, and added the two-headed eagle to Moscow's arms.

The concept of Moscow as a 'third Rome', successor to that city and to Constantinople as centre of imperial might and the orthodox faith, gained currency under Ivan. He established autocratic government and was honoured with the title of tsar (caesar), though never crowned.

The Wars of the Roses: 274–5

Jacqueline, countess of Hainault and Holland

1401–36. Daughter and heiress of William IV, duke of Bavaria and count of Hainault; countess of Hainault, Holland and Zeeland (1417–28). Passed over for the succession to the counties of Hainault, Holland and Zeeland in 1417, Jacqueline sought refuge in England, where she married Humphrey, 2nd duke of Gloucester, in 1422, after her marriage to John, duke of Brabant, the rival claimant to her inheritance, (Philip the Good of Burgundy's nephew) had been annulled. She accompanied Humphrey when he invaded Hainault on her behalf in 1424–5. The duke was defeated by John of Brabant and withdrew, leaving his wife a prisoner of Philip the Good in Ghent. She escaped to Holland, where she carried on the struggle against Philip and John, but at last, in 1428, sealed the Treaty of Delft, naming Philip as her administrator and heir to her lands. Humphrey divorced her in the same year. After failing to incite Holland to rebel against Philip in 1432, Jacqueline finally abdicated her countships to him in 1433.

The Wars of the Roses: 157, 166, 192

Jacquerie

French peasant revolt of 1358, named after *Jacques Bonhomme,* the nickname for French peasants. The rebellion was provoked by the devastation and poverty associated with the Hundred Years War (1337–1453) and by general dissatisfaction with the ruling classes following French defeats in the early stages of the war. Beginning around Beauvais, north of Paris, the uprising spread rapidly to Amiens, the Île de France and Valois. Contemporary

chroniclers described atrocities and rapes inflicted on the nobility by the rebels. Castles were looted and razed. The nobles retaliated, and Charles II, the Bad, king of Navarre, slew Guillaume Karle, the Jacqueries' leader, at the battle of Mello (1358). Thousands of rebels were slaughtered in the reprisals that followed.

Chronicles of the Age of Chivalry/Four Gothic Kings (US edn): 274–6

Jacques de Molay

See: Molay, Jacques de

James, 2nd earl of Douglas

See: Douglas, James, 2nd earl of Douglas

James I, king of Scotland

1397–1437. Second son of Robert III of Scotland and Annabella Drummond; king of Scotland (1406–37). In 1406, as a result of the mysterious death of his elder brother David Stewart four years earlier, James was sent to France for his own safety. En route to France, the child was waylaid by an English ship off Flamborough Head, and for the next 18 years James was held captive in England by the Lancastrian kings.

He received an excellent education in England, and became an accomplished musician and one of the leading poets in the Chaucerian tradition. He was skilled in arms – in 1420 Henry V made him serve in France against the Scots who were fighting for the dauphin Charles (later Charles VII of France) – and he was made a knight of the Garter. In 1424, just before his release from captivity, he married Joan Beaufort, daughter of John Beaufort, 4th earl of Somerset. His poem, *The Kingis Quair,* tells of his love for her.

James was formally crowned on his return to Scotland the same year. His first parliament, also in 1424, passed 27 acts including one that attempted to prevent the Highland clans from warring amongst themselves. He tried and executed Murdac Stewart, 2nd duke of Albany, his chief rival to the throne, along with Albany's principal supporters, in 1425. A vigorous administration was established, the Scottish parliament strengthened, and crown revenues considerably increased. His parliament of 1425–6 regulated weights and measures and the punishment of heretics, and strengthened central criminal jurisdiction. However James also levied heavy taxation to pay the 40,000 pounds demanded by the English for his keep during his captivity. The Scots nobles resented

the strong powers he had built up, and in 1437 he was murdered in the Dominican friary at Perth: a group of nobles, led by Sir Robert Graham, cornered him in a private chamber while he was entertaining the papal legate. Unarmed, he was killed while trying to escape down a sewer. He left one son, James, who succeeded him, and six daughters.

The Wars of the Roses: 106, 117, 178, 180, 182, 184–6

James II, king of Scotland

1430–60. Son of James I of Scotland and Joan Beaufort; king of Scotland (1437–60). James II was seven years old when he succeeded to the Scottish throne; two years later, in 1439, he was kidnapped from his mother by Sir William Crichton and only regained his liberty in 1443. His minority was a time of strife and anarchy, but after his marriage in 1449, to Mary of Guelders, niece of Philip the Good, duke of Burgundy, James took control of Scottish affairs. He strove to enhance royal power at the expense of the magnates, playing off the strong Douglas family against Crichton's followers: in 1452 he murdered the overmighty William, 8th earl of Douglas, and, in 1455, attainted his family and annexed their lands. He also re-enacted much of his father's legislation at his parliament of 1450.

James negotiated with both the sides when conflict arose between the houses of Lancaster and York – the start of the Wars of the Roses. He raided Northumberland and was routed by Richard, 3rd duke of York, in 1456; the next year he concluded a truce with Henry VI of England, and in 1460 he welcomed Henry's queen, Margaret of Anjou, after the Lancastrians' defeat at the battle of Northampton. He was accidentally killed in the same year while besieging Roxburgh castle, and was buried at Holyrood Palace in Edinburgh.

The Wars of the Roses: 186, 222

James III, king of Scotland

1452–88. Son of James II of Scotland and Mary of Guelders; king of Scotland (1460–88). His father's accidental death in 1460 raised him to the throne at the age of eight. After his mother's death in 1466 he was seized by the Boyd family, who ruled Scotland in his name until 1469, when he married Margaret, daughter of Christian I of Denmark, and assumed control of his affairs.

The marriage produced three sons, and enabled James to annex the Orkneys and Shetlands (hitherto Danish) to Scotland in 1472.

James's many enemies included his brothers Alexander Stewart, 3rd duke of Albany, and John Stewart, 13th earl of Mar. In 1479 James arrested them, but Alexander fled to Paris, and in 1482 concluded the Treaty of Fotheringay with Edward IV by which he agreed to rule Scotland as the English king's vassal.

That same year, his brother Edward sent Richard, 3rd duke of Gloucester (the future Richard III of England) to Scotland with 20,000 men to prosecute Alexander's claims. Their army entered Edinburgh unopposed: James had been captured by a band of his own disaffected nobles, who were holding him in Edinburgh castle. The Scots nobility, who had no desire to install Alexander, a puppet of the English, as king, paid the English to leave and allowed James to keep the throne. He recovered his freedom in 1483, and was reconciled with Alexander, who, nevertheless, continued to plot against him until discovered and forced to flee to England in 1484. In 1488, another major uprising, under the nominal leadership of the king's son, the future James IV of Scotland, was provoked by James' extravagance and reliance on favourites. James was defeated in battle near Stirling and murdered.

The Wars of the Roses: 299

James of St George, master

fl.1282. Savoyard architect employed by Edward I of England to oversee the building of 12 castles and ten lesser fortresses to subdue the Welsh principality of Gwynedd. Master James used the latest developments in military engineering, substituting high encircling walls and towers for a single keep.

Chronicles of the Age of Chivalry/Four Gothic Kings (US edn): 109, 117, 121

Jean le Bel

fl.1350s. Canon of St-Lambert at Liège, in Belgium; chronicler. Jean, who was noted for good living and chivalrous interests, had as patron John of Hainault, uncle of Philippa, the queen consort of Edward III of England, and through his auspices went on the young king's Scottish campaign in 1327. He wrote a eulogistic account of Edward's later wars and diplomacy based largely on the accounts of others. His chronicle mixes history with romance and was one of the sources used by the French chronicler Jean Froissart.

Chronicles of the Age of Chivalry/Four Gothic Kings (US edn): 7, 16, 227, 233, 272

Jacquerie Knights kill peasant rebels during the Jacquerie.

Jean Froissart

See: Froissart, Jean

Jean de Meung

1240?–1307? French poet, also known as Jean Chopinel of Meung-sur-Loire, often described as the Voltaire of the Middle Ages. Jean wrote a continuation of the *Roman de la Rose* (c.1270), the epic of courtly love, which rejected its conventions and celebrated nature, the created world and worldly happiness. Jean's work also incorporated anti-religious satire.

Chronicles of the Age of Chivalry/Four Gothic Kings (US edn): 55

Jerusalem

Capital of Israel; as the Holy City, in Palestine, the goal of the medieval crusaders. It was captured in 637 by Arab Muslims, who tolerated Christian pilgrims until the 11th century when the caliph al-Hakim devastated the Church of the Holy Sepulchre. The First Crusade, partly inspired by this event, took Jerusalem in 1099 and made it the capital of the Latin Kingdom of Jerusalem, the chief crusader state in the Holy Land. In 1187 the city was recaptured by Saladin's armies and remained Muslim except between 1229 and 1239, after Holy Roman Emperor Frederick II had regained it temporarily for Christendom by negotiation. After its recapture by the Muslims, Christian pilgrims continued to go to Jerusalem, this being regarded as the most difficult and meritorious pilgrimage. Although the city's recapture remained a Christian dream for many centuries, it stayed in Muslim hands until 1917.

The Plantagenet Chronicles: 21, 25–6, 36–9, 60, 78, 148–50, 153, 177, 185, 204–17, 224, 234, 278
Chronicles of the Age of Chivalry/Four Gothic Kings (US edn): 38, 42, 69, 181

Jews

During the late 11th and early 12th centuries English kings encouraged Jews to settle in England because of their value as money-lenders. However, in the late 12th century, Richard I's preparations for the Third Crusade provoked hostility towards them as the country's only significant religious and racial minority, and Richard's coronation on 3 September 1189 triggered anti-Jewish riots throughout England, culminating in the massacre and mass suicide of some 150 Jews in York castle on 16 March 1190, despite their special status as serfs of the royal chamber. King John protected them, for nearly one-seventh of his income came from taxes on them, but fined them so heavily on top of this that many left England to escape the burden. In 1275 Edward I forbade them to lend money at interest or to be merchants, and in 1290 expelled them from England – Europe's first expulsion of Jews. In 1392 France followed the English example.

The Plantagenet Chronicles: 102, 201–2, 208, 293
Chronicles of the Age of Chivalry/Four Gothic Kings (US edn): 73, 116, 122, 130–1, 187

Joachim of Fiore

c.1132–1202. Cistercian monk and scriptural commentator. Joachim was abbot of Corazzo in Calabria, but between 1190 and 1195 became a hermit, founded his own religious order and developed an involved historical commentary on the scriptures which prophesied a new 'Age of the Spirit'. Relying heavily on the Book of Revelation, he identified the seven heads of the Dragon of Revelation with seven historic persecutors of Christendom; the sixth of whom was Saladin and the seventh Antichrist. Richard I, the Lionheart, of England, met Joachim in Sicily, while en route to the Third Crusade in the winter of 1190–1, and heard from him that he was fated to defeat Saladin – a prophecy that was fulfilled.

Joachim's works were much in vogue for the next three centuries, especially among apocalyptic religious groups, such as the Taborites.

The Plantagenet Chronicles: 187, 208–10

Joan of Arc

1412–31. Also known as La Pucelle, the Maid of Orléans; born to a peasant family in the village of Domrémy on the Meuse. In c.1425, at the age of 13, she began to hear the voices of St Michael, St Catherine and St Margaret, and to see visions which enjoined her to go to the dauphin Charles (later Charles VII of France) and help him save France from defeat by the English in the Hundred Years War. In 1428, she tried, at first unsuccessfully, to persuade Robert de Baudricourt, the dauphin's commander at Vaucouleurs, to take her to Charles. He eventually agreed and, in 1429, dressed as a boy and with six companions, she travelled to Chinon where the dauphin gave her an audience.

The dauphin, convinced by Joan's sincerity and sense of purpose, gave his consent to her mission and after an ecclesiastical commission at Poitiers had established that she was no heretic, she was given a retinue and a suit of white armour. In May 1429 she inspired the French defenders of Orléans, which was under siege by the English, to drive out their foes. In June she took English strongholds along the Loire and defeated the English at Patay. The dauphin marched to Reims in triumph and was crowned king of France, with Joan at his side.

In 1430, however, Joan was captured by the Burgundians at Compiègne. The English bought her from their allies, and put her on trial as a heretic and witch. Charles VII made no move to save her. Theologians condemned her visions as worthless and her male dress as perverted. Although Joan asserted that her obedience was to God alone and not the Church, her constancy and defiance condemned her. She recanted when promised holy communion, but only temporarily. Having resumed her former defiance, in May 1431 she was burned at the stake at Rouen. After the end of the Hundred Years War, in 1456, Charles VII annulled the sentence passed on her; but she was not canonized by Pope Benedict XV until 1920.

The Wars of the Roses: 170–5, 209

Joan of Brittany

1370?–1437. Second daughter of Charles II, the Bad, of Navarre; queen of Henry IV of England (1403–13). Joan married John IV, duke of Brittany, in 1386; he died in 1399 and in 1402 she was married by proxy to Henry IV as his second wife. They were married in person at Winchester on 7 April 1403, Joan having been forced to surrender the regency of Brittany to her uncle, Philip the Bold, duke of Burgundy, and also to leave her four Breton children in Brittany. Henry granted her extensive dower lands. After the accession of Henry V (son of Henry IV and his first wife Mary Bohun) Joan presided at court until 1419, when the king's brother John, 1st duke of Bedford, arrested and imprisoned her as a witch during Henry's absence in France. However, she was allowed to live in comfort in Leeds castle in Kent, after an initial imprisonment at Pevensey, and was released by Henry on his deathbed, in 1422; the whole affair was probably a ruse for the Crown to acquire the income from her lands to finance war with France. She died in 1437, and was buried at Canterbury with Henry IV.

The Wars of the Roses: 102–3

Joan, the Fair Maid of Kent

1328–85. Daughter of Edmund of Woodstock, 4th earl of Kent; 6th countess of Kent (1352–85); wife of Edward, the Black Prince. Joan was famed for her beauty and charm, though her nickname was probably a later invention. In 1349 her marriage of 1340 to William de Montacute, 5th earl of Salisbury, was set aside because of a precontract in 1339 with Sir Thomas Holand, whom she married. Sir Thomas died in 1360, and the following year she married Edward, the Black Prince, to whom she gave two sons: Edward (who died in infancy) and the future Richard II. Both children were born in Gascony, where she lived with her husband from 1362 to 1371. After his death in 1376, she protected John of Gaunt from Londoners who rioted against his support for John Wycliffe the following year. Although 'devoted to pleasure, and so fat from eating that she could scarcely walk', according to the chronicler Thomas Walsingham, Joan mediated between John and Richard II when they quarrelled in 1385.

Chronicles of the Age of Chivalry/Four Gothic Kings (US edn): 282, 290, 293, 296
The Wars of the Roses: 22–3, 39, 46

Joanna, queen of Scotland

1321–62. Youngest daughter of Edward II of England; queen of David II of Scotland (1327–62). Joanna was married to David Bruce in 1327 when both were children, as part of her mother Queen Isabella's attempts to obtain Scots support for her regime. Crowned at Scone in 1331, she accompanied her husband to exile in France the following year, when Edward Balliol seized the Scottish throne. She lived at Château Gaillard from 1334 to 1341, when she and her husband returned to Scotland. In 1346 David invaded England, where he was defeated and captured by Edward III at Neville's Cross. During David's subsequent imprisonment in England from 1346 to 1357, Joanna was permitted by Edward III to visit her husband. She was popular in Scotland, but David's infidelities on his release from prison drove her back to England, where Edward III granted her Hertford castle as a residence.

Chronicles of the Age of Chivalry/Four Gothic Kings (US edn): 230

Joanna, queen of Sicily

1166–99. Third daughter of Henry II of England and Eleanor of Aquitaine; queen of Sicily (1177–89). Henry arranged her marriage to William II, the Norman king of Sicily, sending her to Palermo with an escort on 27 August 1176. When her husband died in 1189, Joanna was detained by Tancred, the new king of Sicily, until 1190, when she was surrendered to her brother, Richard I of England. She accompanied Richard and his betrothed, Berengaria, to Palestine in 1191, and was proposed as a wife for Saphadin, Saladin's brother. In 1196 she married Raymond VI, count of Toulouse. She died at Rouen at the birth of her second child and was buried in the Angevin mausoleum at Fontevrault.

The Plantagenet Chronicles: 112, 130, 146–9, 210, 212, 224–5

John XXIII, antipope

c.1370–1419. Born Baldassare Cossa; cardinal (1402); antipope of the Pisan branch of the Great Schism (1410–15). A pirate before entering the church, Cossa probably borrowed Medici money to buy his cardinalship from Pope Boniface IX in 1402. In 1408, in the hope of helping to end the Schism, he deserted Gregory XII, who represented the Roman branch, to help convene the Council of Pisa. In 1409 this body first elected Peter of Caudia as Pope Alexander V but his reign lasted only until the following year; Baldassare was unjustly accused of poisoning him. The council then elected Baldassare as John XXIII.

John made the Medici family bankers to the papacy and once pawned his mitre to them. Under pressure from Holy Roman Emperor Sigismund III, he convened the Council of Constance in November 1414. In 1415 he reluctantly promised to abdicate if the other two rival popes, Benedict XIII and Gregory XII, also stepped down. However, just before his abdication took effect, he fled Constance, was pursued and captured, tried on accusations of gross misconduct and deposed. A broken man, he was held prisoner by Louis IV of Bavaria until 1419 but bought his freedom, returned to Italy, and died cardinal bishop of Tusculum.

The Wars of the Roses: 110, 126

John (Balliol), king of Scotland

1249–1315. King of Scotland (1292–6). After the death of Margaret of Scotland in 1290 Edward I was called in by the Scottish magnates as adjudicator between the 13 candidates for the throne and chose John Balliol as the successor. As John of Scotland, Balliol swore fealty to Edward and acceded to his claimed right to hear appeals from Scots courts. However, in 1293 he refused to answer such a suit, brought against him by Duncan, earl of Fife, while he was attending Edward's parliament in Westminster; and in 1294 he refused to send men to Edward's aid against Philip IV of France, allying himself with the French king the following year. John renounced his fealty and invaded England in 1296, but surrendered to Edward after a brief campaign. Forced to abdicate in 1296, he was imprisoned in England until 1299; he retired to Château Gaillard in Normandy.

Chronicles of the Age of Chivalry/Four Gothic Kings (US edn): 134–6, 142, 190, 230

John, count of Dunois

1403–68. Illegitimate son of Charles, duke of Orléans, brother of Charles VI of France; commander of Charles VII's troops. Dunois routed the English at Montargis in 1427 and put up a spirited defence of Orléans in 1428. A leading commander in the gradual reconquest of English-held territories in France in the 1430s and 1440s, the closing years of the Hundred Years War, he made a triumphal entry into Paris in 1436. In 1449 Charles VII ordered him into Normandy at the head of three French and Breton armies and by the following year the duchy was freed from English rule. In 1451 he took Fronsac and other English-held fortresses guarding the Gironde estuary in Gascony and occupied Bordeaux on 29 June that year.

The Wars of the Roses: 206, 208–9

John, 1st duke of Bedford

1389–1435. Third son of Henry IV; knight of the Garter (1400); 1st duke of Bedford (1414–35); regent of England (1415, 1417–21); protector of England (1422–9); regent of France (1414–35). John was regent of England for Henry V in 1415 during the king's first French campaign and led a fleet to repel a French raid in 1416. In 1417 he brought Sir John Oldcastle to trial and execution for treason and heresy.

On Henry's death in 1422 Bedford became protector of England and regent of France. The royal council gave him active authority in France, while his brother Humphrey, 2nd duke of Gloucester, exercised immediate authority in England for Henry VI. In 1424 Bedford won a great victory at Verneuil but he returned to London in 1426 to settle a dispute between his brother Humphrey and the chancellor, Henry Beaufort, bishop of Winchester. In 1427 Bedford returned to France, where in 1431 he permitted Joan of Arc to be burned as a witch and arranged to have Henry VI crowned king of France in Notre-Dame. However, he was unable to stem the tide of the French recovery in the 1430s and died in 1435 a disappointed man.

The Wars of the Roses: 133, 140–1, 144, 157, 163, 166, 167–8, 172, 175, 177–80, 192

John, duke of Berry

1340–1416. Son of John II of France; duke of Berry (1360–1416); patron of the arts. A hostage in England from 1360 to 1366, during the Hundred Years War, he became on his return to France king's lieutenant in the Languedoc and a leading figure at court during the minority of Charles VI (1380 to 1388). He was deprived of the lieutenancy of Languedoc in 1390; although it was restored in 1401 he was forced to delegate his authority because of the deep hatred of the people for him. He thereafter made his capital of Bourges a centre of artistic excellence. The richness of the books of hours he commissioned – the *Très Belles Heures du Duc de Berry* from Jacquemarte de Hesdin (c.1402) and the *Très Riches Heures* from the Limbourg brothers (1413–16) – reflect the splendour of his court, Europe's most elegant. The work of the Limbourg brothers includes several portraits of the duke. He, and the brothers, died of the plague in 1416.

The Wars of the Roses: 136–7, 289

John the Fearless, duke of Burgundy

1371–1419. Son of Philip the Bold, duke of Burgundy; cousin of Charles VI of France; count of Nevers (1384–1419); duke of Burgundy (1404–19). John fought for Hungary against the Turks at Nikopolis in Greece (1396) and was imprisoned by Bayezid I, the Turkish leader, until ransomed in 1397. As duke, he continued his father's struggle for power with Louis, duke of Orléans (leader of the Orleanist/Armagnac party), whose assassination in Paris in 1407 he arranged. This act forced his temporary exile from Paris, but he returned in 1408 to exercise authority over the French government and over Charles VI during the king's bouts of madness. Armagnac hostility caused his retirement from Paris in 1410 but he was recalled the following year to protect the city from the ravages of Armagnac supporters. In 1413 the violence of his followers, the Cabochiens, forced him to leave Paris again; he retired to Burgundy and negotiated with both the Armagnacs and the English. In 1418 he took advantage of France's defeats by Henry V of England, and seized Paris and the king. The dauphin Charles (later Charles VII of France) now led the Armagnacs and had John killed when the two met at Montereau in 1419.

The Wars of the Roses: 99, 108, 114–15, 134, 144–6, 148–9

John of Gaunt, 2nd duke of Lancaster

1340–99. Fourth son of Edward III of England and Philippa of Hainault; 5th earl of Lancaster (1361–2); 2nd duke of Lancaster (1362–99); duke of Aquitaine (1390–9). John was born in 1340 at Ghent, from which his name, John of Gaunt, derives. In 1359 he married his cousin Blanche, heiress to the honour of Lancaster; and in 1362, on her father's death, became duke of Lancaster and the greatest landholder in England.

John joined his brother the Black Prince on his Spanish campaign to reinstate Peter III, the Cruel, of Castile after his deposition by his brother Henry of Trastamara in 1365. After Blanche's death in 1369, John married Constance, daughter of Peter the Cruel (1371). The next year he promulgated his claim to the Castilian throne in his wife's right, her father having been murdered by Henry of Trastamara in 1369.

After campaigning against the French around La Rochelle and Bordeaux in the early 1370s, John returned to England in 1375, where he supported the court faction led by Alice Perrers, Edward III's mistress. Widespread opposition to Alice's influence over the king led to the Good Parliament of 1376, which ousted her and

John of Gaunt A dinner at Lisbon (overleaf) given by John's ally John I of Portugal. John of Gaunt is on the left.

her followers, but John was able to reverse most of its decrees in 1377. In an effort to undermine his clerical opponents, he supported John Wycliffe's anti-clerical theology and defended Wycliffe during his trial in 1377. During the Peasants Revolt of 1381, the rebels sacked and burned the Savoy palace, his London home. In 1386 John left England to try to win the Castilian throne. He was unsuccessful, and relinquished his claims to his daughter by Constance of Castile, Catherine, who was married to the future Henry III of Castile in 1388.

On his return to England in 1389, Gaunt acted as a peacemaker between his nephew Richard II and the lords appellant, but his appointment as duke of Aquitaine in 1390 revived the barons' hostility. When Constance died in 1394, he married (1396) his longstanding mistress, Catherine Swynford; her children, the Beauforts, were ancestors of the Tudor monarchs. In his last years John's relations with the king were increasingly strained, and in 1398 Richard exiled John's son Henry Bolingbroke (later Henry IV). When John fell mortally ill in 1399, Richard is said to have left bills on his deathbed. John was buried in St Paul's Cathedral.

Chronicles of the Age of Chivalry/Four Gothic Kings (US edn): 253, 278, 282, 290, 293, 296, 298–303
The Wars of the Roses: 10, 19–23, 25–6, 28, 41–3, 46–7, 58, 62, 71, 82, 124

John II, the Good, king of France

1319–64. Son of Philip VI of France and Joan of Burgundy; king of France (1350–64). John married Bonne of Luxembourg when he was 13 years old. After his accession in 1350, he had the constable of France executed and conferred the office on his favourite, Charles de la Cerda. On 19 September 1356 the French army was overwhelmingly defeated by English forces under Edward the Black Prince at Poitiers, and John was captured. He was taken to London in May 1357, where Edward III of England housed him in the Tower of London and treated him as an honoured guest.

John remained in the English capital while Edward negotiated with his son Charles (later Charles V of France) who acted as his regent. The French king's ransom was set at 700,000 pounds in the first Treaty of London of May 1358, which also called for French recognition of English sovereignty over Aquitaine and parts of northern France. Charles rejected Edward's terms, and John stayed in English hands until 1360, when, at the end of a brief campaign in

France, Edward resumed negotiations at Brétigny. By the Treaty of Brétigny in May 1360 John was ransomed for 500,000 pounds, a sum for which a group of hostages, including Louis his second son, were sent as surety to England until payment had been completed. Louis escaped from English captivity in 1364 and, in accordance with the chivalric code, John returned to England, where he died later the same year. He was succeeded by his son, Charles V.

Chronicles of the Age of Chivalry/Four Gothic Kings (US edn): 262–4, 268–74, 284, 278–80
The Wars of the Roses: 29, 289

John I, the Great, king of Portugal

1357?–1433. Illegitimate son of Peter I of Portugal; king of Portugal (1385–1433). John was elected king by the people of Lisbon. This followed a popular revolt against the efforts of Beatrice, daughter and heiress of his half-brother Ferdinand I, to pass the Portuguese throne to her husband, John I of Castile. A victory against the Castilians at Aljubarrota (1385) secured Portuguese independence, though peace with Castile was not formally concluded until 1411. John allied himself with England in 1386, and married John of Gaunt's daughter Philippa in 1387. His reign saw many administrative reforms and the beginnings of Portuguese colonial and maritime expansion, under the auspices of John's son Henry the Navigator.

The Wars of the Roses: 40, 42–3

John I, king of Castile

1358–90. Son of Henry II of Castile and León; king of Castile and León (1379–90). When Ferdinand I of Portugal died in 1383 John tried to claim the Portuguese throne through his wife Beatrice, Ferdinand's daughter. His troops were defeated by the Portuguese at the battle of Aljubarrota (1385). He defended his Castilian throne against John of Gaunt, who claimed it through his wife Constance, daughter of Peter I, the Cruel, of Castile; in 1387 he arranged for his son Henry to marry John of Gaunt's daughter Catherine, and John relinquished his claims.

The Wars of the Roses: 42–3

John, king of England

1167–1216. Youngest son of Henry II of England and Eleanor of Aquitaine; lord of Ireland (1177–1216), king of England

(1199–1216). Nicknamed John Lackland, because, unlike his brothers, he received no major continental fiefs from his father, John was made lord of Ireland in 1177. He joined his brother Richard, the future Richard I, to conspire against their father Henry II in 1189. On his accession in the same year, Richard rewarded John with lordships in Derby, Dorset, Somerset, Mortain, and elsewhere in England and France. John married Isabella of Gloucester in 1189; the union remained childless and was dissolved ten years later.

John, angered by Richard's choice of his nephew Arthur, duke of Brittany, as his successor, plotted against his brother during his absence on the Third Crusade (1190–92), aided and abetted by Philip II of France. On hearing in 1193 that Richard had been imprisoned in Germany by Holy Roman Emperor Henry VI, he attempted to prolong Richard's captivity and to take the throne for himself, but was thwarted by Eleanor and others loyal to Richard. However, at Eleanor's instigation, Richard pardoned John on his return in 1194; and John was declared Richard's heir in 1199, and took the English throne after his brother's death.

In 1200 John divorced Isabella and married Isabella of Angoulême. She had been betrothed to Hugh, the Brown, count of Lusignan, and John confiscated Hugh's county in 1201, as a gift for Isabella's father Audemar. Hugh appealed for help to the peers of France at Paris, providing Philip II, the king's French overlord, with a pretext for pronouncing John's lands in France confiscated and giving legal validity to Philip's subsequent conquests.

The supporters of Arthur of Brittany, John's nephew and rival claimant to his lands, allied with Philip, posing a dangerous threat. On 1 August 1202 John won a great victory at Mirebeau when he rescued his mother from the castle, under siege by Arthur, the Lusignans and Philip's forces. He captured Arthur and Hugh, but later released the latter. His cruel treatment of Arthur, allegedly murdered at Rouen in 1203, possibly on John's orders, and of his other prisoners, alienated many of his remaining subjects in France, and in 1203–4 the French king was able to dispossess him of Normandy, Maine, Touraine, Anjou and Poitou with relative ease. Although John recovered Gascony and southern Poitou in 1205–6, his overall losses were immense.

In 1205 John's chancellor, Hubert Walter, archbishop of Canterbury, died. The monks of Canterbury, as was their right, elected Stephen Langton as his successor in 1206. John refused to accept Stephen as archbishop, and in July 1207 drove all Canterbury's monks into exile abroad. This so angered Pope Innocent III that in 1208 England was placed under an interdict: for the next six years it was forbidden to hold church services and even to bury the dead with Christian rites. Clergy who published the interdict were outlawed and their property seized.

John led a brief campaign in Ireland in 1210, which successfully established royal authority over its rebellious Anglo-Norman lords. On his return to England in 1211, he faced the threat of French invasion and ever-increasing hostility from his barons, who were further angered by costly and abortive expeditions in 1212 and 1213–14 to recover his French lands. In 1212 John was excommunicated by Innocent III, but in 1213 turned the tables on his baronial opponents when he surrendered his kingdom to the papacy, receiving it back as a papal fief. The excommunication and interdict were lifted, and John had gained the valuable backing of the pope. But when in 1214 Philip of France won a crushing victory against John's ally, Holy Roman Emperor Otto IV, at Bouvines, John's hopes of regaining his lands in France were destroyed.

John, king of England The ill-fated John Lackland with his dogs.

On his return from France in 1214 John attempted to collect scutage (money in lieu of service) from the barons who had refused to accompany him. Enraged by the king's unfavourable interpretation of this and other feudal rights, a group of barons rose against him and forced him to agree to the terms of Magna Carta in June 1215. It was intended as a redress of baronial grievances, regulating specific feudal customs John had misused, such as the fees a baron's heir paid the Crown to enter his inheritance.

Because of clauses binding John to dispense free and universal justice and not to imprison or outlaw anyone except by the law of the land or judgement of his peers, the charter has subsequently become a symbol of freedom.

Magna Carta did not, however, change John's behaviour. Later in 1215 he obtained papal excommunication of his baronial opponents, and began to wage war against them. More of his supporters deserted him when Prince Louis, son of Philip II of France and the future Louis VIII, invaded England in 1216 to wrest the throne from the Plantagenet house. During his campaign against Louis John lost much of his baggage train in the Wellstream, in the Wash in Norfolk. Shortly afterwards he died at Newark, leaving three daughters and two sons, the eldest of whom, Henry III, was only nine years old. John was buried at Worcester Cathedral, near the remains of St Oswald and St Wulfstan, two English saints for whom he had had a particular reverence.

The Plantagenet Chronicles: 114, 124–5, 127, 130, 137, 150, 202, 204–6, 217–24, 226, 232, 245, 259, 261–321, 277, 290, 293–6, 298, 301–2, 304–21, 323
Chronicles of the Age of Chivalry/Four Gothic Kings (US edn): 23–4, 88, 90, 133

John Lackland

See: John, king of England

John of Luxembourg, king of Bohemia

1296–1346. Son of Holy Roman Emperor Henry VII; count of Luxembourg (1309–46); king of Bohemia (1310–46). John was elected king to end the anarchy that had prevailed since his brother-in-law Wenceslas' death in 1306. Rejected as Holy Roman Emperor in 1313 on account of his youth, John temporarily became a supporter of another claimant, Louis IV of Bavaria, against his rival, Philip, duke of Austria. Leaving Bohemia ungoverned, he subsequently fought campaigns all over Europe: against the heathen in Lithuania and Pomerania; against the Poles in Silesia; and in Italy, much of which he captured in 1331. In about 1340 he went blind but continued to campaign in Lithuania. In 1346 he secured a papal deposition of Louis IV, his former ally, who had been crowned Holy Roman Emperor in 1328, and the election of his son, Charles of Luxembourg (later Holy Roman Emperor Charles IV) as king of Germany (Holy Roman Emperor-elect). He then went to France to support Philip VI against the English and died at the battle of Crécy (1346).

Chronicles of the Age of Chivalry/Four Gothic Kings (US edn): 246

John of Marmoutier

*fl.*1160s. Chronicler John, a Cluniac monk at Marmoutier Abbey in the Loire valley in France, composed a new and final version of *The Deeds of the Counts of Anjou* between 1164 and 1173, concluding it with a biography of Count Geoffrey the Fair (Geoffrey Plantagenet), father of Henry II of England. John's treatment is lively though his subject matter is often little more than legend. His panegyric of Geoffrey the Fair may have been written to please Henry II and is certainly lavish, suggesting, for example, in defiance of the known facts, that Geoffrey's conquest of Normandy in 1142–3 was welcomed by the inhabitants.

The Plantagenet Chronicles: 12–13, 19, 43, 60, 62, 80

John, of Oxford, bishop of Norwich

d.1200. Diplomat in the service of Henry II; royal justice (1179); bishop of Norwich (1175–1200). In 1176 John went to Sicily at Henry II's bidding to oversee the wedding of the king's daughter Joanna to William II, king of Sicily. Travelling, according to the chronicler Ralph of Diceto, through a France afflicted with famine and thence down the Tyrrhenian Sea in a variety of craft, John reached Palermo, saw the wedding take place, and returned to report to Henry at Nottingham on Christmas Eve, 1176.

The Plantagenet Chronicles: 146–8, 306

John XXII, pope

1244–1334. Born Jacques Duese; pope (1316–34), at Avignon. John quarrelled with the Holy Roman Emperor Louis IV, the Bavarian, in 1323, over what Louis considered to be John's extreme claims of authority over the Holy Roman Empire, and Louis' support of the Spirituals, an extreme splinter group within the Franciscans, whom John condemned for their insistence on poverty. In 1328 Louis invaded Italy and, with the help of Sciarra Colonna, a senator of Rome, set up an antipope, Nicholas V. But the antipope's position became untenable and he submitted to John in 1330. In 1331–2 John preached four mystical sermons, deemed heretical by many theologians, and he died in 1334 amid calls from Louis IV and his other enemies for his condemnation and deposition by a general council.

Chronicles of the Age of Chivalry/Four Gothic Kings (US edn): 205, 221

John of Salisbury, bishop of Chartres

*c.*1110–80, English scholastic philosopher; bishop of Chartres (1176–80). Born at Salisbury, John studied at Paris and Chartres under Peter Abelard and other notable teachers. In 1148 he was presented to Theobald, archbishop of Canterbury, by St Bernard of Clairvaux and became his secretary. A friend and, later, secretary of Thomas Becket, John supported the archbishop in his feud with Henry II and as a result was forced to leave England in 1164. He returned in 1170, and was with Becket when the archbishop was murdered in Canterbury Cathedral on 29 December that year. John wrote a life of Becket and advocated his canonization. He was the most skilled classical writer of the Middle Ages and an important thinker: his works include the *Polycraticus*, a treatise on government, and the *Metalogicon*, a portrait of contemporary intellectual life.

The Plantagenet Chronicles: 82

Joinville, John, lord of

1224?–1317? Seneschal of Champagne; French chronicler and biographer of Louis IX of France (St Louis). Joinville was a close friend and adviser to the king, whom he accompanied on his crusade of 1248–54. He opposed and refused to take part in the crusade of 1269–70, on which Louis died. His evidence helped Philip IV of France procure Louis's canonization in 1298. Between 1304 and 1309 Joinville dictated a memoir of Louis IX, which he presented to Philip IV's son Louis (the future Louis X of France). It is written in a simple, delightful style. Louis is described with great familiarity yet reverence. Anecdotes about him reveal, for example, his habit of dispensing justice in the public gardens of Paris, his deep piety, his sober tastes in food and dress and his lively sense of humour.

Chronicles of the Age of Chivalry/Four Gothic Kings (US edn): 7, 16, 90, 93

joust

Sporting passage of arms between mounted or dismounted knights; a popular entertainment for the feudal aristocracy and valuable training for war.

Joust *Contestants from a 15th-century English joust. They wear full tilting helms and plate armour, developed for protection against the couched lance, but in a sporting joust their weapons would have been blunted. The elaborate heraldry identifies them to spectators and to other competitors in the joust.*

Justice of the Peace

Local magistrate, selected by the Crown from amongst the gentry and charged to keep the peace and perform other duties; an office introduced throughout England in 1360.

justiciar

Chief judicial and political officer under the Norman and early Plantagenet kings. The justiciar usually acted as regent in the king's absence.

(1452). Much employed on diplomatic missions by Henry V, Kempe became after 1422 one of Henry VI's councillors and a supporter of Cardinal Beaufort against Humphrey, 2nd duke of Gloucester. Gloucester deprived him of the chancellorship in 1432. In 1435 he represented England at the Council of Arras, and in 1438 at Calais; but neither gathering resolved Anglo-French differences. In 1450, when the men of Kent, led by Jack Cade, marched on London, he was instrumental in breaking up the rebellion by making temporary concessions. Named by Richard, 3rd duke of York, in 1452 as an evil councillor threatening the destruction of England, he resisted the duke and the Yorkist party until his death.

The Wars of the Roses: 178, 210

Kempe, John, archbishop of Canterbury

1380?–1454. Bishop of Rochester (1419–21); bishop of Chichester (1421); bishop of London (1421–6); archbishop of York (1432–52); chancellor of England (1426–32, 1450–4); cardinal (1439); archbishop of Canterbury

Kempe, Margery

1373–1438. English mystic and religious writer. Born Margery Brunham at King's Lynn in Norfolk, she was the wife of a prominent burgess, mother of 14 children and author of the first autobiography in the English language, *The Book of Margery Kempe*. She employed a scribe to record these memoirs, which tell of her quarrels with fellow parishioners, pilgrimages to Santiago and Jerusalem, dialogues with God, mystic prayers and visions. Margery was a zealot, unpopular locally because she wept loudly in church and chided her neighbours. Although she was accused of heresy and even, in 1417, of being a Flagellant, her clerical questioners were unable to make their accusations stick.

The Wars of the Roses: 221

Kenilworth

Market town in Warwickshire; noted for its castle, begun *c.*1120 by Geoffrey de Clinton. It was granted to Simon de Montfort in the 13th century and served as his base in the 1260s. On 24 August 1265, at a great parliament held in the town, Henry III proposed the dictum of Kenilworth to Montfort's dispossessed supporters: the terms on which they could receive back their lands. After Edward II's deposition, he was imprisoned in Kenilworth castle over the winter of 1326–7, and in January 1327 relinquished his crown in its Great Hall.

King's College, Cambridge *The fan vault of the college chapel, a masterpiece of late Perpendicular Gothic architecture.*

The castle later passed to John of Gaunt, and he made many alterations to it in the 1390s, transforming a virtually impregnable fortress into a homelike residence as, for instance, raising a great new hall on an undercroft. Kenilworth became royal property when John's son acceded to the throne of England as Henry IV. Eleanor Cobham was held there in the 1440s after her trial for witchcraft.

Chronicles of the Age of Chivalry/Four Gothic Kings (US edn): 75, 98, 100, 214, 217, 224
The Wars of the Roses: 28, 124, 193

Kilwardby, Robert, archbishop of Canterbury

d.1279. Dominican friar; provincial of English Dominicans (1261–72); archbishop of Canterbury (1272–8), cardinal-bishop of Porto in Italy (1278–9); noted teacher of grammar and logic. Kilwardby crowned Edward I and Queen Eleanor in 1274. His voluminous writings on philosophical and theological topics became widely popular with students. When he left England for Porto, he took with him Canterbury's registers and judicial records, none of which were recovered.

Chronicles of the Age of Chivalry/Four Gothic Kings (US edn): 114

King Henry II and King Richard I, The Deeds of

See: *Deeds of King Henry II and King Richard I, The*

King John of England

See: John, king of England

king of the Romans

Title of the emperor-elect of the Holy Roman Empire, who had been elected by the German princes as king of Germany, giving him the right to the imperial throne, but not yet constituted Holy Roman Emperor by a papal coronation. Because of feuds between the empire and the papacy, a king of the Romans might take years to be crowned as emperor: Frederick II Hohenstaufen, who was elected in 1212, waited eight for his coronation. Some emperors-elect were never crowned.

'Kingmaker, the'

See: Neville, Richard, 'the Kingmaker', 16th earl of Warwick

King's Bench

Court of record and supreme court of common law in England. It developed out of the *curia regis* (king's court) in the 13th century and normally sat at Westminster.

The Wars of the Roses: 270

King's College, Cambridge

College founded at Cambridge University in 1440 by Henry VI; it is twinned with a similar foundation at Eton. Henry initially established a rector and 12 scholars at Cambridge but in 1441 was inspired by William of Wykeham's work at Winchester and Oxford to increase his endowments, enabling the college to maintain 70 scholars. The foundation stone of King's College chapel was laid by Henry on 25 July 1446; work was carried out to the design of Robert Westerby, Henry's master mason, whose plans were put in the king's will of 1448. Henry's deposition in 1461 halted building, by which time the chapel had cost 16,000 pounds; but Edward IV and Henry VII later supported its completion. The fan vault was added after 1506, completing a last great example of the Perpendicular Gothic style.

The Wars of the Roses: 169, 192, 195, 303

King's Hall, Cambridge

College founded at Cambridge in the early 14th century by Edward II to provide well-educated, professional civil servants. Study concentrated on civil and Roman law, arousing the suspicions of the common lawyers trained at the Inns of Court. Richard II's new signet office (which issued writs under his signet seal), established in the 1380s, was mostly staffed with graduates of King's Hall.

The Wars of the Roses: 81

King's Lynn

Market town and port on the great Ouse in Norfolk. Lynn (as it was known until 1537) was established as a borough in 1204, by John de Gray, bishop of Norwich, and granted a merchant guild two years later; the bishops of Norwich were its overlords in the Middle Ages. It was from Lynn that Edward IV fled to Flanders on 29 September 1470, to escape the rebellion of Richard Neville, 'the Kingmaker', 16th earl of Warwick.

The Wars of the Roses: 252

knight

Term used from the 9th century to describe a military tenant of land under a nobleman. Originally, a knight was little more than a retainer but by about 1000 his lowly status had begun to improve, as the Church glorified the institution of Christian knighthood in an attempt to curb endemic anarchy in society.

A man-at-arms was created a knight by being dubbed (struck on both shoulders with a sword), which could be done in haste on the battlefield or with great ceremony in church. In return for a grant of land or money, the knight did military service for his lord on a set number of days. By 1100 the chivalrous code of conduct governing a knight's behaviour had developed, and it was refined over the centuries. But there was always a gap between ideal and reality; for example, Edward III of England was renowned throughout Europe for his chivalrous interests yet nevertheless committed acts of great brutality on the battlefield.

Knighton, Henry

d.1396. Augustinian canon of St Mary of the Meadows at Leicester; chronicler. Henry's chronicle extends from the 10th century to 1395 (excepting 1366–77) and is biased in favour of the earls of Leicester and dukes of Lancaster, patrons of St Mary's; for example, he describes Thomas, 2nd earl of Lancaster's life in some detail. He also shows a hostile interest in the Lollards and records London's moral decline in the plague years (1347–50). Knighton went blind in his last years.

Chronicles of the Age of Chivalry/Four Gothic Kings (US edn): 254

Knights Hospitaller

See: Hospitallers

Knights Templar

See: Templars

Krak des Chevaliers

Crusader castle in Syria, built by the Knights Hospitaller about 1131–6. The lordship of Krak was one of the chief baronies in the Latin kingdom of Jerusalem. In 1187 the castle's lord, Reginald of Chatillon, attacked a caravan led by Saladin, the Muslim leader whose growing power was threatening the survival of Jerusalem, and the following year Saladin took the castle. Later recaptured by the crusaders, it finally fell in 1271 to another Muslim leader, Baybars, who added to its fortifications.

The Plantagenet Chronicles: 250

Kublai Khan

1215?–94. Grandson of Genghis Khan; Mongol emperor (1260–94); founder of the Yuan dynasty in China. Before becoming khan, Kublai led military campaigns in China, from 1251 to 1259. The Mongol empire reached its greatest extent in 1279 with Kublai's final defeat of the Sung dynasty in China. He rebuilt the country's Grand Canal, repaired public granaries, extended highways, fostered Chinese scholarship and the arts and founded a new capital at Peking, where Marco Polo met him in 1275. Kublai, who favoured Buddhism but tolerated other religions, sent Marco to Ceylon to buy the Buddha's tooth in the 1290s. He refused to give the Polo family permission to leave China, and only his death freed them to return to Venice.

Chronicles of the Age of Chivalry/Four Gothic Kings (US edn): 82–3

knights *Judges view knights' helms before a tourney, pointing out those entrants disqualified for unchivalrous acts.*

Lackland, John

See: John, king of England

Lacy, Gilbert de

*fl.*1150s. Fourth baron Lacy. Fought for King Stephen when the English routed the Scots at the battle of Northallerton in 1138. However, later that year Gilbert, who had been disinherited by the king of his share of the great Lacy estate, joined the forces of Empress Matilda, Stephen's rival for the throne of England, in an attack on Bath. By 1146 he was back in Stephen's camp.

Gilbert later joined the Knights Templar and went to the Holy Land, becoming the order's preceptor in the county of Tripoli.

The Plantagenet Chronicles: 70

Lacy, Henry de, 9th earl of Lincoln

1249?–1311. 9th earl of Lincoln (1257–1311). Henry commanded a division in the Welsh wars in 1276 and was joint-lieutenant of England during Edward I's absence in France in 1279. He commanded the English army in France in 1296–8, accompanied Edward on his final campaign in Scotland in 1307 and was present at his death. The *Life of Edward II* records that Henry at first supported Edward II's favourite, Piers Gaveston, but that Piers' ingratitude later made Henry Piers' worst enemy and persecutor. Henry was instrumental in securing Piers' exile in 1308, but nevertheless acted as mediator between Piers, the king and the barons on Piers' return in 1309.

In 1310 Henry became one of the lords ordainers, who drew up the ordinances restricting the king's power, and guardian of the kingdom during Edward's absence in Scotland.

Chronicles of the Age of Chivalry/Four Gothic Kings (US edn): 172, 174

Lacy, Hugh de, 1st earl of Ulster

d.1242. Earliest Anglo-Norman peer of Ireland: created 1st earl of Ulster by King John in 1205. Hugh took part in fighting the native Irish in Ulster before 1205 and, with his brother Walter, pacified large areas. Given the authority of a sub-king, he quarrelled with barons loyal to John; and when the king invaded Ireland in 1210, to impose royal authority there, Hugh was banished to Scotland, from where he fled to France. He returned to England in 1221 and joined the rebel Llywelyn ap Iorwerth in Wales. He went back to Ireland in 1226 and died at Carrickfergus.

The Plantagenet Chronicles: 295

Lacy, Walter de

d.1241. Sixth baron Lacy; 2nd lord of Meath (1186–1210); sheriff of Herefordshire (1216–23). Walter joined his brother Hugh in about 1205 to seize and subdue large estates in Ireland. In 1210 he was dispossessed of his estates when King John invaded Ireland to impose royal authority there. Walter later took part in the king's French expedition of 1214, and, as lord of Ludlow, was one of the young Henry III's chief supporters after John's death in 1216.

The Plantagenet Chronicles: 295

Lancaster, Blanche of

See: Blanche of Lancaster

Lancaster, house of

Cadet branch of the Plantagenets, which took its title from Henry, 1st duke of Lancaster. On his death in 1362, John of Gaunt, the fourth son of Edward III who had married Henry's daughter and heir, Blanche of Lancaster, succeeded him as duke. John was married three times: his second wife was Constance of Castile (1372), and his third Catherine Swynford (1396). He produced many descendants, who had a claim to the English throne because they sprang from the Plantagenet royal line through Edward III.

In 1399, shortly after Gaunt's death, his eldest son, Henry Bolingbroke, 3rd duke of Lancaster, son of Blanche of Lancaster, took the throne from Richard II as Henry IV. He was succeeded by Henry V, his son (in 1413), and Henry VI, his grandson (in 1422). Henry was in turn deposed by Edward, 4th duke of York, in 1461 head of the house of York, another line of Edward III's descendants with a rival claim to the throne. Henry was returned briefly to power in 1470 with the help of Richard Neville, 'the Kingmaker', 16th earl of Warwick; but in 1471 both he and his son and heir Edward, prince of Wales, died at the hands of Edward IV's men, finally ending Lancastrian rule in England. The Lancastrian claim to the throne of England now passed to Henry Tudor, later Henry VII, who was descended from the Beauforts, the legitimized progeny of John of Gaunt and Catherine Swynford.

The Wars of the Roses: 263

Lancaster, Humphrey of

See: Humphrey of Lancaster

Lanercost chronicle

Chronicle probably compiled at Lanercost Priory, an Augustinian house on Hadrian's Wall in Cumbria, or possibly at the Franciscan friary at Carlisle. It continues the writings of Richard of Durham, and covers the period 1297–1346. The chronicler writes mostly of northern affairs, vividly describing the sieges of Berwick and Carlisle by the Scots in 1312 and 1315, and giving an eye-witness account of the battle of Bannockburn in 1314. He accuses Edward II of improper relations with Piers Gaveston, of pursuing 'pointless and trivial occupations' such as digging ditches and of failing to defend the north country against the Scots.

Chronicles of the Age of Chivalry/Four Gothic Kings (US edn): 13, 188, 192, 194, 204, 234

Langeais castle

Castle in Anjou, France, built during the 11th century, probably by Count Fulk Nerra as part of his programme of constructing strategically sited strongholds. The remains of its rectangular stone keep still stand.

The Plantagenet Chronicles: 30

Langland, William

1332?–1400? Priest and poet. Langland was probably born at Ledbury in Herefordshire, and educated at Great Malvern Abbey nearby. He may have held minor orders. He later lived in

Leeds castle *The moat and ramparts of Leeds castle, which surrendered to Edward II in 1321 after being assaulted with catapults and other siege engines.*

London, where he probably earned his living by copying documents and singing masses. He began his great poem, 'The Vision of Piers Plowman', in about 1362 and wrote at least two other versions in 1377 and 1392. He may also be the author of 'Richard the Redeless', a poem attacking Richard II's rule.

Chronicles of the Age of Chivalry/Four Gothic Kings (US edn): 275

Langley, Edmund of, 1st duke of York

1341–1402. Fifth son of Edward III and Philippa of Hainault; knight of the Garter (1361), 3rd earl of Cambridge (1362–1402); constable of Dover (1376–81); 1st duke of York (1385–1402). Edmund accompanied his father on campaign in France in 1359 and his brother, the Black Prince, to Spain in 1367. He married Isabella of Castile, daughter of Peter I, the Cruel, of Castile, in 1372.

In 1377 Edmund was appointed to the council of regency for Richard II and in 1385 took part in Richard's campaign against the Scots. The French chronicler Froissart describes meeting Edmund in 1395. Edmund was regent for Richard II once again, from 1394 to 1399, during the king's absences in France and Ireland; in 1399 he summoned Richard's counsellors to decide what action should be taken when the news of Henry Bolingbroke's invasion came. He joined Henry's supporters, and after Bolingbroke's coronation as Henry IV later that year retired from court.

The Wars of the Roses: 70, 72, 84

Langtoft, Peter

d.1307? Augustinian canon of Bridlington Priory in Yorkshire; chronicler. Peter's chronicle, in French verse, covers the history of England from its mythical foundation by Brutus to 1307. Influenced by romance literature, Peter's work was intended to entertain; and it rapidly became popular, especially in the north of England, where the author's violent hatred of the Scots clearly struck a chord. The last part of the poem concentrates on England's struggle with Scotland, celebrates Edward I's victories of 1296, quotes popular anti-Scottish ballads and eulogizes the dead king.

Chronicles of the Age of Chivalry/Four Gothic Kings (US edn): 164

Langton, Stephen, archbishop of Canterbury

d.1228. Cardinal (1206); archbishop of Canterbury (1207–28). A celebrated theologian in Paris, Stephen was a friend of Lothar of Segni (the future Pope Innocent III), who made him a cardinal. After a disputed election at Canterbury remained unsolved, Innocent suggested in 1207 that Langton be chosen archbishop. At first rejected by King John, Stephen remained at Pontigny in France during the resultant papal Interdict on England (1208–13), which forbade the holding of most church services. The monks of Canterbury were exiled by John for supporting Stephen.

When finally received by John in 1213, Stephen publicly absolved him, at Canterbury, from the excommunication that had been pronounced on him in 1212. Tending to support the barons in their struggle against John, Stephen mediated between them and the king when Magna Carta was drawn up, partly through his influence, in 1215. The following year Innocent suspended him for failing to enforce papal censures against the barons and he resided in Rome until 1218. Returning to England, he gave valuable support to the young Henry III. In 1222 he secured crucial religious liberties from the Crown, which form the basis of ecclesiastical freedom in England.

The Plantagenet Chronicles: 137, 265, 288, 290, 304
Chronicles of the Age of Chivalry/Four Gothic Kings (US edn): 27, 34

Langton, Walter, bishop of Lichfield

d.1321. Keeper of the king's wardrobe (1290–5); treasurer (1295–1307, 1312); bishop of Lichfield (1297–1321). One of Edward I's favourite counsellors, Walter was accused in 1301 of various crimes but absolved two years later. He reformed the Crown finances but was known to be dishonest and ruthless. He accompanied Edward I to Scotland in 1307 and was present at his death. Walter made a fortune from his position as treasurer, and in 1308 Edward II imprisoned him for corruption. He was freed and restored to his office of treasurer in 1312. Excommunicated by Robert Winchelsea, archbishop of Canterbury, he appealed to Pope Clement V and travelled to Avignon, returning after Winchelsea's death in 1313. The *Life of Edward II* records that the barons forced Walter's removal from the king's council in February 1315, following England's disastrous defeat by the Scots at Bannockburn.

Chronicles of the Age of Chivalry/Four Gothic Kings (US edn): 113, 164, 165, 190

Languedoc

Region of southern France stretching along the Mediterranean coast from the Pyrenees to the Rhône. The region's name derives from *langue d'oc*, the dialect spoken there. Languedoc was ruled by the counts of Toulouse until its incorporation into the French royal domain in 1271, after the crushing of the Cathars, or Albigensians, a heretical sect centred on the region.

The Plantagenet Chronicles: 97, 304
Chronicles of the Age of Chivalry/Four Gothic Kings (US edn): 65, 69, 266

Las Huelgas

See: Huelgas, Las

Lateran Councils

Five general councils of the Church held at the Lateran papal palace in Rome from the 12th to the 16th century. The most noted is the fourth Lateran Council (1215), summoned by Pope Innocent III. It defined transubstantiation, confirmed previous disciplinary canons, laid down regulations for the trial of churchmen, and called the Fifth Crusade. Among its other business, it laid down annual confession and communion at Easter as the minimum requirement for membership of the Catholic Church.

The Plantagenet Chronicles: 312–13

Latimer, William, Lord Latimer

1329?–81. Knight of the Garter (1361); king's chamberlain (1369); constable of Dover and warden of the Cinque Ports (1374); governor of Calais (1380–1). In 1359 Latimer served with the English army in Gascony in France. A trusted servant of Edward III of England, he became a close adviser of John of Gaunt during Edward's decline into senility in the 1370s. Accused of corruption and fraud by the Commons in the Good Parliament of 1376, he was tried before the Lords, and found guilty, in one of the first recorded impeachments, together with Alice Perrers, the king's mistress, Richard Lyons, a London banker, and several others.

Edward arranged his pardon and he rejoined the royal council, being appointed to Richard II's regency council in 1377. The chronicler Thomas Walsingham records that public disquiet greeted the news of this latter appointment. After being governor of Calais, he served in France from 1380 until his death.

Chronicles of the Age of Chivalry/Four Gothic Kings (US edn): 299
The Wars of the Roses: 28

Launcecrona, Agnes

*fl.*1387. Bohemian lady-in-waiting to Anne of Bohemia, Richard II's queen. In 1387 Robert de Vere, 9th earl of Oxford, Richard's favourite, divorced his wife, Philippa de Couci, and took Agnes as a mistress. Queen Anne obtained the divorce for Robert.

The Wars of the Roses: 39, 52

Leeds castle

Castle in Kent besieged by Edward II in 1321, after its owner, Bartholomew, Lord Badlesmere, had joined Thomas, 2nd earl of Lancaster's opposition to the king. Large 'ballistas' or 'springalds' (huge crossbows hurling darts or boulders) were used to attack the castle. After its surrender, the garrison was imprisoned or put to death. Richard II received the French chronicler Jean Froissart at Leeds castle in 1395, an event that is vividly described by the latter in his *Chronicles*.

Chronicles of the Age of Chivalry/Four Gothic Kings (US edn): 200, 202–3
The Wars of the Roses: 70

Leicester

County town of Leicestershire; from the 13th century a centre for brewing and the manufacture of woollen goods. The town was an early centre of Lollardy: local merchants shielded the Lollard priest William Swynderby from the authorities when he preached there between 1382 and 1393. Richard III assembled his forces at Leicester in August 1485 before the battle of Bosworth.

The Wars of the Roses: 31, 302, 305

Le Mans

See: Mans, Le

Leo IX, St, pope

1002–54. Born Bruno of Egisheim in Alsace; bishop of Toul (1027–49); pope (1049–54). A precursor of the Gregorian reformers later in the 11th century, Leo travelled widely as pope, combating simony (buying or selling of ecclesiastical preferments) and clerical unchastity; it was for this that he was later canonized. In reply to a bitter attack by the patriarch of Constantinople in 1053, Leo's legates excommunicated the patriarch's entire communion, beginning a schism between East and West. In the same year, to protect the papal states against Norman raids, Leo in person led an army against the Normans of southern Italy but was defeated at Civitate. He had to make humiliating concessions to secure his release and died a broken man. But he is remembered as the pope who restored the lost prestige of the papal office.

The Plantagenet Chronicles: 26

Leopold V, duke of Austria

*fl.*1190. In 1190, during the Third Crusade, Richard I of England publicly humiliated Leopold by allowing his banner to be torn down, and Leopold returned home soon afterwards. According to one story, Leopold took Richard prisoner two years later in an inn outside Vienna, when the English king was trying to return to England from the crusade, and handed him over to Holy Roman Emperor Henry VI. The chronicler Ralph of Diceto records how Leopold's foot was amputated after a riding accident on 26 December 1194 and describes this as punishment for his earlier actions against the English king.

The Plantagenet Chronicles: 225–6, 232, 234, 236

Lewes, battle of

Battle on 14 May 1264 at Lewes in East Sussex, at which the forces of Simon de Montfort, 6th earl of Leicester, defeated Henry III. It followed Henry's subjugation of the Cinque Ports, which provoked the barons to armed resistance. The *Waverley Annals* describe the battle in detail, claiming that the king's army numbered 60,000 men; it included a group of London citizens who turned tail as soon as fighting began and were pursued and slain by Henry's son Edward (later Edward I). Henry was deserted by his followers and captured by Gilbert of Clare, 6th earl of Gloucester. Many royal troops were killed when Edward led them back to the field, thinking his father had triumphed. Total casualties were said to number 3,000.

Chronicles of the Age of Chivalry/Four Gothic Kings (US edn): 75, 96–8, 100

Limbourg brothers

*fl.*1380–1416. Franco-Flemish manuscript illuminators, the brothers – Pol, Jan and Herman – were trained as goldsmiths, and in 1411 succeeded Jacquemart de Hesdin as court painters to John, duke of Berry, France's foremost contemporary patron. Their *Très Riches Heures*, painted between 1413 and 1416, contains illustrations of the twelve months and is the finest example of the contemporary international Gothic style. The illuminations depict scenes of courtly and peasant life at Bourges, where John held his court. The brothers died with their patron in an outbreak of plague at Bourges in 1416.

The Wars of the Roses: 137

Limoges

City in western central France, on the River Vienne. Richard I died in battle near Limoges in 1199. In 1370, during the Hundred Years War, Edward the Black Prince burned the city and massacred its inhabitants because they had rebelled against the taxes he had levied and defected to Charles V of France. By the 13th century Limoges supported a flourishing enamel industry.

The Plantagenet Chronicles: 45, 119, 164–5
Chronicles of the Age of Chivalry/Four Gothic Kings (US edn): 90, 296

Lincoln

City and county town of Lincolnshire. Lincoln castle was begun by William I in 1068 and Lincoln Cathedral by Bishop Remigius in 1075. King Stephen of England besieged Lincoln in 1141 and was captured on 2 February when a force under Robert, 1st earl of Gloucester, raised the siege. After an earthquake had destroyed all the cathedral save the front in 1185, St Hugh of Avallon, bishop of Lincoln, rebuilt it, from 1192, in Gothic style, with richly moulded limestone walls and zigzag vaults. Hugh's apse was demolished in the 1250s to provide more space for his relics and the cathedral became a major centre of pilgrimage. Queen Eleanor of Castile's entrails were buried at Lincoln following her death at Harby in Lincolnshire in 1290. The city was an important trading centre, with fairs for six different commodities.

The Plantagenet Chronicles: 69, 72–8, 102, 144, 181, 203, 264, 277, 312, 317
Chronicles of the Age of Chivalry/Four Gothic Kings (US edn): 29, 64, 76, 133, 150, 156
The Wars of the Roses: 187

liturgy

Prescribed rites and forms of service of the Church. Medieval liturgies were in Latin and followed a form fixed in the 8th century.

Livio, Tito

1400?–42? Early humanist writer. Born near Ferrara in Italy, Tito joined the household of Humphrey, 2nd duke of Gloucester, around 1436 as his poet and orator, and introduced humanist learning to his court. In *c*.1438 Tito applied to the chancellor for a new post, pleading poverty. The request was refused and he left England in 1438–9. Both his *Life of* Henry V and a Latin poem detailing Humphrey's campaign in Flanders (1435–6) against Philip the Bold of Burgundy, draw on Humphrey's recollections and favour him. Tito records how, when the duke was wounded in the groin at Agincourt, Henry V stood over him, fighting fiercely until Humphrey was rescued.

The Wars of the Roses: 13, 124, 126

Llywelyn, prince of North Wales

See: Llywelyn ap Iorwerth

Llywelyn ap Gruffyd, prince of Wales

d.1282. Son of Gruffyd ap Llywelyn; prince of North Wales (1246–58), prince of Wales (1258–82). Llywelyn succeeded his uncle, Dafydd, as prince of North Wales in 1246. In 1247 he did homage to Henry III of England, surrendering all his lands east of the River Conway to him. This surrender confined his dominion to Snowdon and Anglesey, where he built up a power base. Profiting from Welsh anger at the encroachments of Prince Edward (later Edward I of England) and the English marcher lords, Llywelyn used popular support

Llywelyn ap Gruffyd The Welsh hero is decapitated at Builth in 1282.

to extend his power gradually into the old Welsh principality of Gwynedd during the 1250s. In 1258 he assumed the title of prince of Wales. When war broke out between Henry III and his barons in 1262, he allied with the king's chief antagonist, Simon de Montfort. He took the field against Prince Edward in 1263, and forced him to a truce. Despite de Montfort's death in 1265, Llywelyn continued to consolidate his power.

By the Treaty of Montgomery in 1267 Llywelyn's title was recognized on the basis that he was a vassal of the English crown, but in 1272 he refused homage to Edward I, who in 1276 invaded Wales. Llywelyn lost all but Snowdonia in the invasion, and in 1277 sealed the Treaty of Conway, by which he retained this territory alone, and only for life. His treacherous brother Dafydd received rights in Snowdonia in return for helping the English. In 1278 Llywelyn married Eleanor de Montfort, his former ally's daughter, in Worcester Cathedral, with Edward's consent and at his expense.

Llywelyn's brother Dafydd, angry that the English had not rewarded his treachery more generously, instigated a fresh Welsh uprising against English rule at Easter 1282. At first Llywelyn held aloof from the revolt since his wife was pregnant and he hoped for an heir. But in June, after his wife's death in childbirth, Llywelyn joined the uprising. He moved south, hoping to revive Welsh resistance there, and on 11 December 1282 was killed in battle near Builth. His head was taken to London and displayed at the Tower of London to public derision. To the Welsh he has remained as a great hero, the last independent ruler of Wales.

Chronicles of the Age of Chivalry/Four Gothic Kings (US edn): 47, 96, 108, 116–22, 124–5

Llywelyn ap Iorwerth, 'the Great', prince of Wales

1173–1240. Son of Owain Gwynedd; prince of North Wales; prince of Wales (1216–40). Llywelyn seized North Wales from his uncle Dafydd ap Llywelyn in 1194 and five years later, he captured the border fortress of Mold from the English, confirming his position as Wales' most powerful magnate. In 1206 King John gave Llywelyn his illegitimate daughter, Joanna, in marriage. With the king's help Llywelyn took over lands in South Wales in 1207, but after 1208 John drove him back into the north of the principality. Llywelyn supported the English barons in their feud with John, and took advantage of the rebellion to reconquer South Wales in 1212–15. His rights as prince of Wales were recognized by John in Magna Carta in

1215. Llywelyn continued his wars with the Norman marcher lords during the minority of Henry III, but did homage to the king as his feudal lord in 1218. Llywelyn was a generous benefactor of the Church, and a noted patron of Welsh bards. In 1239 he retired to a Cistercian monastery, where he died the next year.

The Plantagenet Chronicles: 293, 310
Chronicles of the Age of Chivalry/Four Gothic Kings (US edn): 44–7, 52–3

Loches, Thomas of

See: Thomas of Loches

Lollardy

English movement for ecclesiastical reform, stemming from the teachings of John Wycliffe in the 1370s; it became increasingly popular after 1387, when the Great Schism further discredited the papacy. The *Conclusions*, a Lollard manifesto presented to parliament in 1395, sum up the creed, which condemned transubstantiation, the sacraments, and celibacy for the clergy and supported clerical poverty and the translation of the Bible into English. Many Lollards went beyond Wycliffe's teaching and embraced free love and pacifism. After the publication of the anti-heretical statute *De heretico comburendo* in 1401, the movement was driven underground. Itinerant preachers spread its doctrines, and Lollards were involved in revolts against the Crown, of which the best-known is Sir John Oldcastle's plot of 1414 against Henry V.

Chronicles of the Age of Chivalry/Four Gothic Kings (US edn): 163, 303
The Wars of the Roses: 31, 68, 96, 100, 105, 112–13, 123–4, 141–5

London

Writing in the 12th century, St Thomas Becket's biographer William Fitzstephen claimed that London was more ancient than Rome, for although both had been created by the Trojans, Brutus had founded London before Romulus and Remus had built Rome. London had in reality been inhabited since before Roman times, and was an important provincial capital of the Roman empire. The city lay at the lowest crossing point of the Thames, and served as a port, trading with continental Europe, and as a centre for exchange between northern England and the rich lands and many harbours of the southern coastal region.

London retained its importance after the end of Roman rule, and after his invasion in 1066, William the Conqueror regarded it as the key to control England. During his reign (1066–87), the Tower of London was built as a royal fortress to dominate the city. It was not until the late 12th century, however, that London became the capital of England. Before then, Winchester had housed the principal royal treasury and the Exchequer, but in the late 12th century they were removed to Westminster. A royal bureaucracy and central law courts developed around them.

London's wealth gave its citizens considerable power, both political and economic. Richard I (1189–99) granted the city a form of municipal administration from which its corporation developed. In 1215 King John granted London the right to elect a mayor annually. City government was controlled by craft guilds, such as the mercers (cloth traders) and fishmongers, who formed the richest and best organized section of the populace. Many of London's streets still bear the names of the groups of traders which colonized them, such as Hosier Lane and Carpenter Street. The 35,000 strong population of London, far outnumbering its nearest rival, York (c.8,000), contained many humbler people too, who might form violent mobs – as in 1326 when Londoners murdered Bishop Stapledon (whom Edward II had appointed to control the city), or in 1381 when John of Gaunt's London palace, the Savoy, was burned by Wat Tyler's followers during the Peasants Revolt.

The abbey and palace at Westminster were the seat of government and the focus of royal ceremonial. The palace was begun under Edward the Confessor in the 11th century; the abbey, reconstructed by 1065, was again rebuilt by Henry III from 1245 onwards. Other buildings in later medieval London included Old St Paul's Cathedral with its 520ft spire, the Guildhall, and many monastic and parish churches. However, its most striking construction was Old London Bridge, first built in the years around 1200, and under constant need of attention to prevent its collapse. Lined with shops, chapels and taverns, it was a microcosm of the thriving community which it linked to Kent and Surrey.

The Plantagenet Chronicles: 76, 96–101, 161, 172, 220–1, 232–3, 240, 294–7, 312
Chronicles of the Age of Chivalry/Four Gothic Kings (US edn): 29–30, 58, 80, 82, 97–8, 114, 116, 146, 148, 158, 168, 182, 210–11, 224, 254, 256, 278, 302
The Wars of the Roses: 19, 22, 24–8, 34–6, 40–1, 48, 108–9, 166, 168, 178–9, 190, 260, 266, 292–4

London Bridge

Situated at the then lowest crossing point over the Thames, London Bridge was first built (963–75) as a wooden structure, then replaced (1176–1290) by a stone bridge bearing houses and a chapel. It was the only crossing over the river until the 18th century, and the tolls charged to use it were an important source of revenue to the city. By the late 13th century, when it was rescued from near collapse, its buildings included shops and taverns.

The Plantagenet Chronicles: 297
Chronicles of the Age of Chivalry/Four Gothic Kings (US edn): 211

Longchamp, William, bishop of Ely

d.1197. Chancellor (1189–97); bishop of Ely (1189–97); justiciar of England (1190–1); papal legate (1190). In 1189 William, who served in Aquitaine as chancellor of Henry II of England's son Richard (soon to be Richard I) supported Richard and Henry's other son John (later King John) in an alliance against the king; and that same year, on his accession, Richard made him chancellor and bishop of Ely. Appointed joint justiciar when Richard went on crusade in 1190, William ousted the other justiciar, Hugh du Puiset, was appointed papal legate and so became supreme head of both state and Church in England. Discontent with his rule developed and when, in 1191, his servants exceeded their powers by arresting and maltreating Richard's half-brother, Geoffrey, archbishop of York, opposition from the Church and people was overwhelming: William was removed from office and exiled. In 1193 he joined the captive Richard in Germany, negotiated for his release and thereafter remained Richard's chancellor, visiting England with him in 1194.

The Plantagenet Chronicles: 161, 202, 217–21

Longespee, William, 3rd earl of Salisbury

See: Longsword, William, 3rd earl of Salisbury

Longsword, William, 3rd earl of Salisbury

d.1226. Also known as William Longespee. Son of Henry II and, possibly, Rosamund Clifford;

Limbourg brothers *The month of April (opposite) from the* Très Riches Heures du Duc de Berry, *their greatest work.*

3rd earl of Salisbury (1197–1226) through his marriage in 1196 to the heiress Isabel; warden of the Cinque Ports (1204–6). William counselled his half-brother King John to grant Magna Carta in 1215. In 1216 he joined Prince Louis of France (later Louis VIII), who was trying to seize the English crown from John, but the following year gave his allegiance to Henry III and served the young king faithfully.

The Plantagenet Chronicles: 104
Chronicles of the Age of Chivalry/Four Gothic Kings (US edn): 133

lords appellant

Five lords who rose against Richard II's tyranny and 'appealed' (accused) five of his counsellors of treason. Thomas, of Woodstock, 1st duke of Gloucester, Richard Fitzalan, 9th earl of Arundel, and Thomas Beauchamp, 12th earl of Warwick, issued an appeal after meeting at Waltham Cross on 14 November 1387. Thomas Mowbray, 1st duke of Norfolk, the earl marshal and Henry Bolingbroke (later Henry IV), 9th earl of Derby, joined them in prosecuting their accusations at the Merciless Parliament of February 1388. The counsellors accused were Robert de Vere, 9th earl of Oxford, Alexander Neville, archbishop of York, Michael de la Pole, 3rd earl of Suffolk, Sir Robert Tresilian and Sir Nicholas Brembre.

The Wars of the Roses: 52–3, 57

lords appellant *The five lords' seals: (top l-r) Gloucester, Bolingbroke; (centre) Warwick; (bottom l-r) Mowbray, Arundel.*

Lorris, William of

See: William of Lorris

Louis, duke of Orléans

1372–1407. Brother of Charles VI of France; duke of Orléans (1392–1407). When Charles VI suffered his first bout of insanity in 1392, Louis, who had been his chief counsellor from 1388, began a long struggle with Philip the Bold, duke of Burgundy, to control France. Thomas Walsingham and others credited him with responsibility for the *bal des ardents* (1392), in which the king was almost incinerated during a masque. In his lucid intervals, Charles favoured Louis, but during his periods of madness Philip ruled. Philip died in 1404 and Louis was murdered on the streets of Paris in 1407, on the orders of Philip's son John the Fearless. The killing precipitated civil war between the Orleanists (who became known as Armagnacs) and Burgundians.

The Wars of the Roses: 68, 108, 115, 134

Louis VI, king of France

1081–1137. Son of Philip I of France; king of France (1108–37). Associated with his father as co-ruler from 1100, Louis waged 20 years of warfare against the robber barons in his royal domain. He fought three campaigns against Henry I of England in Normandy (1109–13, 1116–20, 1123–35), despite frequent setbacks. In 1124 he gathered an army under the French royal banner, the *oriflamme*, to oppose an invasion by the Holy Roman Emperor Henry V, an ally of Henry I.

A benefactor of monasteries, Louis was advised later in his reign by Abbot Suger of St-Denis. By the 1120s he had become so fat he could no longer mount a horse and earned the nickame Louis the Fat.

The Plantagenet Chronicles: 36–7, 56–7, 65, 77

Louis VII, king of France

c. 1121–80. Son of Louis VI of France and Adela of Maurienne; king of France (1137–80). Shortly before his accession to the French throne in 1137, Louis married Eleanor, daughter and heiress of William X, duke of Aquitaine. During the early years of his reign he tried to assert his royal authority over Toulouse, and fell out with Theobald, count of Champagne, over the election of the archbishop of Bourges. Geoffrey IV, 'the Fair', count of Anjou, made use of the conflict between the

king and the count of Champagne to overrun Normandy in 1141–4. After his troops had burned the church of Vitry in 1144, killing more than 1,500 people, Louis abandoned his aggressive and unsuccessful campaigning for more pious pursuits.

In 1147 Louis left for the Second Crusade, appointing his influential adviser Abbot Suger, abbot of St-Denis, who had also counselled his father, as regent. Eleanor, who had borne Louis a daughter in 1145, accompanied her husband to the Holy Land. She was suspected of adultery with her uncle Raymond, prince of Antioch, and in an attempt to reconcile the couple on their return journey to France in 1149, Pope Eugenius III arranged for them to sleep in a bed he himself had decked with valuable ornaments. However, on 21 March 1152, four French archbishops granted the couple a divorce, on grounds of consanguinity.

Eleanor married Henry of Anjou (later Henry II of England) in the same year, and Louis, with Henry's brother Geoffrey and King Stephen of England, mounted an unsuccessful campaign against him. As a result of his marriage to Eleanor, Henry of Anjou controlled Aquitaine as well as Normandy and his Angevin dominions, making him lord of a greater territory than the French king, his overlord, could command. In 1154 Henry succeeded Stephen as king of England, and he and Louis warred sporadically from then on. In 1164, Louis received Thomas Becket, archbishop of Canterbury, who had fled from Henry's anger, and gave him leave to shelter at the Cistercian abbey of Pontigny.

In 1165 Louis's third wife, Adela of Champagne, bore a son, Philip (later Philip II Augustus, king of France), thus securing the succession. Margaret, his daughter by his second wife, Constance, had married Henry's son, Henry the Young King in 1160, and in 1173–4 Louis aided the revolt of Henry the Young King, Richard, and Geoffrey against their father Henry II. He besieged Rouen in July 1174, but retreated before Henry, who broke the siege in August. The two kings were later reconciled, and in August 1179 Louis was welcomed by Henry when he came to England to venerate the tomb of the murdered and canonized St Thomas Becket. In his last year Louis left government to his son Philip. Walter Map, the English chronicler, recorded that in his old age Louis was so highly regarded by his people that he could sleep alone in a wood with no fear of harm. He died in Paris on 13 September 1180.

The Plantagenet Chronicles: 38, 55, 57, 78–9, 81, 97, 106, 114, 124, 133, 137, 148, 154–6, 164–5

Louis VIII, king of France

1187–1226. Eldest son of Philip II of France and Isabella of Hainault; king of France (1223–6). Louis married Blanche, daughter of Alfonso VIII of Castile, in 1200 (she later bore him 12 children). In 1214 he defeated King John of England's forces at La Roche-aux-Moines near Angers, and in 1215 he joined the crusade against the Albigensians (followers of the Cathar heresy) in southern France.

Soon afterwards, in May 1216 Prince Louis crossed to England at the invitation of King John's baronial opponents, hoping to seize the throne from the unpopular English king. The papal legate in England excommunicated Louis and his supporters, but he continued his campaign regardless and captured Winchester. John's death on 19 October 1216 left his infant son, Henry III, as Louis' rival, and English support for Louis, a French prince, waned once John was no longer present as a personal focus for discontent. Louis left for France to recoup his strength, and returned to England in 1217 after seven weeks' absence; his forces were defeated by Henry's guardian, William Marshal, at Lincoln. A French fleet sent to relieve Louis was turned back in a battle on 24 August 1217, and on 12 September Louis agreed to relinquish his claims to the English throne in return for 10,000 marks.

Louis returned to France, where, in 1219, he rejoined the Albigensian crusade in the Languedoc region, and was present at a great massacre of Cathar heretics at Marmande. After succeeding his father Philip II in 1223, Louis took Poitou, hitherto Henry III's domain, in 1224. In 1226 he resumed the Albigensian crusade, and conquered most of the Languedoc. He died later the same year.

The Plantagenet Chronicles: 97, 184, 238, 261–2, 314, 316–17, 321
Chronicles of the Age of Chivalry/Four Gothic Kings (US edn): 24, 26, 29–31

Louis IX, king of France

1214–70. Or Saint Louis; eldest son of Louis VIII of France and Blanche of Castile; king of France (1226–70), canonized 1297. Louis succeeded to the French throne at the age of 12. His mother ruled as his regent from 1226 to 1234, and suppressed several rebellions led by Peter I, duke of Brittany, with the help of Raymond VII, count of Toulouse, and Henry III of England. She remained Louis' principal adviser until her death in 1252. Louis married Margaret of Provence, daughter of Raymond, count of Provence, and sister of Eleanor of Provence, Henry III's wife, in 1234, but her influence never matched that of his mother.

The chronicler Salimbene describes Louis as 'thin, slender, lean and tall; he had an angelic countenance and a gracious person'. Salimbene and Louis' biographer, John of Joinville, both record his piety, which manifested itself in 1239 when he purchased, at enormous cost, a purported relic of the Crown of Thorns from the bankrupt Baldwin, king of Jerusalem. Later, in 1241, he obtained part of the True Cross. He built the Sainte-Chapelle in Paris (1234–6) as an enormous reliquary to hold his collection of relics. He was generous to the religious orders and to the poor, at times frustrating his advisers by making what they saw as over-lavish benefactions.

In 1240–3 Louis subdued revolts in southern France, and in 1242 repelled an invasion by Henry III in alliance with Raymond VII of Toulouse. He forced Raymond to sue for peace, and encouraged the extirpation of the Albigensian heresy in the Toulouse region. In 1244, after a near-fatal illness, Louis took the Cross, swearing to go on crusade to the Holy Land. He made careful preparations, in 1247 appointing royal officials to root out corruption at a local level and remedy injuries and exactions against his subjects.

Louis embarked on crusade in 1248, having appointed his mother Blanche as his regent. He left from Aigues-Mortes in southern France, wintered in Cyprus, and, in 1249, landed in Egypt with the aim of seizing Cairo, a strategic key to Palestine. His army was overwhelmed by the Saracens near Mansourah, and on 6 April 1250 he was taken prisoner by the Saracens.

In France, news of his capture prompted the 'Crusade of the Shepherds', when peasant mobs assembled to go to his aid and wreaked havoc until Blanche suppressed them in June 1251. Louis was ransomed after several months, and went on to the Holy Land, where he remained until 1254, strengthening the defences of Christian Outremer.

He returned to France with his reputation enormously enhanced by the prestige of crusading, despite the campaign's military failure. His biographer Joinville records that thereafter he became a piously austere figure who abandoned the royal ermine or squirrel fur trimmings for his clothes, and wore plain grey woollen cloth with a black taffeta cape; that he regularly washed the feet of the poor, and was often seen in summer in the wood of Vincennes, near Paris, dispensing justice to any who cared to put a case before him.

Louis continued to dispute with Henry III over the English king's rights in France, and tried to reach a settlement – even presenting Henry with an elephant as a goodwill gift in 1254. Finally, in February 1259 Louis sent his envoys to England to negotiate with Henry. The treaty that resulted, known as the Treaty of Paris, was ratified in October 1259; by its terms Henry agreed to abandon claims to Normandy, Maine, Touraine, Anjou and Poitou, and agreed that he held Gascony, hitherto a private holding, from Louis as a fief of the French crown. In return Louis made Henry a peer of France, gave him money, certain rights in Périgueux, Limoges and Cahors, and a promise of the reversion to him of the Agenais, Quercy and Saintonge on the death of their lord, Alphonse of Poitiers. The treaty secured peace between England and France until 1293. In 1263 Louis was asked by Henry to arbitrate in his dispute with Simon de Montfort and the rebellious English barons whom he led in their struggle to impose the Provisions of Oxford, limiting Henry's power, on the English king. Louis awarded a judgement in Henry's favour at the Mise of Amiens (25 January 1264); however, his declaration that Henry should be free to govern as he wished and that the Provisions were void, was disregarded by Montfort and his party.

In the 1260s the Mameluke rulers of Egypt began a new offensive against the Christian states in Palestine. Louis set off in 1270 on another crusade to rescue the Holy Land, but on the way launched an offensive against Muslim Tunis, where he died. His body was returned to St-Denis for burial. In 1297 Louis was canonized by Pope Boniface VIII.

Chronicles of the Age of Chivalry/Four Gothic Kings (US edn): 18, 24, 56, 58, 60, 62, 68–9, 78–81, 88, 90, 96, 101, 104, 137, 148, 175

Louis XI, king of France

1423–83. Son of Charles VII of France and Mary of Anjou; king of France (1461–83). Louis married Margaret, daughter of James I of Scotland, in 1436. In 1440 he rebelled against his father for the first time, joining the Praguerie, a coalition of powerful French nobles supported by Philip the Good, duke of Burgundy, which took its name from recent Hussite uprisings in Prague. Charles pardoned his son but in 1446 Louis conspired against his father's influential mistress, Agnes Sorel, and was exiled to the Dauphiné. Louis continued to intrigue against his father, and was exiled anew in 1456 to the court of Philip the Good.

In 1461 he returned to take the throne on his father's death, which, according to some contemporaries, he had hastened by poison. In a bid to win papal support, he immediately revoked the Pragmatic Sanction of Bourges

(1438) by which his father had limited papal rights over the Church in France. As king, Louis was opposed by the autonomous and hostile nobles who had joined the Praguerie; many were former allies whom he had abandoned when he took the throne. In 1464 the first revolt of his reign broke out when his brother Charles led an alliance of nobles called the League of the Public Weal. Other participants included Philip's son Charles the Bold, Francis II, duke of Brittany, and Edward IV of England. Louis was supported by the French lesser gentry and lower classes. The king's brother remained his principal opponent until Charles' death in 1472, while Louis himself was at the centre of a web of alliances intended to neutralize threats from both England and Burgundy.

In 1474 Edward IV and Charles the Bold sealed the Treaty of London, agreeing to divide France between them once Louis had been deposed. Edward invaded France in July 1475, but Brittany and Burgundy failed to provide promised support, and Louis invited Edward to negotiate terms. The Treaty of Picquigny, sealed on 29 August 1475, secured Edward a 75,000 crown (15,000 pound) payment if he left France, plus a 50,000 crown (10,000 pound) annual pension. The English king withdrew, and made alliances against Charles the Bold with the Holy Roman Emperor Frederick III, the duke of Lorraine, and the confederation of Swiss cantons. The Swiss won several victories against Charles, and Louis defeated and killed him at the battle of Nancy in January 1477.

Louis proposed a marriage between the 19-year-old Mary of Burgundy, Charles' only child and heir, and his seven-year-old son. She refused the match when Louis annexed some of her lands, and instead married Maximilian of Austria, later Holy Roman Emperor, who defeated Louis at Guinegate in 1479. Louis had by this time taken Burgundy, Picardy, Boulogne, Artois and the Franche-Comté, considerably reducing Burgundian territories in France. In 1481 Charles of Maine, last of the house of Anjou, died, and Louis added his territories of Anjou, Maine, Bar and Provence to the French royal domain. Maximilian continued to campaign against Louis, but at the Treaty of Arras (1482) finally conceded him the disputed lands he had taken from Mary.

Louis was a virtual recluse in his last years. Dreading assassination, he lived at his château of Plessis-les-Tours, in Touraine, with only his doctors and astrologers for company. In the course of his reign he had increased French royal revenues by 250 per cent, and subjugated almost all the great French nobles to his authority: at the time of his death, only Brittany retained its independence. He died in 1483, and was buried not at St-Denis, as was customary for French kings, but in splendid isolation in a mausoleum at Cléry.

The Wars of the Roses: 178–80, 197, 201, 238–9, 268–9, 274

Lovell, Francis, Lord Lovell

1454–87? Knighted (1482); privy councillor and knight of the Garter (1483); lord chamberlain (1483–5). In 1480 Lovell served with Richard, 3rd duke of Gloucester, the future Richard III, in Scotland. A supporter of the king, he was referred to in subversive ballads as 'Lovell our Dog'. In 1485 he was stationed with the king's fleet near Southampton to prevent Henry Tudor (soon to be Henry VII) from landing there. Lovell survived the battle of Bosworth that year, at which Richard III died, and organized an unsuccessful rebellion against Henry VII in 1487.

The Wars of the Roses: 301–2

Lusignan, Guy of

See: Guy of Lusignan, king of Jerusalem

Lusignans

French noble family, named after a castle in Poitou; 13th–14th-century counts of la Marche; 12th–15th-century kings of Cyprus. Guy of Lusignan, king of Jerusalem (1186–92), became in 1192 the first of the Lusignan dynasty of kings of Cyprus, which lasted until 1475. Another branch of the family ruled in Armenia from 1342 to 1489. Hugh X, the Brown, of Lusignan quarrelled with King John of England when John took Hugh's fiancée, Isabella of Angoulême, in 1200 and seized Hugh's county

Louis IX *The saintly King Louis washes the feet of the poor.*

of La Marche the following year. In the 1240s John's son Henry III of England introduced many of his Lusignan half-brothers (from Isabella's second marriage to Hugh the Brown's son) into English offices, to the annoyance of the native barons.

The Plantagenet Chronicles: 263
Chronicles of the Age of Chivalry/Four Gothic Kings (US edn): 59

Luxembourg, John of

See: John of Luxembourg, king of Bohemia

Lydgate, John

*c.*1370–*c.*1450. English poet, monk of Bury St Edmunds and prior of Hatfield (1421–32). A court poet, Lydgate began his *Troy Book* (1412–20) at the request of Prince Henry (later Henry V). His patron from 1422 was Humphrey, 2nd duke of Gloucester. Having been rewarded with lands and money for his services, he settled at Bury in 1434. Apart from the *Troy Book*, Lydgate, who was an admirer of Chaucer, also wrote *The Fall of Princes* (1430–8), *The Siege of Thebes* (1420–2), short lyrics, saints' lives and philosophical poems.

The Wars of the Roses: 182, 221

Machaut, Guillaume de

c.1300–77. French poet and composer, considered the greatest French musician of the 14th century. Machaut, a priest, acted as secretary to John of Luxembourg, king of Bohemia, and was a canon at Reims (1340–77). From 1350 he was a poet and musician at the court of John II of France. He helped secularize the motet by using French texts of courtly love instead of the Latin liturgy and wrote the first complete polyphonic mass, the *Mass of Notre-Dame* (1364), for the coronation of Charles V of Navarre, to whom he also addressed several poems. His music was chiefly admired for its skilful use of rhythm with counterpoint. Machaut's poetry included *lais* (verse narratives set to music), ballads, rondeaux and long narrative poems.

Chronicles of the Age of Chivalry/Four Gothic Kings (US edn): 284–5
The Wars of the Roses: 134

McMurrough, Art

1357–1417. Irish chieftain and rebel. By the 1390s he had risen in revolt against English rule and was calling himself king of Leinster. Richard II offered a reward for his capture. In 1392 Art attacked the English-held towns of Leinster, precipitating Richard's expedition to Ireland of 1394, which brought the Irish leaders to subjection.

The Wars of the Roses: 82–3

Magna Carta

Charter of English personal and political liberties, granted by King John to his barons at Runnymede in June 1215. The charter's provisos were extorted from John, and presented to him as a draft document on 15 June to which he was forced to put his seal. Several days' negotiations followed, and the final form was fixed on 19 June, then issued as a charter freely granted by John.

Magna Carta is a complex document, and many of its 63 clauses provided redress against John's recent encroachments on baronial liberties: reliefs charged by the king when an estate was inherited were fixed at 100 pounds, widows and under-age heirs were protected from financial exploitation by the Crown, and debtors' lands were safeguarded against unnecessary seizure. The royal court was fixed in one place – in practice Westminster – where justice could always be sought, and the arbitrary excesses of royal officials in the shires were to be curbed. The Church was guaranteed its liberties and the citizens of London their privileges.

The charter also established that no one was to be imprisoned, lose his lands or be outlawed except by the judgement of his equals or the laws of the land. The king also promised not to sell, deny or delay justice to anyone. It was because of these clauses that the charter came to be seen as embodying principles of liberty.

Magna Carta was reissued in 1216 after John's death, in the name of his son, Henry III, with some changes and omissions regarding individual liberty. It was reissued, with amendments, in 1217 and 1225; the 1225 version was incorporated into English statute law.

The Plantagenet Chronicles: 312, 315
Chronicles of the Age of Chivalry/Four Gothic Kings (US edn): 26, 29, 89, 105, 141, 144, 146, 150

Maid of Norway, Margaret

See: Margaret, Maid of Norway

Maine

County in north-west France, south of Normandy. In 1126 it was annexed to the duchy of Anjou. Part of the dominions of Henry II of England and his sons, it was captured by Philip II of France in 1204 and formally relinquished by Henry III of England in 1259. It was, however, held by the English once more (1425–48), during the later stages of the Hundred Years War.

Chronicles of the Age of Chivalry/Four Gothic Kings (US edn): 24, 90
The Wars of the Roses: 209

Malcolm IV, king of Scotland

1141?–65. Grandson and heir of David I of Scotland; king of Scotland (1153–65); 6th earl of Huntingdon (1157–65). On his accession, Malcolm put down a rebellion of the western Gaels, who were supported by the Norwegians. On Henry II of England's insistence, he surrendered his claim to Northumbria in 1157

Art McMurrough *The Irish rebel chieftain bears down on Richard II's troops.*

in return for a re-grant of the earldom of Huntingdon; he fought as an English baron in Henry's expedition against Toulouse (1159) and did homage to the English king in 1163. From 1160 to 1164 Malcolm was occupied in suppressing rebellions in Scotland.

The Plantagenet Chronicles: 104, 110

Malmesbury, William of

See: William of Malmesbury

Malory, Sir Thomas

d.1471. English author; almost certainly Thomas Malory of Newbold Revell in Warwickshire. Knighted in 1442, he was a member of the parliament of 1445. In 1449 he and his men tried and failed to kill Humphrey Stafford, 1st duke of Buckingham; in 1450 he twice committed rape and extortion and in 1451 he terrorized the monks of Combe Abbey in Warwickshire. From 1451 he spent most of his life in prison, where he wrote his prose romance of King Arthur, *Morte d'Arthur*, published by Caxton in 1485. His work, supposedly based on French romances, is noted for the simple beauty of its prose and its narrative drive; it became the standard source for later versions of the legend.

The Wars of the Roses: 233

Maltravers, John, baron Maltravers

1290?–1364. Knighted 1306; constable of Corfe castle in Dorset (1330). Maltravers sided with Thomas, 2nd earl of Lancaster, against Edward II and fled abroad after the battle of Boroughbridge (1322), at which Thomas was captured. He joined the rebellion of Roger Mortimer and Edward II's queen, Isabella, against the king in 1326 and was Edward's gaoler after his deposition that year. The chronicler Geoffrey le Baker implicates him in the murder of Edward, who died in custody in 1327. Maltravers accompanied the young Edward III to France as a steward (and probably warder) in 1329. He was implicated in the death of Edmund of Woodstock, 3rd earl of Kent, in 1330, and after Mortimer's fall that year he fled abroad to escape a death sentence for being an accessory to the murder of Edward II. He was allowed to return in 1345 by Edward III, who subsequently employed him. His estates were restored and he sat in parliament.

Chronicles of the Age of Chivalry/Four Gothic Kings (US edn): 217, 221, 224

Mamelukes

Originally slaves of non-Arab extraction, bought by the rulers of Egypt and used as soldiers from the 10th century onwards. By the 13th century the Mamelukes were powerful enough to challenge their masters, and in 1250 a Mameluke, Aybak, became sultan and inaugurated a dynasty which was to last until the early years of the 16th century. In 1260 the Mamelukes began an offensive against the crusader states of Palestine and by 1291 had ended the crusader presence there.

Chronicles of the Age of Chivalry/Four Gothic Kings (US edn): 69

Mancini, Dominic

*fl.*1483. Italian priest, humanist poet and chronicler. Mancini was a friar, possibly an Augustinian. By 1482 he was in Paris. From autumn 1482 to 6 July 1483 he visited England, witnessing Richard, 3rd duke of Gloucester's seizure of power from the young Edward V (Richard was crowned Richard III on 26 June 1483). On his return to France, Mancini wrote *De Occupatione Regni Anglie*, an account in Latin of what he had seen during his visit. He details the background to the events, ascribes plausible causes to them and describes Edward IV's career and character ('licentious in the extreme'), Richard's deceit and Edward V's imprisonment.

The Wars of the Roses: 13, 232, 253, 273, 284, 286

Mandeville, Geoffrey de, 1st earl of Essex

d.1144. Constable of the Tower of London (1130–43); 1st earl of Essex (1140–4). By supporting alternately King Stephen and Empress Matilda during their struggles over the English throne, he obtained estates and enormous power in south-east England. Arrested by Stephen in 1143, for supporting Matilda, he bought his liberty by surrendering the Tower of London and Walden and Pleshey castles. According to the chronicler Henry of Huntingdon, he afterwards seized and fortified Ramsey Abbey, expelling the monks and using it as a base for banditry. In 1144 he raised a rebellion against Stephen in the fens but was fatally wounded while fighting the king's forces at Burwell.

The Plantagenet Chronicles: 76

Mandeville, William de, 3rd earl of Essex

d.1189. Son of Geoffrey de Mandeville, 1st earl of Essex; 3rd earl of Essex (1166); earl of Aumale (1180); joint-justiciar (1189). William grew up at the court of Philip, duke of Flanders, with whom later, in 1177–8, he went on crusade. He was made earl on the death of his brother Geoffrey, the 2nd earl. During the revolt of Henry II of England's son Henry, the Young King, in 1173–5, William remained faithful to the king. In 1180 he married Hawise, the heiress of Aumale, and took the title of earl of Aumale from her. He was with Henry II when the king died at Chinon in France in 1189 and was afterwards briefly joint-justiciar for Henry's son Richard I of England.

The Plantagenet Chronicles: 200

Manfred of Hohenstaufen, king of Sicily

c.1232–66. Illegitimate son of Holy Roman Emperor Frederick II and Bianca Lancia; prince of Taranto in southern Italy (1250–66); king of Sicily (1258–66). Manfred was regent in Sicily for his brother Conrad IV, until Conrad's death in 1254, when Manfred ousted his son Conradin. The papacy, determined to crush the Hohenstaufen dynasty, sent an army to Sicily in 1254, and Manfred was forced to restore the island to the papacy; he remained duke of Taranto, but only as a papal vassal. In 1258 Manfred rebelled against the papacy, conquered Sicily and southern Italy, became a leader of Italian antipapal opposition and had himself crowned king of Sicily in Palermo. Pope Alexander IV invested Henry III of England's son Edmund with the Sicilian crown in 1258, but the English king, who lacked funds, was unable to prosecute the claim. Pope Urban IV invested Charles of Anjou as king of Sicily in 1266, and Charles invaded southern Italy and slew Manfred at the battle of Benevento.

Chronicles of the Age of Chivalry/Four Gothic Kings (US edn): 86, 125

Manny, Walter

d.1372. Knight of the Garter (1359); one of Edward III of England's ablest soldiers. Born in Hainault in Flanders, Walter came to England as esquire to Queen Philippa of Hainault. Knighted in 1331, he distinguished himself in the Scottish wars of the 1330s and at the battle of Sluys (1340). With Henry of Grosmont, 1st duke of Lancaster, he led a successful campaign against the French forces in Gascony in 1342–3. The French chronicler Jean Froissart describes how he besieged Calais in 1347 and negotiated the town's surrender, pleading with Edward III to spare its inhabitants. Walter was made one of the founder knights of the Garter in 1359. He campaigned with Edward in France in 1359–60 and helped negotiate the Treaty of Brétigny (1360). In 1369 he accompanied John of Gaunt's invasion of France. In 1371 Walter founded a house of Carthusians, the Charterhouse, in London.

Chronicles of the Age of Chivalry/Four Gothic Kings (US edn): 244, 248–52, 262

manor

The basic unit of feudal landholding, with its own court and often a hall. Manors could consist of one or several villages or even fractions of a village.

Le Mans *The interior of the great 12th and 13th century cathedral of Le Mans.*

Mans, Le

Capital of the county of Maine in north-west France. Le Mans Cathedral, built between the 11th and 13th centuries, was the burial place of Geoffrey the Fair, count of Anjou. Henry II of England was born in Le Mans, founded a leper hospital there and was present at the dedication of the cathedral in 1158. When his son Henry, the Young King, died in 1183, the citizens of Le Mans stole his body, seeking the prestige of a royal burial, and would yield it up to the people of Rouen only on Henry II's express command. The town was burned in 1189, during an attack by Philip II of France, and again in 1202 by King John of England. Berengaria of Navarre, widow of Richard I, held the town in the early 13th

century. She endowed the Cistercian abbey of L'Epau, where she was buried on her death. From 1425 to 1448 Le Mans was held by the English during the last stages of the Hundred Years War.

The Plantagenet Chronicles: 34, 36, 48, 80, 131, 140, 165, 172–5, 188, 192, 213, 234, 274

manuscript, illuminated

Illustrated book, copied by hand, generally on religious themes: saints' lives, bibles and psalters. Secular illustrated books included bestiaries, herbals and scientific treatises. The Church held a near monopoly of book production until the 13th century, but from then on an increasing proportion of manuscript illuminators were lay artists rather than monks.

The Plantagenet Chronicles: 158–9

Map, Walter

1140?–1210? English author, archdeacon of Oxford (1197). Map, who studied in Paris during the 1150s, became in 1162 a clerk in Henry II's household and a justice itinerant. Noted for his wit, he was a favourite of the king, accompanying him on his travels in France in 1173 and 1183. One of his works survives: *De Nugis Curialium (On the Trivialities of Courtiers)*, a Latin prose collection of legends, gossip and anecdotes written between 1181 and 1192, 'a little book I have jotted down by snatches at the court of King Henry'. Walter's writing, informed with the spirit of Horace and Juvenal, is strongly satirical, even at his own expense; he likens his book to 'a forest or a timber yard'. He gives a full portrait of Henry, praising his erudition and generosity but decrying his dilatory conduct of affairs. His lost works almost certainly included Arthurian romances; he was often referred to by contemporaries as an expert on the Arthurian legends and may have been the first writer to link the Arthurian cycle proper with the Grail legends.

The Plantagenet Chronicles: 57, 69, 94

Marcel, Etienne

d.1358. French popular leader; provost of the merchants of Paris. In 1355 Etienne bargained with John II of France in the States-General, obtaining governmental reforms in return for funds for the war against the English. After John's capture at Poitiers in 1356, Etienne dealt with John's son Charles (later Charles V). In 1357 he forced him to agree to the *Grand*

Ordonnance, augmenting the States-General's powers. On 22 February 1358 Etienne led a mob which stormed Charles's palace in Paris and murdered two leading nobles. Shortly after, Charles escaped and raised an army. Fearing Charles's retribution, Etienne allied with Charles II, the Bad, king of Navarre, which aroused the hostility of many of his supporters. Charles besieged Paris, and his party within the city assassinated Etienne on 31 July 1358.

Chronicles of the Age of Chivalry/Four Gothic Kings (US edn): 274

marches

Border regions dividing England from Scotland and Wales (the name derives from an old term for national borders), often raided and invaded from both sides. English gentry with estates in the marches were known as marcher lords. Wardens of the marches, paid from the royal treasury, were chosen from the chief marcher families, such as the Percys, to control the borders.

The Wars of the Roses: 61

Marco Polo

See: Polo, Marco

Margaret of Anjou

1430–82. Daughter of René, duke of Anjou, and self-styled king of Sicily, Naples and Hungary; wife of Henry VI of England (1445–71). A niece by marriage of Charles VI of France, Margaret was married to Henry VI of England in 1445 to strengthen ties between the two countries. When their son Edward, prince of Wales, was born in 1453 Henry had already lapsed into insanity and was unable to recognize his heir.

After her marriage, Margaret became embroiled in factional struggles at court and stirred up opposition to the very interests she was trying to protect. She linked herself and the king with William de la Pole, 6th earl of Suffolk, and Edmund Beaufort, 2nd duke of Somerset, who sought peace with Charles VII of France even at the price of giving up English possessions in France, and encouraged Henry to surrender Maine to Charles VII in 1445. Suffolk was popularly blamed for the loss of Normandy to Charles in 1450. Richard, 3rd duke of York, heir presumptive to the throne until Edward's birth in 1453, became her rival and champion of the magnates who opposed her influence over Henry. With the onset of the king's insanity in

1453 Richard had himself made protector of the realm. When Henry recovered in 1454 Margaret persuaded him to dismiss Richard, ending the protectorate. Richard led an armed force to confront Margaret and Edmund Beaufort, and the two sides clashed at St Albans on 22 May 1455, in the first battle of the Wars of the Roses. Somerset was killed, and Richard's protectorate re-established.

Margaret left Henry briefly in 1456, apparently infuriated by his weak character, and was seemingly reconciled to Richard; but after 1458 she began intriguing against him. She despatched a force which clashed with Richard Neville, 'the Kingmaker', 16th earl of Warwick, one of Richard's supporters, near Newcastle under Lyme in 1459. When open war broke out between the king's supporters and Richard's Yorkist allies in 1460 she led the Lancastrian forces. In June that year she fled with her son into Cheshire after her husband's defeat and capture at Northampton. Six months later, in December, she led the Lancastrians to victory at the battle of Wakefield, when Richard of York was killed. Margaret executed her enemies with great brutality after defeating Richard Neville, and liberating her husband, at the second battle of St Albans in February 1461, but failed to seize London and secure a final victory.

On 29 March 1461 Margaret and Henry were defeated by the Yorkists at the battle of Towton, and fled north to Scotland. Richard's son Edward, 4th duke of York, became Edward IV of England. Margaret went to Brittany and Anjou in 1462 and 1464, seeking French help in restoring her husband to the throne. Henry was captured by Edward's forces in 1465 and Margaret never saw him again, but she continued her efforts to regain the throne on behalf of her husband and son, taking refuge with her father in Anjou after 1464. In 1470 she allied with Richard Neville, earl of Warwick, who had fled to France after breaking with Edward IV's regime, and backed his invasion of England which forced Edward to flee to Flanders in September 1470. Henry, who had been imprisoned in the Tower of London, was restored to the throne in October 1470. Margaret led a landing at Weymouth on 14 April 1471, the day of the battle of Barnet at which Neville was killed and her husband recaptured. She was defeated and captured at the battle of Tewkesbury on 4 May 1471, where her son Edward died. Her husband was put to death on 21 May.

For the next four years Margaret remained a prisoner of the Yorkists, until she was ransomed in 1475 as one of the terms in the Treaty of Picquigny between Louis XI of France and Edward IV of England. In return for her freedom, she renounced her royal title and her rights in England. Until her death in 1482, she lived in penury in a small château near Saumur in Anjou. She was buried in the cathedral at Angers.

The Wars of the Roses: 189, 194, 196, 200–1, 212, 217, 222–4, 229–30, 232, 245, 260, 262–3, 268

Margaret, daughter of James I of Scotland

1425?–45. Margaret was betrothed to the dauphin Louis of France (later Louis XI) in 1435, after a French embassy requesting her hand was received in Scotland. An English flotilla sent to intercept the fleet carrying Margaret to France in 1436 was diverted by a convoy of Flemish merchantmen carrying wine, and Margaret arrived safely at La Rochelle and was married at Tours. The marriage was an unhappy one.

The Wars of the Roses: 178, 180

Margaret, Maid of Norway, queen of Scotland

1283–90. Daughter of Eric II of Norway and Margaret, daughter of Alexander III of Scotland; queen of Scotland (1286–90). Recognized as heiress presumptive by the nobles of Scotland in 1284, she became queen under a regency on Alexander III's death in 1286. Edward I of England arranged her betrothal to his son Edward, later Edward II, in 1287; the Scots agreed to the union in the Treaty of Birgham (1290), on condition Scotland remained independent. Margaret, however, fell ill on her way from Bergen to Scotland, and died in the Orkneys. After her death the succession was thrown open to any valid claimant under Edward I's adjudication. In about 1300 an imposter from Leipzig declared she was Queen Margaret; she was burned at Bergen, as a witch.

Chronicles of the Age of Chivalry/Four Gothic Kings (US edn): 132, 134

Margaret of Provence

d.1295. Daughter of Raymond, count of Provence; sister of Eleanor of Provence; wife of Louis IX of France. Margaret attended Eleanor at her wedding to Henry III of England in 1236 and Henry and Eleanor on their visit to France in 1254–5. On the latter occasion, according to the chronicler Matthew Paris, Margaret presented Henry with a peacock-shaped hand basin of mother-of-pearl, inlaid with gold, silver and sapphires. Although her influence on Louis IX was never strong, she played an important role during his first crusade (1248–54), rallying the French troops outside Damietta. After Louis' death in 1270, she entered into a bitter feud with his brother, Charles of Anjou, over the succession to Provence. An invasion of Provence having failed, she returned to her dower lands.

Chronicles of the Age of Chivalry/Four Gothic Kings (US edn): 56, 58, 78, 80

Margaret, queen of Edward I of England

1282?–1318. Daughter of Philip III of France; second wife (1299–1307) of Edward I of England. Margaret and Edward were married at Canterbury on 10 September 1299. She bore him three children: Thomas (later 6th earl of Norfolk), Edmund (later 3rd earl of Kent), and a daughter, Margaret.

Chronicles of the Age of Chivalry/Four Gothic Kings (US edn): 148

Margaret, wife of Henry the Young King

b.1157. Daughter of Louis VII of France, and Constance of Castile; wife (1160–83) of Henry, the Young King, son of Henry II of England; queen to Bela III of Hungary. Margaret was married to Henry on 5 November 1160, when she was aged only three and he five. Under a longstanding agreement between her father and father-in-law, she had been brought from Paris in 1158 and taken under Henry's protection. The marriage gave the English king possession of the Vexin and Gisors castle and was a cause of dispute with Louis, who claimed the wedding had taken place earlier than he wished. After the death of Henry, the Young King, in 1183 Margaret disputed the disposition of her dowry properties with Henry II, a dispute settled by Henry and Louis at Gisors in March 1186. Henry was allowed to keep the Vexin but had to pay Margaret a large annual pension. Margaret returned to Paris on 24 August 1186 and married Bela III of Hungary that year.

The Plantagenet Chronicles: 104, 106, 108, 124, 130, 176–8

---

markets *Market stalls (opposite) by the walls of a medieval town.*

Margaret of York, duchess of Burgundy

1446–1503. Daughter of Richard, 3rd duke of York, and Cicely Neville; sister of Edward IV of England; wife (1468–77) of Charles the Bold, duke of Burgundy. Margaret's marriage was arranged by Edward and Charles and angered Louis XI of France. Her trousseau cost Edward nearly 2,500 pounds, an enormous sum he could ill afford. She arrived at Sluys in Flanders on 29 June 1468, married Charles at Damme and made a splendid entry into Bruges. William Caxton, the printer, led the English reception at Sluys and in 1469 began translating the *Recueilles d'histoires de Troyes* into English for her. Margaret gave refuge to Edward IV when he fled to Burgundy in 1470. The Crowland chronicler records that after Charles's death in battle in 1477, Margaret tried to arrange a marriage between her step-daughter Mary, heiress apparent to Burgundy, and George, 3rd duke of Clarence, but Edward vetoed the union. After the Lancastrian Henry Tudor's accession as Henry VII of England in 1485, Margaret's court became a haven for discontented Yorkists.

The Wars of the Roses: 238–42, 272

Marie de France

*fl.*1155–90. French-born poet; possibly a half-sister of Henry II of England. Marie spent her adult life in the English court and dedicated her work to a 'noble king', probably Henry II. She wrote in Anglo-Norman, drawing on Celtic and Arthurian legends, which she made into *lais*, verse narratives set to music. Many of her tales concern love and feature fairy mistresses, romantic triangles and separated twins.

The Plantagenet Chronicles: 246–7

mark

In England a unit of account, worth two-thirds of a pound sterling (13s. 4d).

markets

Markets in medieval England were usually held once a week and attracted traders from within a 20-mile radius; as far as a cart could travel in a day, with time still left for trading. The right to hold a market was granted by either the Crown or a great lord. It gave the holder of the land on which the market was held the right to charge tolls on goods and fees for stores but also placed on him the obligation to maintain law and order during the day's trading. By the early 14th century there were about 3,000 markets in England. Food was the main commodity.

Chronicles of the Age of Chivalry/Four Gothic Kings (US edn): 195
The Wars of the Roses: 186–7

Marmoutier, John of

See: John of Marmoutier

marquis

Feudal title below a duke and above an earl; not used in England until John of Gaunt made his son John Beaufort the first marquis of Dorset in 1397.

Marshal, John

1170?–1235. Nephew of William Marshal, 5th earl of Pembroke; marshal of Ireland (1207). According to *The Deeds of King Richard*, John was present at Richard I's coronation in 1189, bearing the king's spurs. He accompanied his uncle William Marshal on campaign in Flanders in 1197–8. Appointed marshal of Ireland by King John in 1207, he was given grants of titles and lands. He supported the king in his conflict with his barons, and went on a mission to Rome for him in 1215. In 1217, after the king's death, John fought against the French at Lincoln and prepared against the arrival of the French fleet. He went on to serve Henry III as a justice itinerant, justice of the forest and royal envoy.

The Plantagenet Chronicles: 200

Marshal, William, 5th earl of Pembroke

1145?–1219. Landless younger son of John Marshal; 5th earl of Pembroke (1189–1219); regent of England (1216–19). William's skill at jousting impressed Eleanor of Aquitaine, and he was made guardian of her son Henry, the Young King, with whom he rebelled against Henry II in 1173. On his ward's death in 1183 William went on crusade to Palestine. While safeguarding Henry II's last flight, from Le Mans to Chinon, in 1189, he unhorsed him in a skirmish but saved his life; he was at Richard's coronation as Richard I that same year. William gained his earldom in 1189 through marrying the heiress, Isabella. He helped thwart the revolt of Richard I's brother John against the king in 1193, but backed John in 1199, and was his chief adviser by 1213. On John's death in 1216 William was made Henry III's regent, and led the English

William Marshal *The tomb effigy of the great English warrior.*

forces against the French at Lincoln, despite his advanced years. William's deeds are told in the *History of William the Marshal* (c.1225).

The Plantagenet Chronicles: 154, 200, 217, 220, 235, 278, 281–2, 323
Chronicles of the Age of Chivalry/Four Gothic Kings (US edn): 23–8, 30, 55, 133

Marshalsea

Prison in London. It was demolished during the Peasants Revolt (1381) and its prisoners released, but later rebuilt.

The Wars of the Roses: 36

Martin IV, pope

1210/20–85. Born Simon de Brie; chancellor to Louis IX of France (1260); pope (1281–5). Once elected, Martin supported the power of Charles of Anjou and the Angevin dynasty in southern Italy and in 1281, on Charles's behalf, excommunicated the Byzantine Emperor Michael VIII, thus sundering the union of eastern and western Churches made at Lyons in 1274. He later excommunicated Peter III of Aragon, whom the Sicilians had called on in 1282 to be their king after rising against and expelling Charles of Anjou.

Chronicles of the Age of Chivalry/Four Gothic Kings (US edn): 126

Martin V, pope

1368–1431. Born Oddone Colonna; pope (1417–31). Created cardinal by Pope Innocent VII, he attended the Councils of Pisa (1409) and Constance (1414–18), called to end the Great Schism. He was elected pope at Constance on 11 November 1417, all other popes having been deposed in his favour, ending the schism. Martin settled in Rome, where he devoted himself to consolidating Church unity, papal finances and papal prestige. He denounced the conciliar theory by which he had been elected, and the two councils he summoned, at Pavia (1423–4) and Basel (1431), accomplished little. He succeeded in reviving the power of the papal states by warfare, diplomacy and nepotism.

The Wars of the Roses: 33, 126–7, 141, 156

Mary of Burgundy

1457–82. Daughter and heiress of Charles the Bold, duke of Burgundy, and Isabella of Bourbon. On her father's death in 1477, Mary inherited the Low Countries, Artois, Luxembourg and Franche-Comté. Edward IV of England vetoed the tender for her hand by his disloyal brother George, 3rd duke of Clarence, fearing the marriage would make him too powerful.

In 1477 Louis XI of France offered her in marriage to his seven-year-old son Charles (later Charles VIII), but seized her inheritance. Mary was determined to fight back and in February of that year granted the Great Privilege to her people of Flanders, Brabant, Hainault and Holland, giving them important liberties in exchange for their support. She rejected the dauphin's hand and in August 1477 married Maximilian of Austria (later Holy Roman Emperor), who reclaimed some of her lands from Louis. Mary died prematurely after falling from her horse.

The Wars of the Roses: 239, 265, 272

Masca, Pandulf, papal legate

d.1226. Bishop of Norwich (1215–26); papal legate (1218–21). A Roman by birth, Pandulf was sent to England by Pope Innocent III in July 1211 to negotiate with King John over the succession to the see of Canterbury, which had been in dispute since 1205. John's refusal to accept the pope's candidate, Stephen Langton, led to his earlier excommunication being renewed. The king forced Pandulf to leave England but he returned in 1213 to receive John's submission to the pope: the king accepted Stephen Langton as archbishop and surrendered England as a papal fee.

Elected as bishop of Norwich in 1215, Pandulf remained loyal to John throughout the Magna Carta negotiations and aided his efforts to revoke the charter in 1215–16. In 1218 Pandulf replaced Gualo as papal legate in England, representing Pope Honorius III, and, after William Marshal's death in 1219, became de facto regent for the young Henry III. Stephen Langton viewed him as a rival and secured his recall to Rome in 1221, but after his death there five years later he was buried in Norwich Cathedral.

The Plantagenet Chronicles: 300, 313
Chronicles of the Age of Chivalry/Four Gothic Kings (US edn): 27, 30, 34

Master of Hungary

d.1251. Renegade Cistercian monk and leader of the Pastoureaux movement in France. In 1251 he began preaching in northern France and Flanders to raise an army to aid Louis IX of France in Egypt, claiming he had been sent by the Virgin to lead the *pastoureaux* (shepherds). Some 100,000 commoners and vagabonds followed him to Paris, where his sermons were directed against the Church and the French nobility. He condemned monks and friars for their greed and hypocrisy, and vehemently abused the papal hierarchy. His followers sacked Orléans in June 1251, then Rouen. Later that year he was captured at Bourges by royal officials and hanged.

Chronicles of the Age of Chivalry/Four Gothic Kings (US edn): 72–4

Matilda, Empress

1102–67. Daughter of Henry I of England and Edith of Scotland; wife of Holy Roman Emperor Henry V (1114–25), wife of Geoffrey the Fair, count of Anjou (1128–51). Her father arranged Matilda's betrothal (1109) and marriage (1114) to the Holy Roman Emperor Henry V. On his death in 1125, she returned to England and in 1127 was designated Henry I's heir; her only legitimate brother, William, had drowned in 1120. She was strong-minded and ambitious: a contemporary ecclesiastic described her as 'a woman who has little of the woman in her'.

Soon after Henry's barons accepted her claim (1127), Matilda was married (1128) for the second time, to Geoffrey IV, 'the Fair', count of Anjou, eleven years her junior. A mutual dislike soon developed between them. Matilda and Geoffrey were both unpopular with the barons in England and Normandy, a majority of whom supported her cousin, Stephen of Blois, in a successful coup when Henry I died in 1135.

Matilda, with the help of her half-brother Robert, 1st earl of Gloucester, and others, fought back, invading England in 1139 while Geoffrey concentrated on subjugating Normandy. Matilda and her allies struggled for two years to gain the throne, but she alienated many of her supporters by her high-handed behaviour. In 1141 Stephen was brought captive to her at Gloucester, and a council at Winchester declared her 'Lady of England and Normandy'. She went on to London, where she so angered the citizens by her confiscations and demands for money that she was driven from the city. In 1141 she was forced by her followers to exchange Stephen for Robert, who had been captured that year. She was defeated at Winchester before the end of 1141. Many of the clergy who had declared for Matilda now switched their support back and nominated Stephen, who besieged her in Oxford castle in 1142: she escaped by slipping through his lines at night.

She continued the struggle against Stephen, but with little success and in 1148 she retired to Normandy, which her husband Geoffrey had conquered in 1145. Her son Henry, the future Henry II of England, prosecuted his own claim to the kingdom, to which he succeeded in 1154. Matilda remained thereafter in Normandy, advising her son on the administration of his empire, and making lavish donations to the Church, until her death in 1167.

The Plantagenet Chronicles: 38–40, 45–8, 60–9, 72–5, 102, 113, 131, 144

Matilda, wife of Henry the Lion

1156–89. Daughter of Henry II of England and Eleanor of Aquitaine; wife of Henry the Lion, duke of Saxony and Bavaria. Matilda married Henry at Minden in February 1168, when she was 12 years old, after negotiations which had begun in 1165. The match was supported by Holy Roman Emperor Frederick I Barbarossa, to crown an alliance with England against Pope Alexander III. Matilda, who administered Henry's estates during his absences, bore him two sons, the second of whom, Otto, later became Holy Roman Emperor Otto IV. Henry quarrelled with Frederick in the late 1170s, and he and Matilda took refuge at Henry II's court in 1182. They returned to Germany three years later in 1185.

The Plantagenet Chronicles: 112–14, 225

Matthew Paris

See: Paris, Matthew

Mauger, bishop of Worcester

d.1212. Physician to Richard I; bishop of Worcester (1199–1212). As a papal commissioner, Mauger urged King John to submit to Pope Innocent III over the election of Stephen Langton as archbishop of Canterbury and, when his entreaties failed, pronounced the interdict against him in 1208. He fled to France that same year and died in Pontigny, after attempting a reconciliation with John.

The Plantagenet Chronicles: 300

Maurice, count of Anjou

d.987. Son and heir of Geoffrey Greygown, count of Anjou. The *Chronicle of the Counts of Anjou* describes him as a man who was 'wise, virtuous and peace-loving and who ruled in peace more as a result of wisdom than of fighting battles'. He left his lands to his son, Fulk Nerra.

The Plantagenet Chronicles: 24

Maximilian of Austria, Holy Roman Emperor

1459–1519. Son and heir of Holy Roman Emperor Frederick III and Leonora of Portugal; duke of Burgundy (1477–1519); king of the Romans (1486–1519); king of Germany (1493–1519); Holy Roman Emperor (1493–1519). Maximilian gained his dukedom by marrying Mary of Burgundy in 1477 but the marriage led to wars with Louis XI of France, who that year seized Burgundy and Mary's other possessions. Maximilian won a victory at Guinegate in 1479, and by the time of Mary's death in 1482 had regained more of her possessions: the Low Countries, Artois and the Franche-Comté. However, he yielded the latter two counties to Louis in the Treaty of Arras (1483).

A Habsburg, Maximilian, as emperor, established the family as a powerful dynasty, often at the expense of Germany as a whole.

The Wars of the Roses: 239, 274

Medici family

Florentine banking dynasty. It first became prominent under Giovanni de'Medici (1360–1429), when he lent money to Pope John XXIII, who made the Medici papal bankers. The papal account gave the family prestige (and generated up to half their profits); they became papal office-brokers, with branches across Europe. Cosimo de'Medici (1389–1464), Giovanni's son and friend of three popes, dominated Florence and amassed huge wealth. He was patron of Fra Angelico, Donatello and other Renaissance artists and scholars. Under Piero (1416–69), his son, and Lorenzo the Magnificent (1449–92), his grandson, the family continued to rule Florence and support artists. However, both men were indifferent bankers and the Medici lost the papal account in 1478. The same year Pope Sixtus IV, whose brother Girolamo was closely involved with the Pazzi, enemies of the Medici, backed a plot to kill Lorenzo; it only just failed. Despite such setbacks, the Medici played a leading role in Florentine politics into the 16th century.

The Wars of the Roses: 110–11, 218

Mélisande, queen of Jerusalem

d.1161. Daughter of Baldwin II, king of Jerusalem; wife of Fulk V, king of Jerusalem. Fulk was chosen to be Mélisande's husband by Louis VII of France in 1128, in response to a request from Baldwin to select a son-in-law from the French nobility who could succeed to his throne. The marriage took place in 1129, in Jerusalem, and Fulk duly acceded as king of Jerusalem on Baldwin's death in 1131. Mélisande long outlived her husband, who died in 1143, leaving her as regent for their son, Baldwin III. Mélisande was comforted in her bereavement by St Bernard of Clairvaux, who also preached the Second Crusade (1146) to aid her against the Saracens. Baldwin III played his part in the fighting but left the governance of Jerusalem to Mélisande until 1152, when he forced her to relinquish much of her power.

The Plantagenet Chronicles: 38, 77, 104

Melton, William, archbishop of York

d.1340. Keeper of privy seal (1307–12); archbishop of York (1316–40); treasurer of England (1325–6); keeper of the great seal (1333–4). In 1319 William led a force of clergy and laity against a Scots invasion force but it was crushed at Myton-on-Swale in North Yorkshire. In 1328 he officiated at the marriage of the 15-year-old Edward III of England to Philippa of Hainault. The following year he was acquitted of complicity in the plot of Edmund of Woodstock, 3rd earl of Kent, against Edward's regent, Roger Mortimer.

Devout and austere, William was generous to impoverished northern barons and religious houses, helped fund the nave of York Minster and restored the tomb of St William there.

Chronicles of the Age of Chivalry/Four Gothic Kings (US edn): 196

Melusine

Mythical progenitor of the house of Anjou, according to the chronicler Gerald of Wales. Melusine was a beautiful, mysterious woman who wed an early count of Anjou and bore him two sons. Always absent from Mass at the consecration of the Host, she was one day forced by her husband to see the rite. She flew screaming out of a window and vanished; proof of her demonic origin. A similar tale was told of the house of Lusignan.

The Plantagenet Chronicles: 22

menageries

Henry II founded the first royal menagerie in the 12th century, at his park at Woodstock in Oxfordshire. Its occupants included lions, camels and a porcupine. Richard I owned a crocodile, and Henry III's beasts included a polar bear as well as an elephant given to him by Louis IX of France in 1254; this was kept in a specially built house, until its death in 1258.

Chronicles of the Age of Chivalry/Four Gothic Kings (US edn): 81

Mercers Company

London livery company. Chartered in 1393, it traded in high-quality textiles and other goods. Richard Whittington, lord mayor of London, was elected one of the first masters of the Mercers in 1397.

The Wars of the Roses: 109

Merchant Adventurers

Foreign division of the Mercers Company, incorporated in 1407 and comprising English merchants who exported cloth to the Netherlands. Originally centred in Bruges, the company obtained trading privileges from the duke of Burgundy in 1446 and moved to

---

miracles St John of Bridlington (opposite), whose shrine was noted for miracles and who attracted many pilgrims.

Antwerp. Despite strong competition from the Hanseatic League, the Adventurers flourished, setting up depots in several other cities.

The Wars of the Roses: 109

Merciless Parliament

Parliament which assembled on 4 February 1388, so called because of its ruthless pursuit of those implicated in Richard II's despotism. When, in November 1387, the lords appellant brought a charge of treason against five of Richard's intimates (Michael de la Pole, 3rd earl of Suffolk, Robert de Vere, 9th earl of Oxford, Sir Robert Tresilian, Alexander Neville, archbishop of York, and Sir Nicholas Brembre) the parliament supported the lords and found the accused guilty. Brembre and Tresilian were executed; the others fled abroad. The parliament then impeached Richard's confessor and five knights of the king's chamber (including his former tutor, Sir Simon Burley) and condemned the knights to death without a hearing. This cost the parliament considerable support, and although the session ended with Richard under the control of a governing council, no permanent curbs were put on his power.

The Wars of the Roses: 51, 56–8, 80–1

Merlin

fl. 5th century. Bard and prophet who, according to the chronicler Geoffrey of Monmouth and Celtic myth, ruled western Britain in the 5th century. Legend has it that he set up the Giant's Dance (Stonehenge) and vanished out to sea in a glass boat. Welsh stories mention another Merlin, an insane bard who lived in a forest in *c.*570. Merlin became part of the Arthurian myth common to Scotland, Wales, Cornwall and Brittany. In the 13th century Robert de Borron wrote a popular French romance, *Merlin* (using Geoffrey of Monmouth as a source), upon which Thomas Malory drew for his *Morte d'Arthur*. Merlin's prophecies were often quoted; for example, in 1210 the chronicler Gervase of Canterbury records rumours that King John was the prophesied incompetent sixth king of England (since the Norman conquest) who would 'pull down the walls of Ireland'.

The Plantagenet Chronicles: 280, 293

Middleham castle

Castle in Yorkshire belonging to the Neville family. Edward IV was briefly imprisoned there in 1469, following his capture by the rebellious Richard Neville, 'the Kingmaker', 16th earl of Warwick, until widespread disorder forced Warwick to release him. After the earl's defeat and death at the hands of the Yorkists at the battle of Barnet in 1471, the castle was given by Edward to his brother Richard, 3rd duke of Gloucester (later Richard III), who used it as a centre from which to build a northern power base. Gloucester's claim on traditional Neville loyalties in the region was strengthened by his marriage in 1472 to Anne Neville, heiress to the Neville lands. John Rous records that their only child Edward died at Middleham in April 1484, after a short illness.

The Wars of the Roses: 245, 284, 298

Milan Cathedral

Late Gothic cathedral built between 1385 and 1485. Ignoring the classical trends in contemporary Florence, its planners conceived it as an entirely Gothic five-aisled church. French architects were called in during the 1390s when local Italian ones proved unequal to the building's vast scale. There were furious debates over whether its proportions should be square or triangular. The finished (square) cathedral had 135 pinnacles and over 200 statues.

The Wars of the Roses: 218–19

Milford Haven

Port in Dyfed, on the western tip of Wales, in a vast natural harbour, the 'Haven'. Milford Haven was always a port for trade with Ireland. Henry II invaded Ireland from there in 1172 and Henry Tudor, the future Henry VII, landed his invasion force unopposed at Milford Haven on 1 August 1485 before marching eastwards to Bosworth to do battle with, and defeat, Richard III.

The Wars of the Roses: 302

minstrel

Medieval secular musician, either itinerant or attached to a noble's court. In England minstrels often performed near cathedrals, such as at the north door of St Paul's, London, and in the crypt at Canterbury. Their music was seldom written down and most minstrels were illiterate.

Chronicles of the Age of Chivalry/Four Gothic Kings (US edn): 284

miracles

Miracles were almost universally accepted as genuine occurrences in the medieval world. Shrines, such as St Thomas Becket's at Canterbury and that of St John of Bridlington in Yorkshire, were visited by pilgrims partly in expectation of miracles. The stained glass windows round St Thomas's shrine depict Thomas performing miraculous cures for ailments which ranged from nightmares, swollen feet and blindness, to reviving the dead. St Winefred's shrine at Holywell in North Wales was said to promote fertility.

The Plantagenet Chronicles: 268–9
The Wars of the Roses: 64–5

Mirebeau

Town and castle in Anjou in France, between the River Touet and River Vienne; an important stronghold of the Plantagenet dynasty in the 12th century. Henry II of England's brother Geoffrey Plantagenet was left the castle by his father, but Henry seized it in 1156. Henry's son, Henry the Young King, tried to retain Mirebeau, Chinon and Loudon after the king had conferred them on his brother John in 1173, and rose against his father. On 1 August 1202 John, now king of England, defeated his rival for the throne, Arthur, duke of Brittany, and Philip II of France at Mirebeau, after Arthur had besieged John's mother, Eleanor of Aquitaine, in Mirebeau castle. The castle passed to Philip II in 1204.

The Plantagenet Chronicles: 24, 125, 127, 172, 274–5

Mise of Amiens

See: Amiens, Mise of

Molay, Jacques de

1243?–1314. Last grand master of the Knights Templar. Molay distinguished himself in defending Palestine against the Syrians, and when the Templars were driven from the Holy Land to Cyprus in 1291, tried to organize a new force to recapture the lost territory. Summoned to Avignon in 1306 by Pope Clement V to discuss a new crusade, he was seized by Philip IV of France on 13 September 1307 as part of a carefully planned attack by the king on the Templars. Molay was tortured to extract confessions of sorcery, sodomy and blasphemy, which he later recanted. Philip had Molay

Mirebeau The great castle in Anjou, which was a bone of contention between various members of the Plantagenet dynasty before passing to Philip II of France.

burned in Paris, and legend relates that at the stake he summoned king and pope to appear with him before God: both men were dead within a year.

Chronicles of the Age of Chivalry/Four Gothic Kings (US edn): 181–2, 186

Mongols

See: Tartars

Monreale

Town in Sicily. Its cathedral, one of the masterpieces of Norman-Sicilian architecture, was begun in 1174 by William II of Sicily. He intended it as his burial place, and one of its Byzantine-style mosaics shows him presenting the cathedral to the Virgin. The Eastern influence is also apparent in the twisted, mosaic-decorated columns of the cloister and the building's Arabic-style intersecting arcades.

The Plantagenet Chronicles: 210–11

Montague, Thomas, 9th earl of Salisbury

1388–1428. Son and heir of John, 8th earl of Salisbury (1409–28); knight of the Garter (1414). Thomas served as commander of the rear of Henry V's army in 1419 and as lieutenant-general of Normandy. He invaded Maine and Anjou in 1421 and distinguished himself at the relief of Crevant (1423) and the siege of Montaiguillon (1424). In 1425 he completed the subjugation of Champagne and Maine. He returned to England in 1427 to obtain reinforcements and petition for the settlement of arrears in pay. He returned to France in June 1428 and laid siege to Orléans, where he was struck by a cannon ball and died of his injuries.

The Wars of the Roses: 168, 170

Montague, William, 7th earl of Salisbury

1301–44. Or William Montacute; 7th earl of Salisbury (1337–44); marshal of England (1338); king of the Isle of Man (1341–4). William accompanied Edward III to Scotland in 1327 and to France in 1329. The chronicler Geoffrey le Baker records that he was one of Edward's friends, sworn to protect him during the early years of his reign when he was still a boy and under the control of Queen Isabella and Roger Mortimer. William assisted in Mortimer's arrest in 1330, after rumours of a plot against Edward's life, and was rewarded with some of Mortimer's forfeited lands. He was present at the siege of Berwick and the battle of Halidon Hill (1333). He served in Flanders and in 1340 was taken as prisoner to Paris. Released, he won the Isle of Man from the Scots and was crowned as its king in 1341.

Chronicles of the Age of Chivalry/Four Gothic Kings (US edn): 232

Montfort, Amaury de

d.1292? Son of Simon de Montfort, 5th earl of Leicester; canon and treasurer of York (1265). Amaury lost his preferments on his father's defeat and death as a rebel in 1265, and fled to Italy, where he became chaplain to Pope Clement IV in 1268. He assumed his father's title of earl of Leicester in 1272, but was refused permission to return to England. In 1276 he and his sister Eleanor were captured at sea by Edward I and held prisoner in England, Eleanor until 1278, Amaury until 1282, when he was released on sworn promise that he would never return to England.

Chronicles of the Age of Chivalry/Four Gothic Kings (US edn): 120

Montfort, Eleanor de

1252–82. Daughter of Simon de Montfort. Eleanor was exiled to France in 1265, after her father's fall. In 1275 she was married by proxy to Llywelyn ap Gruffydd, prince of Wales, but the following year, to prevent the actual marriage, Edward I of England had her captured at sea with her brother Amaury on her way from France to Wales. Llywelyn demanded her release as the price of his homage to Edward; the king refused, and condemned him as a rebel against the Crown. Eleanor was imprisoned in England until 1278, after Llywelyn's surrender to Edward. With the king's permission, the marriage between Eleanor and Llywelyn was solemnized in Worcester Cathedral on 13 October, St Edward's Day, 1278. Eleanor died in June 1282 giving birth to a daughter, disappointing Llywelyn's hopes of a male heir.

Chronicles of the Age of Chivalry/Four Gothic Kings (US edn): 120–2

Montfort, Guy de

1243?–88? Son of Simon de Montfort, 6th earl of Leicester. Guy shared command with his father at the battle of Lewes (1264), when their forces defeated those of Henry III; he was wounded and taken prisoner at the battle of Evesham (1265), at which his father was defeated and killed. He escaped to France in 1266 and rose high in the service of Charles of Anjou, king of Sicily, who made him governor of Tuscany in 1268. Declared an outlaw in England, he was unable to inherit his father's earldom of Leicester. In 1271, to avenge his father's death, with his brother Simon, he killed Edward I of England's cousin Henry of Almain at Viterbo in Italy. Edward put pressure on

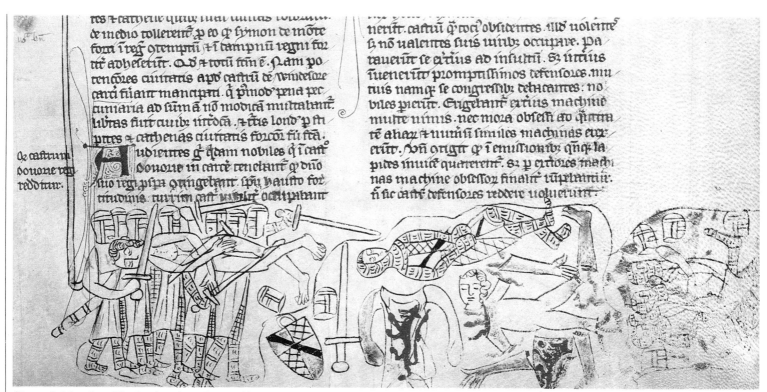

Simon de Montfort The death and mutilation of Simon at the battle of Evesham in 1265. The pieces of his corpse were gathered up by the monks of Evesham Abbey, and buried in their precincts. The cult which grew up around Simon's tomb testifies to his popularity with common people.

Charles of Anjou and the pope, and Guy was excommunicated and outlawed in 1273. He bought his freedom the following year and became captain-general of the papal forces, fighting from 1283 for the Angevins against the Aragonese (by now masters of Sicily). He was captured at Catania in 1287 and died in a Sicilian prison.

Chronicles of the Age of Chivalry/Four Gothic Kings (US edn): 120

Montfort, Simon de, 6th earl of Leicester

1208?–65. Fourth son of Simon IV de Montfort; 6th earl of Leicester (1231–65). Simon was born in Normandy, and went to England in 1229 to revive his mother's claim to the earldom of Leicester for himself. He succeeded in establishing his title to the estates in 1231, and in 1236 officiated at the coronation of Henry III's wife, Eleanor of Provence, as grand seneschal (an office belonging to the earldom of Leicester), although he was too poor to support the dignity of an earl. His closeness to the young king is shown by his marriage to Henry's sister, Eleanor, in 1238. Simon was finally invested with the earldom of Leicester in 1239.

In 1240 he went on crusade and distinguished himself in Palestine. He returned in 1242 to help Henry in his Gascon campaigns of 1242–3 against Louis IX of France. In 1248 Simon took the Cross again with the intention of following Louis IX to Egypt, but was persuaded by Henry to become governor of Gascony instead. He took the post on condition of receiving absolute authority over the Gascon revenues, and governed with ruthless efficiency. He crushed the feuding Gascon barons and stirred up considerable opposition: in 1251–2 he was faced with two baronial revolts. The Gascons complained to Henry, and although in 1252 a formal inquiry cleared Simon of charges of oppression, relations between king and earl were increasingly strained. Simon resigned his governorship that same year and retired to France.

In 1253 Simon returned to Gascony in response to Henry's pleas for assistance to end the continuing revolt there, but was balked in mid-campaign by Henry's insistence that his son, Prince Edward, the future Edward I, should take over the duchy. By 1258 Simon had emerged as the leader of the coalition of barons seeking to impose reforms on the king. He helped draw up the Provisions of Oxford, which were imposed on Henry in the parliament of 1258 to curb royal power, and was one of the 15 counsellors appointed by the Provisions to oversee Henry's government. In 1261 Simon was the only magnate who refused to accept Henry's emancipation from the Provisions. He retired to France once more, only to return in 1263 in answer to a secret summons from the barons, who had denounced the king and declared war on all violators of the Provisions.

Simon agreed to refer the dispute to the arbitration of Louis IX, but, when the French king found for Henry and quashed the Provisions at the Mise of Amiens (1264), Simon resorted to arms, in what became the Barons' War. On 14 May 1264 he and his followers won a major victory at the battle of Lewes, capturing the king. A form of government by council (the 'Mise of Lewes') was forced on Henry, divesting him of real power. Simon became de facto ruler of England, and, in January 1265, summoned commoners to parliament for the first time in an effort to win popular support. However, he quarrelled with his chief ally, Gilbert de Clare, 7th earl of Gloucester, who fled to join Henry's son Prince Edward in the Welsh marches. Edward, the marcher lords and Gilbert took arms against Simon, and defeated him at the battle of Evesham in August 1265. Simon's army was massacred, and he was killed and his body mutilated. The monks of Evesham

music Courtiers and ladies (opposite), fashionably dressed, in a ring dance, an enduring form of secular music.

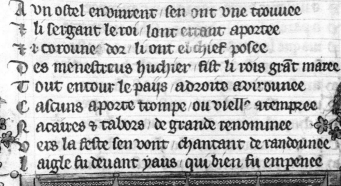

A vn ostel enuirent / sen ont vne trouuee
Et li sergant le roi / lont errant aportee
Et corone dor / li ont eï chief posee
Des menestreus huchier / fist li rois grãt maree
Tout entour le pays / adzoito auironnee
Cascuns aporte trompe / ou vielle atempree
Racaires z tabors / de grande renommee
Uers la feste sen vont / chantant de randonnee
Laigle fu deuant yaus / qui bien fu empenee

A qui que soit dolours / ensi ua qui amours

As mauuais est langours / nos bñs mais nõ porquãt
nsi va qui amours / demaine a son commant

Comment elyos v eniendus v autres
seruit grãt feste z reuel

...edens sa feste entra
...li rois z si siuant
...uent porestendu
...uont le lu comprendant
A force z uiertu
...uont la feste fendant
La charole souuri / si les uont ataignant
Elyos par accort / aloit pardedeuant
Laigle en haut paraument / portoit desor i gant
E menidus laloit / de molt pres costiant
Dautre part martyens / quon apele persant
Qui affaitement / laloient adestrant
z por li alegier / le keute susportant
Les trompes font taisir / si uont en haut cantãt

Ensi ua qui amours / demaine a son commant

En ce point quelyos / aloit la pietiant
Et cascuns a son chant / hautement respondant
Griu z macedonois / saloient meruellant
A quoi ciez faus seruoit / qui ert en aparant
z ciez quile sauoit / loz aloit denonchant
z disoit en basset / z loz aloit nonchant
As dames as pucelles / qui amors uont siuant
En qui amors maint / z font tout sen granant
C est li pris des ueus / qui tant furent parant
Et Elyos laloit / as pludors portendant
po ormetre z rasachier / z puis repouronstant
z de pluseurs autour / saproche en dariant
Par deuant sezonas / va souuent ampassant
z deuers edea / se traist en sousploiant
z puis vers ydorus / sen va ratrauersant
Par deuant porus / ydore z floridant
Caulus z ariste / z gadifer lenfant
Perdicas le baudrain / qui le vis ot luisant
Tout ensement en va / deuant tous remoustrant
Et que plus fort sera / sor aus abandonnant

rescued his corpse and gave it a suitable burial. His tomb at Evesham Abbey became the focus of a flourishing cult.

The Plantagenet Chronicles: 304
Chronicles of the Age of Chivalry/Four Gothic Kings (US edn): 23, 47, 58, 73–6, 86, 89–90, 96–8

Moors

Muslim people of mixed Arab and Berber origin who conquered most of Spain in the 8th century. From the 11th century Spain was gradually retaken by Christians, and the last Moorish kingdom, Granada, fell in 1492.

The Wars of the Roses: 247

More, Sir Thomas

1478–1535. Writer and martyr; lord chancellor (1529–32). His great satire *Utopia* (1516), written in Latin, contrasts an ideal commonwealth with contemporary England. More was eminent in intellectual circles and in Henry VIII's service, but his refusal, as chancellor, to agree to the Act of Supremacy making Henry head of the English Church led to his execution (and to his later canonization). Apart from *Utopia*, More wrote a *History of Richard III*, which contains many informed observations on the Plantagenet era. He described Edward IV as 'of youth greatly given to fleshy wantonness', and his 'merry harlot' Elizabeth (Jane) Shore as 'ready and quick of answer, neither mute nor full of babble'. His account of Richard III formed the basis of Shakespeare's evil king.

The Wars of the Roses: 65, 231, 253, 287

Moreville, Hugh de

d.1204. One of Thomas Becket's murderers. Attached to the court from the beginning of Henry II's reign in 1154, Moreville became an itinerant justice in Cumberland and Northumberland in 1170. During Becket's murder in 1170 he kept back the crowd with his sword while Becket was killed. He did penance in the Holy Land and regained royal favour.

The Plantagenet Chronicles: 118

Mortimer, Edmund, 3rd earl of March

1351–81. Son and heir of Roger, 2nd earl of March; 3rd earl of March (1360–81); earl of Ulster (1368–81); marshal of England (1369–77); lieutenant of Ireland (1379–81). In 1368 Edmund married Philippa, daughter of Edward III's son Lionel, and inherited the earldom of Ulster from him. The House of York later traced part of its claim to the throne to this match; Edward IV was a descendant of Edmund and Philippa. Edmund was an ambassador to France and Scotland in the 1370s and in 1376 led the popular, constitutional party in opposition to John of Gaunt in the Good Parliament. In 1377 he bore the sword and spurs at Richard II's coronation, and was elected to the royal council of regency. Richard made him lieutenant of Ireland but he died at Cork in 1381 while attempting to take over Connaught and Munster.

The Wars of the Roses: 28, 83

Mortimer, Sir Edmund

1376–1409? Youngest son of Edmund, 3rd earl of March. After the death of his brother Roger, 4th earl of March, in 1398, Edmund became the most powerful member of the Mortimer family, since the 5th earl – his nephew Edmund – was still a minor. He supported Henry Bolingbroke's usurpation as Henry IV in 1399 and helped him to suppress Owen Glendower's revolt in 1402. He was captured by Owen in the same year and, when Henry forbade his ransom, because Edmund's sister was wife of the rebel Henry, 'Hotspur', Percy, he joined the rebels and married Owen's daughter. Edmund supported the claim of his nephew Edmund to the throne, and continued to fight on with Glendower even when their Percy allies were defeated in 1403. He died when besieged by royal forces at Harlech castle.

The Wars of the Roses: 101–2

Mortimer, Roger, 1st earl of March

1287?–1330. Son and heir of Edward, 7th baron Wigmore; lieutenant of Ireland (1316–30); 1st earl of March (1328–30). Roger succeeded to his father's vast estates in about 1304. As lieutenant of Ireland, he defeated Edward Bruce's invasion of the country in 1317. His main estates were in the Welsh marches and in 1321 he joined the marcher lords against Edward II and the Despensers. A year later he surrendered to Edward and was imprisoned in the Tower of London. In 1323 he escaped to Paris, where he became the lover and adviser of Edward's queen Isabella. He invaded England with her in 1326 and after Edward II's deposition and during Edward III's minority ruled England through his influence over Isabella, making himself earl of March in 1328. In October 1330 Edward III and William Montague seized Mortimer at Nottingham castle. He was condemned to death and hanged, drawn and quartered at Tyburn in London.

Chronicles of the Age of Chivalry/Four Gothic Kings (US edn): 202, 208–10, 216, 224, 230–4

Mortimer, Roger, 4th earl of March

1374–98. Son and heir of Edmund, 3rd earl of March; 4th earl of March (1381–98); 7th earl of Ulster (1393–8); lieutenant of Ireland (1397–8). Brought up as a ward of Richard II after his father's death in 1381, Roger was proclaimed heir presumptive to the throne by Richard II in 1385. In 1394 he accompanied Richard to Ireland to subdue the rebel Irish chiefains, and to take possession of his Ulster estates there. When Richard made him lieutenant of Ireland in 1397, his liberality and bravery won him some popularity with the Irish. Richard, suspicious of this popularity, summoned him to England in 1398 to attend parliament. Roger complied, gave the king no chance to move against him and returned safely to Ireland. He died at Kells in 1398, fighting the clans of Leinster.

The Wars of the Roses: 101

Mortimer's Cross, battle of

Battle in Herefordshire on 2 February 1461, between Yorkist forces under Edward, 4th duke of York (the future Edward IV) and a Lancastrian army under James Butler, 2nd earl of Wiltshire, and Jasper Tudor, 17th earl of Pembroke. Edward won decisively, and was said to have derived his emblem, a sun in splendour, from an omen which appeared during the battle.

The Wars of the Roses: 223–4

Mortmain, statute of

Statute proclaimed on Edward I's authority in 1279, by which no one could sell or donate lands, revenues or possessions to the clergy without a royal licence. The reason for the statute was to halt the expansion of ecclesiastical lands, which were of little benefit to the Crown, since they were taxed less heavily than lay estates and feudal services were not paid on them.

Chronicles of the Age of Chivalry/Four Gothic Kings (US edn): 122

Morton, John, archbishop of Canterbury

1420?–1500. Master of the Rolls (1473); bishop of Ely (1478–86); archbishop of Canterbury (1486–1500); chancellor (1487–1500); cardinal (1493). Morton was an adherent of the Lancastrians in the Wars of the Roses. He was attainted (that is, he lost his lands and his heirs were disinherited) after the Yorkist victory at Towton in 1461, and lived at Margaret of Anjou's court-in-exile in France. Even though Morton supported Henry VI's brief restoration in 1470–1, Edward IV reversed his attainder after 1471, and he rose to eminence under the Yorkist king. He was arrested in 1483 on Richard III's authority and imprisoned first in the Tower of London and later in Brecknock castle. He escaped, first to Ely then to Flanders. In 1484 he heard of Richard's plans to persuade the Burgundians to yield up Henry Tudor (the future Henry VII) and warned Henry, enabling him to flee to France. Morton was recalled to England after Henry's victory of 1485 and served under him as chancellor.

The Wars of the Roses: 301

Moscow

Capital of the duchy of Vladimir; seat of the dukes of Moscow. Grand Duke Ivan III freed Moscow from Mongol rule in 1480 and it became the capital of the Russian nation-state.

The Wars of the Roses: 275

Mowbray, John de, 2nd duke of Norfolk

1389–1432. Son of Thomas de Mowbray, 1st duke of Norfolk; 10th earl of Norfolk and Nottingham (1405–25); knight of the Garter (1421); 2nd duke of Norfolk (1425–32); hereditary earl marshal of England. Prominent in the French wars under Henry V, John was nominated to Henry VI's regency council in 1422. On 8 November 1428 he was involved in an accident, recorded by the *Brut* chronicler, when his barge collided with one of the piles of London Bridge. Most of the passengers were drowned, but John and a few others leapt to safety on the piles. He attended Henry VI's coronation (1429), as marshal.

The Wars of the Roses: 168

Mowbray, Thomas de, 1st duke of Norfolk

1366?–99. Son of John, 4th lord Mowbray; knight of the Garter (1393); 2nd earl of Nottingham (1383–99); earl marshal (1385–99); 1st duke of Norfolk (1397–9). One of the lords appellant who helped prosecute Richard II's servants in the Merciless Parliament of 1388, Thomas later found favour with the king. He accompanied Richard to Ireland in 1394 and helped arrange his marriage to Isabella of Valois in 1396. In 1397 he was instrumental in the arrest of Thomas of Woodstock, 1st duke of Gloucester, and the earls of Arundel and Warwick, also lords appellant. Gloucester died in his custody, and he received part of Arundel's estates and the dukedom of Norfolk as a reward from Richard. In 1398 Henry Bolingbroke (later Henry IV) accused Thomas of treason. They fought an inconclusive duel at Coventry, and the king banished both men. Thomas died in Venice.

The Wars of the Roses: 80, 82–3

Mowbray, Thomas de, 9th earl of Norfolk and Nottingham

1385–1405. Son of Thomas de Mowbray, 1st duke of Norfolk, and elder brother of John Mowbray, 2nd duke; 9th earl of Norfolk and Nottingham (1399); earl marshal (1399–1405). Thomas joined the Percys' revolt of 1405 against Henry IV, in the company of Richard le Scrope, archbishop of York. Ralph de Neville, 1st earl of Westmorland, tricked Scrope into a parley, seized him and Thomas and beheaded both.

The Wars of the Roses: 104

Murimuth, Adam of

See: Adam of Murimuth

music

Much early medieval music was liturgical, produced by monks or under monastic patronage for use in church services. The traditional Gregorian chanted liturgy, plainsong, emerged at the time of Pope Gregory I (*c.*600) and remained the same until polyphonic composition, exemplified by composers such as the 14th-century Guillaume de Machaut, began to embroider its melodies.

Secular music – both songs and instrumental works – was at first performed from memory by minstrels but gradually became more complex as it was increasingly influenced by ecclesiastical music.

In the 14th century royal courts began to support composers; several were associated with Edward III's Chapel Royal. Henry V was also a patron of music: at least one song, 'Gloria', may have been written by him. The English style of composition, under royal chaplains such as John Dammett and Nicholas Sturgeon, was highly regarded in the 15th century.

The Plantagenet Chronicles: 141
Chronicles of the Age of Chivalry/Four Gothic Kings (US edn): 284–5
The Wars of the Roses: 132–3

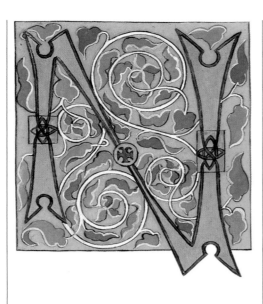

Nájera, battle of

Battle near Burgos, in Castile, on 3 April 1367, at which an army of English, Gascon and mercenary troops led by Edward, the Black Prince, and Peter I, the Cruel, of Castile defeated the forces of Henry of Trastamara, Peter's illegitimate brother who had deposed him. The victory was a spectacular success for the Black Prince, and restored Peter to his throne.

Chronicles of the Age of Chivalry/Four Gothic Kings (US edn): 228, 290–2

Navarre

Region and ancient kingdom of northern Spain, bordering on France; established in the 9th century and a monarchy throughout the Middle Ages.

Chronicles of the Age of Chivalry/Four Gothic Kings (US edn): 290, 293

navy

A royal navy was first organized in England under Alfred the Great in the 9th century. After the loss of Normandy in 1204 King John built a number of royal ships to defend the Channel against the French; even so, most ships used in the English royal fleets in the Middle Ages were either provided by the Cinque Ports or requisitioned from merchants and converted for battle. By the end of the 13th century these makeshift, though often effective, fleets came under the control of one or more admirals, who were appointed by the Crown. In the 15th century Henry V created a sizeable permanent royal fleet; by 1417 it numbered about 30 vessels. This force was dismantled after Henry's death in 1422 but revived under Edward IV, who, by 1480, had seven royal ships. This fleet provided the basis for the great Tudor navy of the following century.

Chronicles of the Age of Chivalry/Four Gothic Kings (US edn): 240–4
The Wars of the Roses: 128–9

Neckham, Alexander

1157–1217. Augustinian canon and scholar; foster-brother of Richard I. Neckham began his career as a distinguished teacher at Paris University (c.1180). He returned to England in 1186 and in 1213 became abbot of Cirencester Abbey in Gloucestershire. He wrote treatises on grammar, natural science and, most notably, navigation: he was the first to record the use of the compass by seamen.

The Plantagenet Chronicles: 271

Neville, Anne

1456–85. Daughter of Richard Neville, 'the Kingmaker', 16th earl of Warwick, and Anne Beauchamp; queen of Richard III. In 1470 Anne was married to Edward, son of Henry VI. But her father's restoration of Henry VI to the English throne in 1470–1 did not prove lasting, and both her father and her husband died in battles with the Yorkists in 1471. Later that year Richard, 3rd duke of Gloucester (the future Richard III), sought to marry her, but his brother George, 3rd duke of Clarence, Anne's sister's husband, opposed the match, seeking to keep all Warwick's vast estates in his own family. Rumour had it that George hid Anne in a London mansion, disguised as a kitchen maid. In 1472 Richard and George debated the issue before Edward IV, and then took it to parliament, which agreed to the marriage and decreed that Warwick's estates be partitioned between the brothers. The marriage took place two years later. Anne died in 1485, the year after the death of her only child, Edward.

The Wars of the Roses: 245, 248, 265–6, 295

Neville, George, archbishop of York

1433?–76. Chancellor of Oxford University (1453–7); bishop of Exeter (1456–65); chancellor of England (1460–7, 1470–1); archbishop of York (1465–76). In 1463 George was an ambassador of Edward IV to Louis XI of France, whom he won away from support of the Lancastrians. He celebrated his installation at York in 1465 with great splendour. In 1469 George secretly performed the marriage ceremony between Isabel, elder daughter of his brother Richard, 'the kingmaker', 16th earl of Warwick, and George, 3rd duke of Clarence, brother of Edward IV and of the future Richard III; this was a seal of alliance in their joint attempt to oust Edward from the throne. In 1470 Edward fled to Flanders and George Neville became chancellor to Henry VI. When Edward returned to England and his throne the following year, George surrendered Henry VI and he himself was imprisoned, though for only two months. But in 1472 Edward, perhaps suspecting him of plotting with Clarence once more, arrested him and had him exiled to Hammes, near Calais, where he remained in prison until 1474, his lands and revenues forfeit. George was a patron of learning and supported Oxford colleges.

The Wars of the Roses: 231

Neville, Hugh de

d.1222. Hugh accompanied Richard I to Palestine in 1190 and was present at the siege of Joppa in 1192. In the same year the king appointed him chief forester, and he continued in this capacity under King John, whose henchman and gaming companion he became. His wife was John's mistress; in 1204 she paid the king 200 chickens to spend one night with her husband. Although Hugh did well out of his association with John, he joined the baronial party in 1216.

The Plantagenet Chronicles: 264

Neville, Isabel

1451–76. Daughter of Richard Neville, 'the kingmaker', 16th earl of Warwick, and Anne Beauchamp. Isabel was secretly married by her uncle George Neville, archbishop of York, to George, 3rd duke of Clarence, brother of Edward IV and Richard, 3rd duke of Gloucester (the future Richard III), at Calais on 11 July 1469. The marriage cemented the alliance between Warwick and Clarence, which was designed to topple Edward from the throne. The two briefly returned Henry VI to power in 1470–1, but Warwick was killed at the battle of Barnet in 1471. The following year his estates were divided between Clarence and Gloucester, husband of Isabel's sister Anne.

The Wars of the Roses: 244–5, 265, 295

Neville, John, 1st marquis of Montague

*c.*1431–71. Younger son of Richard Neville, 8th earl of Salisbury; Yorkist baron; knight of the Garter (1462); 12th earl of Northumberland (1464–70); 1st marquis of Montague (1470–1). John took a full part in Yorkist uprisings in the North in 1453 and 1457 and was imprisoned by the Lancastrians in Chester castle in 1459–60. Following his release he fought at the second battle of St Albans (1461) and was held at York but freed by Edward IV after the battle of Towton (1461). In 1464 he crushed the Lancastrians at Hexham and was made earl of Northumberland for his sterling services to Edward IV. In 1470, however, he was deprived of the earldom of Northumberland, which Edward restored to Henry Percy. The marquisate of Montague proved insufficient compensation, and John deserted to the Lancastrian camp. He died at the battle of Barnet, fighting for his brother Richard, 'the Kingmaker', 16th earl of Warwick, in support of Henry VI.

The Wars of the Roses: 236, 252, 261

Neville, Ralph, 1st earl of Westmorland

1364–1425. Sixth baron Neville (1388–1425); 1st earl of Westmorland (1397–1425); marshal of England (1399); knight of the Garter (1402); warden of the western marches (1403); joint-warden of the northern marches. A close associate of Richard II, Ralph supported him at the trial of the lords appellant in 1397. His reward – appointment as earl of Westmorland – angered the Percy family, his chief rivals. Ralph's second wife, Joan Beaufort, was half-sister of Henry Bolingbroke and in 1399 he turned against Richard, and supported Henry on his return from exile and accession that year as Henry IV. After Henry, 'Hotspur', Percy's death at the battle of Shrewsbury in 1403, Ralph was made warden of the western marches, previously a Percy title. During the revolt against the king of 1405 he routed the main rebel force and took its leaders, Thomas Mowbray and Archbishop Richard le Scrope, prisoner by a false truce. Ralph, who thereafter continued to dominate the North, was an executor of Henry V's will. His daughter Cicely married Richard, 3rd duke of York, and was the mother of two future kings of England: Edward IV and Richard III.

The Wars of the Roses: 61, 84, 104–6

Nájera *The great battle of 1367 in which Edward the Black Prince's forces defeated the troops of Henry of Trastamara, who had usurped the throne of Castile.*

Neville, Richard, 'the Kingmaker', 16th earl of Warwick

1428–71. Eldest son of Richard Neville, 8th earl of Salisbury; 16th earl of Warwick (1449–71), governor of Calais (1455–60), 9th earl of Salisbury (1460), knight of the Garter (1461). Richard married Anne Beauchamp, sole heir to the title and estates of the Beauchamp family, and was created earl of Warwick in 1449 in the right of his wife, becoming one of the most powerful nobles in England.

In 1453 Richard and his father became supporters of the court faction led by Richard, 3rd duke of York and heir-apparent to the English throne, and in 1455 he took up arms, with the duke of York, against Margaret of Anjou and the Lancastrian faction which controlled Henry. Richard was mainly responsible for the Yorkist victory at St Albans on 22 May 1455, the first battle of the Wars of the Roses. He was rewarded with the governorship of Calais, and became a popular hero in England when he attacked a Spanish fleet off Calais in 1458.

In June 1460 Richard returned from Calais to join the Yorkists in renewed fighting and won the battle of Northampton for them in July 1460, taking Henry captive. He became 8th earl of Salisbury when his father was killed at Wakefield in December 1460. In the second battle of St Albans (17 February 1461) he lost Henry to Margaret's forces and left London unprotected, but Margaret failed to make use of the opportunity. In March 1461, he helped to put the duke of York's son Edward on the throne as Edward IV and was instrumental in defeating the Lancastrians at the battle of Towton on 29 March 1461.

Warwick was confirmed in all his offices by Edward, and was de facto ruler of England during the first three years of the new king's reign. Warwick, at the age of 33, had accumulated great estates throughout the country and, with an income of some 3,900 pounds a year, was the richest of all Edward's magnates. However, in 1464, while Richard was negotiating the king's marriage to Bona of Savoy, sister-in-law of Louis XI of France, Edward secretly married Elizabeth Woodville, and subsequently allowed her family great influence at court. Edward also favoured an alliance with the Burgundians rather than with Louis XI of France. Disaffected, Richard withdrew from court in 1467 and began plotting against the king. In 1469 he joined forces with

George, 3rd duke of Clarence, Edward's brother, whom he secretly married to his daughter Isabel Neville, against Edward's orders. Richard was instrumental in Robin of Redesdale's Yorkshire revolt against Edward in 1469, and in July seized and imprisoned the king, first at Warwick, then at Middleham castle.

Richard now tried to rule in Edward's name, but was unable to suppress the widespread revolts which broke out, and was forced to release Edward, who regained power in October 1469. Richard fled to France and, under the auspices of Louis XI, began plotting an attempted coup against the king with his former enemy Margaret of Anjou. He landed at Plymouth in September 1469 and Edward fled to Flanders. When Richard and Clarence entered London in October, they released the captive Henry VI from the Tower and reinstated him as king.

However, Edward returned to England in March 1471 with Burgundian support. Richard was defeated and slain at the battle of Barnet on 14 April 1471.

The Wars of the Roses: 201, 214–17, 220, 222–5, 230, 232, 234–6, 244–6, 248, 252, 260–3, 295

Neville's Cross, battle of

Battle in Durham in October 1346 at which a Scots invasion force, launched at the insistence of the French and including French mercenaries, was intercepted and decisively defeated by Edward III's northern commanders. David II of Scotland, who led the Scots army, was wounded in the head by an arrow and taken prisoner during the battle.

Chronicles of the Age of Chivalry/Four Gothic Kings (US edn): 235, 248, 272

New College, Oxford

Oxford college founded in 1379 by William of Wykeham, bishop of Winchester, who had been planing its inception since 1369. He intended New College as a religious institution to offer prayers for his soul and as a means of raising the calibre of parish clergy by supporting theological students. It was twice as large (at 70 students) as any contemporary college and specially designed buildings (the chapel, dining hall and archives) were erected in William's lifetime. In addition, Winchester College was established as a feeder school. Supported by William's income from the diocese of Winchester, England's richest see, New College

was the finest college of its day. Henry VI later founded King's College, Cambridge, in order to emulate it.

The Wars of the Roses: 62–3, 195

Newcastle upon Tyne

Port on the River Tyne since Roman times. The castle that gave Newcastle its name was constructed in 1080 and the town walls were built during Edward I's reign (1272–1307). The mainly 14th-century St Nicholas's Cathedral (the city's parish church until the 19th century) has a fine 15th-century spire. Newcastle's coal export trade began in the 13th century, and was later supplemented by a monopoly (with Berwick) of the export of coarse north-country wools to the Low Countries.

The Wars of the Roses: 58, 202

Nicholas III, pope

1210/20–80. Born Giovanni Gaetano Orsini; pope (1277–80). Nicholas's main papal objective was to free the Holy See from the domination of Charles of Anjou, king of Sicily. To achieve this he managed to end Charles's appointments as Roman senator and imperial vicar of Tuscany. At the same time he persuaded Rudolf I of Habsburg, Holy Roman Emperor designate, to renounce all control of the Romagna, an agreement which enlarged the boundaries of the papal state. Nicholas, who was the first pope in a century to make Rome his headquarters, extended and modernized the Vatican Palace in order to accommodate his court.

Chronicles of the Age of Chivalry/Four Gothic Kings (US edn): 122

Nicholas IV, pope

1227–92. Born Girolamo Maschi; pope (1288–92). The first Franciscan friar to be elected pope, Nicholas appealed, unsuccessfully, for a crusade after the fall of Acre to the Muslims in 1291 and sent missionaries to the court of Kublai Khan in China. His death was followed by a 27-month election conclave, hampered by competition between the supporters of the Roman Colonna family and those of Charles II, king of Naples. The dispute was resolved by the election of Pope Celestine V.

Chronicles of the Age of Chivalry/Four Gothic Kings (US edn): 150

Nigel, bishop of Ely

d.1169. King's treasurer (*c.*1126–39); bishop of Ely (1133–69). Nigel was one of the last married bishops in pre-Reformation England. In 1139 King Stephen removed Nigel and his uncle, Roger, bishop of Salisbury and justiciar of England, from their key posts in the royal administration, thereby losing the support of the Church. Nigel was driven from his bishopric but restored in 1142. He was brought out of retirement by Henry II, whom he helped to restore the Exchequer.

The Plantagenet Chronicles: 72

Niger, Ralph

*fl.*1170. Clerk to Henry, the Young King, son of Henry II; writer. Educated in Paris, Ralph wrote mainly religious works but late in life compiled two chronicles; largely derivative, these do, however, contain one strikingly original passage – a bitter character-sketch of Henry II, that criticizes him for spending too little time in church and constantly muttering and doodling during Mass.

The Plantagenet Chronicles: 94

Nogaret, William of

See: William of Nogaret.

Normandy

Province of northern France, on the Channel coast opposite Dorset and Hampshire. The region, named after the Normans who had settled there, was a duchy from 911. Duke William of Normandy conquered England in 1066. Geoffrey of Anjou took the duchy in 1144 and made his son Henry (later Henry II of England) duke in 1151. Normandy was joined to the French royal domain after Philip II's invasion of 1203–4, and Henry III surrendered all claims to the region at the Treaty of Paris (1259). The duchy was a major battleground of the Hundred Years War (1339–1453), during which it was frequently raided by sea, and annexed by Henry V in 1419. Henry gave many English nobles lands there, but tried also to win local support. The area was finally returned to France in 1450 and, after the fall of Gascony in 1453, only Calais and the Channel Islands remained in English hands.

Chronicles of the Age of Chivalry/Four Gothic Kings (US edn): 25, 90, 136–8, 244, 264
The Wars of the Roses: 122, 147–9, 202, 209

Northampton

County town of Northamptonshire, whose Norman castle was the seat of parliaments from the 12th to the 14th century. Henry VI was defeated and captured at Northampton by a Yorkist army in July 1460: Richard Neville, 'the Kingmaker', 16th earl of Warwick, attacked the Lancastrian forces during a shower of rain which incapacitated their artillery, and Lord Grey of Ruthin treacherously let the Yorkists into the camp.

The Plantagenet Chronicles: 76, 85, 111–12, 142, 232, 259, 281, 308, 312–14
Chronicles of the Age of Chivalry/Four Gothic Kings (US edn): 81, 125, 133
The Wars of the Roses: 101, 208, 220, 222, 233, 244, 256, 261

Northumberland

Northernmost English county, on the border with Scotland. The county was in dispute between the English and the Scots throughout the Middle Ages; frequent skirmishes and battles took place there, and many castles, including Bamburgh and Dunstanburgh, were built.

The Plantagenet Chronicles: 128, 314
Chronicles of the Age of Chivalry/Four Gothic Kings (US edn): 192

Norwich

County town of Norfolk and a royal borough since the 10th century. The cathedral, founded in 1096 by the city's first bishop, Herbert de Losinga, is mainly Norman in style. Norwich was the scene of a massacre of Jews on 6 February 1190. In the 14th century Edward III's queen, Philippa, sponsored in Norwich a thriving colony of Flemings, emigrants from her native county of Hainault, who taught the citizens how to manufacture cloth.

The Plantagenet Chronicles: 102, 129, 140, 208
Chronicles of the Age of Chivalry/Four Gothic Kings (US edn): 126, 131, 253
The Wars of the Roses: 41, 44, 179

Norwich, William of

See: William of Norwich

Nottingham

County town of Nottinghamshire, settled since Danish times. The town's Norman castle survived a fire which destroyed most of Nottingham in 1153, when the castle garrison burnt the town after its capture by King Stephen's opponents. In the 13th century the town's guild was given trading privileges by King John. Throughout the Middle Ages Nottingham had a famous fair which traded entirely in geese.

In October 1330 Edward III and his supporters seized his mother Isabella of France and her lover Roger Mortimer at Nottingham castle; he later held David II of Scotland there after his capture in 1346. Richard III used the castle as his headquarters before the battle of Bosworth in 1485.

The Plantagenet Chronicles: 85, 232, 298, 316
Chronicles of the Age of Chivalry/Four Gothic Kings (US edn): 29, 194, 231–4
The Wars of the Roses: 22, 52, 220, 298, 302, 305

Novgorod

City in Russia which, at the height of its commercial power in the 14th century, was one of the Hanseatic League's four chief trading centres. It had a population of *c*.400,000 and dealt in furs, honey and wax. The city came under Moscow's control in 1478 and was destroyed by Ivan the Terrible in 1570.

The Wars of the Roses: 274–5

nuns

Between 1216 and 1350 there were about 256 convents and 3,300 nuns and canonesses in England. Some occupied the 19 great abbeys (mainly Benedictine) of the time, such as Amesbury in Wiltshire, but most were housed in small priories. The order of Fontevrault and the Gilbertines (the only English religious order) had monasteries for both nuns and canons, but mixed orders never became popular.

A nun normally professed her vows at 16, but girls of noble birth often entered convents at a much earlier age: Edward I's daughter Mary, for example, entered Amesbury Abbey at the age of seven. Widows frequently retired to convents for practical reasons and paid the nuns for their hospitality. In the later Middle Ages such guests were often criticized for the worldly influence they exerted on the brides of Christ.

Chronicles of the Age of Chivalry/Four Gothic Kings (US edn): 128–9, 266

nuns Mass in a convent. The priesthood being an exclusively male preserve, nuns relied on male priests (here at right) to officiate for them at Mass.

Norwich The west front of Norwich cathedral (overleaf), the great Norman building founded in 1096 by Norwich's first bishop, Herbert de Losinga.

Ockham, William of

See: William of Ockham

Oldcastle, Sir John

1378?–1417. Lollard leader. Oldcastle served Henry IV in his campaigns against Owen Glendower in Wales, during which he befriended Prince Henry, later Henry V. In 1409 Oldcastle married as his second wife Joan, Lady Cobham, and became known as 'the good Lord Cobham'. In 1413 he was attacked by the clergy for supporting Lollard heretics; Henry V tried in vain to restore him to orthodox Catholicism, but he refused to recant and later the same year was tried for heresy before an ecclesiastical court. Here he publicly denounced the pope as antichrist and was sentenced to burning. Granted a stay of execution of 40 days by Henry, who still hoped he would rescind his views, he escaped from the Tower of London and helped organize the abortive Lollard plot of January 1414 which aimed to capture or kill the king. He remained at large, and continued to plot against Henry, until his capture near Welshpool in 1417. Condemned by parliament, he was burned over a slow fire at St Giles's Fields. Shakespeare's great comic character Falstaff is a travesty of Oldcastle, and in the original version of *Henry IV, Part One*, bore the Lollard leader's name until protests forced the dramatist to change it.

The Wars of the Roses: 113–14, 123–4, 141–2, 144–5

omens

Belief in unusual events as signs of God's will persisted throughout the Middle Ages. Halley's Comet, appearing in 1066, was interpreted as foretelling the doom of Harold of England; the Bayeux tapestry shows the comet overshadowing his coronation. In 1196 the chronicler William of Newburgh saw a double sun that he thought presaged war (which duly broke out) between Richard I and Philip II of France. A rain of blood was reputed to have fallen while Richard I was building Château Gaillard in 1196–8, but the king is said to have ignored it. In February 1461 an omen of a golden sun in splendour accompanied Edward IV's defeat of the Lancastrians at Mortimer's Cross and the king later based his badge on it. Omens were by their nature less systematically interpretable as portents than astrological conjunctions.

The Plantagenet Chronicles: 238–9
The Wars of the Roses: 223

ordainers

Twenty-one magnates chosen by a meeting of English barons in February 1310 to impose restrictions on Edward II's royal prerogative (the ordinances). The ordainers included Robert Winchelsey, archbishop of Canterbury, Thomas, 2nd earl of Lancaster, seven other earls and six bishops. Their aim was to curb Edward's incompetent and tyrannous rule by making him accountable to parliament through themselves, and to remove his hated favourite, Piers Gaveston, from power. Parliament enacted the ordinances in September 1311, but Edward evaded their provisions and the ordainers' unity was destroyed when Thomas and others had Gaveston killed in 1312.

Chronicles of the Age of Chivalry/Four Gothic Kings (US edn): 178–80, 186, 190

Order of the Garter

English chivalric order set up by Edward III in 1348, modelled in part on Alfonso XI of Castile's Order of the Band (Europe's first such order, instituted in 1330). Edward took an oath at a 'Round Table' tournament in 1344 to re-establish Arthur's order of knights, and the same year he began building St George's Chapel, Windsor, to house it.

In 1348 the order was founded with 26 knights, including Edward, and St George as its patron. It was organized like an ecclesiastical body, with stalls in the chapel, chapter meetings and a 'college' of knights. Its name and motto are said to have arisen when Edward's mistress, the countess of Salisbury, dropped her garter at a dance in Calais in 1348. To spare her embarrassment, Edward fastened the garter on

Order of the Garter An early Garter knight, his robe decorated with garters.

his knee, declaring 'honi soit qui mal y pense' (evil to him who thinks evil of it).

Chronicles of the Age of Chivalry/Four Gothic Kings (US edn): 262–3
The Wars of the Roses: 171

Order of the Golden Fleece

Chivalric order instituted by Philip the Good, duke of Burgundy, in 1430. It comprised 24 knights, on the model of Edward III's Order of the Garter, and it was partly intended to unite the nobles ruling the duke's disparate lands in common loyalty to him. Burgundy's wealth and importance in the 15th century made the Order of the Golden Fleece one of Europe's foremost chivalric orders. Its badge was a golden ram, often worn hanging from a neck chain.

The Wars of the Roses: 171, 242

ordinances

Directives or regulations. In 1310 an important set of ordinances (decrees) was drawn up by a number of leading English magnates (henceforth known as the ordainers), to place constraints upon Edward II's oppressive and corrupt rule. These ordinances, which were imposed on the king by parliament the following year, made royal officials accountable to parliament, barred Edward from making war without parliament's consent and exiled his favourite, Piers Gaveston.

Chronicles of the Age of Chivalry: 178–80, 186, 190

Orleanists

See: Armagnacs

Orléans

City and dukedom on the River Loire in north France; after Paris, the chief residence of the French monarchy. In June 1251 the city was sacked by Pastoureaux rebels. Joan of Arc's relief of Orléans in 1429, when it was besieged by the English, saved France and turned the tide of the Hundred Years War.

Chronicles of the Age of Chivalry/Four Gothic Kings (US edn): 73, 86
The Wars of the Roses: 168, 170, 172

Orleton, Adam, bishop of Hereford, Worcester and Winchester

d.1345. Bishop of Hereford (1317–27); treasurer (1327); bishop of Worcester (1327–33); bishop of Winchester (1333–45). Adam was a supporter of Roger Mortimer and other opponents of Edward II and the Despensers, and in 1322 was charged with treason and deprived of his lands and revenues. He aligned himself with Queen Isabella, Edward's wife, when she and Roger Mortimer invaded England in 1326 and preached a sermon at Oxford justifying rebellion. As the queen's chief negotiator with Edward during his captivity at Kenilworth, he persuaded the king to abdicate. The chronicler Geoffrey le Baker claims Adam ordered Edward's murder at Berkeley castle in 1327. Under Edward III his possessions were restored, he was briefly appointed treasurer (from January to March 1327) and was later sent on diplomatic missions, as to Paris in 1332.

Chronicles of the Age of Chivalry/Four Gothic Kings (US edn): 202, 208, 214, 216–20, 230

Otterburn, battle of

Battle in Northumberland on 5 August 1388 when a Scots invasion force, led by James, 2nd earl of Douglas, defeated an English army led by Henry, 'Hotspur', Percy. Douglas was killed by Henry Percy in hand-to-hand fighting, and although Percy was subsequently captured by the Scots, the battle helped to establish his reputation for heroism. It also inspired two ballads; the Scottish 'Otterburn' and the English 'Chevy Chase'.

The Wars of the Roses: 58–60

Otto IV, Holy Roman Emperor

1175?–1218. Second son of Henry the Lion, duke of Saxony and Bavaria, and Matilda, daughter of Henry II of England. King of Germany (1198–1218); Holy Roman Emperor (1209–15). Otto was raised at the court of his uncle, Richard I of England, and in 1198 Richard secured his election as rival king of Germany in opposition to Philip of Swabia who had been elected in 1197. In the ensuing warfare Otto was on the verge of defeat but was saved by Philip's murder in 1208 and became king unopposed. He was crowned Holy Roman Emperor in 1209 after he had promised to respect the integrity of the papal states. However, the following year he tried to claim lands he alleged had been annexed by the papacy and Pope Innocent III excommunicated him. In addition, Innocent encouraged Otto's enemies in Germany to revolt and, with the encouragement of Philip II Augustus of France, to elect Frederick of Sicily (later Holy Roman Emperor Frederick II) as king of Germany in 1210.

By the end of that year Otto had lost many of his supporters and relied increasingly on financial help from his uncle, King John of England. In 1214 Otto, in alliance with John, invaded France, where he was defeated by Philip at Bouvines. In 1215 the pope deposed him and Frederick of Sicily replaced him as Holy Roman Emperor; the following year he retired to Brunswick.

The Plantagenet Chronicles: 113, 168, 205, 225, 250, 305–6

Ottoman Turks

Alliance of small nomadic tribes in Asia Minor following the break-up of the Seljuk Turkish empire in the 13th century. It began to absorb neighbouring states, and by the late 14th century controlled much of the Balkans. A crusade against the Ottoman Turks led by Ladislaus III of Poland was defeated at Varna in 1444. On 29 May 1453, after a two-month siege, the Ottomans under Mohammed II took Constantinople, last remnant of the Byzantine Empire. After sacking the city and massacring or enslaving its population, they made Constantinople their capital, and renamed it Istanbul. During the 16th century the Ottomans expanded their empire into Hungary, Persia, Egypt and North Africa.

The Wars of the Roses: 68, 165, 210

Outremer

The crusader states in Palestine: the Latin kingdom of Jerusalem and its dependencies, established in 1099 after the First Crusade. Outremer (which means 'beyond the seas') was dominated by the Norman French, who provided its ruling class. It ceased to exist in 1291, when Acre, the last Christian outpost, fell to the Mameluke Turks.

The Plantagenet Chronicles: 69, 149

Owen Glendower

See: Glendower, Owen

Oxford

County town of Oxfordshire, occupied since Anglo-Saxon times. By the 12th century Oxford had a castle, an abbey and a nascent university, which developed in the early 12th century from the young scholars gathering round the town's monks and teachers. In 1214 the masters elected their first chancellor, and in 1264 the first college, Merton, was established. Oxford hosted a number of parliaments, including that of 1258 which imposed the Provisions of Oxford on Henry III. Monastic houses included St Frideswide's, for Augustinian canons, and Dominican and Franciscan friaries. Noted medieval Oxford scholars included Roger Bacon, Duns Scotus, Robert Grosseteste and John Wycliffe.

The Plantagenet Chronicles: 72, 74, 85, 102, 308, 310, 313–14
Chronicles of the Age of Chivalry/Four Gothic Kings (US edn): 16, 41, 46, 52, 79, 86–9, 96, 105, 125, 154, 177, 185, 210, 254, 302
The Wars of the Roses: 30–1, 62–3, 190, 194–5

Oxford, John of

See: John of Oxford, bishop of Norwich

Oxford, Provisions of

A series of limitations imposed on Henry III's government at the Oxford parliament of 1258. A baronial faction led by Simon de Montfort, angry with Henry's incompetent government, made money grants to Henry conditional on his acceptance of provisions embodying administrative reform. To enforce them, a council of 15 was appointed, who controlled the chancellor and treasury and without whose consent Henry could not act. Regular parliaments were to be held, and errant officials to be punished. Henry's need to finance his son Edmund's claim to the Sicilian crown made him accept the provisions. Louis IX of France, asked to rule on the provisions' validity, declared them void at the Mise of Amiens in 1264, and Simon de Montfort's death at the battle of Evesham in 1265 confirmed their demise.

Chronicles of the Age of Chivalry/Four Gothic Kings (US edn): 86–9, 96, 105

Oxford *The skyline of the university city, already an international centre of learning by the 13th century. Oxford scholars such as William of Ockham and Duns Scotus made decisive contributions to medieval scholastic philosophy.*

papal bull

Papal letter containing an important pronouncement, named after its *bulla* or lead seal. Notable medieval bulls included Pope Boniface VIII's of 1302, declaring all men's duty of submission to the papacy, Gregory XI's of 1377, against Wycliffe's heresy, and Urban VI's of 1382, for a crusade against antipope Clement VII.

The Wars of the Roses: 30, 40, 168, 220, 247

papal states

The domain of the papacy, made up of land given to popes from the 4th century – the so-called Patrimony of St Peter. Varying widely in extent in different eras, the papal states included Latium (though not Rome, whose commune resisted papal government), Romagna, Spoleto and scattered fiefs such as Avignon. The papacy exercised only sporadic control over the states during the Middle Ages.

Paris

Paris grew from a small Roman settlement on the River Seine, and remained relatively obscure and unimportant until 987 when Hugh Capet, count of Paris, became king of France. Under his successors the size and prosperity of Paris increased, as the settlements clustered round the Île de la Cité grew in size and began to merge together. In the 11th century the city spread on to the right bank of the Seine; merchant guilds emerged and soon dominated its commercial life. The rebuilding of Notre-Dame was begun in 1163, and the schools on the left bank supported a flourishing intellectual life, attracting great theologians such as Peter Abelard (1079–1142).

But it was not until the reign of Philip II Augustus (1180–1223) that Paris began to outstrip the other great cities of northern France. The king arranged for the streets to be paved, built a wall round the expanded city, and had the Louvre palace constructed. The markets were concentrated on the site of Les Halles, and two buildings were erected for them. The royal archives and treasury were given a permanent site nearby.

Under Philip's successors Paris continued to grow. Louis IX (1226–70) embellished it by building the magnificent Sainte-Chapelle to house his relic collection. His chaplain, Robert de Sorbon, founded the Sorbonne, the first constituted college of the University of Paris, which opened in 1253. In the 13th century the University of Paris won great intellectual distinction, with scholars such as St Thomas Aquinas (1225–74). Philip IV (1285–1314) reconstructed the royal palace around the Sainte–Chapelle.

The citizens of Paris came to hold an increasingly powerful political role, like their counterparts in London. In the States-General (the French national assembly) of 1355 Etienne Marcel, the provost of Paris, traded money grants for administrative reforms with John II of France, who needed money to fight Edward III of England. After John's capture by the English in 1356, Etienne dealt similarly with the future Charles V, who was a virtual prisoner in Paris until his escape in 1358. Charles besieged the city and Marcel set up an independent commune, but was assassinated by royalists on 31 July 1358, after which Charles re-entered Paris. In 1383, after another insurrection, the city lost its municipal privileges, a state of affairs which lasted until 1412.

During the 15th century internecine strife between Burgundian and Armagnac factions, the Hundred Years War and the disruption to trade that resulted from both reduced the prosperity and the population of the city – there were reputedly some areas where it was unsafe to walk for fear of attack. Paris was occupied by the English from 1419 to 1436, and Henry VI of England was crowned king of France there in 1431. Popular revolts against English rule enabled Charles VII of France to take back Paris in April 1436. However, it was not until the 16th century that the city's decline was reversed and its restoration by the French Renaissance monarchs began.

The Plantagenet Chronicles: 19–24, 34, 96–7, 238, 241
Chronicles of the Age of Chivalry/Four Gothic Kings (US edn): 24, 30, 55, 62–3, 73, 78–80, 86, 90, 101, 112, 115, 274, 276, 280, 296.
The Wars of the Roses: 30, 40, 130, 136, 147–9, 168, 176, 180, 220, 247

Paris, Matthew

c.1200–59. Monk of St Albans Abbey (1217–59); historian and artist. As chronicler to his abbey, Matthew started adapting, in about 1240, the *Flores Historiarum* (Flowers of History), a history of England until 1234 by Roger of Wendover, an earlier St Albans chronicler. Matthew called his adaptation *Chronica Majora* and extended it to cover the years 1235–59. In 1250 he started a more concise history of England, the *Historia Anglorum*, and produced two short chronicles, the *Abbreviato Chronicarum* and the *Flores Historiarum*. His other works include a history of St Albans Abbey and lives of Offa and his fellow kings and of St Edmund and other saints.

Matthew is foremost among English chroniclers for his vigorous and expressive style. He was strongly anti-authoritarian; for example, he roundly denounced the papacy for bestowing English benefices on foreign absentee clergy. He depicts Henry III as weak and naïve, extravagant and a prey to his foreign favourites. His assertions are at times supported by the texts of documents, many preserved solely by him. Matthew illustrated his manuscripts with lively drawings, among them a self-portrait and a sketch of Henry III's pet elephant, and with maps, including a detailed depiction of Britain.

The Plantagenet Chronicles: 265
Chronicles of the Age of Chivalry/Four Gothic Kings (US edn): 7, 13, 16, 35, 44, 47, 56, 68, 72, 81, 84–5

parish

Defined area of ecclesiastical jurisdiction under a priest. In the Middle Ages a parish was in practice normally a village, or cluster of settlements, with its own church and priest, to whom tithes and ecclesiastical duties were paid. Larger parishes might have additional chapels-of-ease to serve outlying areas. Cities like London or Norwich had many small parishes packed closely together. By 1200 there were about 9,000 parishes in England.

The Plantagenet Chronicles: 302, 303

Henry Percy, 4th earl of Northumberland *The earl's statue (opposite), on Beverley Minster in Yorkshire.*

parlement

Judicial meetings of the royal court in France from the late 13th century. The Parlement de Paris emerged in the 14th century as a permanent court of justice to hear appeals from lesser courts. From the 15th century local parlements were set up in the provinces on the same lines. Although primarily judicial bodies, parlements, as assemblies of notables, also had political influence and played their part in law-making.

Parliament

England's legislative assembly. The term was first used in the 1230s to describe the king's *Curia Regis*, the council to which nobles and prelates were summoned and which, over the centuries, developed into the House of Lords. In 1258, 1264 and 1265 county representatives were also summoned – and, in the latter year, burgesses; they met separately from the magnates and formed the embryo House of Commons. Edward I's Model Parliament of 1295 was composed of prelates, nobles, two knights per county, two burgesses per town, and lesser clergy. Edward also encouraged petitions for justice to parliament. During the 14th century, by withholding grants from taxes to the king until he acted on such petitions, parliament gradually increased its powers over taxation. From Edward II's reign (1307–27) statutes were formally enacted only with the consent of parliament; when Edward was deposed, parliament gave legality to the act. The Good Parliament of 1376 produced the first Speaker of the Commons, Sir Peter de la Mare, and the first impeachment, of Lord Latimer and Richard Lyons for corruption. By the 15th century parliament had won considerable power.

Chronicles of the Age of Chivalry/Four Gothic Kings (US edn): 86–90, 96–9, 100, 104, 114, 123, 128, 136, 142, 150, 162, 176–8, 192, 214, 232, 236, 240, 264, 298–9, 302
The Wars of the Roses: 28, 30, 32, 51, 56–8, 78, 80, 88–91, 100, 106, 168, 178, 180, 184, 204–5, 216, 220, 222, 232, 256, 293

Paschal II, pope

d.1118. Born Ranierius. Cluniac monk; pope (1099–1118). Paschal's reign began with the successful outcome of the First Crusade in 1099. In 1102 Paschal renewed earlier papal bans on lay investiture and consequently became embroiled in disputes with Holy Roman Emperor Henry V. In 1111 Paschal was imprisoned by the emperor and was forced to make major concessions to him, including the right to investiture; however, five years later he withdrew these rights. In England a compromise had been worked out in 1107, whereby King Henry I renounced the right to investiture but was paid homage by a bishop-elect for his lands before consecration. This was to be the blueprint for future settlements elsewhere.

The Plantagenet Chronicles: 102

Paston letters

Letters, private papers and other documents, of a middle-ranking Norfolk family, from 1422 to 1529. The Pastons' wealth increased over the period of the correspondence, as the family rose to the status of landed gentry. Written in English (by the 1400s the common tongue of the court and ruling classes) the papers include private letters, instructions to servants and deeds. Agnes Paston wrote in 1458 to her son Clement's tutor: 'truly belash him until he will amend'; and in 1469 the family persuaded the bishop of Norwich to write to their eloped daughter to remind her 'how she was born, what kin and friends she had'.

The Wars of the Roses: 221, 231

Pastoureaux

Members of 'the Crusade of the Shepherds', which began in Flanders and northern France early in 1251. Led by a renegade Cistercian monk, known as the Master of Hungary, around 100,000 shepherds (*pastoureaux*), peasants and vagabonds set off to rescue Louis IX's crusaders in Egypt. Blanche of Castile, Louis' mother and regent of France during his absence, welcomed the Pastoureaux in Paris; but they sacked Orléans when they reached it in June 1251, killing clergy who dared oppose them. In Rouen they slaughtered Jews and attacked priests. The Master of Hungary and other leaders were caught and hanged at Bourges by officials acting on Blanche's orders, and the Pastoureaux dispersed.

Chronicles of the Age of Chivalry/Four Gothic Kings (US edn): 72–4

patent rolls

Documents kept in Chancery from 1199, recording the letters patent by which the king granted privileges or offices such as that of sheriff. The entries were written on parchment membranes sewn end to end and rolled tightly for compactness and ease of carrying.

The Plantagenet Chronicles: 309

Peacock, Reginald, bishop of Chichester

1395?–1460? Fellow of Oriel College, Oxford (1414–24); bishop of St Asaph (1444–50); bishop of Chichester (1450–8); theologian. Peacock distinguished himself by writing against the Lollard heresy; his 'Repressor of over much Blaming for the Clergy' (1455) is a 15th-century English prose classic. However, his emphasis on the authority of reason made him suspect, and when he denied the authenticity of the Apostles' Creed, he alienated every sector of English theological opinion and was accused of heresy. He was expelled from the privy council, and on 4 December 1457 publicly renounced his views at St Paul's Cross in London. His books were burned before his eyes. Peacock resigned his see in 1458 and retired to Thorney Abbey near Cambridge, where it is believed that he lived in total seclusion.

The Wars of the Roses: 218

Peasants Revolt

Revolt of 1381 which began when peasants in Kent and Essex under the leadership of Wat Tyler, Jack Straw and John Ball, briefly rose against Richard II's regents. The unrest stemmed from the hated poll tax introduced the previous year. Late in May 1381 the men of Fobbing in Essex and their neighbours attacked tax commissioners at Brentwood. Around 10,000 rebels from Essex and Kent united in London on 13 June 1381 and Wat Tyler became their spokesman. For two days the rebels looted and burned. On 14 June Richard II met them at Mile End and promised them important concessions, including the abolition of villeinage (which he later revoked). Most rebels were satisfied and dispersed but that night Tyler and other diehards seized the Tower of London and killed the archbishop of Canterbury, Simon Sudbury.

During a second meeting with the king at Smithfield on 15 June, the rebels escalated their demands, asking for abolition of lordship (except the king's), disestablishment of the Church and complete reform of the law. However, Tyler was struck down at the meeting by William Walworth, lord mayor of London, and later killed. Richard managed to prevent further violence and promised the mob a pardon if it dispersed. But later judicial proceedings were brought against the leaders, some of whom were executed.

There were isolated outbreaks of violence elsewhere in the country. The worst were at St Albans and Bury St Edmunds, where the monks were forced to hand over deeds and plate, and in Norfolk, where Geoffrey Litster took over Norwich castle and his mob ran amok. These local uprisings, too, were short-lived.

The Wars of the Roses: 23, 31, 34–40

Penshurst Place, Kent

Manor house built in the 1340s by Sir John Pulteney, then lord mayor of London. Penshurst was built at a time when English magnates were exchanging their castles for more comfortable manors, and its only defensive features were a crenellated roof and fortified walls. The house later passed to John, 2nd duke of Bedford, regent for the young Henry VI, who strengthened its walls in the 1430s.

The Wars of the Roses: 124–5

Percy, Henry, 4th earl of Northumberland

1342–1408. Son and heir of Henry, 3rd baron Percy; knight of the Garter (1366); marshal of England (1377); 4th earl of Northumberland (1377). Henry fought in France in the Hundred Years War (1337–1453) and in border warfare against the Scots. Created earl at Richard II's coronation, he was a supporter of Richard but joined Henry Bolingbroke (later Henry IV) in 1399 after Richard made Ralph Neville, Percy's chief rival, 1st earl of Westmorland. The same year Percy captured Richard in Wales, on behalf of Bolingbroke, by offering him terms on which he could keep the throne and falsely promising him safe passage home: on the journey Richard was ambushed and taken.

In 1402 Percy won the battle of Homildon Hill against the Scots. The following year he rebelled against Henry IV, aiming to put Sir Edmund Mortimer, 5th earl of March, on the throne, but yielded after the death of his son, Henry, 'Hotspur', Percy at Shrewsbury in 1403. He then conspired with Owen Glendower against the king and in 1405 rebelled again in support of the archbishop of York, Richard le Scrope. After le Scrope's defeat, Percy's estates were seized by the king and he fled to Scotland. In 1408 he invaded England with a small force and was slain at the battle of Bramham Moor.

The Wars of the Roses: 26, 28, 60–1, 84, 94, 100, 104–8

Matthew Paris *This self-portrait shows Matthew as a tonsured cleric, but since the gifted artist and chronicler was married he was only in minor orders.*

Percy, Henry, 5th earl of Northumberland

1394–1455. Son of Henry, 'Hotspur', Percy; 5th earl of Northumberland (1416–55). Henry spent his youth in exile at St Andrews, in the company of the future James I of Scotland. He was restored to his family's dignity and estates by Henry V in 1416, and became a member of the council of regency on Henry's death in 1422. A supporter of Henry VI's queen, Margaret of Anjou, he opposed Richard, 3rd duke of York, and his allies the Nevilles, hereditary enemies of the Percys; on 22 May 1455 he fought with the Lancastrians at St Albans and fell fighting the Nevilles.

The Wars of the Roses: 185, 217

Percy, Henry, 6th earl of Northumberland

1421–61. Son and heir of Henry Percy, 5th earl of Northumberland; warden of the eastern marches (1439–61); 6th earl of Northumberland (1455–61). Henry rallied support for the Lancastrians in 1460 and in December that year slew Richard, 3rd duke of York, the Yorkist leader, in battle at Wakefield. On 17 February 1461, with Margaret of Anjou, he defeated Richard Neville, 'the Kingmaker', 16th earl of Warwick, at the second battle of St Albans, avenging his father's death at Neville's hands in that city and freeing Henry VI from Yorkist custody. He was killed at the battle of Towton on 29 March 1461.

The Wars of the Roses: 222–3

Percy, Henry, 7th earl of Northumberland

1446–89. Son of Henry Percy, 6th earl of Northumberland; 7th earl of Northumberland (1470–89); warden of the eastern marches (1470–89). Henry was captured by Yorkist forces at the battle of Towton in 1461 and imprisoned by Edward IV in the Fleet prison and the Tower of London for eight years, forfeiting his earldom to John Neville, 1st lord Montague. In 1470 his earldom was restored, and he was appointed warden of the eastern marches. A follower of Richard, 3rd duke of Gloucester (the future Richard III), Henry executed Anthony Woodville, 2nd earl Rivers, Richard Grey and other supporters of the young Edward V at Pontefract in 1483, to prepare for Gloucester's usurpation. Once crowned, Richard conferred lands and offices on him, but failed to secure his ultimate loyalty: Henry marched with Richard to Bosworth in 1485, to oppose Henry Tudor (soon to become Henry VII), but withheld his men at the battle and submitted to Henry.

The Wars of the Roses: 236, 255, 282, 302, 305

Percy, Henry, 'Hotspur'

1364–1403. Son of Henry Percy, 1st earl of Northumberland; knight of the Garter (1387). From 1384 Henry assisted his father as warden of the eastern marches. Known as 'Hotspur' probably because of his rapid riding, Henry won an outstanding reputation for bravery in border fighting. At the battle of Otterburn against the Scots in 1388, his valour in slaying the Scots leader, James, 2nd earl of Douglas, sealed his reputation – despite his capture. In 1402 he helped his father win the battle of Homildon Hill against the Scots, capturing their leader, Archibald, 4th earl of Douglas. He quarrelled with Henry IV over the king's refusal to exchange Douglas for Sir Edmund Mortimer, brother-in-law of 'Hotspur', and in 1403 he joined his father's plot to replace the king with Edmund. In July that year he died fighting against the king at the battle of Shrewsbury. To prove his death, his head was exhibited at York, his body at Shrewsbury.

The Wars of the Roses: 46, 58–61, 84, 101–4

Penshurst Place, Kent *The house's crenellations (overleaf) are virtually its only defensive features.*

Percy, Sir Thomas, 2nd earl of Worcester

1343?–1403. Son of Henry, 3rd baron Percy, and brother of Henry Percy, 1st earl of Northumberland; knight of the Garter (1376); steward of Richard II's household (1393–9); 2nd earl of Worcester (1397–1403). Thomas served in France from 1369 to 1373 and accompanied Geoffrey Chaucer on a diplomatic mission to Flanders for Richard II in 1377. Despite his position in the king's household and Richard's award of the earldom of Worcester to him in 1397, Thomas joined the rest of the Percy family in supporting Henry Bolingbroke (the future Henry IV) against the king in 1399. In 1401 he was appointed Henry IV's commander in South Wales against Owen Glendower. However, less than two years later he joined his brother the 1st earl of Northumberland's rebellion against the king. Thomas was captured at the battle of Shrewsbury on 21 June 1403 and beheaded.

The Wars of the Roses: 101–2, 104

Périgord

Region of south-west France, enclosing the valley of the Dordogne with Périgueux as its capital. A county from the 9th century, and part of the duchy of Aquitaine, Périgord passed to England in 1152 after the marriage of Henry Plantagenet (the future Henry II of England) to Eleanor of Aquitaine. Philip II of France captured Périgueux in 1204, but the English retook it in 1356. Périgord returned to France in 1370 as part of a general French recovery of lands from the English.

Chronicles of the Age of Chivalry/Four Gothic Kings (US edn): 90, 276

Perpendicular style

Final development in English Gothic architecture, from the late 14th to early 16th century. The name comes from the style's predominantly vertical lines in tracery and panelling. Gloucester Cathedral was England's first Perpendicular building: from c.1330, masons stretched patterned traceries over the old Norman choir to save costly demolition. Fan vaults are another feature of Perpendicular; the first examples were built in Gloucester's choir. The naves of Winchester Cathedral (redesigned 1394–1410) and Canterbury Cathedral (rebuilt 1379–1405), provide other early examples of the style. Later Perpendicular buildings include St George's Chapel, Windsor (rebuilt 1477–83)

and King's College Chapel, Cambridge (built 1446–1506).

Chronicles of the Age of Chivalry/Four Gothic Kings (US edn): 207
The Wars of the Roses: 86–7, 303

Perrers, Alice

d.1400. Reputedly the daughter of a Hertfordshire knight; mistress of Edward III. Alice entered the service of Edward's queen, Philippa of Hainault, at some time before 1366 and married a courtier, Sir William de Windsor. She became Edward's mistress before Philippa died in 1369 and, after the queen's death, had almost complete power over the fast-ageing king, who granted her royal estates, gave her his dead wife's jewels and allowed her to sit on the bench in court and bully the judges. Anger against her influence on the king led to her impeachment for fraud and corruption by the Good Parliament of 1376 and her banishment from court. In 1377 Edward recalled Alice, who remained with him until his death that year; she was rumoured to have stolen rings from the dying king's fingers. The same year Richard II's first parliament confirmed her banishment, but in 1379 it was revoked at the request of her husband William.

Chronicles of the Age of Chivalry/Four Gothic Kings (US edn): 298–300, 304
The Wars of the Roses: 28, 30

Perth

City on the River Tay in central Scotland; county town of Tayside. Called St Johnstoun until the 17th century, it was the country's capital from the 11th to the mid-15th century. James I of Scotland was murdered at the Dominican friary in Perth on 27 February 1437.

The Wars of the Roses: 184–5

Peruzzi

Family of Florentine bankers; with the Bardi family, the English Crown's principal creditors in the 14th century. The Peruzzi were ruined by Edward III of England's bankruptcy of 1340, after he had demanded loans far beyond his income to pay for his 1336 campaign against the French, knowing the Florentine bankers could not refuse.

Chronicles of the Age of Chivalry/Four Gothic Kings (US edn): 281

Peter of Aigueblanche, bishop of Hereford

d.1268. Bishop of Hereford (1240–66). A Savoyard of high rank, Peter accompanied Henry III's queen, Eleanor of Provence, to England in 1236. His appointment to the see of Hereford angered the king's opponents. Unpopular for his financial exactions on the Church, Peter was imprisoned in 1263 in Eardisley castle in Herefordshire by the king's baronial opponents. In 1264 he retired to Savoy.

Chronicles of the Age of Chivalry/Four Gothic Kings (US edn): 72

Peter I, the Cruel, king of Castile

1334–69. Son and heir of Alfonso XI of Castile; king of Castile (1350–69). Peter's repudiation and abuse of his wife Blanche of Bourbon, was one factor which provoked the Castilian nobility to several rebellions, fomented by Peter's illegitimate half-brother Henry of Trastamara. Another cause of revolt was fear and revulsion caused by Peter's cruel murders of several nobles. In 1366 Henry invaded Castile with the mercenaries of the Great Company under Bertrand du Guesclin. Peter fled, and Henry was crowned king of Castile. Peter invoked an alliance he had made with Edward III of England four years earlier, promising to pay his expenses, and Edward, the Black Prince, led an army to his aid, defeating Henry's forces at Najera on 3 April 1367. Restored to the Castilian throne, Peter refused to reimburse the English. In 1369 he was defeated at Montiel by another force under Henry and du Guesclin and killed by Henry in a duel after the battle.

Chronicles of the Age of Chivalry/Four Gothic Kings (US edn): 228, 286 290–3, 296
The Wars of the Roses: 44, 46

Peter the Hermit

1050?–1115. French religious leader. Peter was a popular preacher of the First Crusade and led a peasant army which reached Constantinople in 1096, killing Jews and looting as they travelled. He deserted the crusaders at the siege of Antioch in 1098 but was recaptured and brought back in disgrace. Nevertheless, a few months later he was sent on a mission to Kerbogha, the ruler of Mosul. After the fall of Jerusalem in 1099, he returned to France and founded Neufmoutier Abbey at Liège.

Chronicles of the Age of Chivalry/Four Gothic Kings (US edn): 73

Peter III, king of Aragon and Sicily

1239?–85. Son and heir of James I of Aragon; king of Aragon and count of Barcelona (1276–85); king of Sicily (1282–5). In 1262 Peter married Constance, daughter and heir of Manfred of Hohenstaufen, and through her gained a claim to Sicily and southern Italy. The Sicilians, who had expelled their sovereign, Charles of Anjou, crowned him king in 1282. Pope Martin IV, a supporter of Charles, excommunicated Peter for taking the island, and a crusade was organized against him by the French (whose king, Philip III, was Peter's nephew); they invaded Catalonia in 1485 but were repulsed by Peter. He died under the papal ban but still king of Sicily.

Chronicles of the Age of Chivalry/Four Gothic Kings (US edn): 125–6

Peter of Wakefield

*fl.*1212. The Barnwell annalist describes Peter, a 'simple and rustic man', as a prophet who publicly foretold in 1212 that 'King John's reign would not last beyond the next Ascension Day' (23 May 1213). Although John's men arrested and imprisoned him, his prophecy became common knowledge. When the date passed without incident, the king had Peter hanged and also hanged his son 'in case he was...the author of his father's prophecies'.

The Plantagenet Chronicles: 298, 300, 302, 304

Philip of Alsace, count of Flanders

d.1191. Count of Flanders. One of Henry the Young King's supporters in his abortive revolt against Henry II in 1173. He swore to invade England for the Young King, and in 1174 launched a raid during which Norwich was sacked. The same year he and his allies were forced to retreat before Henry II after attempting to besiege Rouen. Philip was sword-bearer and special official at the coronation of Philip II Augustus of France in 1179 and acted as regent during his minority. In 1184 he visited Canterbury and London and was received by Henry II. In 1191 he accompanied Philip II on the Third Crusade, during which he died.

The Plantagenet Chronicles: 128–30, 140, 164, 166, 168, 172, 188, 212

Philip, the Bold, duke of Burgundy

1342–1404. Younger son of John II of France; duke of Touraine (1360–1404); duke of Burgundy (1363–1404). Philip fought the forces of Edward, the Black Prince, at Poitiers in 1356 and shared his father's captivity in London until 1360. In 1363 John granted him the duchy of Burgundy, and in 1369 he married Margaret, heiress to the counties of Flanders and Franche-Comté. From the accession of the young Charles VI of France until his coming of age in 1388 Philip was regent. In 1382 he aided his father-in-law, Louis of Mâle, count of Flanders, against Flemish rebels and defeated them at Roosebeck. In 1384 he inherited Flanders, Franche-Comté, Artois, Nevers and Rethel from Louis and added to these possessions by buying the county of Charolais. After Charles VI's first bout of insanity in 1392, Philip returned to rule as regent – but a power struggle developed between him and his brother Louis, duke of Orléans, who was Charles's chief counsellor during the king's lucid periods; and from this time dates the long-running conflict between the houses of Burgundy and Orléans. A patron of the arts, Philip had his tomb carved by the Dutch sculptor Claus Sluter.

The Wars of the Roses: 115, 134, 136–7

Philip the Good, duke of Burgundy

1396–1467. Son and heir of John the Fearless, duke of Burgundy; duke of Burgundy (1419–67). After his father's assassination on the orders of the dauphin Charles (later Charles VII of France), in 1419, Philip allied with Henry V of England and in the Treaty of Troyes (1420)

Philip the Good *The duke hosts a picnic on the evening before his wedding in 1430.*

recognized him as king of France in opposition to the dauphin. Philip aided Henry and his successor Henry VI until 1435, when, after a dispute with the English over the succession to the Flemish county of Hainault, he was reconciled with Charles VII in the Peace of Arras (1435). He later sheltered Charles' rebellious son, the dauphin Louis, but refused him aid. In 1436 he led an abortive siege of Calais for Charles.

In 1433 Philip had acquired Brabant and Holland, his mother's lands, and in 1435 had been given Mâcon, Auxerre and Ponthieu by Charles. He thus more than doubled his duchy's size. His court at Bruges was the richest in Europe and had Jan van Eyck as its official painter.

The Wars of the Roses: 128, 148–50, 166, 177, 180, 182, 197, 239

Philip I, king of France

1052–1108. Son and heir of Henry I of France; king of France (1060–1108). Philip controlled little more than his royal domain in the Ile de France and although he tried to enlarge this area by force and diplomacy, royal power remained weak. In 1092 he met Bertrada of Montfort, wife of Fulk Rechin, count of Anjou, at Tours and took her as his second wife. His abandonment of his first wife, Bertha, which was carried out against the Church's laws and wishes, deepened a conflict with Pope Gregory VII which had started over Philip's practice of simony (he sold ecclesiastical preferments) and his opposition to Gregory's reform programme for the Church. Philip was excommunicated by Popes Urban II and Paschal II, but remained defiant over Bertrada until 1104 when he was reconciled with the Church; even then, he did not honour his promise to put her aside. In his last years his son, the future Louis VI, exercised effective power on his behalf.

The Plantagenet Chronicles: 34, 37

Philip II Augustus, king of France

1165–1223. Son of Louis VII of France and Adela of Champagne; king of France (1180–1223). When Philip came to the throne, aged only 15, he inherited a domain little larger than the Île de France and far smaller than Henry II of England's French lands. Seeing the importance of enlarging his territories and the funds he could raise from them, in 1181–6, having crushed a coalition of Flanders, Champagne and Burgundy, he added Amiens, Artois and other lands to his domains.

Philip's major danger was from the Plantagenets, and in 1187 he incited Henry II of England's sons to rebel. In November 1188 he attacked the English king's lands in France with the help of Henry's heir, Richard, and forced the old king to yield up Le Mans and some castles just before his death in July 1189. Philip's first wife, Isabella of Hainault, also died in 1189, two years after bearing him a son (later Louis VIII). Philip accompanied Richard, now Richard I of England, on the Third Crusade in 1190, but quarrelled with him after the capture of Acre, and in 1191 returned to France. Philip conspired against Richard with his brother John (the future King John of England) while the former was imprisoned by Holy Roman Emperor Henry VI from 1192 to 1194. Richard attacked Philip after his release and, by 1199, had forced the French king to return most of the lands he had seized.

In 1193 Philip married Ingeborg of Denmark, but turned against her after their wedding night and abandoned her. In 1196 he married his third wife, Agnes of Meran, who bore him two sons and a daughter; but the match aroused the hostility of Pope Innocent III, who objected to Philip's irregular repudiation of Ingeborg and excommunicated him. But Agnes died in 1201 and in 1213 Philip finally yielded to Innocent III and took Ingeborg back, although the couple produced no children.

On John's accession to the English throne in 1199, Philip took up the cause of Arthur Plantagenet, duke of Brittany, John's nephew and a rival claimant to his inheritance. Philip declared John's French lands confiscate in 1202, and took advantage of local disaffection to win his fiefs away from him. By 1204 Philip had overrun Normandy, Brittany, Anjou, Maine and Touraine, leaving John with Gascony and only a shaky hold on Poitou, which he later lost. Philip had expanded his domain fourfold. He also rebuilt Paris, and had the streets paved and a city wall erected. He introduced salaried crown bailiffs to control local administration and improved the collection of customs and fees due to the Crown, following the Plantagenet example in his system for administering the localities. From 1208, when Innocent III called a crusade against Albigensian heretics in southern France, he allowed his vassals to fight in the crusade. As a long term result the Languedoc was brought under the control of the French crown in 1229.

In 1214 Philip defeated the Holy Roman Emperor Otto IV and the count of Flanders, King John of England's allies, at the battle of Bouvines, a victory which established France as a major power and ended any threat from John. Philip died in 1223.

The Plantagenet Chronicles: 41, 153, 164, 166, 176, 184–6, 188, 193, 195, 204–10, 212, 216, 218, 224, 228, 233, 238, 241, 244–5, 250, 259, 262–4, 272, 278–84, 300, 302, 305–7
Chronicles of the Age of Chivalry/Four Gothic Kings (US edn): 90

Philip III, king of France

1245–85. Son and heir of Louis IX of France; king of France (1270–85). Philip was an ineffectual ruler and factional struggles were rife at his court. In his early years he was aided by his father's advisers, and in 1279 he gained Poitou, Auvergne and Toulouse from Edward I of England. He arranged the marriage of his son, the future Philip IV, to Joan of Navarre and Champagne in 1284, uniting these territories to the Crown of France. The following year he invaded Aragon to win a crown for Charles of Valois, his third son, but the expedition was a disastrous failure; the king was forced to retreat and died on the march home.

Chronicles of the Age of Chivalry/Four Gothic Kings (US edn): 96, 104, 112, 126

Philip IV, the Fair, king of France

1268–1314. Son of Philip III of France and Isabella of Aragon; king of France (1285–1314). In 1284 Philip married the heiress Joan, queen of Navarre and countess of Champagne. All their three sons were to succeed in turn to the throne, as Louis X, Philip V, and Charles IV; their daughter, Isabella of France, married Edward II of England.

From 1294 to 1296 Philip mounted a series of expensive and indecisive campaigns against Edward I of England's domains in Gascony. A long controversy with Pope Boniface VIII began in 1296 when Philip asserted his right to tax the French clergy for purposes of his kingdom's defence. The measure stemmed from the cost of his Gascon campaign and was opposed by Boniface in a bull of 1296. Philip cut off Church revenues normally paid to the pope by France, and Boniface capitulated in 1297. That year also, Philip agreed a truce with Edward. Three of Philip's councillors, William de Nogaret, Pierre Flote and Enguerrand de Marigny, assiduous in building up royal authority, were to the fore during this great quarrel.

In 1301 the conflict with Boniface revived when Philip's councillors arrested Bernard Saisset, bishop of Pamiers, ostensibly for seeking to incite rebellion against the king. Boniface insisted Saisset be returned to Rome for trial, and issued the bull *Unam Sanctam* (1302), setting out his right to intervene in secular affairs. Threatened with excommunication, Philip sent Nogaret to seize Boniface at the papal palace at Anagni in 1303. The pope was freed, but died soon after.

In Flanders, Philip tried to reduce the larger towns to submission but in 1302 his army suffered a humiliating defeat at Courtrai. He conceded Edward's rights in Gascony in 1303, expanding the truce of 1297 into a permanent peace.

In 1307, Philip's officers arrested members of the crusading order of Knights Templar throughout France, producing in justification confessions of sodomy, blasphemy and sorcery supposedly obtained from their captives. In 1309 Clement V, Boniface's successor, took up residence at Avignon rather than Rome, beginning the so-called 'Babylonian captivity' of the *Curia*. A Frenchman, he was virtually the king's puppet and in 1312, after threats from Philip, he disbanded the Templars. In 1314 Philip burned 54 Knights Templar, including the Grand Master of the order, Jacques de Molay. Its assets were transferred to the rival order of Knights Hospitaller, after payment of fictitious 'debts' to Philip.

Also in 1314, Philip attempted once again to suppress the Flemish, eliciting opposition from nobles who protested against royal taxation and the conduct of the administration. The king convened the States-General (the French national assembly) to obtain approval for his plans. The same year, a scandal erupted at court, almost certainly fomented by his daughter, Isabella, Edward II's queen. All three of Philip's daughters-in-law were disgraced as the result of alleged adulterous liaisons, and their supposed lovers publicly executed.

Philip died in 1314. His three sons died in turn soon after, without issue, ending the direct line of Capet. His demise was attributed by many to Jacques de Molay's dying curse – at the stake he had called on Philip and Clement to join him before God's tribunal: within a year, both were dead.

Chronicles of the Age of Chivalry/Four Gothic Kings (US edn): 50, 137, 142, 144, 148, 150–1, 154, 162, 170, 172, 177, 181, 186

Philip V, king of France

1294–1322. Son of Philip IV of France; king of France (1317–22). Nicknamed Philip the Tall, Philip became regent of France when his brother Louis X died before the birth of his only child John I. On the death of the infant king in the same year, Philip took the crown instead of Joan, Louis' infant daughter. This precedent helped establish the Salic law, by which

Philip IV, the Fair *The king of France with his court. Philip was an able, ruthless ruler who attacked both papacy and Templars.*

women were excluded from the French royal succession. Edward II – whose wife Isabella was Philip's sister – did homage to Philip for Gascony in 1319.

Chronicles of the Age of Chivalry/Four Gothic Kings (US edn): 196

Philip VI, king of France

1293–1350. Eldest son of Charles of Valois, third son of Philip III of France; king of France (1328–50). Philip's three cousins, Louis X, Philip V and Charles IV, held the French throne briefly in turn between 1314 and 1328. When Charles died his wife was pregnant, but the child was a girl, and Philip, as the nearest direct male heir, was chosen as king of France under the Salic law; the Capetian line was replaced by the Valois.

His first wife was Joan, daughter of Robert II of Burgundy, who bore him two sons: John II, who succeeded Philip, and Philip of Orléans, count of Valois.

In the early years of his reign, Philip planned an Anglo-French crusade with Edward III of England but Edward withdrew his support and the plan never reached fruition. Friction gradually built up between the monarchs, and when in 1337 Philip declared Gascony confiscated, Edward retaliated by claiming the French crown; he argued that his claim to the throne of France was stronger than that of Charles, since his mother, Isabella, was the daughter of Philip IV of France.

In 1339 the Hundred Years War broke out. The first English victory followed on 24 June 1340 when the French fleet was destroyed at Sluys in Flanders. The two kings signed a three-year truce in 1343, but in 1345 Edward invaded Normandy and, in 1346, defeated the French at the battle of Crécy. Philip was badly wounded. In 1347 the English captured Calais, which they were to hold for the next two centuries.

Philip resorted to extraordinary taxes, including a salt tax (the *gabelle*), to pay for his campaigns, but was unable to stem the English advance. He died in 1350 and was succeeded by his son, John II.

Chronicles of the Age of Chivalry/Four Gothic Kings (US edn): 227, 234, 236–48, 251, 261–4

Philip of Poitiers, bishop of Durham

d.1208? Bishop of Durham (1195–1208). Philip accompanied Richard I on the Third Crusade in 1190, but returned to England before him and was elected bishop in 1195. He was later one of King John's supporters in the king's controversy with Pope Innocent III over the election of Stephen Langton as archbishop of Canterbury.

The Plantagenet Chronicles: 248

Philippa, daughter of Henry IV of England

1394–1430. Daughter of Henry IV and his first wife, Mary Bohun. In 1406 she was married to Eric IX, king of Denmark.

The Wars of the Roses: 108

Philippa of Hainault

1314?–69. Daughter of William, count of Holland and Hainault; queen of Edward III (1328–69). In 1326 Philippa's betrothal to the then Prince Edward of England was negotiated by his mother, Isabella of France, who, using money from the young bride's dowry, paid the wages of knights from Hainault and Germany to assist her in her invasion of England the same year. Edward was Philippa's second cousin, and a papal dispensation had to be obtained before the couple could marry in 1328. She bore Edward 12 children, and was widely respected for her patience and forbearance.

In August 1347 she interceded successfully with Edward to spare the lives of six burghers of Calais, who had brought the town's keys to him and incurred his wrath.

The French chronicler Jean Froissart became Philippa's secretary after his arrival in England in 1361. Edward was not always faithful to Philippa, but his reliance on her is shown by his rapid decline after her death.

Chronicles of the Age of Chivalry/Four Gothic Kings (US edn): 208, 233, 240, 251–3, 280, 294, 298

Philippa, queen of Portugal

1359–1415. Daughter of John of Gaunt; queen of Portugal (1387–1415). Philippa was married to John I, the Great, of Portugal in 1387, as part of her father's attempts to forge a close alliance with the Portuguese king against Castile. She bore him four sons, who included Henry the Navigator and Edward I of Portugal.

The Wars of the Roses: 43

Picquigny, Treaty of

Treaty between Edward IV of England and Louis XI of France, agreed at Picquigny near Amiens in north-east France on 29 August 1475. It ended Edward's brief invasion of France, which had been launched in July 1475 and was aborted when Francis II, duke of Brittany, and Charles, duke of Burgundy, failed to provide promised aid. The two kings met at Picquigny, speaking through a trellis to avoid any attempt at assassination. The treaty called for a seven-year truce, and the English swore to withdraw from France on receipt of 75,000 crowns (15,000 pounds sterling). Louis granted Edward a pension of 50,000 crowns (10,000 pounds) a year and agreed that the dauphin (the future Charles VIII) should marry Edward's daughter, Elizabeth of York. The marriage never took place – Elizabeth became queen to Henry VII – but the treaty kept the peace between England and France until 1483.

The Wars of the Roses: 201, 269, 274

Piero della Francesca

1420?–92. Italian painter. The influence of the early Florentine Renaissance on his work is shown by his grasp of space and mass. Piero's works include the *Baptism of Christ* (c.1450s); a fresco cycle, *The Legend of the True Cross*, in the San Francesco church, Arezzo (1452–66); and profile portraits of Federigo da Montefeltro, duke of Urbino, and his duchess (c.1460s). The regularity and solidity of form in these works reflect Piero's belief in mathematical harmonies described in his theoretical writings on perspective. He worked mostly in the lesser Italian towns and courts.

The Wars of the Roses: 218, 289

Piers Plowman, The Vision of

See: *Vision of Piers Plowman, The*

pilgrimage

Visit to a notable shrine or holy place, which offered spiritual benefits, such as the forgiveness of sins, and, for the sick, the hope of a cure.

pipe rolls

Records of English Crown revenues received and spent, kept by the Court of Exchequer on large parchment membranes sewn at the top and rolled up. The rolls annually recorded the audit of accounts of sheriffs and debtors to the Crown. The oldest extant pipe roll dates from 1129–30. Records in the same form were produced until 1833.

The Plantagenet Chronicles: 161, 309, 325

piracy

Many medieval seamen turned temporary pirate when they met a weaker foreign vessel. The rulers of England, France, Spain and Flanders often issued 'letters of marque', in which they authorized those of their subjects robbed by pirates to plunder ships of the offending nation in turn. The Cinque Ports, core of England's naval strength, were a centre of piracy. Eustace the Monk, based at Winchelsea in the early 13th century, was probably the most notorious medieval pirate; he fought for both England and France before being caught and beheaded by his Cinque Ports fellows in the sea battle of Sandwich in 1217. England and France encouraged pirates to prey on each other's ships during the Hundred Years War. One such pirate was a Breton woman,

Jeanne de Belleville, who harried the French and their ships to avenge her husband's death at their hands.

Chronicles of the Age of Chivalry/Four Gothic Kings (US edn): 200–1

Pisan, Christine de

1364–1430? French poet. Born in Venice of Italian parents, she came to France as a young girl, married Etienne du Castel, a French courtier, when she was 15 years old, and was widowed at the age of 25. Abandoned in Paris with three children and little money, Christine turned the poetry she had written to console herself in her bereavement into a source of income. First Louis, duke of Orléans, then the Burgundian dukes Philip the Bold and John the Fearless, were her patrons. At their courts she wrote works ranging from celebrations of the strengths and virtues of women (the *Book of the City of Ladies*) to love lyrics (*One Hundred Ballads of a Lover and his Lady*). Her writing shows an equal command of narrative verse, lyric verse and prose, as well as great depth of learning.

The Wars of the Roses: 54–5, 134–5

plague

See: Black Death

plainsong

Liturgical music of the medieval Church, usually considered synonymous with Gregorian chant (*cantilena Romana*). Plainsong's texts were the Latin Mass, the psalms, canticles and some hymns; the melody was codified at the time of Pope Gregory I in the 6th century and passed on, and modified, by subsequent generations. The chants were in a free rhythm determined by the metre of the text.

Plantagenet, Arthur

d.1542. Illegitimate son of Edward IV of England and Elizabeth Lucy, daughter of Thomas Wayte, a minor Hampshire gentleman. Their affair lasted from around Edward's accession in 1461 to his marriage to Elizabeth Woodville in 1464. Arthur was brought up at court, and in 1472 the royal tailor was ordered to provide clothes for 'my lord the bastard'. After a period of eclipse, Arthur rose in the service of Henry VIII, was granted the title of Lord Lisle and was captain of Calais in the 1530s. In 1540, however, he was implicated in a plot against the king and imprisoned in the Tower of London, where he died two years later.

The Wars of the Roses: 253

Plantagenet, Geoffrey

See: Geoffrey, the Fair, count of Anjou

Plantagenet, Richard, 5th duke of York

See: Richard, 5th duke of York

Plantagenets, The

Surname used since the 15th century of the English dynasty founded in the 12th by Geoffrey the Fair, count of Anjou (1113–51). *Plantagenet* was originally his nickname, said to derive from the sprig of broom (*genêt*) he wore in his hat. Geoffrey's son, Henry II, became king of England in 1154, and his descendants in the direct male line ruled until 1399: Richard I, John, Henry III, Edward I, Edward II, Edward III and, finally Richard II, who was deposed by Henry Bolingbroke, later Henry IV. There is no evidence that any of them used the name Plantagenet. After Richard's deposition, the line split into the houses of Lancaster and York, both cadet branches of the direct Plantagenet line. The Lancastrian branch, the descendants of Edward III's third son, John of Gaunt, 2nd duke of Lancaster, produced Henry IV, Henry V and Henry VI; the Yorkist branch, from Edward III's fourth son, Edmund of Langley, 1st duke of York, produced Edward IV, Edward V and Richard III.

The surname Plantagenet was first adopted in the 1460s by Richard, 3rd duke of York, father of Edward IV, the first Yorkist king of England, and was used by his family for propaganda purposes – to emphasize the superiority of their claim over the Lancastrians. Shakespeare, and many subsequent writers and historians, have used the name for all the male lines descended from Geoffrey of Anjou: the direct male line, culminating with Richard II, and the two cadet branches of Lancaster and York.

The Plantagenet dynasty ended with Richard III's death in 1485, when Henry Tudor took the throne as Henry VII. Even he owed his claim to the throne partly to his Plantagenet lineage, but in the female line: his mother, Margaret Beaufort, was the great-granddaughter of John of Gaunt. When Henry married Elizabeth of York, Edward IV's daughter, in 1486 both cadet branches of the Plantagenets were reunited in the Tudor dynasty.

Edward IV's illegitimate son Viscount Lisle bore the name Plantagenet, as did the shadowy Richard, a stonemason at Eastwell in Kent, who was said to be the natural son of Richard III and died in 1550.

plays

Mystery (or miracle) plays were a popular form of drama in the Middle Ages. Dramatized renderings of scriptural stories such as the Nativity or the Creation, they were usually performed in the market place by members of one of the town's guilds, often at the Feast of Corpus Christi. Four great cycles of English mystery plays have been preserved: those of Chester, Lincoln, Wakefield and York. Morality plays – dramatized allegories, such as *The Castle of Perseverance* and *Everyman* – were performed from the mid-14th century; and folk plays formed part of the celebrations at village festivals.

Plymouth

Port on the south coast of Devon, inhabited since early medieval times. Plymouth was a centre for the wine trade with Bordeaux in the 14th and 15th centuries, when Gascony was English territory. The town was raided by the French in 1403. Granted a royal charter in 1439, it became in the 16th century a centre for expeditions to the New World.

Chronicles of the Age of Chivalry/Four Gothic Kings (US edn): 266, 296
The Wars of the Roses: 104, 257, 296

Poitiers

Capital of the province of Poitou in western central France, on the River Clain. Near Poitiers, in 732, Charles Martel won a momentous victory against the Muslims. The ancient capital of the duchy of Aquitaine, the city held the brilliant court of Eleanor of Aquitaine. From 1152 when Eleanor married the future Henry II of England in Poitiers Cathedral, to 1204, when Philip II of France seized Poitou from King John of England, Poitiers was under Plantagenet rule. In the 1160s the 11th-century cathedral began to be rebuilt as a Gothic hall-church with aisles as high as the central vessel; it was completed about 100 years later.

Poitiers *The capital of 12th-century Aquitaine and a seat of Plantagenet power.*

On 19 September 1356 Edward, the Black Prince, defeated and captured John II of France and Philip the Bold, duke of Burgundy, when he met their army near Poitiers, and the English held the city until Bertrand du Guesclin took it back for Charles V of France in 1373. During the English occupation of northern France, the beleaguered Charles VII had his court at Poitiers from 1423 to 1436.

The Plantagenet Chronicles: 28, 32, 37, 45, 55, 80–2, 88, 97, 129, 246, 260–1, 271, 277, 279, 304–6
Chronicles of the Age of Chivalry/Four Gothic Kings (US edn): 52, 72, 76, 229, 268–72, 284
The Wars of the Roses: 194

Poitiers, Alphonse of

See: Alphonse of Poitiers

Poitiers, Philip of

See: Philip of Poitiers, bishop of Durham

Poitiers, Raymond of

See: Raymond of Poitiers, prince of Antioch

Poitou, William of

See: William of Poitou

poll tax

Tax levied on every head of the population. It was first granted to Edward III by parliament in 1377, at the rate of a groat (4d) per head. In 1379 the figures were graduated: John of Gaunt, the wealthiest subject, paid ten marks and, at the other end of the scale, peasants over the age of 16 paid a groat. The most notorious poll tax was granted to Richard II in 1380: all men and women aged over 16 were required to pay the substantial sum of one shilling. The tax was hated, as were the commissioners sent out to collect it, and it was an immediate cause of the Peasants Revolt of 1381.

The Wars of the Roses: 32, 34

pollards

Counterfeit English silver pennies issued by lords, counts, bishops and abbots in the Low

Christine de Pisan *The poetess presents her work to Isabella of Bavaria.*

Countries in the 1290s; named after the bare, uncrowned head, or 'poll', on the obverse.

Chronicles of the Age of Chivalry/Four Gothic Kings (US edn): 148, 149

Polo, Marco

1254?–1324? Venetian traveller and writer. A member of a leading merchant family, Marco joined his father Niccolo and uncle Maffeo on a trading expedition to China in 1271 and reached Peking by 1275. He became the favourite of Kublai Khan, China's Mongol ruler, entered the Chinese civil service and later ruled the city of Yangchow for three years. Only Kublai's death in 1292 enabled the Polos to leave China; three years later they returned to Venice. Taken prisoner while fighting for Venice against the Genoans in 1296, Marco dictated his memoirs in prison. In them he tells of places he had seen or heard of on his travels, including China, Persia, Japan, Sumatra and East Africa, and describes coal, asbestos and paper money. His account was the main source of European knowledge of China until the 19th century.

Chronicles of the Age of Chivalry/Four Gothic Kings (US edn): 19, 82–3

Pont l'Evêque, Roger of

See: Roger of Pont l'Evêque

Pontefract

Town in West Yorkshire inhabited since the 8th century and site of a great castle begun in 1069 on the site of a Saxon fort. The vast duchy of Lancaster was administered from the town, making it a centre of regional power. In 1322 Thomas, 2nd earl of Lancaster, was beheaded at Pontefract for treason, when his feud with Edward II ended in his capture at Boroughbridge. Richard II was imprisoned in the castle after his deposition in November 1399 and died there within a few months, from unknown causes. After Charles, duke of Orléans, was captured at Agincourt in 1415, he was held in the castle for more than two decades. Richard, 3rd duke of Gloucester, imprisoned and executed Anthony, 2nd earl Rivers, and the young Edward V's other protectors at Pontefract in April 1483, before usurping the throne as Richard III.

Chronicles of the Age of Chivalry/Four Gothic Kings (US edn): 147, 179, 204
The Wars of the Roses: 46, 89, 97–8, 141, 212, 272, 279, 282

Marco Polo *The celebrated traveller arrives at Hormuz in Iran.*

Ponthieu

Former county in north-east France, around the mouth of the Somme. Edward I gained Ponthieu in 1279 through his marriage to Eleanor of Castile, but in 1326 Charles IV of France seized the county while Edward II was engaged in resisting Queen Isabella's invasion of England. Edward III recovered Ponthieu under the Treaty of Brétigny (1360), but by the end of the Hundred Years War (1453) the English had once more lost the county to the French.

Chronicles of the Age of Chivalry/Four Gothic Kings (US edn): 122, 205–6, 278, 296

Poore, Richard, bishop of Durham

d.1237. Friend, and probably former pupil, of Stephen Langton, archbishop of Canterbury; bishop of Chichester (1214–17); bishop of Salisbury (1217–28); bishop of Durham (1228–37). Richard began the construction of Salisbury Cathedral in 1220, moving the headquarters of the diocese from the high ground of Old Sarum to the valley of the River Avon. The cathedral was consecrated in 1225. As bishop of Durham, Richard ordered the construction of the Chapel of the Nine Altars in Durham Cathedral. The constitutions he issued from 1217 to 1221 to guide his clergy in the diocese of Salisbury were widely copied by later episcopal legislators.

Chronicles of the Age of Chivalry/Four Gothic Kings (US edn): 287

portraiture

The depiction of particular individuals rather than general types in art developed in the 14th century. Edward III's tomb effigy in Westminster Abbey (1377), probably taken from a death mask, is an early attempt to portray an individual. Richard II's painted portrait in the same abbey (*c.*1395) is a more developed example. Donor portraits such as the Wilton Diptych (*c.*1394–6), in which Richard appears with the Virgin, set portraits in a religious context, but Jan van Eyck's *Arnolfini Wedding* (1434) shows that within 40 years people of lesser rank were commissioning purely secular portraits. In the 1460s Piero della Francesca painted his patron Federigo da Montefeltro, duke of Urbino, both as a donor with the Virgin and as a secular figure.

The Wars of the Roses: 18, 74–5, 289–91

Portsmouth

Port in Hampshire used for Channel crossings since ancient times. In the summer of 1346 Edward III assembled his fleet there for the invasion of Normandy.

Chronicles of the Age of Chivalry/Four Gothic Kings (US edn): 244

Portugal

Portugal, overrun by the Moors in the 8th century, became an independent kingdom during the long struggle to expel them. Alfonso I, the first king of Portugal, broke away from the kingdom of León and took his title after a victory over the Moors in 1139. Lisbon, the future capital, fell to him in 1147. In 1383 John I of Castile tried to claim the Portuguese throne, but the people of Lisbon proclaimed John, illegitimate son of Peter I of Portugal, as king; in 1385, aided by an English alliance with John of Gaunt, he defeated the Castilian invasion and was crowned John I. In the 15th century Portugal enjoyed a golden age of colonial expansion: Prince Henry the Navigator and others explored Africa, South America, and the Orient.

The Wars of the Roses: 40–4

Prague

Capital of Bohemia (modern Czechoslovakia) from the 13th century and an important trading centre since the 10th century. From the 14th century Prague was the second residence of the Holy Roman emperors after Vienna, and under Holy Roman Emperor Charles IV (king of Bohemia 1346–78) it became one of Europe's most splendid cities, with a thriving court and famous university. John Hus, the Bohemian religious reformer, was a professor at Prague University, and his teachings won wide support in the city in the early 15th century. Gradually, however, the excesses of the extremist Hussites alienated the citizens, who came to support Hus's opponents.

The Wars of the Roses: 39, 156, 159

Premonstratensians

Members of the order of regular canons (white canons) founded in 1119 by St Norbert at Prémontré near Laon in northern France. They followed the rule of St Augustine and did much preaching and pastoral work. Norbert was a friend of Bernard of Clairvaux, the influential Cistercian abbot, and adopted many of his austere practices and customs for his own order.

The Plantagenet Chronicles: 325

Portugal *John of Gaunt leaving England and arriving at Lisbon.*

priests

One of the major orders of the medieval clergy (bishops, priests, deacons), distinguished from the minor orders (such as acolytes and exorcists) by their tonsure and their celebration of the offices of the Church.

The Plantagenet Chronicles: 302–3
Chronicles of the Age of Chivalry/Four Gothic Kings (US edn): 36–7, 122

printing

Printing with movable metal type was developed in Germany *c.*1450 by Johann Gutenberg, who printed a papal indulgence at Mainz in 1454. His Mazarin Bible, (*c.*1455) was the first book in Europe to be printed this way. Presses were set up in Cologne in 1464, Rome in 1467, Paris in 1470 and Florence in 1473. William Caxton printed the first book in English at Bruges in 1473, and set up a press in London in 1476.

The Wars of the Roses: 240–1

prior

The head of a priory or, in an abbey, the deputy of the abbot. Some priories were dependent offshoots of abbeys; others – for example, Carthusian and Grandmontine houses – were independent.

privy seal

Royal seal used to authenticate Crown documents which were more private or less important than those validated by the great seal or which authorized use of the great seal.

Provence, Eleanor of

See: Eleanor of Provence

Provence, Margaret of

See: Margaret of Provence

Provisions of Oxford

See: Oxford, Provisions of

quadrivium

The scientific part of the seven liberal arts, comprising arithmetic, geometry, astronomy and music. With the trivium (the other three liberal arts), it formed the basis of medieval education.

Quercy

County in south-west France, with Cahors as its capital. Quercy was part of the inheritance of Henry II of England through his wife, Eleanor of Aquitaine; in 1196 their son Richard I gave it to Raymond VI, count of Toulouse, as his sister Joan's dowry. In 1259, by the terms of the Treaty of Paris, Henry III of England was given the reversion to the county, but it was never handed over and by 1290 Edward I had dropped the claim. Quercy was made over to England again in 1360 but finally retaken by the French in 1440.

The Plantagenet Chronicles: 186, 197
Chronicles of the Age of Chivalry/Four Gothic Kings (US edn): 25, 90–1

Radcot Bridge

Site of a battle in Oxfordshire in the winter of 1387. Richard II's favourite Robert de Vere, 9th earl of Oxford, and his allies, were on their way to London to join the army the king had raised against the lords appellant, who had challenged his despotic rule, when they were intercepted by the rebels.

Trapped by the lords, de Vere fled by swimming the Thames under cover of fog, abandoning his allies; one of them, Thomas Molyneux, constable of Chester, died in the fighting.

The Wars of the Roses: 50, 53–4

Ralph, abbot of Coggeshall

fl. 1207–18. Cistercian abbot of Coggeshall in Essex (1207–18); chronicler. Ralph's name is given to a chronicle that describes events from 1066 to 1224, but he was probably responsible only for the years 1187 to 1224. Living within 50 miles of London, and well informed through his Cistercian connections, he kept in close touch with events. He heard of Richard I's battle with the Saracens in 1191 through one of the combatants, Hugh de Neville, and of Richard's capture in Austria from the king's chaplain Anselm. He described the king as warlike and popular but avaricious and hot-tempered. Ralph supported the baronial party against King John, whom he called a coward and a glutton. He also described the Fourth Crusade, Constantinople (from eye-witness accounts) and the massacre in 1190 of York's Jews, whom he said deserved their fate.

The Plantagenet Chronicles: 12, 317

Quercy The fortified medieval bridge over the river Lot at Cahors, historic capital of the county of Quercy and part of Eleanor of Aquitaine's dowry to Henry II.

Ranulf II de Gernon, 5th earl of Chester

c.1100–53, 5th earl of Chester (1135). A great magnate, Ranulf was one of the barons who warred against King Stephen. In 1141, at the battle of Lincoln, he helped the Angevin party capture both king and castle, hoping to get back his lands in Carlisle from the Scottish king, David I. In 1145 he switched sides and the following year helped Stephen besiege Wallingford. Later that year, however, the king, at the behest of his advisers, suddenly turned on him and accused him of treachery. He was arrested and forced to give up his castles. In 1147 Ranulph made an abortive attempt to retake the city. Two years later he became a leading supporter of the young Henry Plantagenet (the future Henry II).

According to the chronicler Ralph of Diceto, Ranulf was poisoned by William Peverel, a Nottinghamshire baron. Another chronicler, Henry of Huntingdon, described him as 'audacious but lacking in judgement, aiming beyond his reach; whatever he begins like a man he ends like a woman'.

The Plantagenet Chronicles: 72–3, 76, 78, 104

ransoms

Ransom demands were common during the Middle Ages, and the more important the captive the greater the ransom. In 1194 Richard I of England was released from imprisonment in Germany by his captor, Holy Roman Emperor Henry VI, only after payment of a 100,000 mark ransom collected by a special tax in England. John II of France was ransomed for 500,000 pounds after his capture at Poitiers in 1356. Lesser figures also paid large sums for their freedom. The French chronicler Jean Froissart records that the French hero Bertrand du Guesclin, captured by Edward, the Black Prince, at the battle of Najera in 1367, was ransomed for 100,000 francs within a month. Ransoms gave medieval soldiers an incentive to keep their prisoners alive and for this reason the English were slow to obey Henry V's orders to slay their prisoners after the battle of Agincourt in 1415.

The Plantagenet Chronicles: 225, 227
Chronicles of the Age of Chivalry/Four Gothic Kings (US edn): 270, 271

Ravenspur

Promontory on the east coast of Yorkshire now known as Spurn Head. Henry Bolingbroke, 3rd duke of Lancaster (the future Henry IV), landed at Ravenspur on 4 July 1399 and was met there by other lords who opposed Richard II's tyranny; they included Henry Percy, 4th earl of Northumberland, and Ralph Neville, 1st earl of Westmorland. The army marched south to depose the king and install Bolingbroke as Henry IV. In March 1471 Edward IV was driven ashore at Ravenspur when he returned from exile in Zeeland to secure his throne against the Lancastrian rebels.

The Wars of the Roses: 84, 256

Raymond VI, count of Toulouse

1156–1222. Count of Toulouse (c.1194). Raymond was frequently excommunicated by Pope Innocent III because of his toleration of the Albigensian heresy in his domains and he was one of the main targets of the Albigensian Crusade of 1211. Attacked by Simon de Montfort, one of the crusade's leaders, Raymond sought help from his brother-in-law Peter II, king of Aragon, but was defeated, with Peter, at Muret in 1213. Raymond fled to England and the protection of King John, his brother-in-law. In 1215 the Fourth Lateran Council gave Toulouse and Montauban to de Montfort and Provence to Raymond's son (later Raymond VII); but in 1217 Raymond returned to France and, by 1222, with his son's help, had recaptured most of his lost duchy from de Montfort. However, by 1229, seven years after Raymond VI's death, his son had lost much of the duchy to the French Crown.

The Plantagenet Chronicles: 206, 304

Raymond of Poitiers, prince of Antioch

d.1149. In 1136 Raymond was summoned from France to Palestine by King Fulk of Jerusalem to rule the crusader state of Antioch. He was one of the leaders of the Second Crusade (1147–9). Rumours of his improper relations with Eleanor of Aquitaine, his niece and the wife of Louis VII of France, another leader of the crusade, caused a rift with the French king in 1149. Raymond died in a skirmish against the troops of Nur-ad-Din, king of Aleppo, and his head was sent in a silver case to the caliph of Baghdad.

The Plantagenet Chronicles: 79, 81, 97, 168

Rayonnant style

The middle period (c.1240–1350) of French Gothic architecture, named after the radiating tracery of its characteristic rose windows. The extensive use of bar tracery windows turned walls into sheets of glass bound in elaborately ornamented stone webs. More intimate than High Gothic, it was especially suitable for smaller churches and chapels. Amiens Cathedral (begun 1220) and the abbey church of Saint-Denis are early examples. Louis IX's Sainte-Chapelle in Paris is a fine example of the style, which spread through Europe.

Chronicles of the Age of Chivalry/Four Gothic Kings (US edn): 62–3

Reading

County town of Berkshire, inhabited since before the 8th century. In 1121 Henry I founded a Benedictine abbey, eventually his mausoleum, in Reading. In 1180 Henry II's rebellious son Henry, the Young King, swore on the abbey's holy relics that he would obey his father.

The Plantagenet Chronicles: 60, 86, 165, 173–4, 221
Chronicles of the Age of Chivalry/Four Gothic Kings (US edn): 284

Redesdale, Robin of

See: Robin of Redesdale

reeve

A medieval official: chief magistrate of a town or district, or a lesser bailiff appointed by a lord to oversee his estates or tenants. The priest was the spiritual leader of a village community, the reeve its lay leader.

Reims

City in the county of Champagne in north-east France, inhabited since Roman times. Its cathedral, begun in 1211 and substantially completed by 1270, is one of the masterpieces

Reims A smiling angel statue on the exterior of Reims cathedral.

of French High Gothic architecture. It incorporates the first-ever bar tracery windows (which were to become the outstanding feature of the Rayonnant style) and its 115ft-high vault is lavishly ornamented with some of the finest of medieval sculpted figures. The cathedral was the coronation church of French kings; one notable coronation was in 1429, when Charles VII was crowned with Joan of Arc at his side.

The Plantagenet Chronicles: 164, 205
Chronicles of the Age of Chivalry/Four Gothic Kings (US edn): 30, 271, 276, 284, 286–9

relic

Allegedly part of the body of Christ or of a saint, or an item connected with either, venerated by the Church. Such sacred mementoes were believed to work miracles, and Catholic teaching that the saint in heaven and not the relic was responsible, did nothing to discourage faith in their potency. Relics such as the body of St Cuthbert in Durham Cathedral or the tomb of St James the Apostle at Santiago de Compostela in Spain were popular goals for pilgrims. Louis IX of France built the Sainte-Chapelle in Paris in the 1240s as a huge reliquary (relic-holder) for part of the True Cross, part of the Crown of Thorns and other relics he had acquired from King Baldwin of Jerusalem.

The Plantagenet Chronicles: 119, 135
Chronicles of the Age of Chivalry/Four Gothic Kings (US edn): 62, 125, 160, 280, 282

relief

Feudal term denoting a payment in money or kind to a dead man's lord by the relatives of the deceased so that they could inherit his estates and titles. King John of England abused the system in the early 13th century by demanding inordinately high payments, thereby fuelling baronial resistance.

Renaissance

Cultural rebirth which began in the Italian city-states in about 1400. Based on the rediscovery of ancient Greek and Roman culture, it revived classical ideals in the arts and learning, encouraged close observation of nature, emphasized man's importance as an individual and gradually replaced the God-dominated world view of the Middle Ages. In painting Masaccio and Piero della Francesca developed perspective; in sculpture Donatello and Michelangelo reintroduced realism; and in politics

Machiavelli formulated in his writings the rules for seizing power, helping to establish the new pragmatism of the age. Supported in Italy by princes such as the Medici in Florence and the dukes of Urbino, the Renaissance spread throughout Europe, where, by the 16th century, it dominated thought and culture.

The Wars of the Roses: 136–7, 218–19

René I, king of Naples

1409–80. Second son of Louis II, king of Naples; duke of Anjou (1434), Bar (1430) and Lorraine (1431); king of Naples and Sicily (1435). René gained title to Bar and Lorraine in 1419 when he married Isabella of Bar, but for most of the time between 1431 and 1437 was imprisoned by Philip the Good, duke of Burgundy, who supported Antoine de Vaudémont, a rival claimant to Lorraine. In 1441 René lost the throne of Naples to Alfonso V, king of Aragon, who had over-run the kingdom. Retiring to the duchy of Anjou, René set up a brilliant court at Angers; he himself was a superb manuscript illuminator and an accomplished poet and musician, and he also encouraged the performance of mystery plays in Saumur, Angers and other towns in Anjou. As one of the counsellors of Charles VII of France, he entered Rouen with him in 1449 on its capture from the English. His sister, Mary of Anjou, was Charles's wife, and in 1445 his daughter Margaret married Henry VI of England.

The Wars of the Roses: 194, 197, 198–9

Reynes, Henry de

*fl.*1245. First architect of the 13th-century rebuilding of Westminster Abbey. Henry was employed by Henry III in 1245 to reconstruct the abbey as a shrine to St Edward the Confessor. It is not known whether he was English or French, but he undoubtedly worked at Reims Cathedral and he built Westminster with high vaults and flying buttresses in the French style.

Chronicles of the Age of Chivalry/Four Gothic Kings (US edn): 101

Reynolds, Walter, archbishop of Canterbury

d.1327. Bishop of Worcester (1307–13); treasurer (1307–10); chancellor (1310–14); archbishop of Canterbury (1313–27). A household official of Edward I, Walter became a

favourite of Edward II, who gave him the bishopric of Worcester in 1307. He was made archbishop of Canterbury by a papal bull, obtained by Edward II, over the head of Thomas Cobham, who had been elected by the Canterbury monks in the customary way. According to the chronicler Adam of Murimuth, Walter owed the king's favour to his talents as a theatrical director. He imposed some church reforms as archbishop and in 1327 he reached accord with Edward II's queen Isabella after she had overthrown the king. That year he crowned the young Edward III.

Chronicles of the Age of Chivalry/Four Gothic Kings (US edn): 171, 186, 227

Rhuddlan castle

Castle in Clwyd, Wales, that was the first of those built by Edward I around 1277 to subdue the Welsh principality of Gwynedd. Like many of them, its gatehouse was made from linked towers that made its entrance its strongest feature. Edward's queen Eleanor had a fish pond built in its courtyard and a lawn laid with 6000 turves. In March 1282 the Welsh rebel Llywelyn ap Gruffydd besieged the castle without success. When he died in combat in December of that year his head was brought to Edward at Rhuddlan.

Chronicles of the Age of Chivalry/Four Gothic Kings (US edn): 116–7, 119, 121, 124

Richard of Devizes

*fl.*1189–92. Benedictine monk of St Swithun's, Winchester; chronicler. Richard's chronicle, much influenced by romance literature, describes the deeds of Richard I from his accession in 1189 to October 1192, when the king left the Holy Land after jointly leading the Third Crusade. He praises the king, 'that fearful lion', and dwells on his prowess in battle. Richard describes London as a cynical, evil city and compares it unfavourably with Winchester.

The Plantagenet Chronicles: 297

Richard, 3rd duke of York

1411–60. Son of Richard, 5th earl of Cambridge, and Anne Mortimer; 3rd duke of York (1415–60), 6th earl of March (1425–60), lieutenant of France (1436–7, 1440–5), lieutenant of Ireland (1447). Richard's father was son of Edmund, 1st duke of York, fifth son of Edward III; his mother Anne was a great-granddaughter of Lionel, 1st duke of Clarence, third son of the same king. Richard's line was known as the house of York and his descent enabled him to put up a strong claim to the English throne in opposition to the ruling house of Lancaster. The Yorkist branch stemmed from John of Gaunt, Edward III's fourth son, and had come to the throne when Henry IV supplanted Richard II, the legitimate king, in 1399. In the years before the birth of Henry's only child, Edward, in 1453, Richard was heir to the throne, by virtue of his royal blood.

He served in France in 1436–7, where he held the post of king's lieutenant. In 1438 he married Cecily Neville, daughter of Ralph Neville, 1st earl of Westmorland. Their first son, Edward, the future Edward IV, was born in 1442. In 1440 Richard was again appointed lieutenant in France, where he remained until 1445. Henry's advisers, led by the queen, Margaret of Anjou, regarded him as a threat because of his power and his opposition to the queen's policy of peace with France, and in 1447 they appointed him lieutenant of Ireland, an informal exile.

Three years later, in 1450, Richard returned from Ireland and, at the head of 4,000 men, forced his way into the king's presence. Henry promised him a seat on the royal council, and for the next two years there was a power struggle between Richard and Margaret's ally Edmund Beaufort, 2nd duke of Somerset, who was discredited by the loss to the French of Normandy (1450) and Gascony (1453). In 1452 Richard marched on London, leading a large force, to protest to Henry at Somerset's misgovernment, and was formally reconciled with the king at Blackheath. He retired from the council for a year. In August 1453 Henry suffered the first of his bouts of madness. In October Richard was appointed protector of the realm during Henry's period of insanity. However, Edward, heir to the Lancastrian line, was born that year, displacing Richard from his position as Henry's heir-apparent, and when the king recovered early in 1455, Richard's protectorship was revoked at the queen's behest. Somerset was freed in March and Richard and his supporters were driven from power.

Richard took to arms, with the support of the Neville family and other magnates. On 22 May 1455 at St Albans he defeated a Lancastrian force led by Margaret of Anjou and Somerset, in the opening battle of the Wars of the Roses, killing Somerset and capturing Henry with the help of Richard Neville, 'the Kingmaker', 16th earl of Warwick. He governed as protector from November 1455 to February 1456, and remained on the king's council after Henry had discharged him from the protectorship. A ceremony of reconciliation arranged by Henry

VI in 1458, in which Richard paraded through London arm-in-arm with Margaret, was no more than a charade; the queen and Somerset's heir, Henry Beaufort, 3rd duke of Somerset, had been fomenting opposition to Richard. In 1459 the duke armed his followers once more, but in October fled to Wales. He was attainted in November, and took refuge in Ireland; Richard Neville was in exile in France.

In June 1460 Richard Neville invaded England from Calais. He defeated the Lancastrians at Northampton in July and captured the king. Richard of York returned from Ireland in September to claim the crown at Westminster. Parliament and the judges would not support Henry's deposition, and Richard was forced to accept a renewed protectorship and his nomination as Henry's heir in place of Henry's son Prince Edward. Margaret and her Lancastrian supporters rallied, and Richard went north to subjugate them. In December 1460 his men were besieged at Sandal castle in Yorkshire, which they left on 30 December, to be defeated by a Lancastrian force at Wakefield. Richard was killed in the fighting and his head displayed on the walls of York, wearing a paper crown. A year later, his son, Edward of York, took the throne as Edward IV.

The Wars of the Roses: 168, 182, 188–9, 194–6, 200, 205–10, 212, 214–17, 220, 222–4, 245, 272

Richard, 5th duke of York

1472–83. Second son of Edward IV; 5th duke of York (1474–83), 6th duke of Norfolk (1478–83). Richard was married at the age of six to Anne Mowbray, daughter of the earl of Norfolk, thus gaining the title. He fled with his mother, the queen-dowager Elizabeth Woodville, to sanctuary in May 1483 after Richard, 3rd duke of Gloucester, had seized his brother, the young Edward V. Cardinal Bourchier persuaded Elizabeth to release Richard from sanctuary on 16 June, on the pretext that he was to attend his brother Edward's coronation. The two boys were taken to the Tower, and were murdered there sometime soon after the duke of Gloucester's coronation as Richard III in July 1483.

The Wars of the Roses: 235, 274, 282, 286–7

Richard, 8th earl of Clare, 6th earl of Gloucester and 5th earl of Hertford

1222–62. Richard succeeded to all his earldoms as a minor in 1230. An important marcher lord, he was twice defeated by the Welsh, in 1244

and 1257. He refused to participate in Henry III's expedition to Gascony in 1253 and five years later joined the baronial opposition under Simon de Montfort which restricted Henry's power through the Provisions of Oxford. In 1259 he quarrelled with Simon and became reconciled with the king.

Chronicles of the Age of Chivalry/Four Gothic Kings (US edn): 86

Richard, 3rd earl of Cornwall, king of the Romans

1209–72. Second son of King John of England; 3rd earl of Cornwall (1227); king of the Romans (1257–68). In 1225, aged only 16, Richard led a successful campaign to recover the English lands in Gascony, but on his return he joined the baronial opposition to his brother Henry III. In the late 1230s he headed popular opposition to the Lusignan faction at court but by 1239 the brothers were reconciled. In 1243 Richard married Henry's sister-in-law Sancia of Provence. In 1257 he was elected king of the Romans (Holy Roman Emperor-elect) but was never crowned as emperor. In the civil war in England of 1264–5 he fought for Henry against Simon de Montfort and the barons and was taken prisoner at the battle of Lewes (1264). He was released after Henry's victory at the battle of Evesham (1265).

Chronicles of the Age of Chivalry/Four Gothic Kings (US edn): 16, 52, 72, 74, 76, 84, 97, 104, 111, 241

Richard of Ilchester, bishop of Winchester

d. 1188. Archdeacon of Poitiers (1162–73); bishop of Winchester (1173–88). A trusted adviser to Henry II and a baron of his Exchequer, Richard was rewarded with the bishopric of Winchester. The king's message to the electoral college was: 'I order you to hold a free election, but forbid you to elect anyone except Richard, my clerk.' Richard was a trusted envoy: in 1174 the king's justices in England sent him to Poitou to beg Henry to return and deal with the rebellious allies of his son Henry, the Young King.

The Plantagenet Chronicles: 129, 165–6, 168

Richard I, Lion-Heart, king of England

1157–99. Third son of Henry II of England and Eleanor of Aquitaine; duke of Aquitaine

(1172–99); king of England (1189–99). In 1160 Richard was betrothed to Alice, daughter of Louis VII of France. Invested as duke of Aquitaine in 1172, he joined his brothers Henry the Young King and Geoffrey in their 1173–4 revolt against their father, aligning with Louis in an abortive alliance.

In 1183 he fought for Henry against his brothers when they supported a revolt against him in Aquitaine. When Henry the Young King died in 1183, making Richard heir to the English throne, Henry ordered Richard to give up Aquitaine to his hitherto landless youngest brother John. Richard compromised by surrendering Aquitaine to his mother in 1185, but suspected a plan to disinherit him, and in 1188 joined Philip II of France against his father. Their forces defeated Henry, shortly before his death in 1189 made Richard king of England. Richard's contemporaries dubbed him 'the lion-heart' in recognition of his valour and prowess in war, but also because of his awesome Plantagenet rages; he inspired fear as much as admiration. He was cultivated, and is known to have composed several songs in company with the troubadour Blondel le Nesle.

Richard spent only six months of his reign in England. He had taken crusading vows in 1187, and in 1190 set off for Outremer on the Third Crusade with Philip II of France. He conquered Cyprus en route, in 1191, and married Berengaria of Navarre in Limassol in May that year, breaking his childhood betrothal to Alice. Richard's marriage was childless, but he had a bastard son, Philip of Cognac: recent theories that he was homosexual are not substantiated in contemporary sources.

Richard was largely responsible for the capture of Acre in July 1191, in company with Philip II, but the French king, his fellow leader and arch-rival, returned to France to plot with Richard's brother John.

Richard won an outstanding victory against Saladin at the battle of Arsuf (1191) and came near to taking Jerusalem twice, in December 1191 and June 1192. However, news of John's intrigues in France disturbed him, and after making a truce with Saladin that allowed Christians access to Jerusalem's holy places, he set off for home. In December 1190 he was apprehended by Leopold V, duke of Austria, who surrendered him to Holy Roman Emperor Henry VI. Imprisoned at the castle of Trifels, Richard waited for his subjects to raise the enormous ransom (150,000 marks) demanded

Richard II After Wat Tyler's fall, Richard placates forces of the Peasants Revolt.

171

by the emperor. It is said his troubadour Blondel found him by singing outside all the castles in Germany, a lay he and Richard had composed together, until his song was answered. The Plantagenet administrators, directed by Richard's chancellor, William Longchamp, employed the efficient bureaucracy established by Henry II, but it was March 1194 before Richard returned to England.

The king now crushed an attempted coup by his brother John, and recouped gains made by Philip II in his absence. He defeated the French king in 1194, then strengthened the defences of Normandy; the magnificent Château Gaillard, his 'saucy castle', was their centrepiece. The castle cost 11,500 pounds to construct – an enormous sum – and Richard supervised its design with minute attention. His war with Philip continued intermittently, until he defeated him again near Gisors in 1198.

Richard died in 1199, in a skirmish against a rebellious vassal at Châlus-Chabrol. He was buried at the great Plantagenet abbey of Fontevrault, at the heart of his continental dominions.

The Plantagenet Chronicles: 22, 41, 93–4, 97, 104, 117, 129, 134, 136, 140, 152–3, 166, 168–73, 185–93, 195–257, 265

Richard II, king of England

1367–1400. Son of Edward, the Black Prince, and Joan, the Fair Maid of Kent; king of England (1377–99). Richard's grandfather Edward III died in 1377, and since his father too had died the year before, Richard became king at the age of ten. During his minority England was ruled by a council, under the guidance of John of Gaunt, 2nd duke of Lancaster, and the young king was put in the charge of Sir Simon Burley. He early developed aesthetic tastes and interests which later gave rise to exquisite portraits such as the Wilton Diptych (1393–4). When the Peasants Revolt, directed against John of Gaunt's unpopular government, broke out in 1381, Richard (aged 14) faced Wat Tyler's followers, negotiated with Tyler and quelled the mob when the peasant leader was killed.

Richard retracted the concessions he made to the mob, but after December 1381 he declared a general pardon, a display of political acumen which did not set a precedent.

Anne of Bohemia, whom he married in 1382, was a moderating influence, but was unable to curb his generosity to his favourites, such as Michael de la Pole, 3rd earl of Suffolk, whom he appointed chancellor in 1383, and the widely detested Robert de Vere, 9th earl of Oxford,

whom he made earl of Ireland (a new title) in 1385. In 1386, as a result of Richard's determination to govern through Pole and de Vere, a group of nobles led by Thomas, 1st duke of Gloucester, imposed a council of 11 magnates to oversee royal government, and forced Richard to dismiss Pole.

In August 1387 Richard obtained a statement from the royal judges that Parliament had acted illegally by imposing a council on him, and raised an army in the north. In response, Thomas, 1st duke of Gloucester and four other magnates – the lords appellant – issued 'appeals' in November 1387 accusing de Vere and Richard's other advisers of treason.

In February 1388 the lords appellant tried and convicted five of Richard's principal advisers for treason in the so-called Merciless Parliament. They also executed the king's much-loved tutor Simon Burley. Richard was again placed under a council of control, but in May 1389 he dismissed the councillors and ruled with the support of John of Gaunt.

In June 1394 Anne, Richard's beloved wife, died. Richard had the royal manor of Sheen, where she had died, pulled down, and assaulted Richard, 9th earl of Arundel (one of the lords appellant), when he inadvertently arrived late at the queen's funeral service. In October that year the king went to Ireland and imposed order on the Irish chieftains, returning in 1395. In November 1396 he married seven-year-old Isabella of Valois, daughter of Charles VI of France.

In 1397 Richard arrested three lords appellant – Gloucester, Arundel and Thomas, 12th earl of Warwick – and, in September assembled a parliament which was coerced into sentencing them to death. Arundel was executed, Gloucester was murdered (perhaps smothered) while in custody at Calais, and Warwick obtained a pardon. The remaining lords appellant, Henry Bolingbroke (John of Gaunt's son and the future Henry IV) and Thomas Mowbray, the earl marshal, quarrelled in 1398 and agreed to settle the dispute by single combat. Richard allowed preparations for this to proceed, then, on the day appointed, stopped the combat and banished both parties. John of Gaunt died in 1399, removing the last restraining influence on Richard.

The king now ruled apparently unchallenged. He strengthened his personal army, raised heavy taxes, and used his personal signet to seal many royal writs. When he went to Ireland in 1399, in another attempt to pacify its warring chieftains, Bolingbroke, who had been dispossessed of the vast Lancastrian inheritance due to him on John of Gaunt's death, invaded England in May that year – an invasion which

met with little resistance. On his return from Ireland, Richard was unable to raise a force against Henry. He was captured outside Conway castle in August 1399 and, in September 1399, abdicated on condition that his life be spared. Henry was crowned as Henry IV; Richard was sent to Pontefract castle where he died in February 1400, probably starved, after a rising to free him had been crushed in January. He was more popular in death than in life, and rumours that he lived on and was about to reclaim the throne were to haunt Henry IV for many years.

Chronicles of the Age of Chivalry/Four Gothic Kings (US edn): 286–90, 296, 300, 306
The Wars of the Roses: 10, 18–89, 92, 108, 113, 144, 289

Richard III, king of England

1452–85. Eleventh son of Richard, 3rd duke of York, and Cecily Neville; 3rd duke of Gloucester (1461–83); king of England (1483–5). Richard was created 3rd duke of Gloucester in June 1461, at the coronation of his brother Edward of York as Edward IV of England. The belief that Richard was hunchbacked is not supported in contemporary sources, which describe him as dark, short and slight, with uneven shoulders. Richard fled with Edward to Flanders in September 1470 after the Lancastrian invasion led by Margaret of Anjou, wife of the deposed Henry IV, and Richard Neville, 'the Kingmaker', 16th earl of Warwick. He commanded the vanguard for Edward at the decisive battles of Barnet and Tewkesbury in 1471, in which the house of York finally crushed the Lancastrian forces. It was rumoured that Richard killed Henry VI's son, Prince Edward, the Lancastrian heir, after Tewkesbury, and murdered the captive Henry VI in the Tower of London soon after.

He was well rewarded for his loyalty by being given the substantial northern estates of the earl of Warwick, who had died in the battle of Barnet, along with the hand in marriage (1472) of his daughter, Anne Neville. Richard disputed the Neville inheritance with his brother George, 3rd duke of Clarence – who had married Anne's sister Isabel in 1469 and hoped to keep all her family's wealth – and retained his portion. George, repeatedly disloyal to Edward IV, was put to death in the Tower of London in 1478.

With Edward's backing Richard became the master of the North. He won admiration for upholding justice and bringing peace to this area, and for leading an effective campaign against the Scots in 1482. However, he resented the domination of Edward's in-laws, the

Woodvilles, at court. When the king died on 9 April 1483, the royal council planned the immediate coronation of his heir, Edward prince of Wales, as Edward V. This would avoid a minority government, exclude Richard from becoming protector and leave power in the hands of the Woodville family, led by Anthony Woodville, earl Rivers, maternal uncle and governor of the royal heir.

To gratify his ambition or to prevent royal authority from being seriously weakened – perhaps both – Richard staged a pre-emptive strike. On 24 April 1483, before a formal coronation could take place, he seized the young king, arrested Earl Rivers, overthrew the Woodville party, and named himself protector. Edward IV's widow Elizabeth Woodville took sanctuary in Westminster Abbey with her younger son, Richard, 5th duke of York. On 13 June Richard took Lord Hastings, a leading member of the council who had backed his coup but now feared his ambition, and had him put to death; Anthony Rivers was executed ten days later on 23 June. Edward V was taken to the Tower of London and, at Richard's behest, Thomas Bourchier, archbishop of Canterbury, persuaded Elizabeth Woodville to relinquish Richard, duke of York, who joined his brother in the Tower. The legitimacy of both children was called into question by an assembly of the realm, and on 26 June Richard took the throne in his nephew's place.

Although many nobles had supported Richard's supplanting of the Woodvilles, by October 1483 he faced a major rebellion when his erstwhile ally Henry Stafford, 5th duke of Buckingham, rose against him, nominating Henry Tudor, a distant offshoot of the house of Lancaster, as king. The rising was crushed and Buckingham executed.

As king, Richard passed a number of statutes which were of benefit to his subjects during his first (and only) parliament, of January 1484, although they were at the same time designed to widen the basis of his support. Land sales and trusts were regulated, and protectionist laws against foreign merchants introduced. The Commons was skilfully managed by the Speaker, William Catesby, a supporter of Richard, and fear of Richard's considerable army kept the Lords compliant. Although Parliament formally confirmed the claim by which Richard had taken the throne, that was not enough to check sedition.

Opposition to Richard focused on Henry Tudor, and was strengthened by rumours that he had arranged the murder of Edward V and his brother Richard of York in the Tower. Although no evidence was ever found, they were assumed to have died in September 1483.

Richard III *A misericord wood carving of Richard Crouchback the usurper king.*

Henry, exiled in France, raised support for an invasion force which arrived at Milford Haven in Wales on 7 August 1485. Richard had already led an army to Nottingham to await Henry's move, and the two forces met at Bosworth in Leicestershire on 22 August 1485.

Richard's army was the larger, but many nobles had stayed away, and morale among his troops was low. Lord Stanley, previously loyal to the king, at the last minute committed his forces on Henry's side and tipped the balance against Richard. The last Plantagenet king died leading a charge against his Tudor rival. Many contemporaries saw Richard's death as just punishment for his evil conduct, and the legend of Richard Crouchback, the evil usurper, began to take shape.

The Wars of the Roses: 11, 225, 234–5, 253, 255–6, 262, 264–6, 274, 279–305

Rievaulx Abbey

Cistercian abbey in the Rye Valley near Helmsley in Yorkshire, founded in 1132 under the sponsorship of St Bernard of Clairvaux. One of 70 new English abbeys built by the Cistercians in the 12th century, Rievaulx had 140 monks and 500 lay brothers and servants by 1167, when its most notable abbot, Ailred, died. In 1323 Rievaulx was despoiled by Scots invaders after Edward II and his troops had deserted the abbey.

The Plantagenet Chronicles: 266, 267
Chronicles of the Age of Chivalry/Four Gothic Kings (US edn): 204–5

Rishanger, William

1250?–1312? Benedictine monk of St Albans Abbey; chronicler. William became a monk at St Albans in 1271. He wrote an account of the civil war of 1264–5 between Henry III and the barons led by Simon de Montfort, and an account of Edward I's reign. A St Albans chronicle of Edward II's reign has also been attributed to him. Rishanger's writings are rather pedestrian but do provide useful information about the period, as, for example, the descriptions of Edward I's subduing of Wales after Llywelyn ap Gruffydd's death in 1282 and the death of Edward's queen, Eleanor of Castile, in 1291.

Chronicles of the Age of Chivalry/Four Gothic Kings (US edn): 13, 107, 124, 132

Rivers, Earl

See: Woodville, Anthony, 2nd earl Rivers

Robert de Beaumont, 2nd earl of Leicester

1104–68. 2nd earl of Leicester (1118–68); justiciar of England (c.1155). Robert's twin brother Waleran, count of Meulan, defected from King Stephen of England to the Empress Matilda in 1141, but Robert remained a close adviser of the king. In the 1140s, as lieutenant of Normandy, he tried to hold the duchy for Stephen but was defeated by the forces of Matilda's husband Geoffrey Plantagenet, count of Anjou. Robert was one of the magnates who in 1153 helped secure Henry II's future accession, and, jointly with Richard de Lucy, held the important post of justiciar. During Henry's absences in France from 1158 to 1163 and in 1165 Robert was regent of England.

The Plantagenet Chronicles: 112

Robert Blanchemains, 3rd earl of Leicester

1130–90. Son of Robert, 2nd earl of Leicester; 3rd earl of Leicester (1168–90). In 1173 Robert joined the rebellion of Henry, the Young King, against his father Henry II, but was defeated and captured by Richard de Lucy, justiciar of England, near Bury St Edmunds. His estates were seized and he was imprisoned at Falaise in 1173–4; but Henry II restored his honours in 1177. Robert took part in Richard I's coronation in 1189 and went on pilgrimage to Palestine that same year. He died in Greece on his way back to England.

The Plantagenet Chronicles: 200

Robert Bruce, king of Scotland

1274–1329. Son of Robert Bruce, 3rd earl of Carrick, in his wife Marjorie's right; 4th earl of Carrick (1292–1306), king of Scotland (1306–29). Robert grew up at the court of Edward I of England. In 1295 he married Isabella of Mar; their daughter, Marjorie, was the ancestress of the Stewart line.

Robert's grandfather, also Robert Bruce, a descendant of David I, was a principal contender when Edward I arbitrated the succession to the Scottish throne in 1290, but Edward awarded the crown to his rival, John Balliol. Scottish politics remained unsettled, and in 1296 Edward forced Balliol to abdicate and took power into his own hands.

The young Bruce at first supported the English king – he swore fealty to him in 1296 and was appointed co-regent of the Scottish kingdom in 1299 – but was in secret contact with Scots patriots during Edward's invasion of Scotland in 1302–4. By 1305 he had decided to prosecute his own claim to be king. He murdered his principal rival, John Comyn, at Dumfries in February 1306 and on 27 March 1306 was crowned at Scone. Edward attacked him with the help of Robert's opponents in Scotland, and the Scottish king, soundly defeated at the battle of Methven in June 1306, went into hiding in Galloway. Edward I died in 1307 and his successor, Edward II, was an infinitely weaker opponent. Robert began to rally support, and was gradually able to build up his powers.

The Scottish Church recognized Robert as sovereign in 1310, and in 1312 the Hebrides, hitherto Norwegian, were ceded to him by the king of Norway. In 1312 and 1313 Robert continued to raid northern England, and by 1314 had captured all but five border strongholds from the English, who were shamed into action only when Sir Philip Mowbray, the English captain of Stirling castle, agreed to cede his castle to the Scots if not relieved by midsummer. Edward II arrived at the head of a large army, but suffered a humiliating defeat at Bannockburn on 24 June 1314. Robert was now undisputed master in his own kingdom. In 1318 he recaptured Berwick from the English and in 1322 threw off an attempted invasion by Edward II and ravaged Yorkshire. In 1323 his sovereignty was recognized by the pope.

The English refused to accept Robert Bruce as king of Scotland, and sporadic campaigns continued until 1327, when his title was recognized by Isabella of France on behalf of her son Edward III. The next year Edward's sister, Joanna, was married to David, Robert's young son by his second wife, Elizabeth de Burgh. By now Robert was ill, possibly with leprosy, and retired to Cardross castle, where he died a year later in June 1329.

Chronicles of the Age of Chivalry/Four Gothic Kings (US edn): 134–5, 145, 157–8, 160, 162, 174, 176, 178, 186, 188–92, 194, 202, 205

Robert II Curthose, duke of Normandy

c.1054–1134. Eldest son of William the Conqueror; duke of Normandy (1087–1106). Robert rebelled against his father in 1077, but the two were reconciled and Robert inherited Normandy, William's patrimony, on his father's death in 1087. He fought with his brother, William II of England, who coveted Normandy, in 1089 and from 1094 to 1096. On the First Crusade he helped defeat the Saracens at Antioch in 1098. He refused the crown of Jerusalem and returned home in 1100 when William died and his younger brother seized the English throne and became Henry I. Robert invaded England in July 1101, but was compelled to recognize Henry. In 1105 Robert's misgovernment of Normandy prompted Henry to invade it. Robert was captured at Tinchebrai in 1106 and imprisoned at Wareham, Devizes, Bristol and finally Cardiff castle, where he remained until his death at the age of about 80. A poem in Welsh containing the line 'woe is him who is too old to die' is attributed to him. He was buried at Gloucester Abbey.

The Plantagenet Chronicles: 63

Robert, 1st earl of Gloucester

c.1090–1147. Illegitimate son of Henry I of England; 1st earl of Gloucester (1120). Robert did homage to King Stephen after he had seized the throne following Henry I's death in 1136, but quarrelled with him in 1138 and had his English and Welsh estates seized. In 1139 he joined Matilda, Henry's daughter and his half-sister, in her attempt to press her claim to the English crown. He captured Stephen at Lincoln in 1141, but was taken prisoner himself at Stockbridge and exchanged for Stephen. Robert defeated Stephen once more, at Wilton in 1143, and, despite Matilda's arrogance, remained her principal supporter until his death.

The Plantagenet Chronicles: 47, 69–70, 73–4, 76

Robert III, king of Scotland

1340?–1406. Eldest son of Robert II of Scotland; 10th earl of Carrick (1368–90); king of Scotland (1390). Known as John before his accession, he changed his name because of its association with John Balliol, the unpopular king of Scotland from 1292 to 1296. Robert had

ruled Scotland for his ineffectual father until 1389, when he was crippled by a fall from a horse. He was supplanted by his younger brother Robert Stewart, 12th earl of Fife and 1st duke of Albany, who continued to rule the country after the disabled king's accession in 1390 until supplanted by the king's son David, 1st duke of Rothesay, in 1399.

Stewart may have been responsible for David's death in 1402: the king sent his second son James (the future James I of Scotland) to be educated in France for his safety.

The Wars of the Roses: 185

Robert, the Magnificent, duke of Normandy

d.1035. Duke of Normandy (1027). Robert aided Henry I of France in wars against his half-brother Robert and Odo II, count of Blois. He also sheltered and supported Edward, the Confessor, claimant to the throne of England, during the rule of Canute of Denmark and his sons in England. The *Chronicle of the Counts of Anjou* records that Robert poisoned his elder brother Richard to obtain the dukedom and that, to atone for this crime, he went on a barefoot pilgrimage to Jerusalem, seven years after becoming duke, but died in Nicaea. The chronicle describes his illegitimate son William as 'an upright man who conquered England'.

The Plantagenet Chronicles: 26

Robin of Holderness

fl.1469. Leader, with Robin of Redesdale, of rebel demonstrations in northern England in 1469 against Edward IV's regime. He may have been Robert Hillyard of Winestead, or his son.

The Wars of the Roses: 245

Robin Hood

Legendary English outlaw, hero of over 30 Middle English ballads. He was said to live in Sherwood Forest in Nottinghamshire and Barnsdale in southern Yorkshire and to fight the tyrannous officials of Prince John (later King John) during Richard I's captivity in Germany in 1193–4. The original Robin Hood may have been a fugitive who failed to appear before royal justices at York in 1225. 'Robinhood' surnames show the legend was known around 1262, but

Robert Bruce *The statue (opposite) of the celebrated Scots king and hero, overlooking the field of Bannockburn.*

the first direct reference to Robin Hood is in 1377, and the earliest recorded legends date from the late 15th century. The *History of Greater Britain* (1521) by the Scottish writer John Major dates Robin to Richard I's reign.

The Plantagenet Chronicles: 298–9
Chronicles of the Age of Chivalry/Four Gothic Kings (US edn): 214

Robin of Redesdale

*fl.*1469. Popular name of the joint-leader, with Robin of Holderness, of a rising in northern England in 1469 against Edward IV's rule. The rebellion was instigated by Richard Neville, 'the Kingmaker', 16th earl of Warwick, and his supporters. 'Robin' was identified by the chronicler John Warkworth as Sir William Conyers (d.1495) but was more probably his brother John, who later made his peace with the king.

The Wars of the Roses: 245

Rochelle, La

Major French port on the Bay of Biscay, in the county of Poitou. It was held by the English until 1224, when it was captured by Louis VIII of France. Restored to Edward III in 1360, it was lost to the French again in 1371.

The Plantagenet Chronicles: 274, 280, 286, 306
Chronicles of the Age of Chivalry/Four Gothic Kings (US edn): 276
The Wars of the Roses: 180, 209

Roches, Peter des, bishop of Winchester

d.1238. Justiciar (1214–15); bishop of Winchester (1205–38). A native of Poitou in France. Peter served both Richard I and King John of England as knight and clerk. As bishop of Winchester, he supported John against Pope Innocent III and the barons in 1215 and excommunicated Prince Louis of France (the future Louis VIII) in 1216 for invading England. He became Henry III's guardian after the young king's coronation in October 1216 and after William Marshal's death in 1219 shared the regency of England with the justiciar Hubert de Burgh and Pandulf Masca, the papal legate, until Henry reached his majority in 1223. In 1227 Peter went on crusade with Holy Roman Emperor Frederick II. After his return, in 1231, he exercised a strong influence at court, helping to secure Hubert de Burgh's dismissal in 1232 and obtaining the post of treasurer of the

household for his son (or possibly nephew) Peter des Rivaux. But by 1234 both had lost power and in 1235 Peter went abroad again, this time to help Pope Gregory IX defeat a rebellion of the Romans at Viterbo.

Chronicles of the Age of Chivalry/Four Gothic Kings (US edn): 27–8, 46, 48

Roches, William des

*fl.*1202. Powerful baron in the county of Anjou, France, who switched his support to King John of England from Arthur, duke of Brittany, John's rival for the Angevin inheritance. In so doing, he enabled John to hold Anjou. On 1 August 1202, at Mirebeau, he led a victorious attack against the French during which Arthur was captured. However, John's refusal to hand Arthur over to William led the baron to rebel against the king later that year; and in 1204 he allied himself with Philip II of France when the French king invaded John's territories in France.

The Plantagenet Chronicles: 275–6, 280

Rochester

City on the River Medway in Kent, inhabited since Roman times. Its cathedral was started in about 1100, and has 12th- to 14th-century Gothic additions. Rochester castle, built in the 12th century, was besieged three times, notably by King John in 1215, when his baronial opponents took refuge there.

The Plantagenet Chronicles: 122, 284, 314, 316
Chronicles of the Age of Chivalry/Four Gothic Kings (US edn): 54, 203, 254
The Wars of the Roses: 205

Roger, bishop of Salisbury

d.1139. Chancellor (1101–2); bishop of Salisbury (1102–39); proto-justiciar of England (*c.*1107–39). Roger began his career in the service of Henry I, whose administration he controlled from about 1107. He supported Stephen of Blois's claim to the English throne, and was largely responsible for his accession in 1135. He was the leading figure in Stephen's administration and – with his nephews Alexander, bishop of Lincoln, and Nigel, bishop of Ely, and with his son Roger le Poer, the chancellor – he controlled both Chancery and Exchequer; this earned him the enmity of Waleran, count of Meulan, and other barons.

In 1139 Roger was summoned to Oxford by the king, who arrested him for a disturbance of the peace engineered by Waleran and

imprisoned him in his own castle at Devizes in Wiltshire. The chronicler Henry of Huntingdon describes how Stephen starved Roger and tortured his son until Roger gave up his castles. He died in disgrace. Contemporaries attributed his fall to trickery and this lost Stephen many supporters.

The Plantagenet Chronicles: 13, 65, 72

Roger I, count of Sicily

*c.*1031–1101. Norman count of Sicily (1072). Roger joined with his brother Robert Guiscard in 1058 to conquer southern Italy; between 1061 and 1091 he took Sicily from the Arabs.

The Plantagenet Chronicles: 210

Roger of Howden

d.1201? Chronicler and royal clerk. His chronicle, related to that attributed to Benedict of Peterborough, describes contemporary events between 1192 and 1201 and also contains much original and valuable material concerning Henry II's reign (1133–89). He undertook diplomatic and administrative duties for Henry II and was present at the siege of Acre (1191).

The Plantagenet Chronicles: 13

Roger II, king of Sicily

*c.*1095–1154. Son and heir of Roger I, duke of Apulia; 2nd count of Sicily (1101–30); 1st king of Sicily (1130). Roger became king as a reward for backing antipope Anacletus II against Pope Innocent II in 1130. In 1139 he defeated Innocent and his allies at Galcuccio and forced Innocent in his turn to invest him with the crown of Naples and Sicily. Between 1135 and 1153 Roger conquered Africa's north coast from Tripoli to Tunis.

The Plantagenet Chronicles: 210

Roger of Pont l'Evêque, archbishop of York

d.1181. Archbishop of York (1154); papal legate for England (1164) and Scotland (1180). One of King Stephen's chaplains and a protégé of Theobald, archbishop of Canterbury, Roger was elected to the archbishopric of York after Henry II's accession in 1154, with the king's backing. Appointed legate for England by Pope Alexander III, he subsequently supported the king against Thomas Becket. On 14 June 1170 he crowned the king's son Henry, the Young

King, at York, despite Becket's protests that this was the archbishop of Canterbury's prerogative and against the express orders of the pope; in December that year Roger was excommunicated by Becket. In 1176 Roger quarrelled with Becket's successor, Richard of Dover, as to whether Canterbury should take precedence over York. The dispute was settled by a Lateran Council ruling of 1179 that York owed no obedience to Canterbury. In 1181, as Scottish papal legate, Roger excommunicated William, the Lion, king of Scotland, for insubordination.

The Plantagenet Chronicles: 112, 116, 132, 142, 166

Roger of Wendover

d.1236. Benedictine monk of St Albans; chronicler. Prior of the cell of Belvoir, Roger was deposed in about 1219 for profligacy. He began his chronicle, the *Flores Historiarum* (Flowers of History), some time after 1204 and continued working on it until 1234. The chronicle, which relates history from the Creation, uses existing sources for events up to 1202; for subsequent history it is original. Roger describes King John as cruel and tyrannical; his judgement that John was a failure was passed on by Roger's fellow chronicler Matthew Paris and became the prevailing opinion. He attacked Henry III as 'simple' and the papacy for providing Italian priests for English livings.

The work is generally unreliable; for example, it has John travelling to the Isle of Wight in 1215, a journey he is known from other sources never to have made.

The Plantagenet Chronicles: 265
Chronicles of the Age of Chivalry/Four Gothic Kings (US edn): 13, 34, 56

Roland, Chanson de

See: *Chanson de Roland*

rolls

See: pipe rolls

Roman de la Rose

French poem of 22,000 lines in eight-syllable couplets, begun *c.*1237 by the French poet William de Lorris and completed by Jean de Meung *c.*1275–80. William's 4,058 lines are a charming poetic allegory of courtly love, with a lover seeking a symbolic rose in a garden ruled by Love personified. Jean's continuation celebrated sex and propagation as fulfilling

Roman de la Rose The Lover, hero of the poem, is led towards the rose.

God's will and included religious and philosophical digressions.

Chronicles of the Age of Chivalry/Four Gothic Kings (US edn): 55

Roman de Rou

Norman-French verse chronicle by the poet Wace, written *c.*1150, celebrating the dukes of Normandy ('Rou' is Rollo, 1st duke of Normandy) and including a famous description of the battle of Hastings in 1066.

The Plantagenet Chronicles: 246

romance

General term for poetic narratives popular in the 11th century, celebrating chivalry and love. The term refers to the vernacular French in which the works were composed. The *Chanson de Roland* is a notable example.

The Plantagenet Chronicles: 55

Romanesque style

Architectural style prevalent in Europe from the 8th to the mid-12th century, combining Roman with Byzantine and Oriental forms. Romanesque buildings generally have barrel vaulting, with minimal wall openings, giving an effect of massive simplicity, often counterpointed by elaborate sculptural decoration. Angoulême Cathedral in France and Durham Cathedral in England are fine examples.

The Plantagenet Chronicles: 55, 122–3, 174, 175

Romans, king of the

See: King of the Romans

Rome

The centre of Western Christendom. Rome was throughout the Middle Ages a city whose control was in dispute between various factions: the great noble families, such as the Colonna and the Frangipani; the commune of the citizens (in effect, a republic); the Holy Roman Emperors; and the papacy.

The commune of the citizens, established in 1145, was recognized the same year by Pope Eugenius III but, even so, remained unruly. Eventually it reached an agreement with Holy Roman Emperor Frederick I (who had repeatedly tried to crush it) in 1187 and with Pope Clement III in 1188; by this its legislative, administrative and legal powers were confirmed – although some popes, such as Innocent III in the early 13th century, were still able to dominate the city's government. In the 13th century the great noble families began to play a leading role in the commune, and from the 1250s one leading aristocrat was periodically elected senator of Rome. Pope Boniface VIII (1294–1303) exerted great influence in the city, and his jubilee of 1300 attracted many thousands of pilgrims. But the 'Babylonian captivity' of the papacy at Avignon (1309–78) and the Great Schism (1378–1417) both diminished Rome's prosperity and authority. Factional fights between noble and popular parties became common. The city recovered only after Pope Martin V re-established the papal court in Rome in 1420 and began to build up papal control of the city, which was fully achieved by 1503.

The Plantagenet Chronicles: 26–7, 104, 177–8, 208
Chronicles of the Age of Chivalry/Four Gothic Kings (US edn): 148, 150–1

Roses, Wars of the

See: Wars of the Roses

Rouen

Capital of Normandy, near the mouth of the River Seine. Rouen became a Plantagenet stronghold when Geoffrey Plantagenet took it in 1144. Henry, the Young King, was buried in its cathedral in 1183 (though only after his body had been recovered from Le Mans, whose citizens, jealous of the honour, had stolen the corpse). Plantagenet rule of Rouen ended when Philip II of France seized it from King John in 1203, but the city was recaptured for the English by Henry V in 1419, after a long siege. Under English influence, Flamboyant architecture flourished in the city. In 1431 Joan of Arc was tried and burned there. In 1449 Rouen fell to Charles VII of France and remained French thereafter.

The Plantagenet Chronicles: 45–6, 63, 113, 133–4, 172–3, 195, 233, 240, 244, 278–80
Chronicles of the Age of Chivalry/Four Gothic Kings (US edn): 73
The Wars of the Roses: 49, 128, 144–7, 176–7, 202, 230

Rous, John

1411?–91. Chaplain, antiquary and chronicler. Rous left Oxford University in 1445 to become chaplain of St Mary Magdalene, a chantry chapel near Warwick set up by Richard Beauchamp. He enjoyed the patronage of the Beauchamp and the Neville families. His chronicles include the *Historia Regnum Anglicae* (1480–6), recounting the history of England from Brutus to Henry VII's accession in 1485. Between 1477 and 1485 he also wrote two rolls (one in Latin, one in English) of the history of the earls of Warwick. Rous changed his texts with the political climate. For example, Richard III, 'The most mighty prince Richard', in the English roll becomes 'like the Antichrist' in the Latin roll, recast after Richard's death in 1485.

The Wars of the Roses: 13, 294, 304

Roxburgh

Scottish town near the English border. Originally part of English Northumbria, Roxburgh was fought over by the English and Scots. In 1417, when it was in English hands, it was besieged by William Douglas, a Scottish ally of the English Lollards. James I of Scotland besieged the town again in 1436, as did his son James II in 1460, dying after he had seized its castle, which was subsequently demolished.

The Wars of the Roses: 141, 182, 222

royal household

Body of officials constituted to look after the king's private needs. They included, among others, the keeper of the wardrobe, steward, butler and almoner, each heading his own department. They organized expenditure on the king's travels, horses, arms and armour, food and drink, plate, clothes, jewels, messengers, and so on. The royal household's extravagances in Edward II's reign caused the curtailment of its powers and finances.

The Wars of the Roses: 81

Russell, John, bishop of Lincoln

d.1494. Keeper of the privy seal (1474–83); bishop of Rochester (1476–80); bishop of Lincoln (1480–94); chancellor of England (1483–5); chancellor of Oxford University (1483). Russell served Edward IV, Henry VI and Richard III in turn and undertook diplomatic missions for them, as when, in 1474, he negotiated a match between Edward IV's daughter Cicely and Prince James of Scotland. He was probably the author of the second continuation of the *Crowland Chronicle*, a major source for the history of the years 1471–85. After his death Sir Thomas More described him as 'a wise man and good, of much experience and one of the best men, undoubtedly, that England had in his time'.

The Wars of the Roses: 12, 293, 301

Rye

Town in East Sussex; from *c*.1350 one of the Cinque Ports, charged with England's maritime defence. (The harbour later became silted up and Rye now lies inland.) Thomas of Walsingham's chronicle records that on 29 June 1377 the French raided and seized the town – although it had been recently walled – and took all the townspeople's possessions. Rye was seized again by the French, and burned, in 1448.

The Wars of the Roses: 22, 24

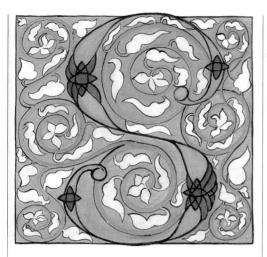

St Albans

Market town in Hertfordshire, founded by the Romans. Its abbey, founded in 793, was one of the greatest of England's Benedictine houses and produced a flourishing school of history in the 13th and 14th centuries; its chroniclers included Roger of Wendover, Matthew Paris, William Rishanger and Thomas Walsingham. In 1381, during the Peasants Revolt, a mob menaced the abbey and was dispersed by the abbot John de la Mare only with difficulty.

St Albans was the site of the first battle of the Wars of the Roses, on 22 May 1455: Richard, 3rd duke of York, stormed the town where Henry VI's party had taken refuge and seized the king. Henry subsequently made Richard found a chantry at St Albans for the souls of the slain. At the second battle of St Albans, on 17 February 1461, a Yorkist force under Richard Neville, 'the Kingmaker,' 16th earl of Warwick, fled before the army of Henry's wife Queen Margaret of Anjou, allowing the king, who had been in Neville's custody, to rejoin Margaret. Her troops then sacked the town.

The Plantagenet Chronicles: 29, 76, 265
Chronicles of the Age of Chivalry/Four Gothic Kings (US edn): 13, 72, 76, 84, 86, 107, 168
The Wars of the Roses: 12, 84, 142, 214–16, 221, 223–4, 233–4, 260

St Andrews

Town in Fife, on the north-east coast of Scotland. Its bishopric was founded in 908 and St Andrews was regarded as the ecclesiastical capital of Scotland. In 1472 its bishopric was elevated to an archbishopric and the holder of the office given the title of primate of Scotland.

The town's university, established in 1413 – one of the proliferation of 15th-century European university foundations – is the oldest in Scotland.

The Wars of the Roses: 194

St David's

Village in Dyfed, on the south-west peninsula of Wales. The 12th-century St David's Cathedral, built of red-violet stone in Romanesque style, contained the 13th-century shrine of St David, Wales's patron saint, and was a popular place of pilgrimage. The Bishop's Palace, now in ruins, was built in the 14th century.

The Plantagenet Chronicles: 121

St-Denis

Township north of Paris. In 626 Dagobert I of France founded a Benedictine abbey near the tomb of St Denis. By the 12th century, the abbey had become the richest and most famous in France. Its church was the burial place for many of the French royal house and from the 12th to the 15th century the oriflamme, the standard of St Denis, was the banner of the kings of France. The noted theologian Peter Abelard became a monk at the abbey early in the 12th century, after Fulbert, uncle of his lover Héloïse, had him castrated. In the 1130s Abbot Suger began rebuilding the abbey church in Gothic style – it became Europe's first truly Gothic building. Suger added a mosaic to the west front, in imitation of Italian churches, but it

soon weathered away. In the 1240s parts of the church were rebuilt in the new Rayonnant style, associated with the French court. During the Hundred Years War (1337–1453) the town was sacked twice by the English, in 1358 and 1406, and Joan of Arc blessed her weapons in the abbey in the 1420s.

The Plantagenet Chronicles: 34, 55, 57–9, 82, 165, 179
Chronicles of the Age of Chivalry/Four Gothic Kings (US edn): 62, 126, 148, 284
The Wars of the Roses: 148, 176

Sainte-Chapelle

Royal chapel in Paris, part of the Palais de Justice (once the royal palace). It was built by Pierre de Montreuil in 1243–6 for Louis IX of France to house various relics, including the supposed Crown of Thorns, brought back from the Holy Land. A supreme example of the Rayonnant style, the Sainte-Chapelle is lavishly painted and gilded, like a huge reliquary, and is split into lower and upper chapels. The walls of the upper are comprised of 15 tall stained-glass windows, supported by thin columns and coloured to combine with the painted interior in a rich display.

Chronicles of the Age of Chivalry/Four Gothic Kings (US edn): 62, 63

St-Omer

Town in Flanders, northern France, which grew up around a monastery founded by St Omer

Sainte-Chapelle *The splendid reliquary chapel built by Louis IX of France.*

in the 7th century. It was given a charter of liberties in 1137 by the count of Flanders, William Clito. In 1360 John II of France, who had been captured by the English at Poitiers four years earlier, was liberated at St-Omer following payment of a 500,000 pound ransom.

Chronicles of the Age of Chivalry/Four Gothic Kings (US edn): 280, 282

Saintonge

Region of western France on the Garonne estuary. Saintonge passed to Henry II of England in 1152 on his marriage to Eleanor of Aquitaine. King John lost the region to Philip II of France in 1204 but recovered it two years later. In 1242 Louis IX regained it for France, taking it from Henry III, but the English recovered part of it in 1289 under the terms of the Treaty of Paris (1259). Ceded to Edward III in 1360, by the Treaty of Brétigny, Saintonge was lost once more in 1371, to the French royal captain, Bertrand du Guesclin.

The Plantagenet Chronicles: 32–4, 37, 45, 55, 198, 261
Chronicles of the Age of Chivalry/Four Gothic Kings (US edn): 25, 90–1, 278

St-Vaast-de-la-Hougue

Port in Normandy, on the Channel coast. Edward III and his forces landed there on 13 July 1346, beginning the campaign which ended in the victory at Crécy. The king's son Edward, the Black Prince, was knighted there after the landing.

Chronicles of the Age of Chivalry/Four Gothic Kings (US edn): 224, 269

Saladin

1138–93. Muslim leader; sultan of Egypt (1171). Saladin declared himself sultan after the death of the Fatimid caliph of Egypt. By the 1180s he had conquered much of North Africa. To further his aim of seizing Syria and Palestine from their Muslim and crusader rulers he brought together a mixed force of Muslim allies. He won a first great victory over the Christians at Hattin in 1187, seizing Jerusalem, and the following year took the vital castle Krak des Chevaliers. The Third Crusade was preached in 1189 in an attempt to reverse his successes, but the crusaders managed to recover only Acre. In 1192 Saladin made the Peace of Ramla with the crusaders, reducing the Latin kingdom of Jerusalem to a coastal strip near Tyre (but

leaving free passage to the Holy City). A learned patron of the arts and sciences, Saladin was respected by the Christians for his generosity and chivalry.

The Plantagenet Chronicles: 148–50, 153, 186, 202, 206, 209, 214, 216, 224, 250

Salimbene

1221–c.1290. Italian Franciscan chronicler. In his work he records that epithets from the Book of Revelation were applied to Holy Roman Emperor Frederick II: 'dragon' or 'beast'; he himself described Frederick, after his death, as 'cunning, avaricious, lustful and wicked' yet also as 'valiant . . . cheerful, sensitive and diligent'. Salimbene dined with Louis IX of France at Sens in 1248, before the king departed on crusade, and gave a highly favourable account of him.

Chronicles of the Age of Chivalry/Four Gothic Kings (US edn): 16, 42, 68, 70, 105

Salisbury

County town of Wiltshire. Salisbury was founded in 1220 when Richard Poore, bishop of Old Sarum, moved his diocese from the

Saladin A European image of one of the great Muslim rulers of Egypt.

highlands of Sarum to the plain of the River Avon and started to build a new cathedral there, using materials from the razed old building. Apart from its tower and spire (the tallest in England), which were added in the 14th century, the cathedral was completed by 1265. The town is notable for its gridded street plan.

Chronicles of the Age of Chivalry/Four Gothic Kings (US edn): 133, 286–9
The Wars of the Roses: 238, 296

Salisbury, John of

See: John of Salisbury

Samson, abbot of Bury St Edmunds

1135–1211. Abbot of Bury St Edmunds (1182–1211). Samson studied in Paris, becoming a monk in 1166. In 1193 he visited Richard I in his prison in Germany. Samson enriched his abbey, adding many new buildings, and wrote theological treatises. His life was written by the chronicler Jocelyn of Brakelond, who paints a vivid portrait of an active and effective abbot.

The Plantagenet Chronicles: 294

Sandwich

Coastal town in Kent, one of the original Cinque Ports, charged with England's maritime defence until the River Stour, on which it stands, silted up in the 16th century. In 1217 four Cinque Ports ships attacked Eustace the Monk, perhaps the most notorious pirate of the Middle Ages, off Sandwich, seizing his vessel and then executing him.

Chronicles of the Age of Chivalry/Four Gothic Kings (US edn): 56, 140, 201

Santiago de Compostela

City in Galicia in north-west Spain where the bones of St James the Greater were miraculously discovered in the 9th century. A shrine built on the site was destroyed by the Moors in the 10th century; its replacement became, after Jerusalem and Rome, the third most popular place of pilgrimage. The pilgrims' route through France and northern Spain was well known and many fine Romanesque churches and hospitals were built along it, culminating in Santiago's cathedral, which was begun in 1078.

The Plantagenet Chronicles: 122, 177

Saracens

Term used by medieval Christians to describe Muslims who fought against them in the crusades.

Chronicles of the Age of Chivalry/Four Gothic Kings (US edn): 42, 60, 62, 68, 254

Savigniacs

Order of reformed Benedictine monks on the border of Normandy and Brittany, founded by St Vitalis in 1105. Its customs were similar to those of the Cistercian order, with which it merged in 1147. Furness Abbey in Lancashire, founded by the future King Stephen in 1127, belonged to the order.

The Plantagenet Chronicles: 77

Savoy

Region of eastern France in the Alps near Lake Geneva. Part of Charlemagne's empire in the 9th century, Savoy, then a county, was ruled by the Holy Roman Emperors in the 10th century. In 1034 it was taken by Humbert the Whitehanded, who held lands north and south of the Alps and who was the founder of the house of Savoy; over the following centuries the dynasty extended its domains in France and into Italy and Switzerland. In 1416 Savoy became a duchy under Amadeus VIII, whose descendants continued to rule the area, although campaigns by the Swiss later led to the duchy's temporary division.

Chronicles of the Age of Chivalry/Four Gothic Kings (US edn): 110

Savoy Palace

Palace in London on the Thames, near the Strand, built in the 13th century as the palace of Peter of Savoy, uncle of Henry III's queen Eleanor of Provence. During the 14th century it belonged to John of Gaunt; it was burnt down by Wat Tyler's mob on 13 June 1381, during the Peasants Revolt.

Chronicles of the Age of Chivalry/Four Gothic Kings (US edn): 300
The Wars of the Roses: 36

Scales, Thomas, Lord

1399?–1460. 7th baron Scales; knight of the Garter (1425). Thomas served against the French in 1422, under John, 1st duke of Bedford; he was captured when the English siege of Orléans was broken by the dauphin Charles in 1429. In 1439 he took part in the capture of Meaux and in the English victory at Avranches. On 5 July 1450 Thomas led a force of London aldermen and others against the Kentish rebels who revolted against Henry VI's misrule and invaded London under Jack Cade. He took the Lancastrian side at the start of the Wars of the Roses and persecuted Yorkist supporters. In July 1460 he unsuccessfully defended the Tower of London for Henry VI against Edward, 7th earl of March (the future Edward IV), and Richard Neville, 'the Kingmaker', 16th earl of Warwick. Although Thomas was released on the capture of the Tower, he was murdered by Yorkists while seeking sanctuary in Westminster Abbey.

The Wars of the Roses: 172, 205, 220

Scone

Village in Tayside, site of the inauguration of the kings of Scotland since Kenneth I in the 9th century. Scottish monarchs were enthroned on the Stone of Scone, supposedly brought from the seat of the High Kings of Ireland at Tara. Until the 14th century the rite was largely pre-Christian and symbolized the king marrying the land; the papacy reserved the Christian privilege of being crowned and anointed for the kings of England. The stone was kept near the high altar of Scone's 12th-century abbey until 1296 when Edward I of England removed it to Westminster Abbey and placed it under the English throne. Robert Bruce was crowned at Scone without it on 25 March 1306. In 1329 the papacy granted the Scots the privilege of a coronation rite and the stone became less important to the Scottish monarchy.

Chronicles of the Age of Chivalry/Four Gothic Kings (US edn): 134, 142–3, 158, 205, 230, 235

Scotland

Independent kingdom throughout the Middle Ages, although heavily under English influence in the 12th and 13th centuries. In 1174, by a treaty extorted from William, the Lion, of Scotland by Henry II of England, Scotland briefly became a fief of England, but in 1189 the Scots purchased their freedom from Richard I of England. In 1292, when the Scottish throne became vacant, Edward I of England, 'the hammer of the Scots', arbitrated between 13 claimants, but his choice, John Balliol, was by 1295 in revolt against the English king and the following year Edward annexed Scotland. A Scottish struggle against the Plantagenets then developed, led first by William Wallace, then Robert Bruce.

The latter earned a considerable measure of independence from Edward II after defeating him at the battle of Bannockburn (1314); but the struggle for domination was revived by Edward III in the 1330s.

Scotland proceeded to align itself with France against the English, an alliance that lasted until the accession of James VI of Scotland to the English throne, as James I, in 1603.

Chronicles of the Age of Chivalry/Four Gothic Kings (US edn): 132, 141–6, 150, 154–62, 174, 178, 188–92, 194–6, 204–5, 230–1, 234–6, 239, 248
The Wars of the Roses: 58–9, 95, 98, 100–2, 106–8, 117, 141, 166, 178–80, 182, 222, 232, 274, 299

Scrope, Sir Geoffrey le

d.1340. Chief justice of the King's Bench (1324–38). Geoffrey was of Norman origin and came from Wensleydale in Yorkshire. He was removed from the office of chief justice after Edward II's deposition in 1327, but was reinstated in 1328. In the same year he acted as ambassador to Scotland for Queen Isabella. He resigned as chief justice in 1338 and joined Edward III's household, following him to France in 1339. He was present at the siege of Tournay in 1340 and died at Ghent.

Chronicles of the Age of Chivalry/Four Gothic Kings (US edn): 236

Scrope, Richard le, archbishop of York

1350?–1405. Chancellor of Cambridge University (1378); bishop of Coventry and Lichfield (1386); archbishop of York (1398–1405). Although Richard was elected archbishop of York at Richard II's request, he supported Henry IV's usurpation of the throne. In 1405 he sided with Henry Percy, 1st earl of Northumberland, against Henry and, with the backing of Lord Bardolf, the earl marshal, and his nephew Sir William Plumpton, called the people of York to take up arms against the king. Their manifesto complained of bad government and excessive taxation afflicting bishops, lay lords and the people alike. The citizen army, led by the archbishop, was intercepted near York by Ralph Neville, 1st earl of Westmorland. The earl, outnumbered by the archbishop's force, tricked him into a truce, then arrested him when his followers dispersed. Richard was executed at

York, where he was venerated as a martyred saint – Saint Richard Scrope – at his tomb in York Minster and celebrated in a folk carol. Bardolf and Plumpton were also executed, and their heads were impaled on the city gates at York.

The Wars of the Roses: 104–6

Scrope, William, 1st earl of Wiltshire

1351?–99. Knight of the Garter (1393); 1st earl of Wiltshire (1397–9); treasurer of England (1398). William served with John of Gaunt against the French at Harfleur in 1369, and spent much of his youth campaigning in France. In 1393 he bought the Isle of Man. William received his earldom for helping Richard II to prosecute the rebellious lords appellant, who had tried to curb the king's tyranny. During the king's absence in Ireland in 1399, William was an adviser to Richard's regent, Edmund, 1st duke of York. When Henry Bolingbroke invaded England later that year, William was arrested at Bristol and beheaded by popular demand.

The Wars of the Roses: 84

scutage

Tax paid by a knight to his feudal lord in lieu of the military service he owed him. Literally meaning 'shield money', scutage was commonly used by the Crown as a tax on the nobility.

The Plantagenet Chronicles: 325
Chronicles of the Age of Chivalry/Four Gothic Kings (US edn): 126

Second Crusade

Crusade of 1147–9, preached by St Bernard of Clairvaux and others after the Turks took Edessa, capital of the crusader state of the same name, in 1144. It was led by Louis VII of France and the Holy Roman Emperor-elect, Conrad III. Their joint armies prepared an attack on Damascus (a Muslim emirate which had lent support to the crusader states) but it was an ignominious failure and Conrad returned home in 1148, Louis in 1149.

The Plantagenet Chronicles: 78–9, 81, 153

seignorial court

Court held by the feudal lord of a manor to try his tenants. The Provisions of Westminster (the

Second Crusade The attack on Damascus during the Second Crusade, which proved a débâcle for the Christian forces, and left Louis VII of France and Conrad III of Germany to return home in disgrace after their campaign's failure.

judicial reforms of 1260) made the proceedings of such courts subject to English common law.

Chronicles of the Age of Chivalry/Four Gothic Kings (US edn): 96

seisin

Feudal term for being in possession ('seized') of an estate.

Sempringham, Gilbert of

See: Gilbert of Sempringham

Senlis

City of Picardy in northern France. Its cathedral of Notre-Dame (built 12th–13th century) is an early Gothic masterpiece.

The Wars of the Roses: 151, 173

Senlis, Simon de, 4th earl of Northampton

d.1153. 4th earl of Northampton (1109–53) and Huntingdon (1152–3). Simon fought for King Stephen against the forces of Ranulf II de Gernon, 5th earl of Chester, and other powerful nobles at the battle of Lincoln in 1141; and he remained loyal to Stephen throughout the king's reign. He was described in Henry of Huntingdon's chronicle as doing 'everything that was unlawful and indecent'.

The Plantagenet Chronicles: 73, 85

serf

Lowest rank of peasant, legally bound to a lord's estate and transferred with it if it changed hands. Common in England (especially in the West Country) in the 11th century, serfdom declined over the succeeding three centuries and serfs gradually merged into the great class of unfree peasants known as villeins.

The Wars of the Roses: 34–40

Shakespeare, William

Plantagenet monarchs are the subjects of nine of Shakespeare's plays: *King John*, *Richard II*, *Henry IV* parts I and II, *Henry V*, *Henry VI* parts I, II and III, and *Richard III*. For his material Shakespeare drew mainly on 16th-century historical works that glorified the Tudor dynasty: Ralph Holinshed's *Chronicles*, Sir Thomas More's *History of Richard III*, and Edward Hall's *Union of the Two Noble and Illustre Families of Lancaster and York*.

The Wars of the Roses: 145, 217

Sheen

Royal palace in Surrey, on the Thames. Once a manor house, it was converted into a palace by

St Denis The Benedictine abbey (opposite) and burial place of French kings who bore its oriflamme standard into battle.

Edward III, who died there on 21 June 1377. A favourite residence of Richard II and his queen, Anne of Bohemia, it was extended by Richard, who built private apartments with a tiled bathroom for Anne on an island called La Neyt in the river. She died at Sheen in June 1394 and, in April the following year, the griefstricken king ordered the entire palace razed. He never revisited the site. After his accession in 1413, Henry V ordered a new palace to be built there.

Chronicles of the Age of Chivalry/Four Gothic Kings (US edn): 157, 304
The Wars of the Roses: 19, 64, 69, 122, 202

sheriff

Representative of royal authority in a shire. Literally the 'shire-reeve', the sheriff administered the shire for the Crown, safeguarded royal interests in it, presided over its court and accounted for the king's revenues and debts from it.

The Plantagenet Chronicles: 161, 309, 325

shire

Unit of local government in medieval England, administered by a sheriff. Shires originated under the Anglo-Saxons; after the Norman Conquest they were known also as counties. Their subdivisions were called hundreds in south and west England and wapentakes in the north and east.

The Plantagenet Chronicles: 161

shire court

County court, presided over by a sheriff, at which he dispensed justice and administered his shire.

The Plantagenet Chronicles: 161

Shore, Elizabeth (Jane)

d.1527? Daughter of a wealthy London mercer named Lambert, Elizabeth married William Shore, a goldsmith. In about 1470, she became mistress of Edward IV, and in 1476 had her marriage annulled on the grounds of William's impotence. Her beauty and wit were famous, and, in the words of Sir Thomas More, she influenced Edward, 'to many a man's comfort and relief'. After Edward's death in 1483 she became mistress of Thomas Grey, 4th marquis of Dorset, then of William, Lord Hastings. Richard III executed Hastings in June 1483, and

had Elizabeth accused of sorcery. She was imprisoned in the Tower of London and made to do public penance as a harlot, walking through London in her kirtle carrying a lighted taper. She was freed when Thomas Lynon, a royal official, fell in love with her. She later died in poverty.

The Wars of the Roses: 253

Shrewsbury

County town of Shropshire and the centre of the important medieval earldom of Shrewsbury. A castle and abbey were built there in the 11th century. On 21 July 1403 Henry IV defeated rebel forces under Henry, 'Hotspur', Percy in the battle of Shrewsbury, on a plain two miles outside the town. The king displayed Hotspur's body to the people of Shrewsbury as proof of his death.

Chronicles of the Age of Chivalry/Four Gothic Kings (US edn): 124–5, 202
The Wars of the Roses: 61, 101–2

shrine

Holy place that owed its sacred status either to a specific relic or a saint's body, or to tradition or legend. During the Middle Ages the shrine of St James at Santiago de Compostella in Spain was second only to Rome as Europe's most popular place of pilgrimage. Thomas Becket's tomb in Canterbury Cathedral was England's foremost shrine; others included St Winifred's spring at Holywell in North Wales, and an ampoule of the Virgin's milk at Walsingham in Norfolk. Local shrines often supported cults for uncanonized saints, partly a relic of pre-Christian folk belief. One example, at North Marston in Buckinghamshire, was the shrine of Master John Schorne, who was believed to have conjured the devil into a boot and was said to help sufferers from gout. Tombs of leaders of failed rebellions against the Crown – such as those of Simon de Montfort and Richard le Scrope, archbishop of York – sometimes also became popular shrines.

The Plantagenet Chronicles: 176–7
The Wars of the Roses: 64–5

Sicily

In the 9th century Sicily was conquered by Arabs, who ruled the island until its conquest, from 1060 to 1091, by the Normans, led by Roger Guiscard. His son Roger II became first king of Sicily in 1130. The heritage of Arab

bureaucracy made Sicily the most sophisticated European monarchy of its time. Holy Roman Emperor Frederick II, whose mother, Constance, was heiress to the island, was brought up there and was king of Sicily from 1197 to 1250. After defeating Frederick's heirs, Charles I of Anjou was crowned king of Sicily in 1266, but his unpopular government led to a revolt known as the Sicilian Vespers in 1282, when the people chose Peter III of Aragon as their king. Sicily was ruled by the house of Aragon for the rest of the Middle Ages.

The Plantagenet Chronicles: 15, 146, 148–9, 159, 174, 208, 210–1, 236
Chronicles of the Age of Chivalry/Four Gothic Kings (US edn): 35, 42–4, 59, 86, 88, 110, 125–6

Siena

City-state in Tuscany, central Italy. Siena gained a commune (a self-governing association of citizens) in the 12th century and grew into a powerful republic. The cathedral, a superb example of High Gothic style, was built in the 13th century. A programme to extend it, begun in 1339, was cancelled in 1348 when the Black Death struck Siena and only the new west front was built. From the 14th century, the city was a centre of the Tuscan Renaissance.

Chronicles of the Age of Chivalry/Four Gothic Kings (US edn): 30–1, 197

Sigismund, Holy Roman Emperor

1368–1437. Son of Holy Roman Emperor Charles IV; elector of Brandenburg (1376–1415); king of Hungary (1387); king of Germany (1410); king of Bohemia (1419); Holy Roman Emperor (1433). Sigismund led a disastrous European crusade against the Turkish invasion of Hungary in 1395; it was defeated at Nicopolis the following year. As emperor-elect, he persuaded Pope John XXIII to convene in 1414 the Council of Constance, which formally ended the Great Schism. In 1415, the council also condemned to death two Bohemian religious reformers, John Hus and Jeremy of Prague, and when Sigismund succeeded to the Bohemian crown in 1419 his subjects rebelled against him. He was not accepted as king of Bohemia until 1436 – three years after he had been crowned Holy Roman Emperor.

The Wars of the Roses: 126–7, 133, 136–40, 142–3, 156, 158–9, 171

signet

Personal seal, particularly the English royal seal used by late medieval monarchs for both private purposes and to validate certain official documents.

The Wars of the Roses: 81

Simon de Montfort

See: Montfort, Simon de, 6th earl of Leicester

Sixtus IV, pope

1414–84. Born Francesco della Rovere; general of the Franciscan order (1464–7); cardinal (1467–71); pope (1471–84). As pope, Sixtus quarrelled with Louis XI of France over whether papal decrees should be subject to royal approval before promulgation. He also quarrelled with Lorenzo de' Medici, cancelling the papal account with the family's bank and approving an abortive plot by rival bankers, the Pazzi, to murder Lorenzo. Lorenzo's brother Giuliano was assassinated by the conspirators in Florence Cathedral in 1478 and Sixtus became involved in a fruitless war with Florence until 1480. He approved the establishment of the Spanish Inquisition in 1478 but soon rebuked the Spanish for illegalities in the methods used by the Inquisitors and sheltered the Jews expelled from Spain. Sixtus founded the Sistine Chapel, added to the Vatican Library, and did much to improve and adorn Rome.

The Wars of the Roses: 111

Sluys, battle of

Naval battle off Sluys harbour, in the Scheldt estuary in the Netherlands, in which the fleet of Edward III of England defeated that of Philip VI of France on 24 July 1340. The first major battle of the Hundred Years War (1337–1453), Sluys resulted in the loss of almost the entire French fleet. The French admirals chained their ships together in three squadrons, like land forts, and were raked with fire from the mobile English vessels while fighting English boarders hand-to-hand. The battle lasted from 9 a.m. until after dark. Thirty French ships escaped during the night, but more than 200 were captured, and the French maritime threat against England was dispelled. Edward III directed the battle from his great ship, the 'Cog Thomas'.

Chronicles of the Age of Chivalry/Four Gothic Kings (US edn): 136, 138, 240, 242–3

Smithfield

District of the City of London; from the 12th century a site for markets, jousts and executions. William Sawtry, the first Lollard to be burned for heresy, died at Smithfield in 1401. Wat Tyler and his rebels met Richard II on 15 June 1381, during the Peasants Revolt, and Tyler was struck down there by William Walworth, mayor of London, and later killed by one of the king's squires.

The Wars of the Roses: 31, 35, 38, 100, 112–13

Snowdonia

Mountainous region in Gwynedd, north-west Wales, around Mount Snowdon, Wales' highest mountain. In the 13th century Snowdonia was a stronghold of resistance to English rule, and the princes of Gwynedd were the last Welsh nobles to hold their lands by right, rather than as English vassals. Edward III drove the Welsh rebels into Snowdonia in 1277, and its strongholds yielded to him in 1282 after the death of Llywelyn ap Gruffyd, prince of Wales, in a battle near Builth.

Chronicles of the Age of Chivalry/Four Gothic Kings (US edn): 47, 116, 124

Song of Roland

See: *Chanson de Roland*

songs

Some 30 English or Anglo-French songs survive with their music from before 1377. One example is *Sub Arturo Plebs*, performed at Windsor in 1358 to celebrate the English victory at Poitiers. Before the advent of composers such as Guillaume de Machaut (d.1377) most secular music was not written down and songs were usually transmitted by memory and sung by minstrels or troubadours. Others were commissioned by royal and noble courts.

Chronicles of the Age of Chivalry/Four Gothic Kings (US edn): 284–5

Southampton

Port in Hampshire; a royal borough since Anglo-Saxon times. Until the 16th century it had a lucrative trade with Venice in goods from the East. Richard I and his fleet left from Southampton for the Third Crusade in 1190. In 1414 Henry V launched his invasion of France from the port, and in 1447 it was created a county by Henry VI.

The Wars of the Roses: 28, 123, 248, 302

Spain

In the Middle Ages the Spanish peninsula was divided between the Moorish states, known collectively as al-Andalus, and the Christian kingdoms of Castile, Navarre, Aragon and Portugal, which grew as they gradually annexed lands from the Islamic princes. In 1212 Alfonso VIII of Castile defeated the Moors at Las Navas de Tolosa and overran Andalusia, leaving the Moors only Granada in the south. In 1479 the marriage of Isabella of Castile and Ferdinand of Aragon united all Christian Spain, the prelude to the fall of Granada in 1492, and the completion of the Reconquista. In that same year, the Jews were expelled from Spain.

The Plantagenet Chronicles: 294
The Wars of the Roses: 42–3, 182, 246–7

spices

In the Middle Ages spices such as ginger, cinnamon, nutmeg and cloves, were imported from the East to offset monotonous fare and obscure the taste of ill-preserved foods. Overland trade with India and China prospered and spices commanded high prices. When land routes were severed as a result of Mongol and Turkish invasions of Asia in the 14th and 15th centuries, sea routes were opened up in their place.

Wars of the Roses: 152–3

squire

Originally, a young man of good birth attending a knight, often as an apprentice. In the later Middle Ages 'esquire' became a title which was used to denote a man ranking below a knight in society.

Stafford, Edmund, bishop of Exeter

1344–1419. Keeper of the privy seal (1389–96); bishop of Exeter (1395); chancellor of England (1396–9, 1401–3). Although Edmund served Richard II as chancellor, he consented to his deposition in 1399 by Henry Bolingbroke (later Henry IV), whom he later served in the same office. He refounded Stapledon Hall, Oxford, as Exeter College.

The Wars of the Roses: 84

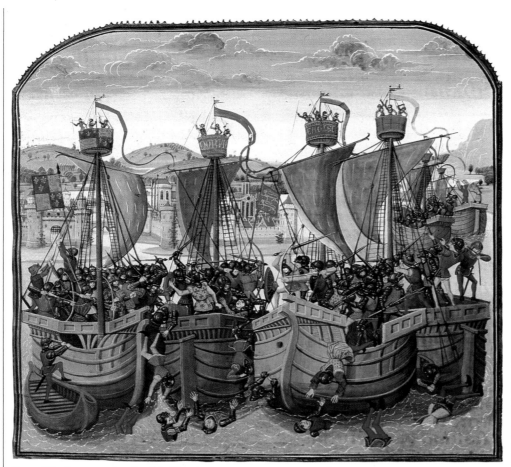

Sluys *The first major battle of the Hundred Years War, and a significant English naval victory.*

Stafford, Henry, 2nd duke of Buckingham

1454?–83. Grandson of Humphrey, 1st duke of Buckingham; 2nd duke of Buckingham (1460); chief justice and chamberlain of North and South Wales (1483). In 1478 Henry passed sentence in parliament on George, 3rd duke of Clarence, for treason against Edward IV, condemning him to death. The wealthiest magnate in England, he joined Richard, 3rd duke of Gloucester (later Richard III) in 1483, to capture Edward V, and provided troops to back Richard's usurpation of the throne. He subsequently circulated Richard's opinion that Edward and his brother were illegitimate, and, as constable of the Tower of London, he may have had some part in the brothers' murder there in 1483.

Richard gave Henry great power in Wales and western England, but in October 1483 Henry rose against the king with the intention of replacing him with Henry Tudor. The rebellion failed and Henry was beheaded on 2 November 1483.

The Wars of the Roses: 273, 287–8, 293–4, 296–7

Stafford, Humphrey, 1st duke of Buckingham

1402–60. Earl of Stafford (1403); 4th earl of Buckingham (1402–44); 1st duke of Buckingham (1444–60). Humphrey inherited the earldom of Buckingham through his mother Anne, countess of Buckingham; the title was raised to a dukedom in 1444. In 1430 he accompanied Henry VI when the king travelled to France for his coronation in Paris and served there against the French. Humphrey supported Henry in the Wars of the Roses and was taken prisoner fighting for the Lancastrians against Richard, 3rd duke of York, in the first battle of St Albans on 22 May 1455. He died fighting against the Yorkists at Northampton on 10 July 1460.

The Wars of the Roses: 205, 214, 216, 220, 233

Stafford, Humphrey, 15th earl of Devon

1439–69. Privy councillor to Edward IV (1460s); 15th earl of Devon (1469). Humphrey fought for Edward IV against Margaret of Anjou and her Lancastrian forces at the battle of Towton on 29 March 1461 and was knighted for his services. Edward's chief supporter in south-west England, Humphrey had held the earldom of Devon for six months when in 1469 Edward sent him to Yorkshire with William Herbert, 18th earl of Pembroke, to oppose Robin of Redesdale's revolt. Humphrey quarrelled with Pembroke about billeting arrangements for their troops and withdrew his men. As a result Pembroke lost the battle against Redesdale. Humphrey escaped but was captured by the citizens of Bridgwater in Somerset and beheaded.

The Wars of the Roses: 244, 255

Stamford

Town in Lincolnshire, site of an ancient Benedictine priory. Stamford was famous in the Middle Ages as a seat of learning: in 1333 a group of Oxford scholars founded Brasenose College (later removed to Oxford) in the town. Stamford was sacked in 1461, the only town to suffer this fate during the Wars of the Roses.

The Wars of the Roses: 233

Stanley, Thomas, Lord Stanley, 10th earl of Derby

1435?–1504. 2nd baron Stanley (1459); chief justice of Cheshire (1461); lord steward (1471–83); knight of the Garter (1483); constable of England (1483); 10th earl of Derby (1485–1504). Thomas married Eleanor, sister of Richard Neville, 'the Kingmaker', 16th earl of Warwick, and in 1460 joined Richard's campaign against Henry VI. Ten years later Thomas supported Richard's restoration of Henry VI but continued to serve Edward IV after Richard's death in 1471. In about 1482 Thomas married, as his second wife, Margaret Beaufort, mother of Henry Tudor, the Lancastrian claimant to the throne. In 1483 Richard III briefly imprisoned Thomas for supporting Edward V, but later the same year appointed him constable of England. Richard forced Thomas to join him against Henry Tudor in 1485 by seizing his son George, Lord Strange, but Thomas held aloof at Bosworth, and placed Richard's battered crown on Henry's head after Richard's defeat and death.

The Wars of the Roses: 297, 302, 305

Savoy Palace *The palace was the residence of John of Gaunt (opposite). Hostile peasant rebels burned it down in 1381*

EDVARDI·TERTII·REX
CASTELLÆ·ET·LEGI
DVX·LANCASTRIÆ
CONSTABVLARIVS·C
DE·QVEENSBOVR·C
TO·OCTOBRIS·AN
REGNI·EDW·TERTI
GLIÆ·50·FRANCIÆ

HONI·SOIT·QVI·MAL·Y·PENSE

Stapledon, Walter, bishop of Exeter

1261–1325. Bishop of Exeter (1308–26); lord treasurer (1320–1, 1322). He founded Stapledon Hall (later renamed Exeter College) at Oxford University and also commissioned a new nave for Exeter Cathedral. In 1310 he joined the ordainers (a group of magnates who imposed restrictions on Edward II's royal prerogative). In 1321 Walter tried to mediate in the continuing conflict between the king and Thomas, 2nd earl of Lancaster, former leader of the ordainers. When Thomas's death in 1322 ended opposition to the king, Walter, with the chancellor Robert Baldock, carried out unpopular fiscal reforms instigated by the king's favourite, Hugh Despenser the son. Edward made Walter guardian of London in 1325, but the following year he was murdered when the citizens revolted and his head was sent as a trophy to Queen Isabella's camp at Gloucester.

Chronicles of the Age of Chivalry/Four Gothic Kings (US edn): 189, 206, 208, 210–11

Statute of Labourers

Statute passed by Edward III's parliament of 1351, fixing wages for various trades and compelling labourers to work for their lord for those rates. It aimed to hold them to levels prevailing before the Black Death. The plague had killed about a third of England's population in 1348 and 1349, resulting in a labour shortage and an attendant, alarming rise in wages. According to the statute, ploughmen were to be hired by the year, at 10d. per wheat bushel harvested; master masons and carpenters were to receive 4d. per day; other masons 3d. All landless men under 60 had to accept the terms, and their lord had first claim on their work. During the 1350s commissioners went four times a year to each county to enforce the statute, aided by local gentry. However, both lords and labourers preferred a freer market, and the statute gradually fell into disuse over the next two decades.

Chronicles of the Age of Chivalry/Four Gothic Kings (US edn): 256, 264

Stephen, king of England

1097–1154. Son of Adela, daughter of William I, the Conqueror, and of Stephen, count of Blois; king of England (1135–54). He grew up at the court of Henry I of England, his uncle, and in 1126 was the first baron to swear to accept Henry's daughter the Empress Matilda as heir to the English throne. He repeated this oath in 1131 and 1133, but when Henry died in 1135 he went to London and secured the support of the city's notables. Stephen was crowned king of England at Westminster, and was also accepted as duke of Normandy.

Matilda appealed to Pope Innocent II, who nevertheless declared for Stephen in 1136. The king tried to win support by making concessions to his barons, but severely weakened his position in the process. In 1137 he made a temporary truce with Matilda's husband, Geoffrey, the Fair, count of Anjou, and in the following year he fought off an invasion by David I of Scotland in the battle of the Standard. However, in 1139 when he arrested Roger, bishop of Salisbury, and his nephews Alexander, bishop of Lincoln, and Nigel, bishop of Ely, he lost the Church's support and fatally discredited himself. Matilda invaded England within the month, and years of strife between the two ensued. The inheritance dispute was further complicated by the attempts of many English barons to increase their own powers and lands at the expense of royal authority. But fighting during Stephen's reign was sporadic and localized, if disruptive to law and order and damaging to the royal administration.

In 1140 Stephen quelled a revolt of the Isle of Ely and took Bungay castle, but was defeated and captured at Lincoln on 2 February 1141 by Matilda's half-brother Robert, 1st earl of Gloucester, while leading the siege of Lincoln castle. Robert took the king prisoner only after he had worn out a battleaxe and a sword defending himself. Stephen was imprisoned at Bristol, and a Church council declared him deposed. However, Matilda's arrogance alienated many of her supporters, and she was forced to exchange Stephen for Robert, who had been captured later in 1141.

Stephen was recrowned but, during the next few years, western and central England were devastated in a series of inconclusive campaigns. Stephen blockaded Matilda in Oxford castle in 1142, but she escaped, and in 1143 the king was routed near Wilton. In 1145 Geoffrey, the Fair, of Anjou, completed his conquest of Normandy, while Stephen was occupied subduing rebellious barons in Norfolk and Essex. Although in 1146 Stephen regained Bedford and Lincoln, at no time was he able to win a decisive victory. In 1147 he started a feud with the papacy which led to the whole country being laid under interdict in 1148. However, Robert of Gloucester had died in 1147, and Matilda, bereft of her main ally, left England soon afterwards.

In 1149 Matilda's son Henry of Anjou (the future Henry II) invaded England to pursue his mother's claim for himself. Stephen had quarrelled with Theobald, archbishop of Canterbury, and in 1152 the papacy refused to sanction the coronation of Stephen's son Eustace as his successor to the English throne. Eustace died in 1153, and Stephen was forced to agree to the Treaty of Wallingford, under which he retained the crown for life but named Henry as his heir. In 1154 Stephen died, and was buried in his own abbey at Faversham, 'having', said a chronicler, 'reigned unhappily and with great labour'.

The Plantagenet Chronicles: 43, 45, 52, 62–3, 65–88, 93

Stewart, Alexander, 3rd duke of Albany

1454?–85. Second son of James II of Scotland; 1st earl of March (1455); 3rd duke of Albany (c.1458–79, 1482–3); high admiral of Scotland; warden of the marches; lieutenant of Scotland (1472–82). Alexander was mistrusted by his brother, James III of Scotland, who imprisoned him in 1479. He escaped to France and thence to England, where, in 1481, he agreed to rule Scotland as the vassal of Edward IV. The following year he invaded Scotland with an English army but agreed to remain James's loyal subject if his lands and titles were returned. The brothers were reconciled, but Alexander continued to intrigue against James, who in 1483 sentenced him to death. He fled to England, handing his castle of Dunbar over to the English. After one abortive raid into Scotland in July 1484, he took refuge in France, where he died in a jousting accident.

The Wars of the Roses: 299

Stewart, Murdac, 2nd duke of Albany

1362?–1425. Son and heir of Robert, 1st duke of Albany; 13th earl of Fife (1420–5); 2nd duke of Albany (1420–5); regent of Scotland (1420). Murdac was captured by the English at the battle of Homildon Hill in 1402, and held prisoner until his exchange for Henry Percy, 5th earl of Northumberland, in 1415. Suspected of delaying the release of James I of Scotland in 1424 (after 18 years' imprisonment by the English), Murdac was arrested and executed after James's restoration the following year.

The Wars of the Roses: 185

Stewart, Robert, 1st duke of Albany

1340?–1420. Second son of Robert II of Scotland; 12th earl of Fife (1371–1420);

chamberlain of Scotland (1382–1407); 1st duke of Albany (1398–1420); regent of Scotland (1389–99, 1402–20). Robert led several plundering expeditions in England in the 1380s. In 1389 he became regent for his aged father Robert II, supplanting his crippled elder brother John in this position, and after their father's death in 1390, he also ruled for his brother (now Robert III). Forced to yield the regency to the king's son David, 1st duke of Rothesay, in 1399, Robert regained it in 1402 after David's mysterious death. He continued as regent after Robert III's death in 1406 and remained so until his own death: the rightful heir, James I, had been taken prisoner by the English after being sent abroad to escape his brother David's fate.

The Wars of the Roses: 185

Stewart, Walter, 20th earl of Atholl

1360?–1437. Third son of Robert II of Scotland; keeper of Edinburgh castle; 20th earl of Atholl (1404–37); 14th earl of Caithness (1431–7); 15th earl of Strathearn (1427–37). In 1437 Walter headed a conspiracy to kill his nephew James I of Scotland and replace him. After the king's murder at Perth on 27 February 1437, Walter was arrested with the other conspirators, tortured and executed.

The Wars of the Roses: 184–6

Stirling

County town in Central Scotland. Stirling castle, built in the 12th century, was the strategic key to the country, and a royal residence; James II, III and IV of Scotland were born there.

Edward I of England seized the castle in 1296 and held it despite a crushing defeat nearby in 1297. The Scots regained the castle the same year but Edward seized it again in 1304. Robert Bruce besieged Stirling in 1313, and its commander, Sir Philip Mowbray, agreed to surrender the town if he was not relieved after a year. The relief force, led by Edward II, met disaster at Bannockburn in 1314: Mowbray surrendered Stirling to Robert Bruce while Edward escaped to Dunbar and ignominiously returned home. From 1334 to 1339 the castle was once more held by the English.

Chronicles of the Age of Chivalry/Four Gothic Kings (US edn): 142, 144–5, 156, 188, 190–1

Strasbourg

City on the River Rhine in eastern France; capital of the province of Alsace. Part of the Holy Roman Empire from 923, Strasbourg became a free imperial city from 1262, after its burghers had risen against its ruling bishops. From 1332 it was governed by guilds. Strasbourg was a centre of the flagellant hysteria which followed the Black Death (1348–9). It is believed that Gutenburg invented his printing press there in the 15th century.

Chronicles of the Age of Chivalry/Four Gothic Kings (US edn): 256, 258, 260

Stirling Castle *The strategic key to Scotland, Stirling Castle changed hands often between English and Scots in the Middle Ages; perhaps the most famous instance was the occupation which led the English to Bannockburn and defeat in 1314.*

Straw, Jack

*fl.*1381. One of the leaders of the Peasants Revolt of 1381. Jack's identity and role in the rising are unclear, and he may actually have been Wat Tyler, a known leader of the revolt, under another name.

The Wars of the Roses: 34, 36

Sudbury, Simon, archbishop of Canterbury

d.1381. Bishop of London (1361–75); archbishop of Canterbury (1375–81); chancellor of England (1380). Simon officiated at Richard II's coronation in 1377. In 1378, at Lambeth, he tried John Wycliffe for heresy. He was seized and beheaded by a mob in London after the Peasants Revolt.

Chronicles of the Age of Chivalry/Four Gothic Kings (US edn): 302
The Wars of the Roses: 26

sugar

A valuable commodity in medieval Europe, sugar was shipped from the Middle East. At first a rare luxury, it became more widely available in the 15th century.

The Wars of the Roses: 152

Suger, abbot

1081–1151. Abbot of St-Denis (1122–51). From 1127 until his death Suger served both Louis VI and Louis VII as an adviser on the government of France and the administration of royal lands. His emphasis on the sacred and ceremonial aspects of kingship did much to enhance the image of the French monarchy. As head of the council of regency Louis VII appointed during his absence on the Second Crusade (1147–9), Suger ruled well and was noted for his financial skill. He rebuilt and greatly enriched St-Denis in the new Gothic style, and left a written account of his

Abbot Suger A window in St-Denis Abbey depicting Abbot Suger kneeling before the Virgin. Suger made St-Denis one of the richest early Gothic buildings.

renovations which is an authoritative guide to Gothic taste. One stained glass window depicts him kneeling before the Virgin. Suger also wrote a life of Louis VI, and part of a life of Louis VII.

The Plantagenet Chronicles: 56–8
Chronicles of the Age of Chivalry/Four Gothic Kings (US edn): 62

Swynford, Catherine

1350?–1403. Duchess of Lancaster (1396). Catherine's first husband was Sir Hugh Swynford, a member of the retinue of John of Gaunt, 2nd duke of Lancaster. Chaucer's wife, Philippa Roet, was her sister. After Hugh's death in 1372 she became John of Gaunt's mistress and governess of his children by his second wife, Constance of Castile. She bore John four children, who were given the name

Beaufort after one of his estates, and who were to become a powerful noble line; the eldest was created earl of Somerset. On Constance's death in 1396 Catherine married John, and their children were legitimized by act of parliament in 1397, with the proviso (inserted in 1407) that they had no claim to the throne.

Chronicles of the Age of Chivalry/Four Gothic Kings (US edn): 301
The Wars of the Roses: 47, 71, 78

Syon

House of Brigettine nuns (followers of the order of St Bridget of Kildare) on the Thames, in Surrey. Founded by Henry V on his accession in 1413, it was generously endowed by him.

The Wars of the Roses: 122

Taborites

Radical wing of the Hussite movement (followers of the early-15th-century Bohemian religious reformer John Hus). The Taborites, named after their Bohemian stronghold of 'Mount Tabor' (which took its name from the scene of Christ's transfiguration) combined early Protestantism with political radicalism. Mainly peasants, they believed in only two sacraments (communion and baptism), rejected the cults of saints and images and aimed to establish a communistic society. From 1420 to 1436 the Taborites allied with moderate Hussites to defeat Holy Roman Emperor Sigismund III's crusades against them (1421 to 1431), using such formidable military equipment as armoured wagons bearing guns. In 1436 the moderates were reconciled with the Catholic Church. The Taborites consequently became isolated but survived until the Reformation in the 16th century.

The Wars of the Roses: 156, 159

Talbot, John, 4th earl of Shrewsbury

1388?–1453. Lieutenant of Ireland (1414–19, 1445–7); knight of the Garter (1421); 4th earl of Shrewsbury (1442–53). Suspected of being a Lollard heretic, John was imprisoned by Henry V in 1413 but was released the following year. From 1421 to 1424 he fought in France, where he became a leading English captain. In 1429 he was captured at Patay by the French, remaining a prisoner until 1431. Between 1434 and 1440 he won many daring victories against the French, including the capture of Ivry and Harfleur in 1440, and was given an earldom as reward.

After the fall of Rouen in 1448 John was once more held hostage by the French and was released the following year only on condition he went on pilgrimage to Rome. When he returned in 1451 Henry VI sent him to Gascony to aid the duchy's resistance to the French under Charles VII. By November the following year John had recovered Bordeaux and its environs for the English. However, on 10 August 1453, while he was trying to relieve the town of Castillon, which was under siege by the French, his army was defeated and he was killed, ending English hopes of recovering Gascony.

The Wars of the Roses: 188, 202, 209–10, 214

tallage

Feudal tax levied by the English Crown on royal lands and boroughs. Resisted by townspeople, it was virtually abandoned by the 15th century.

Tancred, king of Sicily

1130?–94. Grandson of Roger II of Sicily; king of Sicily (1190). Tancred was crowned in 1190, on the death of his cousin, William II of Sicily, whose aunt, Constance, wife of Holy Roman Emperor Henry VI, also claimed the crown. In 1191 Henry made an unsuccessful attempt to depose Tancred. Richard I of England, whom Tancred entertained en route to the Third Crusade, supported the Sicilian king against the emperor and, as a token of friendship, gave him a sword said to be Excalibur. Soon after Tancred's death, three years later, Henry deposed Tancred's infant son, William III of Sicily, in favour of Constance.

The Plantagenet Chronicles: 204, 210, 212, 225

Tartars (or Tatars)

Name used in the Middle Ages to describe the Mongols and their Turkish and Oriental allies, who from 1206 fought under the leadership of Genghis Khan. The name derived from one tribe from north-east Mongolia, the Tata, or Dada. The Tartars formed tightly disciplined cavalry armies, employed deadly archery, Chinese siege engineers and hardy steppe ponies to create the most powerful medieval military force of the Middle Ages. Under Genghis Khan the Tartars ruled Eurasia from the Black Sea to the Pacific. In 1241 Genghis' successor Batu Khan invaded Hungary and Germany, but was repulsed. However, he overran most of Russia in about 1240, establishing a Tartar state known as the Golden Horde, which lasted until the 1390s.

Chronicles of the Age of Chivalry/Four Gothic Kings (US edn): 60–1, 112
The Wars of the Roses: 275

Templars

Abbreviated name of the Knights Templar, also known as the Poor Knights of Christ and the Temple of Solomon; a military monastic order dedicated to the crusades. Founded in about 1118 by nine knights to protect pilgrims in the Holy Land, the order was named after its headquarters in Jerusalem: the El-Aqsa mosque, known as Solomon's Temple. St Bernard of Clairvaux helped to draw up the order's rules, which combined the rule and discipline of Benedictine monasticism with special ecclesiastical powers and privileges.

Pope Honorius II recognized the Templars in 1128 and they rapidly began to amass riches in the crusader states in the East and in Western Europe. Their wealth, and the security of their strongholds, made them valued bankers to royalty – for example, Henry II of England and Louis IX of France. But, above all, the Templars' main function was to protect and defend the Holy Places; and although they became embroiled in many bitter disputes with their rivals, the Hospitallers, thus endangering the defences of the Holy Land, their bravery in combat, as at the siege of Damietta (1219), won admiration from Christians and Muslims alike.

In 1187, when Jerusalem fell to Saladin, the Templars moved their headquarters to Acre, then, when this in turn fell – to the Mamelukes of Egypt in 1291 – to Cyprus. In 1307 advisers to Philip IV of France tortured the Templars to obtain confessions of heresy from them. Five years later Philip compelled Pope Clement V to dissolve the order and in 1314 had its last grand master, Jacques de Molay, burned to death. The French king then divided the Templars' wealth with the Hospitallers.

Chronicles of the Age of Chivalry/Four Gothic Kings (US edn): 42, 54, 137, 180–2, 186

tenant-in-chief

Feudal lord, whether baron or bishop, who held land directly from the king. The tenant-in-chief in his turn granted land to under-tenants.

Tewkesbury

Town in Gloucestershire on the River Avon. Tewkesbury Abbey, a wealthy and celebrated Benedictine house, was founded *c.*715 and refounded in the 12th century; the abbey church was completed in 1123. On 4 May 1471

Edward IV's Yorkist army defeated Queen Margaret of Anjou's Lancastrians at 'Bloody Meadow' south of the town, ending the short Lancastrian restoration of Henry VI. Henry's son Edward, prince of Wales and the Lancastrian heir, died in the battle.

The Wars of the Roses: 201, 220, 225, 233, 262–3

Thames, River

London owed its medieval importance as a port to the Thames, which was navigable, even for large vessels, as far as the city. London Bridge, built at the river's lowest crossing point, was the only bridge over the river throughout the Middle Ages. Thomas Walsingham's chronicle records that on Christmas Day 1391 a dolphin swam up the Thames as far as the bridge, where it was caught and put on display by the citizens.

The Wars of the Roses: 66, 292

Theobald, archbishop of Canterbury

d.1161. Archbishop of Canterbury (1138–61). Theobald crowned King Stephen in 1141 but was exiled in 1148 after attending Pope Eugenius III's council at Reims against Stephen's wishes. Theobald and Stephen were reconciled in about 1150, but in 1152 the archbishop was imprisoned for refusing to crown Stephen's son Eustace king. He escaped to Flanders, from where he was recalled by Stephen in 1153. In the same year he helped resolve the conflict between the king and his Plantagenet rival Henry, duke of Normandy (later Henry II) who as a result became the accepted heir to the throne. For six weeks between Stephen's death in 1154 and Henry II's arrival from France, Theobald kept the peace in England. In 1140 he had taken Thomas Becket into his household (which also included Vacarius, who became an eminent jurist, and John of Salisbury, the future scholar and historian) and in 1154 he recommended Becket to Henry II as chancellor. On Theobald's death Becket succeeded him as archbishop.

The Plantagenet Chronicles: 72, 85, 94, 96, 102, 108, 110

Third Crusade

Crusade launched in 1189, in response to the Muslim leader Saladin's capture of Jerusalem and Acre from the Franks two years earlier. Holy Roman Emperor Frederick I died on his

Templars The Temple Church in London; English headquarters of the Knights Templar.

way to the crusade and most of his German troops dispersed, leaving Richard I of England and Philip II Augustus of France as its leaders. Reaching Acre by sea in 1191, they helped Guy of Lusignan, king of Jerusalem, who had been besieging the city for two years, to recover it from the Muslims. Philip returned to France the same year, while Richard continued campaigning from his base at Jaffa. In 1192 he made a truce with Saladin by which the Christians kept Antioch, Tripoli, Cyprus, Jaffa and a strip of coast (the remains of the Latin kingdom of Jerusalem) and were permitted free access to the Holy Sepulchre in Jerusalem. The Crusade ended when Richard left the Holy Land in October 1192. Jerusalem remained in Muslim hands until the 20th century, except for a short time after 1229 when Holy Roman Emperor Frederick II briefly regained it for Christendom.

The Plantagenet Chronicles: 153, 187, 202, 206

Thomas, Bastard of Fauconberg

See: Fauconberg, Thomas, Lord Fauconberg

Thomas of Brotherton, 6th earl of Norfolk

1300–38. Son of Edward I and his second wife Margaret; half-brother of Edward II; 6th earl of

Norfolk (1312–38); marshal of England (1316). Thomas supported Edward II in 1321, when Thomas, 2nd earl of Lancaster, marched on the king in London and forced him to dismiss his favourites, the Despensers; but he was one of the first to join Edward's queen Isabella and her lover Roger Mortimer when they invaded England in September 1326. After Edward's abdication the following year Thomas was granted lands that had once belonged to the Despensers and married his son to Roger's daughter. By 1330, however, he had turned against Isabella's government and welcomed Edward III's seizure of power.

Chronicles of the Age of Chivalry/Four Gothic Kings (US edn): 200, 208

Thomas, 2nd duke of Clarence

1388?–1421. Second son of Henry IV and his first wife, Mary de Bohun; lieutenant of Ireland (1401–13); 2nd duke of Clarence (1412–21); lieutenant of France (1421). In 1405 Thomas commanded a fleet which burnt French ships at Sluys and raided Normandy. He replaced his brother Henry, prince of Wales (later Henry V), on Henry IV's council in 1412, when the prince's policy of aiding the Burgundian faction in France was reversed. In 1412 Thomas led an expedition to aid the Armagnacs (Orleanists) in France but withdrew to England when the two factions made peace. He fought for Henry V at Harfleur in 1415, and two years later joined his brother's campaign against Charles VI of France, entering Paris in 1420. He remained in France as Henry's lieutenant when the king returned to England in 1421. Anxious to win a victory like Agincourt, Thomas died attacking the French, with cavalry only, at Baugé, that same year.

The Wars of the Roses: 114–15, 156

Thomas, 2nd earl of Lancaster

1277?–1322. First son of Edmund, 1st earl of Lancaster and brother of Edward I; earl of Lincoln (1294–1322), 8th earl of Leicester (1298–1322); 2nd earl of Lancaster (1298–1322). Thomas's high rank, wealth and ambition made him a natural leader of the ordainers, the lords who in February 1310 drew up ordinances to limit Edward II's power. In 1311 Thomas and his fellow-ordainers banished Piers Gaveston, Edward's favourite, and on his return to England the following year had him executed. The king was greatly angered but eventually forgave Thomas, who submitted to him and received a full pardon in October 1313.

However, later that year Thomas refused to accompany the king on his campaign in Scotland and, after the débâcle of Bannockburn in 1314, again wrested control of the kingdom from Edward.

In 1318 Thomas and the king were once more reconciled, and they campaigned together in Scotland. Their attempts to regain Berwick from the Scots failed and many barons suspected Thomas of conniving with the Scottish king, Robert Bruce. Edward and Thomas were estranged again, and in 1321 the earl led an army of marcher lords to London, and forced Edward to dismiss his hated favourites, the Despensers, both the father and the son. The king finally defeated him at the battle of Boroughbridge in 1322 and Thomas was taken to Pontefract, where he was executed as a traitor.

Chronicles of the Age of Chivalry/Four Gothic Kings (US edn): 176–9, 184–5, 192–4, 196, 200, 202–4

Thomas of Loches

*fl.*1130. Chronicler. Thomas served as chaplain to Fulk V, count of Anjou and Latin king of Jerusalem, and wrote part of *The Deeds of the Counts of Anjou*. This 11th- and 12th-century chronicle recounts the history of the Angevin dynasty and was compiled by several hands at Marmoutier Abbey in the Loire valley.

The Plantagenet Chronicles: 13, 19, 22

Thomas, lord of Berkeley

See: Berkeley, Thomas, Lord Berkeley

Thomas More, Sir

See: More, Sir Thomas

Thomas of Woodstock, 1st duke of Gloucester

1355–97. Seventh son of Edward III and Philippa of Hainault; uncle of Richard II; 14th earl of Essex (1374–97); constable of England (1376); 3rd earl of Buckingham (1377–97); 1st duke of Gloucester (1385–97). In 1377 Thomas successfully opposed John of Gaunt's candidacy for the regency during Richard II's minority but in the 1380s allied with Gaunt in opposition to Richard's arbitrary rule. In 1387 he and other lords appellant laid a charge of treason against Richard's favourite, Robert de Vere, 9th earl of Oxford, and other ministers; the lords routed the earl and his followers at Radcot Bridge.

Thomas led the Merciless Parliament's attack on Richard and his advisers in 1388, and with the king under the control of a council, dominated government until Richard resumed power in 1389. In 1397 the king arrested Thomas at Pleshey in Essex and imprisoned him at Calais, where he died, probably murdered on Richard's orders.

The Wars of the Roses: 22, 52, 56–7, 78, 80

Thurstan, archbishop of York

d.1140. Clerk in the royal household under William II and Henry I; archbishop of York (1119). Thurstan was elected archbishop in 1114, on Henry I's command, but Ralph, archbishop of Canterbury, withheld his consecration since Thurstan refused to take an oath of obedience which would have submitted his see to that of Canterbury. Although the king opposed his stand, Thurstan gained the support of Louis VI of France and of Pope Calixtus II, who at Reims in 1119 consecrated him as archbishop of York. Henry I refused to allow him to return to England but eventually they were reconciled and he returned to his see in 1121.

In 1123 Thurstan refused to acknowledge William, Ralph's successor at Canterbury, as his superior; despite visits to Rome by both in 1123 and 1125, to seek papal mediation, the dispute was not settled. In 1138 Thurstan called together the forces of northern nobles who defeated David I of Scotland at the battle of the Standard. He joined the Cluniacs, an order of Benedictine monks, in 1140 and died the same year at Pontefract Priory.

The Plantagenet Chronicles: 70, 142

Tintern Abbey

Abbey in the Wye valley, now in Gwent, Wales. Founded by Walter de Clare for the Cistercians in 1131, it became, like other Cistercian abbeys, a centre of high-quality wool production, and the imposing remains of its church reflect its wealth in the 12th and 13th centuries. In the 1290s, for example, it sold its wool to Italian merchants for the highest price in either England or Wales: £18 13s.4d. a sack.

Chronicles of the Age of Chivalry/Four Gothic Kings (US edn): 147

Tiptoft, John, 4th earl of Worcester

1427?–70. 4th earl of Worcester (1449–70); treasurer (1452–5); deputy of Ireland (1456–7,

1467); constable of England (1462–7, 1470). In 1457 John travelled on pilgrimage to the Holy Land and on his return journey lived for two years in Italy, where he became a noted Latin scholar and translator of Cicero, well versed in Renaissance thought. In 1461, with his brother-in-law, Richard Neville, 'the Kingmaker', 16th earl of Warwick, John backed Edward IV's accession. Known as 'the butcher of England', he was merciless in putting down opposition to the Crown; as Edward's constable of England, he put to death many of the king's Lancastrian opponents, including John de Vere, 12th earl of Oxford, in 1461; in 1468, as deputy of Ireland, he executed Thomas Fitzgerald, 8th earl of Desmond, and his two infant sons; and in 1470, at Southampton, recommended 20 rebels to be hanged and mutilated. That same year, during Henry VI's brief return to power, he was brought to trial for treason on the orders of Richard Neville. His judge, John de Vere, son of the earl of Oxford whom John had put to death, found him guilty and he was executed at Tower Hill on 19 October.

The Wars of the Roses: 248, 256

tournament

Public combat between knights, governed by the rules of chivalry, with the purpose of training participants in the skills of warfare. Tournaments began in France in the 11th century and spread throughout Europe. They usually started with single contests (jousts) between mounted knights and ended with a general mêlée. Although combatants used blunted weapons, deaths and injuries were common; anyone who was captured had his harness taken and paid a ransom. Tournaments were watched by noble ladies, one of whom might be elected 'queen of beauty' for the day. William Marshal's rise from poverty to regency started when his jousting skill impressed Eleanor of Aquitaine. Edward I was described as 'the best jouster in the whole world'.

The Plantagenet Chronicles: 234–5
Chronicles of the Age of Chivalry/Four Gothic Kings (US edn): 112, 125, 160–1, 170
The Wars of the Roses: 40

Tours

Capital of the province of Touraine, on the River Loire in western central France. Charles

---

tournament *A famous tournament (overleaf): the jousts of St Ingilbert.*

Martel, king of France, halted the Muslim conquest of Europe there in 732. In 1044 Geoffrey Martel I, count of Anjou, took Tours by attacking it from an encirclement of forts which his father, Count Fulk Nerra, had constructed; in so doing, he added Touraine to the Angevin domains. The town passed to Henry II of England on his marriage in 1152 to Eleanor of Aquitaine. King John of England, Henry's son, burned most of Tours in 1202 after it had supported his nephew Arthur's claims to Touraine. Philip II of France took Tours in 1204, and it remained a French royal town, especially loved by Louis XI of France.

The Plantagenet Chronicles: 24–5, 30, 32, 33, 34, 37–8, 43, 60, 136, 165, 188, 233, 236, 274
The Wars of the Roses: 206

Tower of London

Fortress on the north bank of the Thames, east of the old City of London. In 1067 William I, the Conqueror, began to fortify Tower Hill, the site of earlier British and Roman strongholds. The White Tower was begun for the king in about 1078, the work being supervised by Gundulf, bishop of Rochester. Subsequent monarchs added to the defences, so that by the end of the 13th century this great fortress covered 13 acres.

A royal castle and residence in the Middle Ages, the Tower was also a gaol. Henry VI was imprisoned there after his deposition by Edward IV in 1461, as were Edward V and his brother Richard of York after their capture by the future Richard III in 1483. Executions of high-ranking prisoners took place in the Tower, or on Tower Hill, and the heads of traitors and rebels were displayed over its gates. The Tower's massive fortifications made it admirable for safeguarding royal records (mainly those of Chancery), money, jewels and regalia. The royal menagerie, too, was kept there; in 1237 Henry III built a special house at the Tower for his leopards.

The Plantagenet Chronicles: 76, 98, 240, 312
Chronicles of the Age of Chivalry/Four Gothic Kings (US edn): 52, 54, 81, 100, 121, 124–6, 130, 202, 208–11, 234
The Wars of the Roses: 25, 225, 286–7, 292

Towton, battle of

Battle fought in West Yorkshire on 29 March 1461, in which the Lancastrian army of Henry VI and Margaret of Anjou was decisively beaten by Edward IV's Yorkist force. Each side numbered about 50,000 men. The battle, long and bloody, was fought in driving snow and ended in a Lancastrian rout in which Henry Percy, 6th earl of Northumberland, and other prominent Lancastrians died. Henry VI and Margaret escaped but the leading Lancastrian families had been crushed and Towton marked the end of armed resistance to Edward.

The Wars of the Roses: 201, 223–4, 227, 230, 245

Tracy, William de

d.1173. One of the four knights who killed Thomas Becket at Canterbury Cathedral on 29 December 1170. After the murder William, who, when Becket had been chancellor, had served him as a knight, granted his manor of Doccombe in Devon to the chapter of Canterbury to expiate his sin. He then set out on a penitential pilgrimage to the Holy Land but died en route in Sicily.

The Plantagenet Chronicles: 118, 120

Trastamara, Henry of

See: Henry of Trastamara

travel

Although travel in the Middle Ages was often slow and arduous, people of all ranks, including traders, diplomats and pilgrims, regularly made long journeys across Europe; the three pilgrimages to Jerusalem made by Fulk Nerra, count of Anjou (987–1040), for example, were in no way exceptional.

On land travellers went by foot, horse or pack mule. On water they travelled by river barge, by cog (a popular single-masted sailing ship) or, in Mediterranean waters, by oared galley. Long journeys were arduous, and on the pilgrim route to Santiago de Compostella in Spain hospices were erected at regular intervals. Routes to the Holy Land could be dangerous: the two military monastic orders, the Templars and the Hospitallers, were originally founded, in the early 12th century, to protect and heal pilgrims. Journeys further East than Palestine were rare, and Marco Polo's trading mission from Venice to China in the 1270s was exceptional.

The Plantagenet Chronicles: 153, 214, 241
Chronicles of the Age of Chivalry/Four Gothic Kings (US edn): 82–3

Tresilian, Sir Robert

d.1388. Chief justice of the king's bench (1381). In the aftermath of the Peasants Revolt of 1381 Tresilian tried John Ball and his followers and condemned some of them to death. Thomas Walsingham's chronicle states that he was party to Richard II's plot against John of Gaunt in 1385, undertaking to convict John of treason if he was brought before him. He himself was accused of treason in 1387 by the lords appellant, Richard II's opponents, and was found guilty by the Merciless Parliament in 1388. He was dragged on a hurdle to Tyburn, where he was hanged.

The Wars of the Roses: 46, 52–3, 57

Trevet, Nicholas

1258?–1334? Dominican friar and chronicler. Nicholas studied at Oxford, and by 1297 had won a reputation as a scholar. He joined the Dominican friary in London in about 1315. Nicholas, whose biblical and classical commentaries were known throughout Europe, wrote a history in Anglo-Norman extending from the Creation to 1285, and the chronicle *Annales Sex Regum Angliae* (Annals of Six Kings of England), dealing with English kings from Stephen to Edward I. Much of his work was compiled from existing sources but was enlived by anecdotes and vignettes gleaned from his knowledge of court affairs. He wrote the one known description of Henry III: 'medium height, of compact build, with the lid of one eye drooping'. He described Edward I as 'elegant in form, of commanding height'. His amusing style made his work popular and much used by later chroniclers.

Chronicles of the Age of Chivalry/Four Gothic Kings (US edn): 35, 113

Trevor, John, bishop of St Asaph

d.1410. Bishop of St Asaph (1394–1410); chamberlain of Chester, Flint and North Wales (1399). John served Richard II, but in 1399 deserted him for Henry Bolingbroke, who on his accession as Henry IV gave John his chamberlainship. He fought for the king against the rebellious Percy family at the battle of Shrewsbury in 1403, but in 1404 joined Owen Glendower, a Percy ally. When the rebellion ended in 1405, John fled to Scotland.

The Wars of the Roses: 104

Trifels

Castle in western Germany where Richard I was imprisoned in 1193–4 by Holy Roman Emperor Henry VI after his capture in Austria in 1192.

According to legend he bemoaned his 'doleful plight' in song, and was found at Trifels by his minstrel Blondel, who had travelled throughout Germany and sung outside every castle wall until recognized by his master.

The Plantagenet Chronicles: 224–5, 227

trivium

Division of the seven liberal arts: grammar, rhetoric and logic. With the other four arts (the quadrivium), the trivium formed the basis of the medieval university curriculum.

troubadours

Poet-musicians who flourished in Provence, southern France, in northern Spain and in northern Italy from the 11th to 13th century. They composed poems in the southern French *langue d'oc* dialect and these were performed to music. The social status of troubadours varied considerably – from kings, such as Richard I of England, to men of the humblest birth, such as Bernart de Ventadorn, the son of a scullion. Troubadour poetry declined in the mid-13th century after the Languedoc region was devastated by the Albigensian Crusade; the last troubadour, Guiraut Riquier, died in 1294.

In northern and central France aristocratic poets known as *trouvères* wrote poetry, largely about love, for royal and princely courts. The language they used was the *langue d'oïl*, the ancestor of modern French. Like the troubadours, they declined in the 13th century.

The Plantagenet Chronicles: 228–9, 246–7, 273

Troyes, Chrétien de

*fl.*1170–95. French poet; author of the earliest surviving Arthurian romances. Chrétien lived at the court of Marie of Champagne, Eleanor of Aquitaine's daughter. Between 1170 and 1185 he composed a series of Norman French verse romances which drew on Celtic legend – the first great literary treatment of the Arthurian legends. His poems are a sophisticated combination of Breton Celtic folk tales and contemporary ideas of chivalry and courtly love.

The Plantagenet Chronicles: 246

Troyes, Treaty of

Agreement concluded at Troyes, in north-east France, in May 1420, between Henry V of England, Charles VI of France and Philip, the Good, duke of Burgundy. The treaty was intended to settle the disputes between the French and English over the French throne that had brought about the Hundred Years War. Its clauses made Henry heir to the throne on Charles VI's death and arranged the English king's marriage to Charles's daughter Catherine; meanwhile, until the French king's death, Henry was to rule France as regent. Charles's son, the dauphin Charles, was disinherited by the treaty, but on his father's death in 1422 he laid claim to the French throne as Charles VII.

The Wars of the Roses: 148–51

Tudor, Edmund, 13th earl of Richmond

1430?–56. First son of Owen Tudor and Catherine of France; 13th earl of Richmond (1453–6). Edmund served his stepbrother Henry VI as a privy councillor and was raised by him to the earldom of Richmond. In 1455 he married Margaret Beaufort, great-granddaughter of John of Gaunt; their son Henry, the future Henry VII, was born after Edmund's death.

The Wars of the Roses: 151

Tudor, Henry, 14th earl of Richmond

See: Henry VII, king of England.

Tudor, Jasper, 17th earl of Pembroke

1431?–95. Second son of Owen Tudor and Catherine of France; 17th earl of Pembroke (1453–61, 1470–1, 1485–95); knight of the Garter (1459); 3rd duke of Bedford (1485). Jasper fought for his stepbrother Henry VI against the Yorkists at the first battle of St Albans (1455) and at Mortimer's Cross (1461), when he was defeated by Edward IV. He fled abroad and Edward annulled his title. He regained it briefly in 1470 when he returned to England to join Richard Neville, 'the Kingmaker', 16th earl of Warwick, in his restoration of Henry VI to the throne. In 1471, after the Lancastrians had been defeated he fled England once more, with his young nephew, Henry Tudor (later Henry VII), whom he had cared for since 1469. He returned in 1485 to aid Henry's attack on Richard III, and was present at Bosworth on 22 August 1485 when Henry became the first Tudor king of England.

The Wars of the Roses: 151, 254, 297

Tudor, Owen

d.1461. Second husband of Catherine of France; grandfather of Henry VII. Owen was a squire at Henry V's court, and after the king's death in 1422 became clerk of the wardrobe to his widow, Catherine of France. The couple married secretly in 1429, and Catherine bore Owen four children. He was twice imprisoned in Newgate by Humphrey of Lancaster, 2nd duke of Gloucester, because he had married Catherine before her son Henry VI had reached an age to grant permission for the marriage. Owen pleaded his case before Henry VI's council in 1437, and was forgiven. In the Wars of the Roses Owen fought for Henry and the Lancastrians and was part of the army defeated by Edward IV at the battle of Mortimer's Cross in 1461.

He fled as far as Hereford, where Edward caught up with him and had him beheaded in the market place.

The Wars of the Roses: 151

Tyler, Wat

d.1381. One of the leaders of the Peasants Revolt (May–June 1381), Wat was an Essex man, perhaps a roof tiler, who had, according to the French chronicler Froissart, served in Edward III's French wars. On 10 June 1381 he led a force of Essex men to London, to protest against the poll tax. On 13 June they united with rebels from Kent to form a 10,000-strong force. Richard II, aged 14, met the rebels at Mile End the following day and promised to abolish the tax and serfdom. Many of the men returned home, but Tyler and a hard core of supporters seized the Tower of London and killed Simon Sudbury, archbishop of Canterbury. On 15 June, Tyler and the king met again at Smithfield. Tyler presented additional radical demands and addressed the king with such familiarity that William Walworth, mayor of London, struck him down with a dagger. He was killed soon after by John Standish, one of Richard's squires.

The Wars of the Roses: 34–6, 38

Tyre

Ancient city in southern Lebanon, on the Mediterranean coast. The Christians took Tyre from the Saracens during the First Crusade (1095–99). It was besieged by Saladin in 1188, but the following year the Third Crusade broke the siege. An earthquake devastated it in 1202. In 1291 the Saracens recaptured and razed the city.

The Plantagenet Chronicles: 185–6, 202, 238, 278

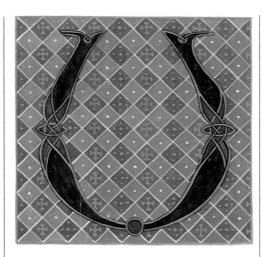

under-tenant

Feudal tenant holding land from a tenant-in-chief, rather than directly from the king.

Urban II, pope

1042?–99. Born Odo in Châtillon-sur-Marne, France; prior of Cluny Abbey, France (c.1075); cardinal bishop of Ostia in Italy (c.1088); pope (1089–99). Odo went to Rome early in Gregory VII's pontificate (1073–85), and became his trusted assistant. As Pope Urban, he continued to follow Gregory's reforming policies, although he was hampered by opposition from Holy Roman Emperor Henry IV, Gregory's great enemy, and his puppet antipope, Clement III. From 1088 Urban was constrained to reside in southern Italy under the protection of the Normans but in 1093 managed, with their help, to return to Rome, where the following year he regained the Lateran Palace by diplomatic means. In November 1095, at the Council of Clermont, he preached the First Crusade. Other councils were held under his auspices at Bari (1098) and Rome (1097, 1099).

The Plantagenet Chronicles: 36, 38–9

Urban V, pope

1310–70. Born Guillaume de Grimoard; Benedictine canon lawyer; pope (1362–70).

Attempting to end the papacy's residence at Avignon (the 'Babylonian captivity'), Urban, with the support of Holy Roman Emperor Charles IV, returned to Rome in 1367. A patron of the arts, he founded universities at Orange, Cracow and Vienna. While in Rome, he repaired many neglected churches and palaces. Urban found the papal states difficult to govern and some of the great Roman families, such as the Visconti, dangerously hostile. He hoped to launch a crusade but needed first to make diplomatic moves to halt the recent renewal of the Hundred Years War. In 1370 he therefore returned to Avignon but died soon afterwards.

Chronicles of the Age of Chivalry/Four Gothic Kings (US edn): 286

Urban VI, pope

1318?–89. Born Bartolomeo Prignano in Naples, Italy; archbishop of Acerenza (1364–77) and Bari (1377–8); pope (1378–89). On the death of Pope Gregory XI in April 1378 the college of cardinals, split by three opposing factions, elected Urban as a compromise candidate; they proclaimed him at the fortified palace of Anagni to avoid the Roman mob, who wanted a Roman-born pope. Urban returned to Rome, where his zeal for purging the Church of clerical luxury, his violent temper and his profane vocabulary combined to alienate the cardinals.

They declared him deposed, and in August 1378 elected a new pope, Clement VII, claiming that the Roman mob had intimidated them into making Urban pope.

However, Urban was recognized by Hungary, the Holy Roman Empire, most of Italy, Flanders and England, and Clement moved to Avignon. So began the Great Schism, which lasted until 1417. The murder of five cardinals in 1384, allegedly at Urban's behest, horrified many contemporaries. Urban himself may have met his death from poisoning.

The Wars of the Roses: 30, 32–3, 40, 46

usury

Charging interest on money loans; it was regarded as a sin by the medieval Church.

usury The medieval Church and state both strictly forbade Christians to practise usury, confining the practice to the Jews, at least in principle.

Although only Jews were permitted to practise usury, banking houses like the Medici evaded the prohibition by disguising interest payments.

Chronicles of the Age of Chivalry/Four Gothic Kings (US edn): 130

Utrecht, Treaty of

Agreement of 1474 between Edward IV of England and the Hanseatic League (a trading association of north European towns). In 1468, Edward had removed the trading privileges enjoyed by London's Hanseatic merchant colony, to placate English merchants, who did not receive similar privileges abroad. However, the king's plan to invade France in 1474 required 14 Hanseatic ships to ferry his troops across the Channel, and to ensure safe passage for his forces and his invasion fleet: consequently, in the treaty he restored the League's privileges. In return, the League promised English merchants Baltic trading privileges – which, however, they never received.

The Wars of the Roses: 267

Valence, William de, earl of Pembroke

d.1296. Half-brother of Henry III of England; titular earl of Pembroke by right of his wife Joan (1247–96). William was one of Henry III's Lusignan half-brothers; the fourth son of their mother Isabella of Angoulême, who, after King John of England's death, had married Hugh of Lusignan. In 1247 William came to Henry's court, where he married Joan, daughter of William Marshal, 1st earl of Pembroke, and took the title of earl of Pembroke. Like the other Lusignans, William was unpopular with the English; the chronicler Matthew Paris accuses him of 'injuries inflicted' on the abbot of St Albans. In 1264 he fought for Henry III against the barons at Lewes, fled to France when the king was defeated by Simon de Montfort, 6th earl of Leicester, and taken prisoner, but returned to England on Henry's restoration in 1265. He accompanied Prince Edward (later Edward I of England) on crusade in 1270–3.

In 1279 William presided over the transfer of the Agenais from France to England. He supported Edward I's invasion of Wales and was given military command in South Wales in 1282; he held the region for the king during a Welsh revolt in 1295.

Chronicles of the Age of Chivalry/Four Gothic Kings (US edn): 59, 72, 88

Valois

French royal house that reigned from 1328 to 1589, named after the duchy of Valois, a small region in northern France. Philip VI was the first of the dynasty to ascend the French throne, after the death in 1328 of Charles IV, last of the direct Capetian line.

Chronicles of the Age of Chivalry/Four Gothic Kings (US edn): 228, 274

Valois, Isabella of

See: Isabella of Valois

vassal

Feudal tenant of a monarch or lord, who, in return for fighting for him, received a fief (usually land) and military protection. The ceremony of homage, in which the vassal knelt before the lord and vowed his obedience, confirmed the vassalage.

The Plantagenet Chronicles: 40

Vaughan, Sir Thomas

d.1483. Edward IV appointed Thomas his personal servant in 1461, after his accession. In 1470 Thomas was made chamberlain to the king's infant son Edward, prince of Wales (later Edward V). He was knighted in 1475. After the young Edward V's accession in April 1438, Richard, 3rd duke of Gloucester (later Richard III), imprisoned Thomas in Pontefract in Yorkshire and executed him there before usurping Edward's throne in June the same year.

The Wars of the Roses: 279, 282

Venice

Established in the 7th century, Venice was ideally sited to trade between western Europe and the Byzantine Empire. By the 10th century it had taken most of the Dalmatian coast and dominated the Adriatic. The cathedral of San Marco (built 1063–73) shows the Byzantine influence on Venice.

The city became a wide-ranging eastern trading empire, where merchants from the north-west of Europe could purchase eastern silks and spices. But in 1203, with its trade damaged by Byzantine hostility, Venice diverted the armies of the Fourth Crusade to Constantinople to depose the Byzantine emperor, and received much of the loot from the crusaders' sack of the city in 1204. Venice conquered many Greek islands, notably Crete in 1216, and became Europe's main naval power after crushing its rival Genoa at Chioggia in 1380. The 15th century saw the zenith of its power and wealth.

The Plantagenet Chronicles: 167, 178–9, 224, 237, 282
Chronicles of the Age of Chivalry/Four Gothic Kings (US edn): 70–1, 82, 195

Vere, Aubrey de, 10th earl of Oxford

1340?–1400. Chamberlain of Richard II's household (1381); 10th earl of Oxford (1393–1400). His nephew was Richard II's favourite, Robert de Vere, 9th earl of Oxford. In 1388, during the Merciless Parliament, Aubrey was removed from court by the king's opponents, but in 1393, the year after Robert's death in France, Richard gave Aubrey his nephew's earldom.

The Wars of the Roses: 23

Venice Rich mosaics in the Byzantine style adorn the ceilings of San Marco, Venice's cathedral.

Vere, John de, 13th earl of Oxford

1443–1513. 13th earl of Oxford (1464–75, 1485–1513); chamberlain of England (1485); constable of the Tower of London (1485). In 1462, on the execution of his father John de Vere, 12th earl of Oxford, a prominent Lancastrian, John forfeited his earldom, but two years later received it back from Edward IV. However, his loyalty to the Yorkists was suspect and in 1468 he was briefly imprisoned in the Tower of London. In 1470 he helped Richard Neville, 'the Kingmaker', 16th earl of Warwick, to restore the Lancastrian Henry VI to the throne, but after the Yorkist victory at the battle of Barnet (1471) he fled abroad.

In 1473–4 John landed with a Lancastrian expeditionary force in Cornwall, marched north and besieged Oxford. Captured by Edward IV's army, he was held prisoner in Hammes castle near Calais from 1474 to 1484, and during his imprisonment the king once more removed his earldom from him. In 1484 John escaped from prison and in Paris joined Henry Tudor, 14th earl of Richmond, inheritor of the Lancastrian claim to the throne and the future Henry VII. The following year he took part in Henry's invasion of England and fought beside him at Bosworth. After his accession, the king restored John's earldom and rewarded him with offices.

The Wars of the Roses: 302

Vere, Robert de, 9th earl of Oxford

1362–92. 9th earl of Oxford (1381–8); 1st marquis of Dublin (1385–8); 1st duke of Ireland (1386–8). The favourite of his boyhood friend Richard II. Robert married Philippa de Couci, the king's first cousin, in 1378. Between 1382 and 1385 Richard gave him the castles of Okehampton, Queenborough and Berkhamsted. Contemporary sources record Richard's foolish infatuation with him, which aroused baronial opposition to them both.

Robert divorced Philippa in 1387 to marry his mistress, Agnes Launcecrona, provoking an outcry from his wife's relations. Under threat of impeachment as a traitor by the lords appellant in 1387, he escaped from London, raised troops at Chester and marched back towards the capital. At Radcot Bridge he was ambushed by Thomas of Woodstock, 1st duke of Gloucester; he deserted his men, swam the Thames in fog and fled to Paris. Sentenced to death for treason by the Merciless Parliament in his absence, Robert was killed by a boar while hunting at Louvain in 1392.

The Wars of the Roses: 39, 50–8, 83

Vesci, Eustace de

1170?–1216. In 1195 Eustace served with Richard I on crusade in the Holy Land and in 1199 was a royal envoy to William, the Lion, king of Scotland. In 1212 he conspired against King John of England with Robert FitzWalter and others. The plot was discovered and he fled to Scotland, where he married one of William the Lion's illegitimate daughters. Eustace returned to England in 1213. Two years later he became a leading member of the baronial party and was one of the 25 executors of the Magna Carta. When John harried the eastern counties of England in 1215–16 Eustace made overtures for peace. However, in 1216 he died supporting the Scottish king, Alexander II, in his siege of Barnard castle.

The Plantagenet Chronicles: 296

Vexin

Region of north-east France, east of Rouen. In the 12th century the Vexin was a vital strip of land, since it divided the duchy of Normandy, held by the English kings, from the French royal lands. Part of the region, north of the River Epte and controlled by the great castle of Gisors, was attached to the duchy and known as the Norman Vexin. The area south of the Epte was the French Vexin, controlled by the fortresses of Pontoise, Chaumont and Mantes, the keys to the northern defence of Paris.

In 1144 Geoffrey Plantagenet ceded Gisors to Louis VII of France as the price of French recognition of Geoffrey's conquest of Normandy, and in 1151 the rest of the Norman Vexin was made over to the French. In 1158 Henry, the Young King, Henry II's heir, was betrothed to Louis' daughter Margaret, and Louis promised Henry II the Norman Vexin as part of her dowry. When this was not forthcoming on the couple's marriage in 1160, the English king seized it that year. Thereafter the Plantagenets held the region until Philip II Augustus of France overran it in 1192–3.

In 1196–8 Richard I built Château Gaillard in eastern Normandy as a base to recover the Vexin and the French king's other gains in Normandy. King John of England returned the recaptured areas to Philip, who took Château Gaillard in 1203.

The Plantagenet Chronicles: 92–3

Vézelay

Small town in Burgundy, France, dominated by its great abbey, founded in the 9th century. It was at Vézelay that St Bernard of Clairvaux preached the Second Crusade in 1146 and that Richard I of England and Philip II Augustus of France vowed to launch the Third Crusade. Vézelay Abbey is a superb example of 12th-century Burgundian architecture.

The Plantagenet Chronicles: 112, 192, 205, 208

Victor IV, antipope

d.1164? Born Ottaviano of Monticelli. Antipope (1159–64). He was established as antipope by Holy Roman Emperor Frederick I Barbarossa and his imperialist supporters in Italy, who refused to accept Pope Alexander III on his election in 1159.

The Plantagenet Chronicles: 113

Vienne, Jean de, admiral of France

*fl.*1385. Admiral of France (1373). From his appointment as admiral, Jean built up a major fleet for operations against the English. In May 1385 he took an army to Scotland to assist Robert II, the Scottish king, against an English force led by Richard II of England and John of Gaunt. Jean's troops had no opportunity to engage the English, since the Scots pursued a successful scorched-earth policy. This drove out the English but disgusted the French, who turned violently on their Scottish allies. Jean was held captive in Scotland as a surety for French payment for the damage his men had caused.

Chronicles of the Age of Chivalry/Four Gothic Kings (US edn): 248, 250–2
The Wars of the Roses: 58–9

villein

In feudal times the highest-ranking unfree peasant. He was bound to the manor of his lord and owed him set services and payments in return for justice and protection. The term is Norman French for 'villager'.

The Wars of the Roses: 37

Villon, François

1431–63? French poet. François was adopted as a child by Guillaume de Villon, chaplain of St-Benoît-le-Bétourné in Paris, and took his name. He became a student at the Sorbonne, killed a priest in 1455, robbed the college of Navarre in 1456 and fled Paris, leaving the witty poetic *Lais* (Legacies) to his friends. He roamed France, visiting the court of René of Anjou at Angers in

1457, and perhaps joined the Coquillard bandits. In the early summer of 1461 the bishop of Orléans jailed him for robbery at Meung-sur-Loire but he was pardoned in October by Louis XI, who had just succeeded to the throne. In 1462 he was condemned to death, but the parlement commuted his sentence to one of ten years' banishment from Paris. His end is unknown. His greatest work, the *Testament*, written in prison in 1461–2, is remarkable for its irony, directness and passion. He also wrote many ballads, some in Coquillard slang.

The Wars of the Roses: 196–7

Virgin Mary, cult of

From the 12th century the Virgin Mary was a focus of adoration second only to Christ in the medieval Church and was prayed to as an intercessor. Images of Mary were much revered and centres of the cult were the goals of many pilgrimages.

The Plantagenet Chronicles: 134

Vision of Piers Plowman, The

English allegorical poem written *c.*1362–77 by William Langland. Composed of about 7,000 lines of unrhymed alliterative verse, it is the greatest Middle English poem before Chaucer. It consists of three dream visions of Piers the Plowman. In the first, Holy Church and Lady Meed (wealth) woo Piers; in the second, he leads a group of penitents; in the third, he sees and practises the ideal virtues. Langland's Lady Meed is thought to embody social upheavals following the Black Death. The poem castigates the age's evils in a conservative, pious vein and exhorts all classes to follow the callings ordained by divine and natural law.

Chronicles of the Age of Chivalry/Four Gothic Kings (US edn): 275

Robert de Vere *Richard II's favourite was gored to death by a boar in 1392 whilst hunting at Louvain.*

Wace

*fl.*1160. Clerk of Caen; canon of Bayeux; chronicler and poet. Wace was made a canon of Bayeux by Henry II of England, who also asked him (*c.*1160) to write the *Roman de Rou*, a verse history of the dukes of Normandy in Norman French. He also composed the *Roman de Brut*, a verse history of England from the time of Brutus the Trojan, mythical founder of the English nation, to Wace's own age; in this work the legend of King Arthur's Round Table first appears.

The Plantagenet Chronicles: 246
Chronicles of the Age of Chivalry/Four Gothic Kings (US edn): 262

Wakefield

Town in West Yorkshire; a centre of the wool trade in the 14th century, and, on 30 December 1460, site of a battle in the Wars of the Roses in which Richard, 3rd duke of York, Yorkist claimant to Henry VI of England's throne, died. Richard aimed to crush Lancastrian support for the king in the north but was defeated by Henry Beaufort, 6th earl of Somerset, outside Wakefield. After the battle, Richard's head was displayed at York wearing a paper crown.

The Wars of the Roses: 222–4

Wakefield, Peter of

See: Peter of Wakefield

Wales

In the 11th century Gruffydd ap Llywelyn (d.1063) gained mastery over all the British and Celtic peoples of Wales. Later that century the Normans gained control of South Wales and the marches, but the Welsh princes managed, with some difficulty, to remain independent of English rule for another two centuries. In the 12th century Welsh people and culture were recorded and celebrated by Gerald of Wales, who found his compatriots 'more shrewd than any other Western people'.

In the 13th century English designs on Wales grew stronger and Llywelyn ap Iorwerth (d.1240) and other Welsh princes had to fight hard to repel English invasion. Eventually, in 1282, Edward I of England conquered the principality and enforced his rule with ten great and 12 lesser castles, purpose-built to subdue the Welsh heartlands in Snowdonia. The king made his son Edward (later Edward II) prince of Wales in 1301, to appease Welsh pride.

A Welsh rising begun by Owen Glendower in 1400 failed three years later when Henry IV crushed Owen's allies, the Percy family. Later in the 15th century Henry Tudor, 14th earl of Richmond, whose paternal family was Welsh, gained considerable backing from the principality in his bid for the English throne, to which he succeeded in 1485 as Henry VII.

The Plantagenet Chronicles: 141, 293, 296
Chronicles of the Age of Chivalry/Four Gothic Kings (US edn): 44, 47, 96, 116–21, 124–5, 138, 150, 200, 202, 264
The Wars of the Roses: 95, 98, 100–1, 104, 106, 108

Wales, Gerald of

See: Gerald of Wales

Wallace, William

1272?–1305. Warden of Scotland (1298); Scots national hero. In May 1297 Wallace led 30 men who burned Lanark and slew its English sheriff, in the name of John Balliol, who the previous year had been deposed as king of Scotland by Edward I of England. Wallace drove the English from Perth, Stirling and Lanarkshire in August 1297, routed them at Stirling Bridge in September, then laid waste Northumberland, Westmorland and Cumbria. On 22 July 1298 Edward I crushed his forces at Falkirk, and Wallace resigned as warden of Scotland to wage guerilla war against the English. In August 1299 he went abroad to seek aid from France, Norway and Pope Boniface VIII. He returned to Scotland in 1303, was outlawed by Edward I in 1304 and was betrayed to the English in 1305. Taken to London in August that year, he was hanged, drawn and quartered as a traitor, and his quarters were sent to Scotland.

Chronicles of the Age of Chivalry/Four Gothic Kings (US edn): 134, 144–5, 156

Wallingford

Town in Oxfordshire, near Oxford, built in the 9th century by King Alfred, where the Ridgeway, an ancient track, crosses the Thames. In 1066 it was one of the first places secured by William the Conqueror in his subjugation of England. King Stephen of England besieged Wallingford castle in 1152, when it was held by supporters of Henry, duke of Normandy (later Henry II). Henry broke the siege in 1153, and he and Stephen made terms at Wallingford the same year. On 2 December 1307, in honour of his favourite, Piers Gaveston, Edward II of England held a tournament there, in which Piers routed Earl Warenne and other magnates.

Richard II of England's ten-year-old widow, Isabella, was kept at Wallingford from 1399 to 1401 by Henry IV before he allowed her to return to France. The Yorkist Edward IV held Margaret of Anjou, Henry VI's queen, there after her capture in 1471, until Louis XI of France ransomed her in 1475. Wallingford's prosperity was diminished in the early 15th century by the building of two bridges across the Thames further upriver at Abingdon, which took away much of the town's traffic, trade and tolls.

The Plantagenet Chronicles: 74, 76, 82, 84, 86, 88
Chronicles of the Age of Chivalry/Four Gothic Kings (US edn): 98, 170, 174, 176
The Wars of the Roses: 77, 96, 201

Walsingham, Thomas

d.1422. Benedictine monk; precentor and mentor of the St Albans Abbey scribes; prior of Wymondham (1394–6); chronicler. Thomas revived the St Albans tradition of producing chronicles, as exemplified by Matthew Paris in the 13th century. To this end he continued Paris's *Chronica Majora* (Greater Chronicle), extending the period it covered from 1259 to 1422, and wrote a short history of the world from the Creation to 1392. His other historical works included the *Ypodygma Neustriae*, a chronicle of England and Normandy from 911 to 1419. His chronicles are the principal authority for the period 1377–1422, when he was recording current events. His work is often moralistic; for example, he called the Peasants

Wakefield *The site of the battle of Wakefield Bridge on 30 December 1460, in which Richard, 3rd duke of York and pretender to the throne, was killed.*

Revolt God's punishment for the sins of the English, and wrote of a dolphin that appeared in the Thames in 1392 as an omen of strife between Richard II and London. He also attacked Wycliffe as 'the mouthpiece of the devil'.

Chronicles of the Age of Chivalry/Four Gothic Kings (US edn): 13, 227, 282, 294, 306
The Wars of the Roses: 12, 30, 40, 46, 53, 91, 98, 126, 140

Walter of Coutances, archbishop of Rouen

d.1207. Keeper of the great seal of England (1173–89); bishop of Lincoln (1183–4); archbishop of Rouen (1184–1207); justiciar of England (1191–3). Walter attended Richard I of England on the Third Crusade in 1189, but in 1191 Richard sent him back from Sicily as chief of his council of regency in England; there Walter took Nottingham and other castles from Richard's brother John, who was plotting against the king.

In 1193 Walter collected the 100,000-mark ransom needed for Richard's release after his capture by Holy Roman Emperor Henry VI; and the following year he went to Germany to negotiate the king's release. There he was made a hostage in place of Richard. The king paid a 10,000-mark ransom for him and Walter returned to England in May that year. The same month he went to Normandy where, in 1196, he quarrelled with Richard over the king's building Château Gaillard on church land; Richard made

good for this act by paying Walter substantial compensation. In 1199 Walter invested John as duke of Normandy (before he was crowned as king of England) and in 1204 did the same for Philip II Augustus of France, when he seized the duchy.

The Plantagenet Chronicles: 217, 226, 228, 232–3, 236, 240, 244, 259

Walter of Guisborough

*fl.*1312. Augustinian canon of Guisborough Priory in Yorkshire; chronicler. Walter wrote a chronicle of events from 1066 to 1312, using contemporary sources for the final 22 years. National events, including Edward I of England's Welsh campaign of 1282 and relations with the Scots from 1291 to 1300, are usually described from a north of England perspective. Walter also records Guisborough Priory's destruction by fire in 1289. The work is lively and not wholly reliable; even so, the accounts of the wars with the Scots in 1296–8 are historically valuable.

Chronicles of the Age of Chivalry/Four Gothic Kings (US edn): 107, 132, 142, 157, 162

Walter, Hubert, archbishop of Canterbury

d.1205. Baron of the exchequer (1184–5); bishop of Salisbury (1189–93); archbishop of Canterbury (1193–1205); chancellor (1199–1205). Hubert accompanied Richard I to

Palestine in 1189 and negotiated with Saladin for him. In 1193 he visited Richard in prison and returned to England to collect his ransom. He suppressed Prince John's attempt at revolt, and officiated at Richard's second coronation (1194). Hubert developed Henry II's legal and financial system, and began the system of keeping legal records in the Chancery rolls. He also caused land tax to be assessed with the help of locally elected landowners and representatives and stressed the elective character of English monarchy at John's coronation in 1199.

The Plantagenet Chronicles: 214, 226, 232, 236, 244, 252, 262, 284, 309

Waltham

Town in Essex, with an abbey founded in 1030. Built to house a cross with the figure of Christ, miraculously discovered at Montacute in Somerset, it was refounded by the future King Harold in 1060 and again by Henry II of England on a massive scale in 1177. Henry III was a frequent visitor to the abbey, whose church was one of the longest in England. Edward I erected a cross (which still stands) at Waltham, one of 12 that marked the route of the funeral procession of his wife Eleanor of Castile in 1290; and his body lay in the abbey after his death in 1307. On 14 November 1387 the lords appellant met at Waltham to issue accusations of treason against Richard II's ministers. The abbey was the last to be dissolved by Henry VIII in 1540.

The Plantagenet Chronicles: 131
Chronicles of the Age of Chivalry/Four Gothic Kings (US edn): 133, 164
The Wars of the Roses: 52

Walworth, Sir William

d.1385. Sheriff of London (1370); mayor of London (1374, 1381); knighted 1381. Walworth, probably from Durham and originally a fishmonger, became an alderman of London in 1368 and sheriff in 1370. From 1377 he lent money to the young Richard II of England and supported John of Gaunt as regent for the king. In about 1380 he built a chantry chapel with ten priests at St Michael's, Crooked Lane. On 13 June 1381, as mayor, he held London Bridge against Wat Tyler's men during the Peasants Revolt. At Richard's meeting with Tyler at Smithfield, two days later, Walworth, enraged by Tyler's familiar manner towards the king, struck him down with a dagger (which is preserved by the Fishmongers' Company in London). Richard knighted Walworth immediately after the event. He later served on two commissions of the peace to restore peace in Kent. On his death, he was buried at St Michael's, Crooked Lane.

The Wars of the Roses: 35, 38

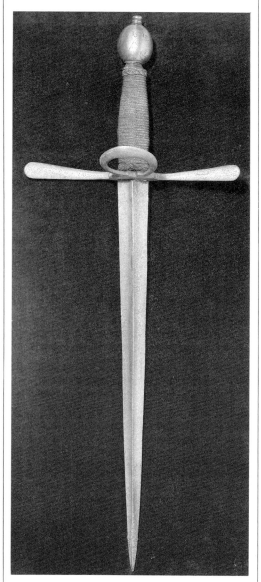

Walworth *The dagger with which William Walworth is reputed to have struck down Wat Tyler in 1381.*

wapentake

Subdivision of an old English northern or eastern shire: York, Lincoln, Leicester, Nottingham, Derby and Rutland. The name derived from Old Norse – many inhabitants of these shires were of Danish descent. Like hundreds (shire subdivisions in the south and west), wapentakes each had their own court.

Wardlaw, Henry, bishop of St Andrews

d.1440. Bishop of St Andrews (1403–40). Wardlaw, who had lived at Avignon before his preferment in 1403, was made a bishop by the Avignonese pope Benedict XIII during the Great Schism (1378–1417). He was tutor to Prince James of Scotland (later James I). Wardlaw completed the restoration of St Andrews Cathedral, which had been destroyed, and founded St Andrews University in 1411. In 1424 he crowned James I and his queen, Joan Beaufort. He burned Lollard heretics in 1407 and 1432.

The Wars of the Roses: 185

Warenne, Earl

Title interchangeable with the earldom of Surrey; associated with the Warenne family, hereditary earls of Surrey from 1088 to 1347.

Warenne, John de, 6th earl of Surrey

1231?–1304. Son of William de Warenne, 5th earl of Surrey; 6th earl of Surrey (1240–1304); styled earl of Sussex (1282); warden of Scotland (1296–7). A ward of Henry III of England after his father's death in 1240, John supported the king against his rebellious barons in 1258. He aided the barons from about 1260 to 1263, but rejoined Henry and fought for him at Lewes in May 1264. The king was captured during the battle and John fled to France. He returned to England with the future Edward I in 1265, and freed Henry at the battle of Evesham. In 1282 he assumed the title of earl of Sussex but his claim was uncertain. He joined Edward I's invasion of Scotland in 1296, took Dunbar castle in April that year and became warden of Scotland in August. On 11 September 1297 his troops were routed by William Wallace at Stirling Bridge, but the following year he helped Edward defeat Wallace at Falkirk.

Chronicles of the Age of Chivalry/Four Gothic Kings (US edn): 142, 144

Warenne, John de, 7th earl of Surrey

1286–1347. Grandson of John de Warenne, 6th earl of Surrey; 7th earl of Surrey (1304–47) and styled earl of Sussex (1304). In 1310 John joined Edward II of England's invasion of Scotland, but in 1312, with other barons, he rebelled against Edward's extravagance and misgovernment and took the king's favourite Piers Gaveston prisoner at Knaresborough. Gaveston was afterwards

executed, but John was reconciled with Edward, who pardoned him in 1313.

In 1316 John was excommunicated by Pope John XXII for adultery. The following year he helped Alice Lacy, wife of Thomas, 2nd earl of Lancaster, to elope with her lover; as a result, between 1317 and 1319, Thomas seized much of his land. However, in 1322, Thomas was defeated by John and the king at a battle near Burton-on-Trent and John regained some of his estates. He recovered the rest in 1326 when he supported Edward during his wife Isabella's invasion of England. After Edward's forced abdication in 1327 John made his peace with Isabella.

Chronicles of the Age of Chivalry/Four Gothic Kings (US edn): 174, 176

Warenne, William de, 5th earl of Surrey

d.1240. 5th earl of Surrey (1202–40); warden of the Cinque Ports (1216). William's family estates in Normandy were confiscated in 1204, when Philip II of France seized the duchy. He supported King John of England against the barons and in 1215 acted as one of the king's guarantors for the keeping of the Magna Carta. However, the following year he supported Prince Louis, son of Philip II of France, when he tried to wrest England from John; even so, after the king's death later that year he declared himself a loyal vassal of his infant son and successor, Henry III. His lands were restored in 1221. During the 1220s and 1230s John took an active part in politics, and in 1238 he was appointed a treasurer of royal taxes.

Chronicles of the Age of Chivalry/Four Gothic Kings (US edn): 52

Warkworth castle

Stronghold in Northumberland acquired by the Percy family in the 14th century. Despite the Yorkist leader Edward's triumph over the Lancastrians in 1461 and enthronement as Edward IV that year, Lancastrian forces in Northumberland under Margaret of Anjou retained Warkworth and other castles. However, after besieging Warkworth the following year, Edward's forces took it in 1463.

The Wars of the Roses: 61, 232, 255

Warkworth, John

d.1500. Master of Peterhouse College, Cambridge (1473); chronicler. The only copy of

Warkworth's chronicle, which he probably wrote after 1478, is an English manuscript appendix to a volume of the earlier *Brut* chronicle (published by Caxton in 1482). Warkworth produced an informed account of events from 1460 to 1474, with special attention to events in the north and written mainly from the Lancastrian point of view. He records the Yorkist Edward IV's conquest of Northumbria in 1462, the Lancastrian Henry VI's capture at Ribblesdale in Lancashire in 1465 and the Lancastrian defeat at the battle of Tewkesbury on 4 May 1471. He complains of 'one battle after another, and much trouble and great loss of goods', and blames this on Edward's failure to establish peace.

The Wars of the Roses: 12, 230, 234, 244, 252

Wars of the Roses

Struggle for the English throne fought intermittently from 1455 to 1487 between the houses of York and Lancaster. The wars were so named because the opposing factions' badges were believed to have been a white and a red rose respectively.

The Wars of the Roses: 10–11, 212, 214–25, 233

Warwick

County town of Warwickshire, on the River Avon. Warwick castle, built in the 14th century on the site of a stronghold constructed in 915, belonged to the earldom of Warwick. Richard Neville, 'the Kingmaker', 16th earl of Warwick, imprisoned the Yorkist Edward IV there briefly after capturing him at Edgecote in July 1469.

The Wars of the Roses: 244–5

Waurin, Jean de

1394?–1471? Lord of Forestal; Flemish chronicler. The illegitimate son of a noble Artois family, Jean served John, the Fearless, duke of Burgundy, and fought with the duke's English allies against the French at Agincourt in 1415. He left the army when the Treaty of Arras ended the Anglo-Burgundian alliance in 1435 but served two more dukes of Burgundy, Philip the Good and Charles the Bold, as a diplomat. From about 1450 until his death he wrote his *Recueil des Croniques et Anchiennes Istories de la Grant Bretaigne, à présent nommé Engleterre*, a French history of England from earliest times to his own. Aiming to record the 'lofty enterprises' of the English, he wrote a romanticized version of England's past, using his own memory for

events, such as John, 1st duke of Bedford's 'marvellous feats of arms' at Verneuil in 1424.

The Wars of the Roses: 13, 184, 194, 238

Waverley annals

Anonymous annals written at the Cistercian monastery at Waverley in Surrey. A history of the period from the Incarnation to 1291, they are valuable mainly for their descriptions of 13th-century events. They record local and national happenings and include documents, such as Henry III of England's submission to his rebellious barons in 1265. Their accounts are often brief, because 'the affair is so public that nearly anyone who wishes can learn about it'. The annals support 'the saner party' of Simon de Montfort, 6th earl of Leicester, and the barons against Henry III; the barons are said to 'renew ancient laws and customs', and Simon de Montfort is called 'a glorious martyr'.

Chronicles of the Age of Chivalry/Four Gothic Kings (US edn): 7, 96

Welfs

See: Guelphs

Welles, John, 1st viscount Welles

d.1499. Brother of Richard, 7th baron Welles; 1st viscount Welles (1487). A Lancastrian who fled to Brittany in 1483 when Richard III usurped the throne of England, John joined

Wells The richly sculpted west front of Wells Cathedral, built 1220-30.

Henry Tudor, 14th earl of Richmond (the future Henry VII), in his invasion of England in 1485 and fought against Richard at Bosworth. After his accession, Henry created him Viscount Welles.

The Wars of the Roses: 302

Welles, Richard, 7th baron Welles

1431–70. Baron Welles (1461). Richard fought for the Lancastrians at the second battle of St Albans in 1461 but submitted to the Yorkist Edward IV later that year. In 1470 he raised a force in Lincolnshire against Edward IV, but was taken hostage by the king after meeting with him under a promise of safety. Richard was beheaded when his son Sir Robert Welles refused to end the rebellion.

The Wars of the Roses: 246, 247

Wells

Cathedral city in Somerset; with Bath, joint seat of a bishopric. Wells Cathedral has a fine sculpted west front, built 1220–30 as a screen at the end of an earlier (12th-century) building and containing over 300 sculpted figures. In the early 14th century the east end was rebuilt in the Decorated style and the crossing was strengthened with inverted arches to support a higher and heavier tower. The plan is complex, with stone traceries running across surfaces and windows. Fine woodwork was added to Wells Cathedral in the 15th century.

Chronicles of the Age of Chivalry/Four Gothic Kings (US edn): 48–51, 206
The Wars of the Roses: 147

Welsh marches

Lands in Wales bordering England, ruled by English barons who had seized estates in East Wales with royal approval and who owed allegiance only to the king. Frequent Welsh risings, such as those of 1400, made the marches a lawless and troubled area. In 1471 Edward IV of England set up the Council of Wales and the Marches to try to control the rebellious Welsh lords of the region.

Wenceslas IV, Holy Roman Emperor

1361–1419. Son of Holy Roman Emperor Charles IV; elector of Brandenburg (1373–6); king of Bohemia (1378–1419); German king and Holy Roman Emperor (1378–1400). In 1387 Wenceslas helped his half-brother

Sigismund seize the throne of Hungary. In 1394 a group of hostile Bohemian nobles imprisoned him and, although he was released the following year, he had to concede most of his power in Bohemia to his cousin Jobst. His neglect of German affairs caused a revolt among the German princes, who deposed him in 1400. Wenceslas retired to Bohemia, and in 1411 surrendered his rights in Germany to Sigismund. In 1402–3 he was imprisoned again by rebellious Bohemians under Sigismund's leadership and thereafter was little more than a puppet king. Wenceslas encouraged the religious reformer John Hus and continued to support him after he was placed under papal interdict in 1412. When Hus was burnt for heresy in 1415 a mass revolt arose which Wenceslas did not attempt to suppress until 1419. That year a mob threw the Catholic councillors of Prague from the town hall windows, which caused Wenceslas to die of shock.

The Wars of the Roses: 142, 156, 159

Wendover, Roger of

See: Roger of Wendover

Wenlock, John, Baron Wenlock

d.1471. Chamberlain to Henry VI of England's queen, Margaret of Anjou (1450); knight of the Garter (1461); Baron Wenlock (1461); lieutenant of Calais (1469). John fought for the Lancastrian Henry VI at the first battle of St Albans in 1455, but later that year became Yorkist Speaker of the House of Commons. He fled to France in 1459, when the Lancastrians were in the ascendant, but returned in 1460 and fought for the Yorkists at Towton in 1461. The victorious Edward IV created him baron, but in 1471 John again changed sides, aiding Margaret of Anjou's revolt against Edward. He was slain, fighting on her side, at the battle of Tewkesbury.

The Wars of the Roses: 262

Westminster

Area two miles west of the city of London, containing England's foremost royal palace and seat of government.

Westminster Abbey

Benedictine abbey church in London, the coronation church of the English monarchy, built by Edward the Confessor in 1050–65, on the site of a 7th-century church. After Edward was canonized in 1161 his tomb became the abbey's principal relic. In 1245 Henry III began rebuilding the abbey's choir, using a French architect, Henry de Reynes; the reconstruction was consecrated in 1269. (The nave was rebuilt in the same early English style over the following two centuries.) In 1272 Henry III was buried in the abbey, in St Edward's old tomb. Many later sovereigns were also entombed at Westminster, and the abbey became the principal English royal mausoleum.

In 1292 Edward I ordered a new Chapel of St Stephen to be built in the Decorated style. Four years later Edward captured from the Scots their coronation stone, the Stone of Scone, and placed it under the abbey's royal throne, where it still remains.

The Plantagenet Chronicles: 108, 110, 136, 142, 172–3, 178, 226
Chronicles of the Age of Chivalry/Four Gothic Kings (US edn): 30, 35, 58–9, 82–4, 100–5, 132, 143, 146, 158–60, 206, 211, 230, 282, 284
The Wars of the Roses: 25–6, 69, 72, 189, 192, 289

Westminster Palace

Principal English royal palace from the reign of Edward the Confessor in the 11th century to that of Henry VIII in the 16th; and from 1265 the seat of Parliament. Edward the Confessor (d.1066) built the palace on the site of an earlier one. In about 1100 William II constructed the Great Hall; the hammer-beam roof of this was added in the 1390s and is virtually the only part of the medieval palace to have survived the fire of 1834 (following which the present palace, or Houses of Parliament, was built, in the Gothic style). The great complex of buildings once housed Chancery, the Exchequer, the treasury, the royal household and the courts of King's Bench and Common Pleas. Many medieval accounts describe the expensive work carried out on the palace to make it fit for royalty.

The Plantagenet Chronicles: 98, 112, 160, 297
Chronicles of the Age of Chivalry/Four Gothic Kings (US edn): 54, 58, 114, 146, 148, 154, 158, 169, 176, 211, 224, 240
The Wars of the Roses: 25–6, 72, 81, 105, 124

Wharram Percy

Village in Yorkshire noted for well-preserved traces of its 12th-century layout. Lying in a valley, it had a water-mill to grind corn, a stone church and a thatched-roof stone manor house. The mud-walled peasants' cottages, also roofed with thatch, had solid wooden doors with locks and sheds outside to house pigs and other livestock.

The Plantagenet Chronicles: 310–11

Whittington, Richard

1358–1423. Son of Sir William Whittington; alderman of London (1393); sheriff (1394); mayor of London (1397–8, 1406–7, 1419–20). Born in Gloucestershire, Richard was apprenticed to Sir Ivo Fitzwaryn, a London mercer, around 1371. He prospered in the lucrative high-quality textile trade, and married Ivo's daughter, Alice. As lord mayor, he loaned Richard II of England money. When the king was deposed by Henry Bolingbroke (later Henry IV) in 1399, Richard was called to the usurper's council; the old debts were repaid and Richard loaned the new king £666.

During Richard's second term as mayor he was head of the Calais Staple, an association of merchants that virtually controlled the wool trade. In 1406 he captured an impostor posing as Richard II. He lent money to Henry V of England and, in his will, endowed Christ's Hospital and Whittington College. A sculpture on the old Newgate prison, rebuilt by Richard, shows a man and cat, and a medieval carving of a boy and cat was found in what is thought to be the Whittington family home. But it is uncertain how the legend of Dick Whittington and his cat evolved. The earliest literary version dates from the 17th century.

The Wars of the Roses: 109, 179

William, archbishop of Canterbury

d.1136. Augustinian canon; prior of St Osyth in Essex (c.1120); archbishop of Canterbury (1123–36); papal legate in England and Scotland (1126). William was elected archbishop by the Canterbury chapter under pressure from Henry I of England; Thurstan, archbishop of York, unsuccessfully opposed his claim at Rome in 1124. In 1126 William swore to ensure Empress Matilda's succession to Henry's crown. He completed and dedicated Canterbury Cathedral in 1130 and helped build Rochester castle and cathedral. In 1135, despite his earlier oath to Matilda, William consented to Stephen's accession to the English throne and crowned him that year.

The Plantagenet Chronicles: 65

Wars of the Roses *The Neville family (opposite), powerful supporters of the house of York.*

William I, the Conqueror, king of England

1027–87. Illegitimate son of Robert I, duke of Normandy; duke of Normandy (1035); king of England (1066–87). William visited England in about 1051, when Edward the Confessor may have promised to make him his heir. In 1064 Harold Godwinson, earl of Wessex, was shipwrecked off Ponthieu in France and taken to William, who made him swear to uphold his, William's, claim to the English throne. In 1066, on hearing that Harold had been crowned king, William invaded England and defeated Harold at Battle near Hastings. He was crowned in London on Christmas Day, 1066.

Between 1066 and 1072 William crushed the opposition of the English nobles; he built castles and called in English titles to noble estates and reassigned them on a feudal basis to his Norman followers. In 1085 he ordered a general survey of lands and their holders that resulted in *Domesday Book*.

The Plantagenet Chronicles: 26, 37, 149

William I The conqueror of England; he is represented by the artist wearing dress adorned with three gold lions, part of the later Plantagenet dynasty heraldry from the time of Henry II.

William, count of Maine

1103–20. Only son and heir-apparent of Henry I of England and his first wife, Matilda. William received the homage of the Norman barons in 1115 and of the English in 1116, confirming him as Henry's heir. In 1120, as future duke of Normandy, he did homage to Louis VI of France. On his return voyage to England his ship was wrecked off Barfleur in France and he was drowned, leaving Henry I's daughter,

Empress Matilda, as the sole legitimate heir to the throne.

The Plantagenet Chronicles: 37–8

William VIII, duke of Aquitaine

d.1086. Also known as William of Poitou and Guy-Geoffrey. Duke of Aquitaine and count of Poitou. In 1042 William, whom the *Chronicle of the Counts of Anjou* describes as 'second to none in daring', seized the county of Saintonge, but Geoffrey Martel I, count of Anjou, crushed his troops near Chef-Boutonne and took the county from him. However, William retook the county 20 years later in 1062, while Fulk Rechin, Geoffrey's successor as count of Anjou, was campaigning against his brother, Geoffrey the Bearded. The following year William added Gascony to the duchy of Aquitaine.

The Plantagenet Chronicles: 32–4, 37

William IX, duke of Aquitaine

d.1126. Duke of Aquitaine (1086). The first great troubadour of the Languedoc region of France, William wrote love-lyrics in the Provençal dialect that were amoral, erotic and irreverent. He was a noted crusader, who was said to have had his wife painted on his shield, as 'it was his will to bear her in battle, as she had borne him in bed'.

The Plantagenet Chronicles: 45, 55, 60, 228

William X, duke of Aquitaine

d.1137. Duke of Aquitaine (1126). William's daughter Eleanor of Aquitaine, the future queen of Henry II of England, was his heiress when he died without male heirs.

The Plantagenet Chronicles: 45, 55, 97

William II, king of Sicily

1153?–89. Son of William I of Sicily; king of Sicily (1166–89). William married Joanna, daughter of Henry II of England, in 1177. In that same year, he founded the cathedral of Monzeale near Palermo one of the richest churches built in the Middle Ages. He joined Pope Alexander III's campaign against Holy Roman Emperor Frederick I, but in 1184 made peace with the emperor in order to attack the Byzantine Empire. He seized the Byzantine cities of Salonica and Durazzo in 1185 but the same year was defeated by the Byzantine Emperor Isaac Comnenus and withdrew. William's navy, under his admiral Margarito, supported the beleaguered Franks against

Saladin in the Holy Land and forced the Muslim leader to retreat from Tripoli in 1188.

The Plantagenet Chronicles: 146, 148–9, 204, 210–11, 225

William I, the Lion, king of Scotland

1143–1214. Son of Henry, 6th earl of Northumberland, and grandson of David I, king of Scotland; king of Scotland (1165–1214). William succeeded his brother Malcolm IV as king. In 1168 he joined forces with Louis VII of France against England in what was the first Franco-Scots alliance. Anxious to regain Northumberland, lost to England in 1157, he supported the sons of Henry II of England in their revolt against the king in 1173. He invaded England, was captured near Alnwick in Northumberland and in 1174 sealed the Treaty of Falaise, which made Scotland an English fief. Freed the following year, he asked the papacy to declare the Scottish Church independent; after considerable delay, in 1188 Pope Clement III declared the Scottish Church subject only to Rome. In 1189 William paid Richard I of England 10,000 marks to annul the Treaty of Falaise. On King John's accession to the English throne in 1199 William demanded Northumberland anew but in 1209 he abandoned his claim.

The Plantagenet Chronicles: 128, 140, 166, 204, 232, 264, 268, 292, 296, 306

William Longchamp

See: Longchamp, William, bishop of Ely

William of Lorris

1215?–78? French poet. William was the author of the *Roman de la Rose*, a popular allegorical verse romance composed in the 1230s. He left the work unfinished, and Jean de Meung completed it around 1270.

Chronicles of the Age of Chivalry/Four Gothic Kings (US edn): 55

William of Malmesbury

1095?–1143. Benedictine monk and librarian of Malmesbury Abbey in Wiltshire; chronicler. William wrote hagiographies and histories that include the *Gesta Regum Anglorum* (Deeds of the Kings of England), which deals with the period 449–1127, and the *Historia Novella* (Recent History), which covers the years 1128–42. Although sometimes biased and inconsistent,

William II of Sicily The king of Sicily in *Monreale cathedral, shown offering the cathedral to the Virgin.*

his work shows fine style and sound historical method and gives a dramatic account of events, such as the abuse of the church by William II of England ('he did nothing that was not bad').

The Plantagenet Chronicles: 266

William Marshal

See: Marshal, William, 1st earl of Pembroke

William of Newburgh

1136–98? Augustinian canon of Newburgh in Yorkshire; chronicler. William wrote the *Historia Rerum Anglicarum* (History of English Affairs), which covers the period 1066 to 1198, the probable date of the chronicle's composition. His vivid style, rational approach and relative impartiality make the chronicle one of the finest of the 12th century. He mourned the Jews killed at York in 1190, describing one as 'a worthy man and a friend of Christians', and included anecdotes and supernatural tales.

The Plantagenet Chronicles: 91

William of Nogaret

1265?–1313. French statesman; counsellor to Philip IV of France. William denounced Pope Boniface VIII during his feud with Philip from 1296 to 1303 concerning clerical taxation and royal rights over the French Church. In September 1303 William and Sciarra Colonna, member of a powerful Roman family, led a force against Boniface at his palace at Anagni. The pope fled to Rome, where he died soon afterwards. In 1304 Pope Benedict XI issued a bull against William, but it was lifted in 1311. In 1313 he helped Philip in his suppression of the Knights Templar.

Chronicles of the Age of Chivalry/Four Gothic Kings (US edn): 137, 150

William of Norwich, 'Saint'

1132?–44. In 1142, when he was about ten years old, William was apprenticed as a skinner (dealer in skins) in Norwich. In 1144 his mutilated body was found in a wood outside the city and five years later it was claimed that he had been the victim of a ritual murder by Jews. His tomb in Norwich Cathedral became a place of pilgrimage, even though he was never canonized and there was no evidence that Jews were implicated in his murder.

Chronicles of the Age of Chivalry/Four Gothic Kings (US edn): 131

William of Ockham

1285?–1349? English Franciscan monk; scholastic philosopher. William studied and taught at Oxford from *c.*1310 until 1324, when he was summoned to Pope John XXII's court at Avignon to answer a charge of heresy. He was confined to his convent at Ockham in Surrey until 1328 while his works were examined by leading theologians. In 1328 his championship of the Spiritual Franciscans, an extremist wing of the order, brought him into conflict with the pope once more, and he took refuge with Holy Roman Emperor Louis IV at Pisa.

William was expelled from the Franciscans in 1331 and a papal decree of *c.*1338 charged him with 70 errors and seven heresies. He died in Munich.

William's teaching, which marked a break with traditional medieval philosophy, was nominalist – that is, opposing the doctrines of St Thomas Aquinas, it denied the validity of universals, or abstract concepts, dismissing them as mere names; refused to accept the competence of reason in matters of faith; and saw the Creation as a result, not of God's intellect, but of His will.

The Wars of the Roses: 67

William II, Rufus, king of England

d.1100. Second son of, and heir to, William I, the Conqueror; king of England (1087–1100). In the first year of his rule William crushed a plot spearheaded by his uncle Odo of Bayeux to supplant him with his elder brother Robert Curthose, their father's successor as duke of Normandy. In 1090 he invaded Normandy, secured some of his brother's lands and then agreed to help him regain other lands, such as Cotentin and Maine, that he had lost to his barons. In 1091 he marched against Malcolm III of Scotland, forced him to do homage and seized the city of Carlisle. He invaded Normandy again in 1094 and persuaded Philip I of France to withdraw his support from Robert. In 1096–7 he led an abortive campaign against the Welsh. He quarrelled with Anselm, archbishop of Canterbury, about lay investiture (the right of a king to invest a bishop and control episcopal elections) and in 1097 exiled him. His harsh rule and pillaging made him widely hated.

In 1096 Robert pledged his duchy of Normandy to William for 10,000 marks, to enable him to go on the First Crusade (1095–9); in his absence, William campaigned unsuccessfully against the French king. William was killed (probably murdered) while hunting in the New Forest and was buried at Winchester, where the clergy refused him the last rites.

The Plantagenet Chronicles: 36–7

William of Sainte-Mère-Eglise, bishop of London

d.1224. Bishop of London (1198–1221). A baron of the Exchequer under Richard I of England (*c.*1192), William was one of the three bishops who in 1208 pronounced Pope Innocent III's interdict (prohibiting clergy from administering the sacraments and burying the dead) against King John of England and he was banished in consequence. Thereafter he mediated between Innocent and John until 1213, when he returned to England on John's yielding to the pope's demand that Stephen Langton be elected archbishop of Canterbury. William resigned his see to Pandulf, the papal legate, in 1221, because of old age.

The Plantagenet Chronicles: 304

William, son of Henry II

1153–6. First child of Henry II of England and Eleanor of Aquitaine. William died in infancy.

The Plantagenet Chronicles: 97

William of Wykeham, bishop of Winchester

1324–1404. Bishop of Winchester (1366–1404); chancellor of England (1367–71, 1389–91). William entered Edward III of England's service in 1347. Clerk of works at Windsor and two other royal castles by 1356, he was not ordained priest until 1362. His first appointment as chancellor ended with his dismissal, brought about by rising anticlericalism. In the Good Parliament of 1376 William was a leading opponent of Lord Latimer and Alice Perrers, who, with John of Gaunt's support, had exercised a dominance – deemed malign by their critics – over the senile Edward III. Their power subsequently waned, but on the death of John of Gaunt's brother Edward, the Black Prince, in 1376, it revived and they charged William with abuses while he had been chancellor and harassed him until Richard II pardoned him on his accession to the English throne the following year.

From then on William took an active part in politics – he was made chancellor for a second term – and in massive and prestigious building projects. In 1379 he founded New College, Oxford, and in 1382 Winchester College as its feeder school, using his see's rich revenues to finance them; and in 1394 he began rebuilding the nave of Winchester Cathedral.

The Wars of the Roses: 22, 62, 104, 195

William of Ypres

d.1165? Son of Philip, count of Ypres. As grandson of Robert I, count of Flanders, William claimed Flanders in *c.*1125, but Louis VI of France installed another claimant, William Clito. In 1127 William of Ypres joined a league of English nobles against Clito but was captured by Louis and Clito at Ypres and imprisoned. He was freed when Clito died in 1128. In 1133 William fled to England, where he supported King Stephen against his rival, Empress Matilda. He became Stephen's principal military commander, fighting for him at the battle of Lincoln in 1141 and at Winchester in 1142. In 1143 he founded, on the proceeds of his plunder, a Cistercian monastery at Bexley in Kent.

The Plantagenet Chronicles: 73–4

Wilton Diptych

Picture consisting of two folding panels, painted in oils for Richard II of England *c.*1394–6; named after Wilton House in Wiltshire, where it was preserved. The diptych folds shut, and was probably designed as a portable altarpiece to be taken on campaigns. The inside of the left-hand panel shows a profile portrait of a kneeling Richard II, with three patron saints – St John the Baptist, St Edmund and St Edward the Confessor – who present the king to the Virgin and Child on the inside of the facing panel. With the Virgin are angels (one for each year of Richard's reign), one of whom bears the banner of St George. On the outside of the panels are Richard's white hart badge (also shown on the inside of the panels) and his personal coat of arms.

The Wars of the Roses: 22, 23, 72–3, 74–5, 289

Winchelsea

Port on the south-east English Channel coast; one of the Cinque Ports. The old town, overwhelmed by the sea in 1297, was rebuilt by Edward I of England, on a site further inland. In 1380 the town was burned by French raiders.

The Wars of the Roses: 49

Winchelsey, Robert, archbishop of Canterbury

d.1313. Rector at Paris University (1260s); chancellor of Oxford University (1288); archbishop of Canterbury (1293–1313). In 1297 Robert led the opposition of the English Church to the taxes levied on the clergy by Edward I of England to finance his war with France. The previous year Pope Boniface VIII had forbidden them to pay such taxes but when Edward impounded Church property they were forced to do so. However, Robert continued to lead demands for reform and to resist taxation of the Church, and in 1306, at the king's request, Pope Clement V suspended him from the archbishopric and summoned him to Avignon to answer charges. Two years later he was able to return to England where he resumed his appointment.

In 1308 he pronounced that the banished Piers Gaveston, Edward II of England's favourite, would be excommunicated if he failed to leave England for Ireland by 24 June. When Gaveston returned, that same year, as regent, Robert refused to take part in the parliament that had restored him to power.

In 1310 he was one of the ordainers, magnates chosen by the English barons to place restraints on Edward II's administration; and two years later he sided with the barons in their war with the king and excommunicated Gaveston again.

His death removed a dangerous opponent of the king. Miracles were reported at his tomb in Canterbury Cathedral, but he was never canonized.

Chronicles of the Age of Chivalry/Four Gothic Kings (US edn): 140, 144–6, 165, 178, 184–6

Winchester

County town of Hampshire. Winchester was made the capital of Anglo-Saxon England by Alfred the Great in the 9th century and gave way to London as the national capital only in the late 12th century. The town had a Norman castle, now in ruins; and a Norman cathedral, replacing a Saxon church, was consecrated in 1093. Famous as a centre of learning, Winchester was also the centre of one of England's richest sees. In 1394 William of Wykeham, bishop of Winchester, began rebuilding the cathedral nave, to the design of William Wynford, in the Perpendicular style. Winchester College was also founded by Wykeham, in 1382, as a feeder school for New College, Oxford. It was opened in 1394 as a free school for 70 pupils.

The Plantagenet Chronicles: 69, 72, 74, 85, 102, 117, 122, 125, 157, 159, 195, 232, 282, 288, 316–17.
Chronicles of the Age of Chivalry/Four Gothic Kings (US edn): 29, 48–9, 58, 100, 104, 116, 125–6, 128, 232, 254
The Wars of the Roses: 62, 86, 104, 195

Winchester Bible

Illuminated bible produced in Winchester *c.*1160–80, probably commissioned by Henry of Blois, bishop of Winchester. It is perhaps the finest book produced in England in the Middle Ages. Although five or more artists worked on it, it was never finished.

The Plantagenet Chronicles: 87, 157, 159

Windsor

Town in Berkshire on the Thames; site of Windsor castle, one of England's principal royal residences since William I, the Conqueror's, accession to the English throne in 1066. In the 12th century Henry II built the castle's Round Tower. Edward III extended the chapel in 1344–8, rededicating it to St George to house his new chivalric order, the Order of the Garter, which he established at Windsor in 1348. He also constructed new apartments in the castle (*c.*1359–60).

Windsor *The interior of St George's Chapel, rebuilt in late Perpendicular style by Edward IV as his mausoleum.*

In 1474 Edward IV began rebuilding St George's Chapel as his mausoleum, devoting over 1,000 pounds a year to it between 1477 and 1483. A vast aisled building in late Perpendicular style, it was intended as a shrine for the Yorkist kings. The Chapel was finished under Henry VII and Henry VIII, but without the black marble tomb Edward had intended to build for himself: Edward's successors made no attempt to complete this glorification of Yorkist kingship.

The Plantagenet Chronicles: 220–1, 317
Chronicles of the Age of Chivalry/Four Gothic Kings (US edn): 35, 98, 100, 168–9, 262–3, 284
The Wars of the Roses: 62, 94, 225, 231, 303

Windsor, Treaty of

Treaty signed in 1386 between Portugal and England and still in force. It created a perpetual alliance between the two countries, including a guarantee of mutual defence in wartime. John of Gaunt was its prime English mover: he wanted Portuguese help to press the claim of his second wife Constance to the Castilian crown; she was sister to Peter I of Castile, slain in 1369. John I of Portugal in his turn wanted English help to fend off the rival claim of John I of Castile to the Portuguese throne.

The Wars of the Roses: 42–3

Wonderful Parliament

Parliament of 1386 which impeached Richard II of England's chancellor, Michael de la Pole, 3rd earl of Suffolk, who was identified with the king's despotism. Richard was forced to accept a council appointed by parliament to oversee his rule. However, when the parliament ended, the king restored Suffolk as his adviser, ignored the council, and manipulated the judiciary to deny the legality of the Wonderful Parliament's actions.

The Wars of the Roses: 57

Woodstock

Royal palace from the 11th to the 17th century, set in royal forest in Oxfordshire. From *c.*1173 to her death in 1176, it was the home of Henry II of England's mistress, Rosamund Clifford. Legend has it that she was hidden there in a secret chamber within a maze, but that Henry's jealous wife, Eleanor of Aquitaine, found her and bled her to death in a hot bath. Henry also kept a menagerie at Woodstock, which included lions, leopards, lynxes, camels and a porcupine.

In 1238 an assassin broke into Henry III's room at the palace to find it empty: the king was sleeping in the chamber of his wife, Eleanor of Provence. Edward III's son, Edward, the Black Prince, was born at Woodstock in June 1330; for this reason he was also known as Edward of Woodstock. The palace was destroyed in the late 17th century and was replaced by Blenheim Palace in the 18th.

The Plantagenet Chronicles: 104–5, 118
Chronicles of the Age of Chivalry/Four Gothic Kings (US edn): 59, 81, 168–9, 234, 269

Woodstock, Edmund of

See: Edmund of Woodstock, 3rd earl of Kent

Woodstock, Edward of

See: Edward of Woodstock, the Black Prince

Woodstock, Thomas of

See: Thomas of Woodstock, 1st duke of Gloucester

Woodville, Anthony, 2nd earl Rivers

1442?–83. Son of Richard Woodville, 1st earl Rivers; Baron Scales (1462); knight of the Garter (1466); 2nd earl Rivers (1469). Anthony fought for the Lancastrians at the battle of Towton (1461), but switched his allegiance to the Yorkist Edward IV, who married Anthony's sister Elizabeth in 1464. During the Lancastrian restoration of 1470–1 Anthony fled with Edward to Flanders, and in 1473 he became guardian of Edward's son, Prince Edward. He was the translator from the original French of the first book off Caxton's Westminster press, *Dictes and Sayings of the Philosophers* (1477).

After Edward IV's death in 1483 Anthony's ward became Edward V and Anthony was arrested by Richard, 3rd duke of Gloucester, (the future Richard III), who saw him as a threat to his plans for usurpation. He was held at Pontefract and executed on a trumped up charge of treason. At his death he was found to be wearing a hair shirt next to his skin.

The Wars of the Roses: 235, 240, 244, 248, 255, 279, 282–3

Woodville, Elizabeth

1437?–92. Daughter of Sir Richard Woodville, later 1st earl Rivers, and Jacquetta of Luxembourg (widow of John, 1st duke of Bedford); wife of Edward IV of England (1464–83). Elizabeth in her youth was a maid of honour to Henry VI's queen, Margaret of Anjou, and in 1452 married Sir John Grey, by whom she had two sons. Sir John died fighting for the Lancastrians in 1461, the year that her future second husband, Edward of York, took the English throne as Edward IV, the first Yorkist king.

Elizabeth and Edward were secretly married at Grafton Regis, her family home, on 1 May 1464 and news of the marriage leaked out, just as Richard Neville, 'the Kingmaker', 16th earl of Warwick, Edward's most powerful subject, had successfully negotiated his marriage to the niece of Louis XI of France. The king's advisers reacted to the match with dismay: Elizabeth was five years Edward's senior, and her family was of a relatively modest station.

Elizabeth was crowned in 1465 and bore Edward three sons and seven daughters; the future Edward V, her first son and the Yorkist heir, was born in 1470. Although beautiful, she was widely resented for the rewards Edward heaped on her five brothers and seven unmarried sisters, distorting normal patterns of royal patronage: her sisters were married off to England's most wealthy and eligible nobles, further angering the earl of Warwick, who had daughters of his own to provide for. The king also tampered with the laws of inheritance to endow Elizabeth's sons by John Grey with estates. The Woodville family had considerable influence at court, and when, in July 1469, Warwick rebelled and seized Edward, he issued a manifesto claiming that the king's reliance on the Woodvilles was jeopardizing the Yorkist dynasty.

Elizabeth remained in England in September 1470 when Warwick, forced into exile after his abortive rebellion, invaded and drove Edward abroad. She took sanctuary in Westminster Abbey, where the future Edward V was born, and was left unharmed to greet Edward's triumphant return in May 1471. Woodville dominance was unchecked for the remainder of Edward's reign; Elizabeth's brother Anthony, Lord Scales (later 2nd earl Rivers) became tutor to Edward, prince of Wales.

Edward IV died on 9 April 1483. Fears that his heir would be dominated by the Woodvilles during his minority led many nobles to support the king's brother Richard, 3rd duke of Gloucester (the future Richard III), when he seized Edward V in April 1483 and declared himself protector of the realm. Elizabeth took sanctuary in Westminster once again, with her younger son, Richard, 5th duke of York. Richard of Gloucester had her brother Anthony and her son, Richard Grey executed, and on 16 June, persuaded her, through Thomas Bourchier, archbishop of Canterbury, to allow the duke of York to attend Edward V's supposed coronation later that month. Richard placed both her sons in the Tower of London, and declared them illegitimate on the grounds that Edward IV had been precontracted to Lady Eleanor Butler (who had died in 1468) at the time of his marriage to Elizabeth and that the match was therefore invalid. Elizabeth's captive sons disappeared in the autumn of 1483, probably killed at the behest of Richard, now Richard III, and in January 1484 parliament confirmed their illegitimacy. Soon after, Richard persuaded Elizabeth to leave her sanctuary by promising to provide for her and her daughters, and gave her a generous pension. During 1484 she began to promote the betrothal of her eldest daughter, Elizabeth of York, to Henry Tudor (the future Henry VII). Their marriage in 1486 reunited the warring houses of Lancaster and York in the Tudor line, and Elizabeth was restored to prominence as queen dowager. However, after a short period at court, she retired to Bermondsey Abbey, where she died in 1492 aged 55.

The Wars of the Roses: 2, 4, 232–5, 245, 253–4, 261, 274, 282

Woodville family

Baronial family elevated (by means of titles, offices and advantageous marriages) by Edward

IV of England after his secret marriage in 1464 to Elizabeth Woodville, daughter of Richard Woodville, Baron Rivers. Elizabeth and her five brothers and seven sisters dominated Edward IV's court, and when Richard Neville 'the Kingmaker', 16th earl of Warwick, led a revolt against Edward in 1469, he claimed that it was the king's reliance on the Woodvilles that had made him rebel. After Edward's death in April 1483, the royal council left the new young king, Edward V, under the control of his guardian Anthony Woodville, 2nd earl Rivers, rather than his uncle Richard, 3rd duke of Gloucester (later Richard III). Richard seized Edward V in May and executed Anthony. Three years later Elizabeth Woodville's daughter, Elizabeth of York, married Henry VII, but by then the Woodvilles' power had long since ended.

The Wars of the Roses: 234–5, 245, 255, 277, 282–3

Woodville, Richard, 1st earl Rivers

d.1469. Baron Rivers (1448–66); knight of the Garter (1450); 1st earl Rivers (1466); treasurer of England (1466), constable of England (1467). In about 1436 Richard secretly married Jacquetta of Luxembourg, widow of Henry V's brother John, 1st duke of Bedford, in whose army Richard had served. He became a privy councillor to Henry VI in 1450, after assisting in the suppression of Jack Cade's revolt against the king's misrule. He fought for the Lancastrians at the battle of Towton (1461), but afterwards went over to the Yorkist Edward IV, who in 1464 married his daughter Elizabeth. In 1469 Richard was captured by a Lancastrian force in the Forest of Dean and was beheaded soon after.

The Wars of the Roses: 234, 255

Worcester

Cathedral city and county town of Worcestershire. The city, which first became the seat of a bishopric in about 680, was burned by King Stephen of England in 1150 because it supported his Plantagenet rivals, but he was unable to take its castle (which no longer exists).

The cathedral, founded in the 10th century as a monastery by Saxon St Oswald, began to be rebuilt in 1084 by Wulfstan, bishop of Worcester, as a repository for saints' relics. He

himself was canonized in 1203, and 13 years later King John of England was buried before his altar in the cathedral. The cathedral's Benedictine monks, determined to mark the burial suitably, gave the king a fine tomb of Purbeck marble – the oldest royal effigy in England. In the 13th and 14th centuries the cathedral was rebuilt in the Gothic style; it is dominated by its massive tower.

The Plantagenet Chronicles: 80, 104, 257, 265, 320
Chronicles of the Age of Chivalry/Four Gothic Kings (US edn): 121–2, 125, 133
The Wars of the Roses: 65, 101, 106, 220

Worcester Chronicle

The *Chronicon ex Chronicis* (Chronicle of Chronicles) describes events from the Creation to 1140. Begun at the Benedictine cathedral priory of Worcester before 1095, it was long known as the chronicle of Florence of Worcester, but his authorship is unlikely. The cathedral priory also had later chroniclers; the annals from 1281 to 1307 are a valuable source for both local and national history, providing, for example, interesting details about the war between England and Scotland in 1296.

Chronicles of the Age of Chivalry/Four Gothic Kings (US edn): 7, 124–5

Worde, Wynkyn de

d.1534? Born Jan van Wynkyn, in Alsace; printer. It is probable that Wynkyn met William Caxton in 1472 in Cologne, where the latter had gone to learn printing, and accompanied him to England in 1476. He continued the business after Caxton's death in 1491.

The Wars of the Roses: 241

Wycliffe, John

1328?–84. Religious reformer; master of Balliol College, Oxford (1361). At Oxford, where he taught theology, Wycliffe evolved a theory that the bible was the only true religious authority and that only souls in a state of grace could be true members of the Church; because no one could know who these souls were, members of

the clergy, and even the pope, were possibly not among them. From 1377 Wycliffe wrote pamphlets attacking various Christian dogmas, such as the central doctrine of transubstantiation, and sponsored 'poor priests' to spread his beliefs. He became leader of anticlerical opinion in England and a tool of John of Gaunt's efforts to tax the clergy.

In 1377 Wycliffe was tried for heresy at the bishop of London's court at St Pauls; but John of Gaunt stood next to him in court, causing the trial to break up in confusion. In 1378 he escaped conviction again when Joan, the Fair Maid of Kent, widow of Edward the Black Prince, enjoined the court at Lambeth to acquit him. In 1380, and again in 1382, he was eventually condemned as a heretic but was allowed to retire to Lutterworth in Leicestershire, where he translated the Bible into English. His followers were known as Lollards. In 1428, more than 40 years after his death, his body was dug up and cast into a river.

Chronicles of the Age of Chivalry/Four Gothic Kings (US edn): 302–3
The Wars of the Roses: 30–1, 39, 44–6, 112, 126

Wykeham, William of

See: William of Wykeham

Wykes, Thomas

1222?–93? Augustinian canon of Osney Abbey in Oxfordshire (1282); official abbey chronicler (1285–93). Wykes was about 60 years old and a man of substance before becoming a canon. His continuation of an existing abbey chronicle starts from 1256 and gives royalist accounts of Henry III of England's wars with his barons (1259–65), Henry's last years and death (1272) and Edward I's coronation and early reign.

Thomas criticized Henry for squandering money 'on aliens', but also berated his enemy Simon de Montfort, 6th earl of Leicester, as too ready 'to rule his king'. He loved London, but hated its fickle people, who in 1263, 'forgetful of humanity', murdered Jews. He admired Edward I, 'of leonine courage', for ending the disturbances that stemmed from 'his predecessors' impotence'.

Chronicles of the Age of Chivalry/Four Gothic Kings (US edn): 13, 104, 107, 114

Yarmouth

Port on the Norfolk coast; also known as Great Yarmouth. During the Middle Ages ships from Yarmouth fished around Norway and Iceland, and every year the town held a herring fair. It was one of the trading posts of the Hanseatic League (a mercantile association of German towns) and traded with Baltic fleets who came each year to fish herring. Bartholomew Cotton's chronicle records that a flood devastated the port in 1287.

Chronicles of the Age of Chivalry/Four Gothic Kings (US edn): 60–1, 128, 138, 140
The Wars of the Roses: 41, 187, 266

Yevele, Henry

d. 1400. Master-mason; director of the king's works at Westminster and the Tower of London. Henry signed contracts to build bridges as well as buildings, and was probably a contractor as much as an architect. In 1378 he was appointed by Richard II to oversee works at Southampton. He completed the nave of Westminster Abbey *c.* 1378, and in 1379 began rebuilding the nave of Canterbury Cathedral. In 1395 Richard commissioned Henry to produce a painted and gilded tomb in Westminster Abbey for himself and his queen, Anne of Bohemia, who had died the previous year. Henry also rebuilt the walls of Westminster Hall in *c.* 1395, adding larger windows.

The Wars of the Roses: 72, 86

York

Cathedral city and county town of Yorkshire. An important Roman city, York became an archbishopric in the 7th century and in the 8th was one of Europe's great centres of learning. The Minster, its cathedral, was destroyed at the Conquest, rebuilt between 1070 and 1154 and again, in its present magnificent form, from the 13th to the 15th century. York was England's second largest medieval city after London, with a population of *c.* 10,000. Each year it performed notable mystery plays, accompanied by music.

On 16 March 1190 there was a massacre of Jews in the city, and 150 Jews allowed themselves to be burned alive in York castle rather than be captured. York was a centre of the wool trade until its decline in the 15th century. After his victory at the battle of Towton in March 1461 the Yorkist Edward IV was welcomed and feasted in the city.

The Plantagenet Chronicles: 80, 102, 142, 202, 208, 262, 266, 299
Chronicles of the Age of Chivalry/Four Gothic Kings (US edn): 13, 125, 146, 184, 190, 194, 196, 204–5, 211, 230, 236, 249, 284
The Wars of the Roses: 61, 68, 179, 212, 225–7

York, Elizabeth of

See: Elizabeth of York

York, house of

English royal house, an offshoot of the Plantagenet royal line; descended in the male line from Edmund, 1st duke of York, fifth son of Edward III, and in the female line from Lionel, 1st duke of Clarence, third son of Edward III. In the 1450s opposition to Henry VI, of the house of Lancaster, focused on Edmund's grandson, Richard, 3rd duke of York, who emerged as a rival claimant to the throne. He died at the battle of Wakefield in December 1460, fighting the Lancastrian forces, and his son Edward became the first Yorkist king as Edward IV, in 1461, driving the Lancastrian monarchy into exile.

Edward ruled until 1483, apart from an eight-month interval in 1470–1, when the rebellious Richard Neville, 'the Kingmaker', 16th earl of Warwick, drove him abroad and briefly restored Henry VI to the throne. Edward's son Edward V was named as his

York The statues of the Plantagenet kings stand on the choir screen of York Minster, York's magnificent Gothic cathedral. Here, the three Edwards. From left to right: Edward I, Edward II, Edward III.

successor, but, with his brother Richard of York, disappeared in the Tower of London, probably murdered at the behest of Edward IV's brother, Richard III. In 1485 Richard, the last Yorkist monarch, was defeated and killed at the battle of Bosworth by Henry Tudor, the leading claimant to the throne on the Lancastrian side. Shortly afterwards, in 1486, Henry married Edward IV's daughter, Elizabeth of York, uniting the houses of Lancaster and York. Another leading claimant to the throne, but on the Yorkist side, Edward, 18th earl of Warwick, son of George, 3rd duke of Clarence (Edward IV's brother), was held captive by Henry VII, who finally executed him in 1499.

The Wars of the Roses: 217

York, Margaret of

See: Margaret of York, duchess of Burgundy

Ypres, William of

See: William of Ypres

Europe in 1485

Map showing the principal political divisions of Western Europe in 1485. By the time the last of the Plantagenet kings, Richard III, died at the battle of Bosworth, England had lost all its possessions in France except Calais.

SCOTLAND

Edinburgh

North Sea

UNION OF CALMAR

Baltic Sea

Copenhagen

IRELAND

Dublin

Hamburg

Warsaw

ENGLAND

London

POLAND

Thames

THE EMPIRE

Calais

Atlantic Ocean

Seine

Paris

Danube

Vienna

Rhine

Munich

HUNGARY

FRANCE

Rhone

Milan

Venice

BOSNIA

Avignon

Genoa

Adriatic Sea

Florence

PAPAL STATES

PORTUGAL

SPAIN

Ebro

Corsica

Rome

Madrid

NAPLES

Lisbon

Tagus

Naples

Balearic Islands

Sardinia

Granada

Mediterranean Sea

SICILY

Tunis

BIBLIOGRAPHY

Adair, J., *The Pilgrims' Way*, London, 1978

Aers, D., *Chaucer, Langland and the Creative Imagination*, London, 1980

Allmand, C., *Henry V*, London, 1968

Allmand, C., *The Hundred Years War*, Cambridge, 1988

Arts Council of Great Britain, *English Romanesque Art 1066–1200*, London, 1984

Bagley, J. J., *Margaret of Anjou, Queen of England*, London, 1948

Baker, D., ed., *Medieval Women*, Oxford, 1978

Baker, J. H., *An Introduction to English Legal History*, 2nd edn., London, 1979

Barber, R. W., *The Knight and Chivalry*, London, 1970

Barber, R. W., *The Life and Campaigns of the Black Prince*, Woodbridge, 1986

Barlow, F., *The English Church, 1066–1154*, London 1979

Barraclough, G., *The Medieval Papacy*, London, 1968

Barraclough, G., ed. and trans., *Medieval Germany, 911–1250, 2 vols.*, Oxford, 1938

Barraclough, G., ed., *The Times Atlas of World History*, London, 1978

Barrow, G. W. S., *Feudal Britain: The Completion of the Medieval Kingdoms, 1066–1314*, London 1956

Barrow, G. W. S., *The Kingdom of the Scots: government, church and society from the 11th to the 14th century*, London, 1973

Barrow, G. W. S., *Kingship and Unity: Scotland 1000–1306*, London, 1981

Barrow G. W. S., *Robert Bruce and the Community of the Realm of Scotland*, Edinburgh, 1976

Bautier, R. H., *The Economic Development of Medieval Europe*, London, 1971

Bautier, R. H., ed., *La France de Philippe August: le temps des mutations*, Paris, 1982

Bellamy, J. G., *Crime and Public Order in England in the Later Middle Ages*, Cambridge, 1973

Bennett, J. M., *The Battle of Bosworth*, Gloucester, 1985

Beresford, M. W., and St Joseph, J. K. S., *Medieval England: an Aerial Survey*, Cambridge, 1958

Bertrand, G., and others. *Histoire de la France rurale des origines à 1340.* Paris, 1975

Blake, N. F., *Caxton and his World.* London, 1969

Bloch, M., *Feudal Society*, trans. Manyon, L. A., 2nd edn., London, 1962

Boase, T. S. R., *Death in the Middle Ages.* London, 1972

Boase, T. S. R., *English Art, 1100–1216*, Oxford, 1953

Bolton, B., *The Medieval Reformation*, London, 1983

Brooks, F. W., *The English Naval Forces, 1199–1272*, London, 1933

Brown, R. A., *English Castles*, 4th edn., London, 1976

Brown, R. A. *The Normans and the Norman Conquest*, London, 1969

Brown, R. A., and Colvin, H. M., and Taylor, A. J., *The History of the King's Works; vol. 1: The Middle Ages*, London, 1983

Burne, A. H., *The Agincourt War*, London, 1956

Buxton, M., *Medieval Cooking Today*, Waddesdon, 1983

Cam, H. M., *The Hundred and the Hundred Rolls*, London, 1930

Carus-Wilson, E. M., *Medieval Merchant Venturers*, London, 1967

Centre National de la Recherche Scientifique, *Bibliographie annuelle de l'histoire de France*, Paris, 1953–89

Chailly, J., *Histoire musicale du Moyen Age*, Paris, 1969

Chaytor, H., *From Script to Print: an Introduction to Medieval Literature*, London, 1966

Chrimes, S. B., *An Introduction to the Administrative History of Medieval England*, 2nd edn., Oxford, 1959

Chrimes, S. B., Ross, C. D., and Griffiths, R. A., eds., *Fifteenth-century England, 1399–1509*, Manchester, 1972

Clanchy, M. T., *England and its Rulers, 1066–1272*, London, 1938

Clanchy, M. T., *From Memory to Written Record, England, 1066–1307*, London, 1979

Clarke, B., *Mental Illness in Earlier Britain*, Cardiff, 1975

Cobban, A. B., *The Medieval Universities, Their Development and Organization*, London, 1975

Coleman, J., *English Literature in History, 1350–1400: Medieval Readers and Writers*, London, 1981

Contamine, P., *Guerre, état et société à la fin du Moyen Age*, Paris, 1972

Contamine, P., *War in the Middle Ages*, Oxford, 1984

Cowdrey, H. E. J., *The Cluniacs and the Gregorian Reform*, Oxford, 1970

Cox, J. C., *The Royal Forests of Medieval England*, London, 1905

Croft Dickinson, W., *Scotland from the Earliest Times to 1603*, 3rd edn., revised and ed., Duncan, A. A. M., Oxford, 1977

Crombie, A. C., *Augustine to Galileo*, Harmondsworth, 1959

Cronne, H. A., *The Reign of Stephen, Anarchy in England, 1135–54*, London, 1970

Crosland, J., *Medieval French Literature*, Oxford, 1956

Crowder, C. M. D., *Unity, Heresy and Reform 1378–1460: the Conciliar Response to the Great Schism*, London, 1977

Cuttino, G. P., *English Medieval Diplomacy*, Bloomington, Indiana, 1985

Daiches, D., and Thorlby, A., *Literature and Western Civilization, The Medieval World*, London, 1973

Davies, R. G., and Denton, J. H., eds., *The English Parliament in the Middle Ages*, Manchester, 1981

Davis, R. H. C., *A History of Medieval Europe from Constantine to Saint Louis*, London, 1957

Davis, R. H. C., *King Stephen*, London, 1977

Davies, R. R., *Lordship and Society in the March of Wales*, Oxford, 1978

Deacon, R., *William Caxton, the First English Editor*, London, 1976

Dobson, R. B., ed., *The Peasants' Revolt of 1381*, 2nd edn., London, 1981

Dodwell, C. R., *Painting in Europe, 800–1200*, Harmondsworth, 1971

Donaldson, G., *Scottish Kings*, 2nd edn., London, 1977

Douglas, D. C., and Greenaway, G. W., eds., *English Historical Documents*, vol II, 1042–1189, London, 1953

Douie, D. L. *Archbishop Geoffrey Plantagenet*, York, 1960

Duby, G., *Rural Economy and Country Life in the Medieval West*, trans. Postan, C., London, 1968

Dufournet, J., *Nouvelles recherches sur Villon*, Paris, 1980

Dunbabin, J., *France in the Making, 843–1100*, Oxford, 1985

Duncan, A. A. M., *Scotland: the Making of the Nation*, Edinburgh, 1975

English Romanesque Art, 1066–1200 (Exhibition catalogue), London, 1984

Evans, J., *English Art, 1307–1461*, Oxford, 1949

Evans, J., *A History of Jewellery, 1100–1870*, London, 1953, repr. 1970

Evans, J., ed., *The Flowering of the Middle Ages*, London, 1966

Falkus, M., and Gillingham, J., *Historical Atlas of Britain*, London, 1981

Favier, J., *Francois Villon*, Paris, 1982

Fawtier, R., *The Capetian Kings of France, Monarchy and Nation, 987–1328*, trans. Butler, L., and Adam, R. J., London, 1966

Finucane, R. C., *Miracles and Pilgrims: Popular Beliefs in Medieval England*, London, 1977

Fowler, K., *The Age of Plantagenet and Valois*, London, 1967

Fox, J., *The Lyric Poetry of Charles d'Orléans*, Oxford, 1969

Fox, J., *The Poetry of Villon*, London, 1982

Frankl, P., *Gothic Architecture*, London, 1962

Fryde, N., *The Tyranny and Fall of Edward II*, London, 1979

Ganshof, F., *Feudalism*, trans. Grierson, P., 3rd edn., London, 1964

Gentil, P. le, *Villon*, Paris, 1982

Gillingham, J., *The Angevin Empire*, London, 1984

Gillingham, J., *Richard the Lionheart*, London, 1978

Given-Wilson, C., *The Royal Household and the King's Affinity; Service, Politics and Finance in England 1360–1413*, Newhaven, 1986

Godfrey, J., *1204: the Unholy Crusade*, London, 1980

Goodman, A., *The Loyal Conspiracy: the Lords Appellant under Richard II*, London, 1971

Goodman, A., *The Wars of the Roses*, London, 1981

Gottfried, R. S., *The Black Death*, London, 1983

Gottfried, R. S., *Doctors and Medicine in Medieval England*, Princeton, 1986

Gransden, A., *Historical Writing in England*, 2 vols, London, 1974 and 1982

Grant, A., *Independence and Nationhood: Scotland 1306–1469*, London 1984

Griffiths, R. A., *The Reign of King Henry VI*, London, 1981

Griffiths, R. A., and Sherborne, J. W., *Kings and Nobles in the Later Middle Ages*, Woodbridge, 1986

Gross, C., and Graves, E. B. *A Bibliography of English History to 1485*, Oxford, 1975

Guillot, O., *Le comte d'Anjou et son entourage au XIè siècle*, 2 vols, Paris, 1972

Hale, J. R., Highfield, J. R. L., and Smalley, B. ed., *Europe in the Late Middle Ages*, London, 1965

Hallam, E. M., *Capetian France, 987–1328*, London, 1980

Hallam, E. M., ed., *Chronicles of the Crusades*, London 1989

Hallam, E. M., ed. *The Plantagenet Chronicles*, London, 1986

Happe, P., ed., *English Mystery Plays*, Harmondsworth, 1975

Harding, A., *The Law Court of Medieval England*, London, 1973

Hargreaves-Mawdsley, W. N., *A History of Legal Dress in Europe until the End of the 18th Century*, Oxford, 1963

Harris, G. L., *King, Parliament and Finance in Medieval England to 1369*, Oxford, 1975

Harris, G. L., ed., *Henry V: the Practice of Kingship*, Oxford, 1985

Harvey, J. H., *The Black Prince and his Age*, London, 1976

Harvey, J., *The Medieval Architect*, Gloucester, 1972

Haskins, C. H., *The Renaissance of the 12th Century*, New York, 1927

Hatcher, J., *Plague, Population and the English Economy*, London, 1977

Hay, D., *Europe in the 14th and 15th Centuries*, London, 1966

Hayter, W., *William of Wykeham, Patron of the Arts*, London, 1970

Heer, F., *The Holy Roman Empire*, trans., Sondheimer, J., London, 1968

Hewitt, H. J., *The Black Prince's Expedition, 1355–57*, Manchester, 1958

Hewitt, H. J., *The Organisation of War under Edward III*, Manchester, 1966

Hibbert, C., *Agincourt*, London, 1968

Hibbert, C., *The Rise and Fall of the House of Medici*, London, 1977

Hicks, M. A., *False, Fleeting, Perjured Clarence*, Gloucester, 1980

Hill, G., *A History of Cyprus*, 2 vols, Cambridge, 1940

Hillgarth, J. N., *The Spanish Kingdoms, 1250–1516*, 2 vols, Oxford, 1978

Hilton, R. H., *Bond Men Made Free*, London, 1973

Hilton, R. H., and Aston, T. H., eds., *The English Rising of 1381*, Cambridge, 1984

Hindley, G., *England in the Age of Caxton*, London, 1979

Holmes, G., *Dante*, Oxford, 1980

Holmes, G., *Europe: Hierarchy and Revolt, 1320–1450*, London, 1975

Holmes, G., *The Good Parliament*, Oxford, 1975

Holt, J. C., *King John*, London, 1963

Holt, J. C., *Magna Carta*, Cambridge, 1965

Holt, J. C., *The Northerners*, Oxford, 1961

Holt, J. C., *Robin Hood*, London, 1982

Horrox, R., ed., *Richard III and the North*, Hull, 1986

Howard, D. R., *The Idea of the Canterbury Tales*, Berkeley, 1976

Jacob, E. F., *The Fifteenth Century*, Oxford, 1961

Jacob, E. F., *Henry V and the Invasion of France*, London, 1947

Jordan, W. C., *Louis IX and the Challenge of the Crusade*, Princeton, 1979

Jusserand, J. A. A. J., *English Wayfaring Life in the Middle Ages*, London, 1920

Keen, M., *Chivalry*, Yale, 1984

Keen, M., *England in the Later Middle Ages*, London, 1970

Kenny, A., *St Thomas Aquinas*, Oxford, 1980

Kidson, P., Murray, P., and Honour, H., *A History of English Architecture*, London, 1967

Kingsford, C. L., *English Historical Literature in the 15th Century*, Oxford, 1915, repr. New York, 1962

Knowles, D., *Thomas Becket*, London, 1970

Knowles, M. D., *The Monastic Order in England, 940–1216*, 2nd edn., Cambridge, 1966

Koch, H. W., *Medieval Warfare*, London, 1978

Labarge, M. W., *Gascony, England's First Colony*, London, 1980

Lambert, M., *Medieval Heresy*, London, 1977

Lander, J. R., *Conflict and Stability in 15th-century England*, London, 1969

Lander, J. R., *Crown and Nobility, 1450–1509*, London, 1969

Landstrom, B., *The Ship*, London, 1961

Lapsley, G. T., Cam, H. M., and Barraclough, G., *Crown, Community and Parliament in the Later Middle Ages*, Oxford, 1951

Lasko, P., *Ars Sacra, 800–1200*, Harmondsworth, 1972

Lawrence, C. H., *Medieval Monasticism*, London, 1984

Leff, G., *Heresy in the Later Middle Ages*, Manchester, 1967

Leff, G., *Medieval Thought: St Augustine to Ockham*, Harmondsworth, 1958

Legge, M. D., *Anglo-Norman Literature and its Background*, Oxford, 1963

Lemarignier, J. F., *La France médiévale, institutions et sociétés*, Paris, 1970

Lewis, C. S., *The Allegory of Love*, Oxford, 1936

Lewis, P. S., *Later Medieval France, the Polity*, London, 1968

Lindbergh, D. C., ed., *Science in the Middle Ages*, New York, 1978

Lloyd, T. H., *The English Wool Trade in the Middle Ages*, Cambridge, 1977

Lloyd, J. E., *A History of Wales, from the earliest times to the Edwardian Conquest*, 3rd edn., London, 1939

Lloyd, J. E., *Owen Glendower*, Oxford, 1931

Lodge, E. C., *Gascony under English Rule*, London, 1926

Longnon, A. *Atlas Historique de la France*, 2 vols, Paris, 1885–9

Loomis, L. R., *The Council of Constance*, London, 1962

Lucas, A., *Medieval Women*, Brighton, 1983

Lucas, H. S., *The Low Countries and the Hundred Years War*, Ann Arbor, 1929

Macdougall, N., *James III: a Political Study*, Edinburgh, 1982

McFarlane, K. S., *John Wycliffe and the Beginnings of English Nonconformity*, London, 1966

McFarlane, K. B., *Lancastrian Kings and Lollard Knights*, Oxford, 1972

McFarlane, K. B., *The Nobility of Later Medieval England*, Oxford, 1973

McKay, A., *Spain in the Middle Ages, from Frontier to Empire, 1000–1500*, London, 1977

McKisack, M., *The Fourteenth Century, 1307–1399*, Oxford, 1959

Mackinney, L., *Medical Illustrations in Medieval Manuscripts*, London, 1965

McNiven, P., *Heresy and Politics in the Reign of Henry IV*, Woodbridge, 1987

Maddicot, J. R., *Thomas of Lancaster*, Oxford, 1970

Madox, T., *The History and Antiquities of the Exchequer of England*, London 1769

Małe, E., *Religious Art in France; The 12th Century*, Princeton, 1978

Marcus, C. J., *A Naval History of England*, London, 1961

Mayer, H. E., *The Crusades*, trans. Gillingham, J., Oxford, 1972

Mead, W. E., *The English Medieval Feast*, London, 1967

Miller, E., and Hatcher, J., *Medieval England: Rural Society and Economic Change, 1086–1348*, London, 1978

Mitchell, S. K., *Taxation in Medieval England*, ed., Painter, S., New Haven, 1951

Moore, R. I., *The Origins of European Dissent*, London, 1977

Moorman, J. R. H., *Church Life in England in the 13th Century*, Cambridge, 1946

Morris, J. E., *The Welsh Wars of Edward I*, Oxford, 1901

Morris, W. A., *The Medieval English Sheriff to 1300*, Manchester, 1927

Muir, L., *Literature and Society in Medieval France: The Mirror and the Image*, London, 1985

Munz, P., *Frederick Barbarossa*, London, 1969

Newhall, R. A., *The English Conquest of Normandy, 1416–1424*, London, repr., 1971

Nicholson, R., *Scotland: the Later Middle Ages*, Edinburgh, 1974

Nicol, D. M., *The End of the Byzantine Empire*, London, 1979

Oman, C., *A History of the Art of War in the Middle Ages, 378–1485*, 2 vols, 2nd edn., London, 1924

Oman, C. W. C., *The Coinage of England*, Oxford, 1931

Orme, N., *From Childhood to Chivalry*, London, 1984

Ormrod, W. M., ed., *England in the 14th Century*, Woodbridge, 1985

Otway-Ruthven, A. J., *A History of Medieval Ireland*, 2nd edn., London, 1980

Pacaut, M., *Louis VII et son royaume*, Paris, 1967

Packe, M., *King Edward III*, London, 1983

Painter, S., *William Marshall*, Baltimore, 1933

Pantin, W. A., *The English Church in the 14th Century*, Cambridge, 1955

Parsons, J. C., *The Court and Household of Eleanor of Castile*, Toronto, 1977

Patourel, J. le, *The Norman Empire*, Oxford, 1976

Pernoud, R., *Christine de Pisan*, Paris, 1982

Pernoud, R., *Eleanor of Aquitaine*, London, 1967

Perroy, E., *The Hundred Years War*, trans. Wells, W. B., London, 1951

Petit-Dutaillis, C. *The Feudal Monarchy in France and England from the 10th to the 13th Century*, trans. Hunt, E. D., London, 1935

Phillips, E. D., *The Mongols*, London, 1969

Platt, C., *The English Medieval Town*, London, 1976

Plucknett, I. F. T., *The Legislation of Edward I*, Oxford, 1949

Poirion, D., *Le Poète et le Prince: l'évolution du lyrisme courtois de Guillaume de Machaut à Charles d'Orléans*, Paris, 1965

Pollard, A. J., *The Wars of the Roses*, London, 1988

Poole, A. L., *From Doomsday Book to Magna Carta*, 2nd edn., Oxford, 1955

Poole, A. L., *Medieval England*, Oxford, 1958

Postan, M. M., *The Medieval Economy and Society*, London, 1972

Power, E., *Medieval English Nunneries*, Cambridge, 1922

Power, E., *Medieval Women*, Cambridge, 1975

Power, E., and Postan, M. M., *Studies in English Trade in the 15th Century*, London, 1933

Powicke, F. M., *King Henry III and the Lord Edward*, 2 vols, Oxford, 1947

Powicke, F. M., *The Loss of Normandy*, 2nd edn., Manchester, 1961

Powicke, F. M., *Military Obligation in Medieval England*, Oxford, 1962

Prawer, J., *The Latin Kingdom of Jerusalem*, London, 1972

Prestwich, M. C., *The Three Edwards*, London, 1980

Prestwich, M. C., *War, Politics and Finance under Edward I*, London, 1972

Rashdall, H., *The Universities of Europe in the Middle Ages*, ed. Powicke, F. M., and Emden, A. B., 3 vols, Oxford, 1936

René d'Anjou, *Le Cuer d'Amours Espris*, ed. Wharton, S., Paris, 1980

Richard, J., *St Louis*, Paris, 1983

Richardson, H. G., *The English Jewry under the Angevin Kings*, London, 1960

Rickert, M., *Painting in England in the Middle Ages*, London, 1954

Riley-Smith, J., *The Crusades; A Short History*, London, 1987

Riley-Smith, J., *the Knights of St John in Jerusalem and Cyprus*, c. 1050–1310, London, 1967

Ross, C., *Edward IV*, London, 1974

Ross, C., *Richard III*, London, 1981

Ross, C., *The Wars of the Roses*, London, 1976

Roth, C., *A History of the Jews in England*, Oxford, 1964

Rothwell, H., ed., *English Historical Documents III, 1189–1327*, London, 1965

Royal Historical Society, *Annual Bibliography of British and Irish History*, London, 1976–89

Rubin, S., *Medieval English Medicine*, Newton Abbot, 1975

Runciman, S., *The Fall of Constantinople*, Cambridge, 1965

Runciman, S., *A History of the Crusades*, 3 vols, Cambridge, 1951–4

Russell, P. E., *The English Intervention in Spain and Portugal at the Time of the Black Prince*, Oxford, 1955

Saltmarsh, J., *King Henry VI and the Royal Foundations*, Cambridge, 1972

Sanders, I. J., *English Baronies: A Study of their Origin and Descent, 1086–1327*, Oxford, 1960

Sauerlander, W., *Gothic Sculpture in France*, London, 1972

Sayles, G. R., *The King's Parliament of England*, London, 1975

Scammell, G. V., *The World Encompassed*, London, 1981

Schramm, P. E., *A History of the English Coronation*, trans. Wickham Legg, G., Oxford, 1937

Scofield, C. L., *The Life and Reign of Edward IV*, London, 1923, repr., 1967

Scott, M., *The History of Dress: Late Gothic Europe, 1400–1500*, London, 1980

Scott, M., *A Visual History of Costume: the 14th and 15th Centuries*, London, 1986

Setton, K. M., and others, *A History of the Crusades*, vols 1–11, Madison, 1962

Seward, D., *Henry V as Warlord*, London, 1987

Seymour, M. C., ed., *Sir John Mandeville's Travels*, London, 1968

Shrewsbury, J. F. D., *A History of Bubonic Plague in the British Isles*, London, 1970

Simpson, O. von, *The Gothic Cathedral*, London, 1956

Smail, R. C., *Crusading Warfare, 1097–1193*, Cambridge, 1956

Smith, J. H., *Crusading Warfare, 1097–1193*, Cambridge, 1956

Smith, J. H. *The Great Schism*, London, 1970

Southern, R. W., *The Making of the Middle Ages*, London, 1953

Southern, R. W., *Robert Grosseteste*, Oxford, 1986

Southern, R. W., *Western Society and the Church in the Middle Ages*, Harmondsworth, 1970

Steel, A., *Richard II*, Cambridge, 1941

Stenton, F. M., *The First Century of English Feudalism*, 2nd edn., Oxford, 1961

Stone, L., *Sculpture in England, the Middle Ages*, London, 1954

Stones, E. L. G., *Edward I*, Oxford, 1968

Stones, E. L. G., and Simpson, G. G., *Edward I and the Throne of Scotland, 1290–1296*, 2 vols, Oxford, 1979

Storey, R. L., *The End of the House of Lancaster*, London, 1966, repr., Gloucester, 1986

Strayer, J. R., *The Reign of Philip the Fair*, Princeton, 1980

Sumption, J., *The Albigensian Crusade*, London, 1978

Tait, J., *The Medieval English Borough*, Manchester, 1936

Talbot, C. H., *Medicine in Medieval England*, London, 1967

Thomson, J. A. F., *The Later Lollards, 1414–1520*, Oxford, 1967

Thomson, J. A. F., *The Transformation of Medieval England*, Harlow, 1983

Thrupp, S. L., *The Merchant Class of Medieval London*, Chicago, 1948

Tierney, B., *The Crisis of Church and State, 1050–1300*, New York, 1964

Tout, T. F., *Chapters in Medieval Administrative History* 6 vols, Manchester, 1923–35

Tout, T. F., *The Place of Edward II in English History*, 2nd ed., Manchester, 1936

Tuck, A., *Crown and Nobility, 1272–1461*, London, 1986

Tuck, A., *Richard II and the English Nobility*, London, 1973

Ullmann, W., *Principles of Government and Politics in the Middle Ages*, London, 1961

Vale, J., *Edward III and Chivalry*, Woodbridge, 1982

Vale, M. G. A., *Charles VII*, London, 1971

Vale, M. G. A., *War and Chivalry*, London, 1981

Vaughan, R., *Valois Burgundy*, London, 1975

Verbruggen, J. F., *The Art of Warfare in Western Europe during the Middle Ages*, Oxford, 1977

Warren, F., ed., *The Dance of Death*, Oxford, 1981

Warren, W. L., *Henry II*, London, 1973

Warren, W. L., *King John*, London, 1961

Warren Hollister, C., *The Military Organisation of Norman England*, Oxford, 1965

Webb, G., *Architecture in England: the Middle Ages*, Harmondsworth, 1954

Willard, C. C., *Christine de Pisan, her Life and Works*, New York, 1984

Williams, E. C., *My Lord of Bedford, 1389–1435*, London, 1963

Williams, G. A., *Medieval London from Commune to Capital*, London, 1963

Wilson, A., *Food and Drink in Britain*, 3rd edn., London, 1984

Wolffe, B. P., *Henry VI*, London, 1981

Young, C. R., *The Royal Forests of Medieval England*, Leicester, 1979

Zarnecki, G., *English Romanesque Sculpture, 1066–1140*, London, 1951

Zarnecki, G., *Later English Romanesque Sculpture, 1140–1210*, London, 1953

Zarnecki, G., *Romanesque Art*, London, 1971

Ziegler, P., *The Black Death*, London, 1969

MANUSCRIPTS

INDEX OF NAMES

This index lists leading men and women featured in *The Plantagenet Encyclopedia*.
Page numbers in *italic* refer to the illustrations, **bold** page numbers refer to the main entries.

ACKNOWLEDGEMENTS

The Beaufort Collection, Badminton: 187
Bibliothèque Municipale, Lyon: 182
Bibliothèque Nationale, Paris: 19, 20, 23, 38, 55, 57, 77, 86, 99, 117, 126, 143, 159, 164, 186, 207
Bibliothèque Royale Albert, Brussels: 131
Bodleian Library, Oxford: 105, 139
British Library, London: 15, 16, 18, 21, 24, 35, 41, 42, 43, 58, 79, 83, 101, 103, 107, 110/111, 113, 114, 121, 127, 135, 138, 145, 147, 153, 162/163, 165, 170/171, 177, 180, 194/195, 198, 201, 208
British Museum, London: 47, 53

Bulloz, Paris: 157

Musée de Dijon, France: 34

Landesbibliothek, Fulda: 78

Giraudon, Paris: 123, 209

Staatsarchiv, Hamburg: 91

Marianne Majerus: 6/7, 10, 27, 39, 40, 50/51, 60, 62/63, 65, 67, 70, 71, 75, 89, 93, 95, 96, 115, 119, 129, 132, 137, 146, 149, 151, 154/155, 161, 167, 173, 175, 179, 183, 189, 190, 192, 203, 205, 211, 214

National Library of Scotland, 59

Public Record Office, London: 28, 44, 68, 124

Tim Scott: 166

Sotheby's, London: 30/31

Cecilia Walters: 200
The Worshipful Company of Fishmongers: 204